CLARENDON ANCIENT HISTORY SERIES

General Editors

The aim of the CLARENDON ANCIENT HISTORY SERIES is to provide authoritative translations, introductions, and commentaries to a wide range of Greek and Latin texts studied by ancient historians. The books will be of interest to scholars, graduate students, and advanced undergraduates.

XENOPHON

Poroi

REVENUE-SOURCES

Translated
with Introduction and Commentary by
David Whitehead

OXFORD
UNIVERSITY PRESS

OXFORD
UNIVERSITY PRESS

Great Clarendon Street, Oxford, OX2 6DP,
United Kingdom

Oxford University Press is a department of the University of Oxford.
It furthers the University's objective of excellence in research, scholarship,
and education by publishing worldwide. Oxford is a registered trade mark of
Oxford University Press in the UK and in certain other countries

First Edition published in 2019
Impression: 1

Published in the United States of America by Oxford University Press
198 Madison Avenue, New York, NY 10016, United States of America

British Library Cataloguing in Publication Data
Data available

Library of Congress Control Number: 2018951238

ISBN 978–0–19–883442–7

Printed and bound in Great Britain by
Clays Ltd, Elcograf S.p.A.

Preface

'One of the greatest men that ever antiquity produced, and the only ancient author upon this subject which is now extant' (Walter Moyle, in the dedication prefacing his translation of Xenophon's *Poroi*: 1697). 'Xenophon's *Ways and Means* deserves more credit from us than his contemporaries were willing or able to accord it, as a bold and original intellectual construct' (Paul Cartledge, in his introduction to Robin Waterfield's translation: 1997). In the three hundred years between these glowing testimonials, others damned *Poroi* with much fainter praise—or simply damned it. No matter. Its interest and importance, nowadays beyond dispute, are dealt with in my General Introduction. I can therefore confine myself here to explaining why this is a work well-suited to the *Clarendon Ancient History Series*, offering a new English translation with full historical commentary.

As regards a *translation*, Anglophone readers might seem well-served already. In 1925, fresh from editing an Oxford Classical Text (its life latterly prolonged by being the text available on the online *Thesaurus Linguae Graecae*), E. C. Marchant issued a facing text and translation in the Loeb Classical Library. It too, nowadays, reaches a wider readership by electronic means: first the Perseus website, then the digital LCL itself. Marchant was an able translator with a happy turn of phrase. So too was H. G. Dakyns, sometime tutor to the children of Alfred, Lord Tennyson; his even earlier (London 1897) translation comes with very brief endnotes. Yet increasingly few readers nowadays can be expected to fathom the more archaic locutions of translators born in the Victorian era. (A recent work that I happened to notice presents Marchant's 'fraught with weal' as 'fraught with wealth'.) Though latest is not always best in enterprises like theirs, problems of comprehension are apt to be kept to a minimum if translators are no more than two generations older than their readership.

Myself aside, I know of two individuals who currently meet that criterion where *Poroi* is concerned. One is Ralph Doty, Professor in Classics at the University of Oklahoma. Since the mid-1990s Doty has specialized in translating Xenophon, mainly for the Edwin Mellen Press of Lewiston NY; his *Poroi* appeared in 2003. (Potential readers should note, with pleasure or pain as their nationality determines, his contention that 'American English'—his chosen medium—'has replaced British English as the world's principal second language'.) The other, one of the best present-day translators of any genre of ancient Greek, I have mentioned already: Robin Waterfield. His version of *Poroi* was published in a volume entitled *Hiero the Tyrant and Other Treatises* (1997, updated 2006). And thus, as stated, English translations of *Poroi* to suit every taste are already in existence.

A *commentary*—for Anglophone readers—is another story: the cupboard is bare. Matters improve on the continent, but not as much as they might have done. At the risk of over-simplification, the treatments by Gabriella Bodei Giglioni (Florence 1970) and Eckart Schütrumpf (Darmstadt 1982, repr. 1987)—both of them introduction-heavy, commentary-light—are conceptually oriented; they are thus most useful to readers who approach Xenophon's treatise from the standpoints of philosophy and/or politics. For an historian's *Poroi*, with a commentary that leaves far fewer stones unturned, one must look elsewhere: to France.

Forty-five years ago I was a PhD student in Cambridge, working on the metics (free immigrants) of Athens—Xenophon's topic in *Poroi* Chap.2—under the supervision of Moses Finley. He passed on to me a typescript copy of a dissertation which a French scholar, Philippe Gauthier, had submitted in 1970 for the Doctorat d'État degree at the University of Nancy: *SYMBOLA: les étrangers et la justice dans les cités grecques*—later (1972) the book of the same name. Part of Gauthier's study was instrumental in shaping my own approach; we corresponded briefly but appreciatively; and in 1976 he sent me a copy, inscribed with his 'amical hommage', of his *Commentaire historique des* Poroi *de Xénophon*.

Gauthier's treatment of the *Poroi* in that book—introduction, commentary, appendices (but no continuous text or translation)—is superb. Specialists, when consulting it, do so with the assurance that it is a research tool of the highest calibre, especially for the relevant documentary evidence. But non-specialists, even if they can follow Gauthier's usually crystalline French, are apt to be disheartened by the level at which his analysis flows. There is little 'background', few concessions to the novice. Accordingly, whatever else the present volume manages to achieve, one of its aims has been to salute Philippe Gauthier (1935–2013) by opening up his *Commentaire*, a treasure-house of erudition and good judgement, to a wider circle of readers. In the process, more generally, I hope to have produced here a scholarly but user-friendly *Poroi* for historians who want to make the most of this Tardis-like creation, larger on the inside than external appearances suggest.

A further, twenty-first-century incentive for doing so lies in the fact that *Poroi*-studies have 'moved on', and are now nothing short of fashionable. Some of the manifestations of this do not strike me as very substantial, but two that are, without question, are the PhD dissertations of Joseph Jansen and Janet Powell. I am grateful to both these scholars for permission to cite their fine work. (Likewise, for the same service, to Peter Fawcett on taxation and to Matthew Kears on metics.) Sympathetic, up-to-date analysis of this kind has been essential for me personally, to open up an appropriate degree of distance from Gauthier, and an opportunity to perceive where the conceptual framework within which he viewed *Poroi* (crucial facets of it shaped by Finley) sometimes might—and sometimes must—be challenged.

Neither my General Introduction nor my Commentary require an ability to read ancient Greek; what little they include is transliterated. The (selective) 'Notes on the Text' do, unavoidably, require it. Nevertheless I would invite even Greekless readers to venture into this section, if they want an insight into the often precarious process by which the words of an ancient author such as Xenophon reach the translator's desk. As regards the secondary literature cited, it is heavily slanted towards the Anglophone, though I have included items in other mainstream languages where that seemed appropriate.

Two anonymous readers for the Press examined a penultimate draft of what follows here. Their overall approval and some suggestions for improvement were equally welcome. At the Press itself it has been a pleasure to work with Charlotte Loveridge, Georgina Leighton, Eleanor Chilvers, and my copy-editor Deborah Blake.

David Whitehead

Belfast, June 2018

Contents

Conventions and Abbreviations

1. Xenophon is generally abbreviated to X. Without mention of a work, cross-references (in the range between **1.1** and **6.3**) refer always to his *Poroi*. The titles of the thirteen other surviving works by X. are abbreviated as follows:

Ages. = *Agesilaos*

Anab. = *Anabasis*

Apol. = *Apologia* (*Defence-speech of Sokrates*)

Cyrop. = *Education of Kyros*

Eq. = *De equitandi ratione* (*On Horsemanship*)

Hell. = *Hellenica*

Hier. = *Hieron*

Hipp. = *Hipparchikos* (*Cavalry-Commander*)

Kyn. = *Kynegetikos* (*On Hunting*)

Lac.Pol. = *Constitution of the Spartans*

Mem. = *Memorabilia* (*Recollections of Sokrates*)

Oec. = *Oeconomicus* (*Economics*)

Symp. = *Symposium*.

Most other ancient writers and, where applicable, the titles of their works are abbreviated in accordance with the system used in the *Oxford Classical Dictionary* (4th edition), but fuller ones are used where that seemed desirable. See also below, section 4.

Square brackets enclosing a writer's name indicate that the work in question is wrongly attributed to him. (In that category, [Plut.] *Orat.* refers to the work whose full title is *Lives of the Ten* (*Attic*) *Orators*.) The author of the Aristotelian *Ath.Pol.* (*Constitution of the Athenians*), who may or may not be Aristotle, is designated ?Aristotle.

2. The following editions or translations of *Poroi* are cited by author's name only:

Bodei Giglioni — Gabriella Bodei Giglioni, *Xenophontis De Vectigalibus: introduzione, testo critico, traduzione ed indici* (Florence: La Nuova Italia, 1970)

(Cartledge See under Waterfield)

Dakyns *Xenophon*, Ways and Means: *a pamphlet on revenues*, translated by H. G. Dakyns (London: Macmillan, 1897) [available on the University of Adelaide's website (http://ebooks.adelaide.edu.au) and also in a 2013 reissue by the Floating Press]

Doty Ralph E. Doty, *Xenophon*, Poroi: *a new translation* (Lewiston and Lampeter: Edwin Mellen, 2003)

Gauthier Philippe Gauthier, *Un commentaire historique des* Poroi *de Xénophon* (Centre de recherches d'histoire et de philologie de la IVe Section de l'École pratique des Hautes Études) (Geneva and Paris: Librarie Droz, 1976)

Marchant Edgar Cardew Marchant, *Xenophon vol. VII: Scripta Minora* (Loeb Classical Library) (London and Cambridge, MA: Harvard University Press, 1925)

Rühl Franciscus [Franz] Rühl, *Xenophon, scripta minora* (Bibliotheca scriptorum graecorum et romanorum Teubneriana) (Leipzig: Teubner, 1912)

Schütrumpf Eckart Schütrumpf, *Xenophon, Vorschläge zur Beschaffung von Geldmitteln oder über die Staatseinkünfte*, eingeleitet, herausgegeben und übersetzt (Darmstadt: Wissenschaftliche Buchgesellschaft, 1982) [reprinted with corrections 1987]

Thiel Johannes Hendrik Thiel, *XENOPHONTOS POROI* (Diss. Amsterdam) (Vienna: Österreichische Staatsdruckerei, 1922)

Waterfield *Hiero the Tyrant and Other Treatises*, translated by Robin Waterfield, with introduction and notes by Paul Cartledge (Penguin Classics) (Harmondsworth: Penguin, 2006 ['reissued with a new Chronology and additional material' from the 1997 edition])

3. Other conventions and abbreviations used:

AAHung *Acta Antiqua Academiae Scientiarum Hungaricae*

ABSA *Annual of the British School at Athens*

Agora 16 *The Athenian Agora, XVI: Inscriptions: The Decrees*, edited by A. G. Woodhead (Princeton: American School of Classical Studies at Athens, 1997)

Agora 19	*The Athenian Agora, XIX: Inscriptions: Horoi, Poletai Records, Leases of Public Lands*, edited by G. V. Lalonde, M. K. Langdon, and M. B. Walbank (Princeton: American School of Classical Studies at Athens, 1991)
AIO	*Attic Inscriptions Online* (http://www.atticinscriptions.com)
AJAH	*American Journal of Ancient History*
AJN	*American Journal of Numismatics*
AJPh	*American Journal of Philology*
AncSoc	*Ancient Society*
AO	R. Develin, *Athenian Officials 684–321 BC* (Cambridge: Cambridge University Press, 1989)
APF	J. K. Davies, *Athenian Propertied Families 600–300 BC* (Oxford: Oxford University Press, 1971)
ASNP	*Annali della Scuola Normale Superiore di Pisa*
BE	*Bulletin épigraphique*
BICS	*Bulletin of the Institute of Classical Studies*
BMCR	*Bryn Mawr Classical Review* (online at http://bmcr.brynmawr.edu)
BNP	*Brill's New Pauly: Antiquity*, edited by H. Cancik and H. Schneider, 21 volumes (Leiden: Brill, 1996–2010)
CA	*Classical Antiquity*
CAH	*The Cambridge Ancient History* (2nd edition)
CCJ	*Cambridge Classical Journal*
CJ	*Classical Journal*
C&M	*Classica et Mediaevalia*
(Comm.	the Commentary section of the present book)
CPh	*Classical Philology*
CQ	*Classical Quarterly*
CSCA	*California Studies in Classical Antiquity*
CW	*Classical World*
EA	*Epigraphica Anatolica*
FGrH	F. Jacoby, *Die Fragmente der griechischen Historiker* (Leipzig: various publishers, 1923–)

FRA M. J. Osborne and S. G. Byrne, *The Foreign Residents of Athens. An Annex to the Lexicon of Greek Personal Names: Attica* (Leuven: Peeters, 1996)

G&R *Greece and Rome*

GRBS *Greek, Roman and Byzantine Studies*

HCT A. W. Gomme, A. Andrewes, and K. J. Dover, *A Historical Commentary on Thucydides*, 5 volumes (Oxford: Clarendon, 1945–1981)

HPTh *History of Political Thought*

HSCPh *Harvard Studies in Classical Philology*

IACP *An Inventory of Archaic and Classical Poleis*, edited by M. H. Hansen and T. H. Nielsen (Oxford: Oxford University Press, 2004)

I.Eleusis K. Clinton, *Eleusis: The Inscriptions on Stone: Documents of the Sanctuary of the Two Goddesses and Public Documents of the Deme*, 3 volumes (Athens: The Archaeological Society at Athens, 2005–2008)

I.Erythrai H. Engelmann and R. Merkelbach, *Die Inschriften von Erythrai und Klazomenai* (Bonn: R. Habelt, 1972–1973)

IG *Inscriptiones Graecae*

JAH *Journal of Ancient History*

JEBH *Journal of Economic and Business History*

JHS *Journal of Hellenic Studies*

JRS *Journal of Roman Studies*

LGPN M. J. Osborne and S. J. Byrne, *A Lexicon of Greek Proper Names, volume II: Attica* (Oxford: Clarendon, 1994)

LSJ H.G. Liddell, R. Scott, and H.S. Jones, *A Greek-English Lexicon*, 9th edition with Supplement (Oxford: Clarendon, 1968)

MH *Museum Helveticum*

ML R. Meiggs and D. M. Lewis, *A Selection of Greek Historical Inscriptions to the End of the Fifth Century* BC, 2nd edition (Oxford: Clarendon, 1988)

OCD S. Hornblower, A. Spawforth, and E. Eidinow, eds., *The Oxford Classical Dictionary*, 4th edition (Oxford:

	Oxford University Press, 2012) [Page references are to this print edition. Readers may wish, as well or instead, to consult the corresponding entries in the online 5th edition (2016), edited by T. Whitmarsh and others.]
OR	Robin Osborne and P. J. Rhodes, *Greek Historical Inscriptions 478–404* BC (Oxford: Oxford University Press, 2017)
OCT	*Oxford Classical Texts*
passim	throughout a cited passage or work; as in '*Ajax* passim' , or '7–9 and passim'
PCPhS	*Proceedings of the Cambridge Philological Society*
POP	D. Nails, *The People of Plato: A Prosopography of Plato and other Socratics* (Indianapolis: Hackett, 2002)
RBN	*Revue belge de numismatique et de sigillographie*
RC	C. B. Welles, *Royal Correspondence in the Hellenistic Age* (New Haven: Yale University Press, 1934)
RE	A. Pauly, G. Wissowa, and W. Kroll et al., eds., *Real-Encyclopädie der klassischen Altertumswissenschaft* (Stuttgart: Metzler, 1893–)
Reinmuth	O. W. Reinmuth, *The Ephebic Inscriptions of the Fourth Century* BC (Leiden: Brill, 1971)
RhM	*Rheinisches Museum für Philologie*
RIDA	*Revue Internationale des Droits de l'Antiquité*
RO	P. J. Rhodes and Robin Osborne, *Greek Historical Inscriptions 404–323* BC (Oxford: Oxford University Press, 2003)
RPh	*Revue de Philologie*
SCI	*Scripta Classica Israelica*
SEG	*Supplementum Epigraphicum Graecum*
SIG	*Sylloge Inscriptionum Graecum*, 3rd edition
SO	*Symbolae Osloenses*
TAPhA	*Transactions of the American Philological Association*
TLG	*Thesaurus Linguae Graecae*
WJA	*Würzburger Jahrbücher für die Altertumswissenschaft*

WoA Joint Association of Classical Teachers, *The World of Athens: An Introduction to Classical Athenian Culture*, 2nd edition, revised by Robin Osborne (Cambridge: Cambridge University Press, 2008)

WS *Wiener Studien*

ZPE *Zeitschrift für Papyrologie und Epigraphik*

4. By contrast with (e.g.) the *OCD*, I favour the presentation of most proper names—both of persons and of places—in a Greek transliterated form, rather than Latinized. Since this conflicts with how *authors* are named (above, section 1), some inconsistency has resulted.

5. When an Athenian is presented here as 'of' somewhere, e.g. Euboulos of Probalinthos, the toponym given is that of his Kleisthenic *deme* (inherited from 508/7, and still applicable whether or not he still resided there). On the demes see generally Traill (1975); Whitehead (1986), with a checklist at 369–73.

6. Two distances expressed in 'stades' (*stadia*), in 4.46, have been tacitly converted into their kilometre equivalents. But all sums of money are left in the original units: *obolos*, *mna* (= 600 *oboloi*), *talanton* (= 60 *mnai*). (*Poroi* expresses no sums by the drachma (= 6 *oboloi*), the denomination often found most convenient in modern work, including mine here.) See 3.9–10, 4.14–15, 4.23–4. Orientation: daily rates for various types of worker, and for jurors, ranged between three and fifteen *oboloi* (Loomis (1998) 232–9); at the other extreme the trierarchy liturgy—equipping a warship—might cost anything up to a whole *talanton* (*APF* xxi–xxii).

7. All ancient dates are BC(E) unless otherwise indicated.

General Introduction

1. THE MAN AND THE WORK: BASICS

Xenophon (*OCD* 1580–83 s.v.1, *POP* 301–4) is a name well-known to historians of classical antiquity, ancient and modern. This would still be true if he was known only for joining—eventually leading—the Ten Thousand. An army of Hellenic mercenary soldiers, they were recruited in the late fifth century to help Prince Kyros of Persia unseat his brother King Artaxerxes II and take the imperial throne. Kyros failed, dying in the attempt at the battle of Kounaxa, in 401, not far from present-day Baghdad. The subsequent adventures, and eventual return, of the Ten Thousand were chronicled by Xenophon himself, in a seven-volume narrative entitled *Anabasis*: the *Journey Up-Country* (a perilous one for men accustomed to sea air in their nostrils).

But X. was, and did, much more than that.[1] There was more soldiering, through the 390s and perhaps into the 380s. This time it was in the service of the then dominant power in Hellas, Sparta, a fact probably relevant to his being formally exiled from his native city.[2] And during what turned out to be a protracted exile—in the Peloponnese: mainly at Skillous, near Olympia—there was to be more writing, lots of it.

A general *History of Greece*, the *Hellenica*, begins its narrative in autumn 411, almost exactly where the magisterial account by Thucydides had prematurely broken off. (On the chronological disjunction see

[1] A brief but learned 'life' of X., replete with the relevant sources, is given by Krentz (1989) 1–4 (again Krentz (1995) 1–4). See also Pomeroy (1994) 1–5.

[2] The date of X.'s exile has been a matter of debate—as between 399 and 394—for almost two centuries. Green (1994) 215 n.2 has a convenient checklist. Tuplin (2017) 338 re-states his preference for 394 (fully in Tuplin (1987)). Green (1994) makes a strong case for 399. Without new evidence, the matter is likely to remain beyond resolution. So Badian (2004) 40–2, who himself goes even later than 394.

Krentz (1989) 86.) The *Hellenica* carried events a further half-century, to the summer of 362.[3] Otherwise, much of X.'s large and varied literary output stems from interests that he had acquired in his later teens and twenties, while still in Athens. For instance,[4] his association with Sokrates and its reflection in several works, including discursive *Memorabilia* (*Recollections*) of that charismatic figure, would have made X. for posterity Sokrates' most important pupil, were it not for the superior claim generally accorded to his exact contemporary Plato.[5] (X. was included in Diogenes Laertius' *Lives and Opinions of Eminent Philosophers*, probably written in the third century CE. Diogenes' treatment of him there, 2.48–59, immediately follows that of Sokrates, 2.18–47. Plato required a whole volume to himself: 3.1–109.) X.'s love for horses and dogs generated short treatises on equine and canine topics. His admiration for Sparta and the Spartans found expression in both the *Agesilaos*, a duly admiring biography of the dominant Spartan king of the era, and the *Constitution of the Spartans* (*Lac.Pol.*), a general assessment of the Lykourgan underpinnings of Spartan society.

At some point, however, X. fell out of love with Sparta. Such, especially, is the standard interpretation placed on *Lac.Pol.* chap.14, a disapproving afterword to the treatise. In any case the growth of anti-Spartan sentiments throughout southern Hellas, up to and following the Spartans' defeat at the battle of Leuktra in 371, rendered life uncomfortable for one who had for so long been their cheerleader. A northwards move was made, in the first instance to Corinth. At some indeterminable date in, probably, the early or mid-360s, the Athenians rescinded the decree of banishment (Diog.Laert. 2.59, citing fr.32 of the third-century historian Ister: *OCD* 749, *FGrH* 334). Whether, in the light of that, X. ever returned to his native city or not is a question for section 3, below. Either way there are clear signs of what Tuplin calls 'a reconciliation with Athens'.[6]

[3] Formally so; however, some slightly (but significantly) later material is inserted into the narrative. See below, section 3.

[4] For a complete listing see Conventions and Abbreviations, 1.2. None of X.'s works, it is believed, have failed to survive.

[5] Plato (*OCD* 1155–8 s.v.1) was born in 429/8 or 428/7 (*APF* 333 has the details). X.'s birth-year, it is universally agreed, cannot be calculated by subtracting forty from the year (401/0) when Diog.Laert. 2.55 says that he 'flourished'. In *Anab.* 3.1.14 he describes himself as still young and inexperienced then—probably younger than his Theban friend Proxenos, who died at 'about thirty' (2.6.20). See Anderson (1974) 9–10.

[6] Tuplin (2012) 1581. See also Tuplin (2017) 343–4.

On one level this expressed itself in the fact that X.'s two sons Diodoros and Gryllos—a.k.a. the Dioskouroi, Castor and Pollux (Diog.Laert. 2.52)—joined the Athenian army[7] and fought at the battle of Mantineia in 362. Gryllos, named after his father's father, died during the preliminary cavalry skirmish there.[8] Also, and more important for present purposes, X.'s own thoughts and writings became Athenocentric once more.[9]

Two of his short works—quite possibly his final two—fall into that category. One is the *Hipparchikos* (*logos*), *Cavalry-commander's handbook*. Under that generic title it in fact proffers suggestions for (non-radical) reform of the *Athenian* cavalry-corps, specifically. Because the immediate threat to Athens (in *Hipp*.7.1–4) comes from her northern neighbour Thebes, the treatise is generally thought to date from the mid-360s (though Jansen (2007) 42 with n.40 argues for the early 350s). The other item, recently described as 'perhaps the most remarkable of Xenophon's small works,'[10] is our business here: *Poroi*.

2. AUTHORSHIP AND TITLE

When determining whether a given work should or should not be ascribed to a given author, it is proper to start from what the ancients themselves say—though not necessarily to accept it. The wisdom of this caveat is borne out nowhere better than in the oeuvre of X. himself, to whom, at one time, one work was attributed which he almost certainly did not write: the (almost certainly fifth-century) *Constitution of the Athenians*, or *Ath.Pol.*[11] That said, where *Poroi* is

[7] Spence (1993) Appendix 5 nos.55 & 72. (X. himself is no.192 there.)

[8] An inscription published in 1982 (*SEG* 33.192) shows Diodoros' son—another Xenophon—as the recipient of a citizenship-grant from the city of Ephesos (*OCD* 509, *IACP* no.844) in the late fourth century. Unfortunately (and untypically of the era), no background is given.

[9] In saying 'once more' I have chiefly in mind the fact that *Hell.* books 1–2, in sharp contrast to 3–7, do place Athens centre stage.

[10] Dillery (2017) 216.

[11] See Tuplin (2012) 1583: 'the non-Xenophontic *Constitution of the Athenians*, conceding that democracy, though repellent, was rational in Athenian circumstances, was allowed into the corpus by a later editor as a companion piece', i.e. to the *Lac.Pol.* (Diog. Laert. 2.57 records the doubts, surrounding both works, expressed by the first-century scholar Demetrius of Magnesia, *OCD* 433 s.v.16.) In any event, X.'s purported

concerned the attribution to X. is in fact unproblematic.[12] The formal evidence is of two kinds, (*a*) 'free-standing' *testimonia* and (*b*) manuscript rubrics.

Category *a* consists, first and foremost, of three reputable authors from the third century CE. They are:

Athenaeus of Naukratis (*OCD* 194–5 s.v.1), who at one point in his compendious *Deipnosophists* cites an identifiable passage (4.14) of X.'s '*On poroi*';

Diogenes Laertius (*OCD* 457 s.v.6), already mentioned, whose full list of X.'s works in his 2.57 likewise includes '*On poroi*'; and

Menander 'Rhetor' of Laodikeia-on-the-Lykos (*OCD* 931 s.v.4), one of whose treatises on epideictic (display) oratory had occasion to cite 'Xenophon in the *Poroi*'.

We then fast-forward to the (?)twelfth century, where an entry in the so-called *Etymologicum Magnum* dictionary (*OCD* 541) cites 'Xenophon in the *On poroi*' for the use of a rare noun, *opheilê*, said to mean debt (644.4–6).[13]

Given all this, the category-*b* evidence fills the role of corroboration. It need not be paraded in full here. Suffice it to say that three of the four principal manuscripts present the work as 'Xenophon's'.

To this formal, itemized evidence, two larger considerations in favour of Xenophontic authorship can be added. One is that the language and style of the treatise are in every way congruent with the rest of X.'s oeuvre.[14] The other—more subjective, but nevertheless contributory to the orthodox view—is that a corresponding compatibility is to be seen in the treatise's subject-matter itself.[15]

The objection might be made that any half-decent forger would have attended to both of these matters. But nobody has suggested

Ath.Pol.—not to be confused with the Aristotelian work of the same name—has long since taken on its own life, and bibliography, as the 'Old Oligarch': see *OCD* 1035.

[12] Likewise e.g. Jansen (2007) 30–2.

[13] In fact the manuscripts of *Poroi* nowhere include that word. Either the lexicographer or his source is probably making a mistaken reference to *ophelos* (meaning advantage) in 4.35; cf. Thiel xxix.

[14] So at length e.g. Thiel xv–xxiii; in brief Gauthier 1. We shall pay attention to this criterion here only when its manifestations can be appreciated in translation (such as his penchant for things in groups of three: see initially in the Comm. to **1.4 from which**).

[15] So e.g. Gauthier 1–4. He notes that modern scholars sceptical or agnostic about X.'s authorship are economic historians with anachronistic conceptions of X. See further below, section 7.

forgery in this instance.[16] The author of this work comes across like X. for the most straightforward of reasons: he *was* X.

* * * *

The exact title that X. himself gave to the work, and what he aimed to convey by doing so, are matters that need examination in rather more detail.

In this regard, the discrepancy that has come to light here already, between *On poroi* (i.e. in Greek *Peri porôn*, a prepositional phrase with the noun in the genitive plural) and simple *Poroi*, is of no consequence. It is the sort of thing amply paralleled elsewhere—in, for instance, the Aristotelian *Problems* (*Problêmata*) which Diog.Laert. 5.23 calls '*On problems*' (*Peri problêmatôn*). Nowadays, *Poroi* is the preferred title for X.'s treatise, and I share that preference. (The *Peri porôn* alternative is harmless enough, except in as much as, long ago, it spawned the Latin translation *De vectigalibus*, on which see below.)

Equally unimportant in itself is the fact that the manuscripts which confirm Xenophon's authorship give what might be termed a subtitle, a secondary title as well as a primary one: '*Poroi* or *Peri prosodôn*', the latter phrase meaning *On revenues*. This again is a familiar phenomenon. The list of X.'s own compositions in Diog.Laert. 2.57, for example, includes '*Hieron* or *Tyrannikos* (*logos*)', i.e. *Hieron* (generally regarded nowadays as the title proper) also known as (*Treatise on*) *Tyranny*. Also, Diogenes' discursive catalogue of the dialogues of Plato in 3.57–62 actually gives most of them two-for-the-price-of-one titles in this same way: '*Gorgias* or *On rhetoric*', '*Meno* or *On excellence*', '*Republic* or *On justice*', etc. Consequently, Gauthier was right to castigate the view that X.'s own, original title was *Poroi tôn prosodôn*.[17] X.'s title was *Poroi*. It was ancient scholars and scribes, in subsequent centuries, who appended the explanatory gloss *On revenues*.

Why the gloss, or subtitle, was added is not hard to fathom. X. uses the noun *prosodos*, in singular or plural, no fewer than nineteen times (excluding the gloss itself: 1.2, 2.1, 2.7, 3.6 twice, 3.10, 3.14 twice, 4.1, 4.17, 4.23 twice, 4.25, 4.39, 4.40, 4.50, 5.1, 5.12 twice). The topic is at the very heart of his concerns; and 'revenue(s)', (public) income, is an

[16] Schwahn (1931) 257 protested that the author of *Poroi* could not be the same man who had written *Mem.*2.5.2 (the latter corroborated, in his view, by Plut. *Nik.*4.2); but in truth there is no conflict. See further in the Comm. to **4.14 He contracted**.

[17] Gauthier 7–8, against Breitenbach (1967) 1753 and Bodei Giglioni xi n.22. Likewise Schütrumpf 119.

unexceptionable English translation for the term. However, as Gauthier points out, when Karl von der Lieck gave *Einkünften* as the title of the treatise itself, that is a German rendering of the gloss, not of the title proper. The same goes for Gabriella Bodei Giglioni, who chose to reproduce the Latin *De vectigalibus*. That time-hallowed version, abbreviated to *Vect.*, is still perpetuated by works of reference such as LSJ and the *OCD*, as well as by individual scholars.[18] In my view the time has come to jettison it. We should accustom ourselves to using, instead, either Xenophon's own noun *Poroi* or, if translation is preferred, a better one. Of *single-word* translations (into English) which are in current use, probably the least worst is *Revenues*, as favoured in Oxford[19]—though again Gauthier's objection applies. My own suggestion, which meets that objection, is *Revenue-sources*. Alternatively, if reduction to a single word is not felt to be imperative, there have always been attractions in *Ways and Means*; sources and methods of income-generation (*prosodoi* being the income thus generated).[20]

Whether or not we ourselves choose to cite the work by the title X. himself gave it, an obvious question arises: what did he mean by entitling it so? By contrast with *prosodoi*, above, he never once uses the noun *poroi* within this treatise itself. (The closest he gets is with two *eupor-* compounds: the adjective *euporos* in 4.51 and the verb *euporein* in 6.1—both of them conveying the idea that Athens (4.51) or its demos (6.1) will be well-supplied with routes that lead to its financial goals.) A search of the rest of X.'s writings comes up with passages where generals or the like, who need to feed and/or pay their troops, undertake a '*poros* of *chrêmata* (money)' (*Hell.*1.6.12, 5.1.2)[21] or a '*poros* of *prosodos*' (*Cyrop.*1.6.10). Instances of *poroi* in the plural are irrelevant, illustrating

[18] e.g. Hansen (1991), Gabrielsen (1994), Reed (2003), Liddel (2007), Papazarkadas (2011), Pritchard (2015).

[19] I make this assumption from its use by (e.g.) Cawkwell (1963), Davies (1993), and Hornblower (2002).

[20] For *Ways and Means* see e.g. Rhodes (2010), following Marchant's Loeb. Gauthier 8 adds the German equivalent *Mittel und Wege* (though oddly not the French *Voies et Moyens*; for that see Jansen (2007) 24). Modern institutions which illustrate the phrase include the Committee of Ways and Means (1641–1967) of the UK House of Commons and the US House of Representatives Committee on Ways and Means. Athens in X.'s day had no such committee, but the assembly did from time to time address matters under that head. See e.g. Demosthenes' *First Philippic* speech (of 351): almost half-way through it he backs up his proposal for military measures against the Macedonians by presenting a statement, not preserved, of how the money for this was to be found (*porou apodeixis*: Demosth. 4.29–30).

[21] Compare [X.] *Ath.Pol.*3.2; Demosth. 1.19, 4.29, 18.309.

as they do a more general sense of the word. However, once other evidence is fully brought in, full enlightenment dawns. Gauthier 9–19 is definitive here. Citing and discussing literary testimony from Hyperides to Polybius[22] and a wealth of early Hellenistic inscriptions (from Athens and elsewhere),[23] he situates a financial or fiscal *poros*, as a means of revenue-raising, in two possible conceptual models. One of them relates to its place in a regular budget, where ordinary revenues flow in and are then spent. The other describes situations where the expenditure happens first and unexpectedly, and revenue must be found to offset it. (See also Hakkarainen (1997).)

In entitling his work *Poroi*, then, X. was giving the word much the same sense and implications that he had already given it in *Cyrop*.1.6.9 (where the young Kyros speaks of 'any *poros*' for furnishing an army's supplies). And although he chose not to say as much in his title, what he meant by it—as the contents of the treatise demonstrate—was nothing abstract. His topic is 'ways and means' by which *the Athenians*, specifically, might ameliorate their financial situation at the time of writing.

3. DATE AND PLACE OF COMPOSITION

The orthodox dating for *Poroi* is the mid-350s. In my opinion this is correct, but how it is arrived at, and what alternatives there are to it, will benefit from some unpacking.

A purported *terminus ante quem* is provided by Diogenes Laertius, who writes (2.56) that X. 'died, according to Stesiclides of Athens in his list of (Athenian eponymous) archons and Olympic victors, in the first year of the 105th Olympiad, in the archonship of Kallidemides, the year in which Philip the son of Amyntas [*OCD* 1128 Philip (1) II] became ruler of the Macedonians'. Setting aside problems with two of

[22] Hyp. *Eux*.37; Aristot. *Rhet*.1.4.7–9 = 1359b19–32; [Aristot.] *Rhetorica ad Alexandrum* 2.20 = 1425b19–25 (= Anaximenes *Ars Rhetorica* 2.33); [Aristot.] *Economics* 2.1346a25–9, as introduction to book 2 as a whole; Polybius 30.31.

[23] I will not cite them all here, especially as some are hard to find and/or unavailable in translation, but pride of place goes to Austin (2006) no.48 (*RC* 3–4, *SIG* 344): letters, in *c.* 303, from king Antigonos I of Macedon (*OCD* 102) to the city of Teos (*OCD* 1440, *IACP* no.868), concerning its proposed merger with nearby Lebedos (*IACP* no.850). The last letter (lines 109–26) begins with the topic of ordinary and extraordinary revenues, using both *prosodos* and *poros* vocabulary.

the names there,[24] this triangulation of the date from multiple starting-points looks impressive. It is nevertheless wrong. Whenever X. did die, it was later than 360/59. This is a certainty because *Hell.*6.4.33–37 summarizes Thessalian history from the death of Jason of Pherai (*OCD* 771–2 Jason (2)) up to and beyond the accession of Tisiphonos; thus the material was written between 358/7 (Diod.Sic. 16.14.1) and 353/2 (when Diod.Sic. 16.35.1–3 mentions only the latter's younger brother Lykophron).

The only *terminus ante quem* which stands up to scrutiny, therefore, occurs in 4.25. There X. makes a passing appeal to any readers old enough to remember how much 'the tax on slaves' brought in to Athenian public coffers 'before the events at Dekeleia'; that is, before 413 (see Thuc. 7.19.1–2 & 27–8). It has been suggested, by analogy, that this means in practice any readers who are octogenarians, but even if that is correct, 4.25 as a dating criterion is too elastic to be of any practical use. See further in the Comm. to the passage.

Other internal evidence from the treatise itself includes two *termini post quem*, this time firm ones. First, 3.7 refers to large property-taxes (*eisphorai*) which had bankrolled Athenian military operations in the central Peloponnese under the command of Lysistratos and, later, Hegesileos. Those two generals are known to have held office in 366/5 or (more probably) 364/3 and 363/2, respectively. Second, when 5.9 refers to the Phokians abandoning their control of the shrine and oracle of Apollo at Delphi, that presupposes, obviously, the prior imposition of such control, an event which occurred in 356 (*CAH* 6.739–41; Rhodes (2010) 340). Both of these passages are discussed further in the Comm.; and for 5.9 see also Notes on the Text.

To go beyond that, a broader perspective—which can then be narrowed down—is required. *Poroi* presupposes a context of peace, *eirênê*, which has very recently succeeded a period of war, *polemos*: thus (above all) 4.40 and 5.12, with reiteration throughout 5.1–6.1. How

[24] The correct name of the Athenian eponymous archon in question was Kallimedes (*AO* 270, RO 543). More important, the name of the (lost) primary authority whom Diog.Laert. cites is problematic. Wilamowitz corrected 'Stesikleides' to Ktesikleides, but even that is not quite the 'Ktesikles' mentioned twice in Athenaeus' *Deipnosophists*: 6.272C, 10.445D. For *FGrH* 245 Jacoby prints the name as Ktesikles when quoting Athenaeus (a footnote offers the tentative emendation Stesikles), Stesikleides when quoting Diog.Laert.; his heading is 'Stesikleides (Ktesikles)'. In *LGPN* likewise 'Stesikleides' is favoured. If that is correct, he is the only known Athenian bearer of the name.

does that fact map onto Hellenic history from 363/2 onwards? In theory, three options present themselves: *c.* 361, *c.* 355, and *c.* 346.

Concerning the first of these possibilities: X. himself famously ends his *Hellenica* in anti-climactic mode, commenting that the battle of Mantineia in summer 362 had settled nothing: *Hell.*7.5.27. He writes of increased 'confusion and turmoil' (*akrisia* and *tarachê*),[25] and he mentions no peace-treaty. Later sources do mention one—Polybius (4.33.8–9), Diodorus (15.89.1), Plutarch (*Agesilaos* 35.3–4), and, if correctly dated here, the fragmentary Athenian inscription RO 42 (Harding (1985) no.57); and modern accounts accept this.[26] Nevertheless, nobody to my knowledge has suggested that *Poroi* should be dated in *c.* 361. Had they done so, several compelling objections would arise. One of them has been mentioned above: the Phokian seizure of Delphi in 356 (5.9) is already a thing of the past. Here are two more. 5.5 refers to 'some who want Athens to take back the leadership (*hêgemonia*)'. Athens still had such a position in the late 360s and on into the 350s. Similarly, 5.12 uses the phrase 'ever since there has been peace at sea'. Whenever exactly it is deemed to have begun (J. Roy in *CAH* 6.207 refers to 'a decade of warfare'), the period of *polemos* that ended with Mantineia and the ensuing peace was no naval war.

For practical purposes, then, argument is joined between the proponents of a date for *Poroi* in the **mid-350s** or the **mid-340s**. The first option places it immediately after the so-called Social War (357–355: War of the 'Allies'—Latin *socii*), which brought about the collapse of most of the Second Athenian Confederacy. Alternatively, it belongs directly after the Third Sacred War (356–346) in central Hellas. Though clear majority opinion does favour the first of these choices, the second too has its champions, and the position brings up points and controversies that merit brief mention here.[27]

[25] Though the first of this pair of nouns is noteworthy in being, here, the only extant occurrence before the Hellenistic period, the second has the greater bearing on the present question—because *Poroi* 5.8 uses the phrase '*tarachê* has arisen in Hellas at present'; cf. Tuplin (1993) 33, 162. At first sight this might look like a strong pointer for dating *Poroi* in c.361. Not so, however, on three counts. X. uses a similar phrase about the mid-380s (*Hell.*5.2.35); his narrative in *Hell.* comes to an end before 355/4; and another writer refers to 355/4 as a time of *tarachê* among the Hellenes (Demosth. 14.36).

[26] See e.g. Ryder (1965) appendix 8; *CAH* 6.207–8 (J. Roy) & 888 (chronological table).

[27] Proponents, before Cautadella (1984), of *c.* 346: Holzapfel (1882), Sealey (1955). Some rejections thereof: Zurborg (1874) 2–18; Thiel viii–xiii; Gauthier 4–6; Bloch (2004); Jansen (2007) 54–6.

The most long-standing of them stems from a passage which has been taken to show that the Third Sacred War had not merely begun already but was over already. 5.9, cited above, urges the Athenians to employ Pan-Hellenic diplomacy to protect the autonomy of the shrine of Delphian Apollo against anyone who made a move against it '*eklipontôn Phôkeôn*'—literally, 'the Phokians having abandoned (it)'. The transmitted text of that clause as a whole has appeared, to some scholars, to warrant the conclusion that the Phokians have already done so; thus the context would have to be summer 346 (with Thebes as the unnamed potential aggressor likely to exploit such a Phokian-created vacuum). The orthodox rejection of this position finds the Greek unsatisfactory, and emends the form of the verb to one that allows both it and the participial phrase *eklipontôn Phôkeôn* to describe not a past situation but a possible future one. In fact, no emendation is needed. (See further in Notes on the Text, and the Comm. to the passage.)

Independently of how 5.9 should be understood, 4.40 is adduced in the attempt by Cautadella (1984) to revive the later dating of *Poroi*. X. refers there to very heavy *eisphorai* during the recently concluded war. As the plural is used, Cautadella (reasonably) argues, this must imply more than one such levy—yet Demosth. 22.48–9 (dating from 355/4) could be taken to indicate that only one *eisphora* was imposed during the Social War; and if that was the case, the war in question would have to be the Sacred War (when at least two *eisphorai* are attested).[28] However, Bloch (2004) has shown that other interpretations of the Demosthenes passage are possible, even preferable. In any case it is prudent to remember the paucity of the evidence overall.[29]

The arguments for a date in the immediate aftermath of the Social War, then, continue to prevail over any challenges to them. *Poroi* belongs in 355/4.[30]

* * * *

We have proceeded this far by assembling the relevant *termini ante* and *post quem* and then conducting a summary process of elimination

[28] In 352 and 347/6: see Thomsen (1964) 232, 237–8.

[29] Bloch (2004) 11–15 (and briefly already Tuplin (1993) 32 n.81). The broader point is added by Jansen (2007) 55.

[30] The attempt by Schorn (2006) to refine this even further, to May/June 354, is unconvincing; see Powell (2015) 27.

among the theoretical possibilities they create. Now it should be added that a mid-350s context for *Poroi*—or at least for its completion, if several years of composition is allowed for: Jansen (2007) 46–50, 117—makes an excellent fit on positive grounds, too, with other evidence and considerations.

First and foremost, as stated already, the Social War did bring about Athens' loss of *naval* hegemony, her position (since 377) of Aegean thalassocrat-in-chief; and the ensuing peace-treaty recognized this as a *fait accompli*.[31] That is X.'s background concern here, especially in 5.5, 5.8, and 5.12. Concerning the last of these passages, Sealey (1955) 76 sought to highlight X.'s remark that *prosodoi* had increased since the arrival of peace in the Aegean, claiming that such an increase would not have been discernible until long after 355. The point is refuted by Cawkwell (1963) 63 n.90 (whose dictum is approvingly quoted by Gauthier 5): '[t]he whole work is concerned with Athens' impoverishment and how to overcome it, and by 346 the city was no longer impoverished'. There are figures to back this up. In (probably) 356/5 Athens' income was 130 talents: Demosth. 10.37. A decade later the figure had risen to 400 talents: Demosth. 10.38; Theopompus *FGrH* 115 F166.

The mid-350s, then, was the time *par excellence* for these matters to be addressed by thoughtful Athenians, whether those active in public life or opinion-formers of a more detached kind. In the former domain, reference has already been made to Demosthenes 22, a law-court speech written in 355/4 for one of the prosecutors of a man, Androtion of Gargettos (*LGPN* s.v. no.2, *OCD* 86, *FGrH* 324), who among other things had allegedly been brutal in his collection of *eisphora*-arrears. One can also adduce Demosthenes 14, probably his earliest speech to the Athenian assembly (354/3). Later given the title *On the symmories*, it is principally concerned with further reforms to the system—already overhauled some four years earlier—for group-financing of the Athenian war-fleet.[32] The closest match to X. and his concerns in *Poroi* comes, though, not from a front-line politician but from an armchair pundit: Isocrates of Erchia (*LGPN* s.v. no.13, *OCD* 747–8, *APF* 245–8); specifically his 'speech' 8 *On the peace*, alternatively titled (*Discourse*) *about the allies*.

[31] Ryder (1965) 90: not a Common Peace treaty. Neither Diodorus (16.22.1–2) nor any of the orators (such as Isoc. 8.16 and Demosth. 15.26) quote it, or from it, but according to an ancient scholiast (annotator) of Demosth. 3.28 the Athenians swore to respect the autonomy of all their allies.

[32] See generally Gabrielsen (1994) 182–99.

Whether Isoc. 8 was actually *written* in 355 can be debated, along with its literary and rhetorical sophistication,[33] but *On the peace* is incontrovertibly *set* then. First-time readers of it are likely to be struck by its overall length and verbosity, and the overall lack of concrete proposals. An unkind reaction would be that Isocrates serves up an airy meringue, as opposed to X.'s dense triple-decker sandwich. Look again, though, and the parallels with *Poroi* are plain to see.[34] As here, peace—of a sort—has already, seemingly, been made (Isoc. 8.15–16), and this presents the Athenians with a golden opportunity. Isoc. 8.19–22 spells it out. They can, and should, redeem their bad reputation for aggression and give up their residual hankering after imperialism (Isoc. 8.19 & 64–9; cf. *Poroi* 1.1, 6.1) which has necessitated heavy *eisphorai* (Isoc. 8.12 & 20; cf. *Poroi* 3.7–8 & 6.1). Instead of that, it is Athens' income which will increase (Isoc. 8.21; cf. *Poroi* 3.5 & 5.12); the polis will once again be bustling with metics, merchants, and foreigners (Isoc. 8.21; cf. *Poroi* 2–3). On the 'international' scene the Athenians will regain allies in droves (Isoc. 8.21; cf. *Poroi* 5.9 & 13) and will take the lead in peaceful diplomacy (Isoc. 8.22; cf. *Poroi* 5.9).[35] There is also much in common between a later stretch of *On the Peace*—Isoc. 8.136–40—and *Poroi* Chap.5.

* * * *

That X. wrote *Poroi* with Athens in mind is self-evident. Whether he was actually *in Athens* when he did so is a much harder question.

Two possibilities—neither of them Athens—are proffered in the ancient evidence. Diog.Laert. 2.56 reports his first-century predecessor Demetrius of Magnesia (above, n.11) as recording that X. died in Corinth. The credibility of that is not spoiled by the erroneousness of Diogenes' statement that X. died in the year 360/59, which comes from another source (see the beginning of this section). Another account is preserved by the second-century CE traveller and antiquarian Pausanias

[33] Some discussions: Gillis (1970), Harding (1973); Moysey (1982), Davidson (1990); Michelini (1998).

[34] They do not extend, however, to Isoc. 8.82 on the fifth-century Athenian Empire: some manuscripts give the phrase 'the surplus of the *poroi*' but a papyrus preserves the true reading 'the surplus of the *phoroi*' (tribute-payments). See Meiggs (1972) 433–4 (endnote 19); Gauthier 8 n.6.

[35] The orthodox view of these parallels (summarized in Thiel x) is that X. is responding to Isocrates here; so e.g. Marchant's Loeb xxviii with n.1. But Jansen (2007) 46 n.50 espouses the opposite possibility; and see in general Tuplin (1993) 33–4.

(*OCD* 1097 s.v.3). He claims that X. was buried in his long-time home Skillous (again cf. section 1), in a tomb bearing a statue carved in Pentelic—i.e. best Athenian—marble (Paus. 5.6.6). Since Pausanias does not report his sources as stating that X. had actually *died* at Skillous,[36] both of these traditions could be true. Or neither of them. What is to be noted, at any rate, is that no extant ancient writer believed that X. died in Athens—where, at any time after the revocation of his decree of banishment, he was legally entitled to return.

That he did return to Athens, whether merely as a visitor or as a resident, is nevertheless a cherished idea for many modern scholars. A version of it expressed without caveats is 'Xenophon was reared in Athens and died there'.[37] Compare and contrast 'there is no evidence that he returned to Athens', or, even more baldly, 'he did not . . . return to his native city'.[38] Why the discrepancy? The theory of X's return to Athens is more than a mere wish for a happy ending; for the same sort of pleasing ring-composition effect produced by the claim that the proposer of the abrogation of X.'s exile was the very man, Euboulos, who had proposed it in the first place—a chronological impossibility.[39] Thankfully, the issue does involve respectable academic criteria, judged differently by different scholars.

The theory's most recent exponent is Jansen. Setting it out in unprecedentedly full fashion, he marshals six 'areas of evidence that strongly support the conclusion that Xenophon not only returned to Athens but also took up residence there and had an active role in the intellectual and political life of the city'.[40]

Five of the six are circumstantial. They are:

(*a*) the signs that Corinthian hostility towards Athens grew in the 360s would have meant that, at some point, X.'s presence in Corinth would have no longer been tolerated;

(*b*) the fact that X.'s sons Diodoros and Gryllos (as I have mentioned already) fought at Mantineia 'indicates that the Athenians had

[36] Contrary to the summaries in (e.g.) Anderson (1974) 195–6 and Krentz (1989) 4.

[37] Pomeroy (1994) 8. She had been somewhat more circumspect earlier, but still certain that X. was by now 'visiting Athens regularly' (Pomeroy (1994) 4).

[38] Marchant's Loeb xxvi and Krentz (1989) 4, respectively.

[39] Diog.Laert. 2.59, citing Ister *FGrH* 334 F32; see already above, section 1. On Euboulos (whose birth-date was *c.* 405) and X. see in full below, section 6.

[40] Jansen (2007) 32–50, esp. 35–50; quotation from 32. See also e.g. Delebecque (1957) 334–41; Tuplin (1993) 32.

not only recalled Xenophon by this time, but that the two parties were completely reconciled';

(*c*) 'the aftermath of Mantineia provides tantalizing clues'—i.e. mainly the 'panegyrical movement', in art and literature, surrounding the dead Gryllos—'regarding Xenophon's whereabouts and status among his fellow citizens';

(*d*) X.'s *Cavalry-commander* (and by extension its sequel *On horsemanship*) and *Poroi* are works 'addressed directly to his fellow citizens', as again we have noted here already; and

(*e*) X.'s 'relationship to his (*sc.* intellectual) contemporaries', such as Isocrates and Plato, in these years betokens more than long-distance contact with them.

There is much of interest here but (in my opinion) nothing conclusive, either individually or even in aggregate.

This leaves the crux of the matter as Jansen's sixth and final criterion: the actual content and language of these late, Athenocentric works, *Poroi* itself above all. Given the importance of avoiding subjectivity in assessments of this kind,[41] Jansen focuses his attention on demonstrative or 'deictic' vocabulary in *Poroi*, meaning 'words that specify identity, spatial location, or temporal location relative to the speaker or hearer'.[42]

Some of it, one is bound to say, does not advance his argument a great deal. For instance, in 6.1 (already noted by Thiel xxv) X. uses the first-person plural phrase '*we* will live in greater security'. Indeed 6.1 unleashes a burst of such first-person plurals (eight of them altogether) to express the benefits that 'we' will enjoy if his ideas are implemented. But what of it? One need not be an actual denizen of Fifth Avenue to join in a rendition of (*We'll Have*) *Manhattan*.[43] Much more to the point is the fact that in 1.3, which again had already struck Thiel, X. uses the adverb 'here', in Greek, *enthade*; twice over, in fact.[44] With

[41] Of the kind, in fact, uncharacteristically displayed by Gauthier 64 (asserting that X. had seen for himself that 'many' metics were non-Hellenes: 2.3).

[42] Jansen (2007) 47.

[43] Compare the courteous protest of Dillery (2017) 210 n.58, against Gauthier (1984) 199 n.26 = Gauthier (2010) 135 n.26.

[44] 1.3 also uses *entautha*, which (depending on context) can either mean 'here' or 'there'. Note also the two occurrences of *ekei*, which unambiguously means 'there', in 4.26 and 4.49. Jansen (2007) 49 points out that in those two passages X. is referring to

that, however, we may contrast a form of words such as 'those holding positions of leadership in Athens' (1.1; see also 2.6, 2.7, 5.4).

One issue not addressed by Jansen (or others who share his position) is why, if X.'s rehabilitation in and by Athens was so all-embracing, there is no evidence for his being buried there, reunited with his ancestors; nor his descendants, either. In the light of that, it seems to me prudent to remain agnostic on the question of whether he was. On the other hand, of the fact that in the 350s he was an Athenian again—psychologically as well as legally ('de corps et de coeur': Gauthier 241) —there can be no shadow of a doubt.

4. STRUCTURE AND CONTENTS: A BRIEF SYNOPSIS

In modern printed editions the works of X., as of others, are kitted out with divisions and subdivisions, aids to easy reading and to convenient reference and cross-reference. The four lengthy works (*Anab.*, *Cyrop.*, *Hell.*, *Mem.*) have a three-level division into 'books', chapters, sections. For the others, *Poroi* included, chapters and sections suffice.

When more than one system of such subdivision exists for an ancient writer, 'convenient reference' risks becoming its opposite.[45] That problem does not arise with the works of X. Thus, in *Poroi* itself, X.'s modestly sized body of material—3,935 Greek words, according to the *TLG*; his shortest work apart from the *Apology*—is divided into six chapters of disparate lengths, as follows: 1: six sections; 2: seven; 3: fourteen; 4: fifty-two; 5: thirteen; 6: three.

Whether X. himself constructed it (or would have deconstructed it) in this manner, or anything like it, is neither here nor there. The practical fact is that, for the purposes of modern readers, this arrangement does assist the task of absorbing *Poroi* as well as, when required, making reference to it.[46]

the mining district of Laureion (*OCD* 800), which might indeed be a distant 'there' for many Athenians.

[45] An example is Plutarch's *Lives*: the chapter divisions are the same in all editions; their subsections vary.

[46] In the latter connection it should be noted that Dakyns' translation suppresses the section-numbers, though the Floating Press re-issue inserts them.

My earlier characterization of the work as a sandwich was not flippancy.[47] Chap.1 and Chaps.5–6 do represent a sort of outer wrapping for chapters 2–4 with their denser, meatier content. A treatise consisting *only* of Chaps.1 and 5–6 (had X. felt obliged, for whatever reason, to have it so) would not have been nonsensical. Even that could have got across, effectively enough, his central underpinning idea: that his fellow-citizens should put war and imperialism behind them and embrace the 'peace dividend'. On the other hand he is unlikely to have called such a work *Poroi*, because Chap.1 makes no more than a start on explaining the 'ways and means' that will generate the revenues needed to bring the new post-imperialist Athens into being.

Chapter 1 announces the overall theme. If unjust treatment of imperial allies is to be avoided,[48] the Athenians must find ways of supporting themselves from their own domestic resources. In the first instance this means better appreciation and exploitation of the natural resources of Attica itself: what the land can grow (and the encircling seas yield), and the mineral deposits on and below it—marble and, especially, silver. (On this last see below, *Chapter 4*.)

Chapter 2 extends the search for *poroi* to an under-exploited human resource: metics, the free immigrant population. X. here offers ideas for improving metic-status, both negatively (by removing some disobliging features of it) and positively, so as to attract to Athens not only more but 'better' foreign residents.

Chapter 3 naturally moves from foreign residents, via (in 3.1) another acknowledgement of natural assets, to foreign visitors,[49] especially those visiting for purposes of trade. Again, ideas for increasing and incentivizing this are suggested. Most striking among them are two that (by contrast with *Chapter 2*) carry significant financial implications for the citizen-body: the creation of start-up capital (*aphormê*) and a publicly owned merchant fleet.

Chapter 4 takes up at length (from 1.5) the topic of Athens' silver resources. Working on the assumption that they are limitless, X. wants a massive increase in the number of those working in the mining

[47] To anyone finding it so, I cite in my defence p.2 of Rhodes with Lewis (1997), one of the least flippant books imaginable: Rhodes describes his material as 'organised as a sandwich', with catalogues of data as its 'filling'.

[48] It should not be forgotten that Athens still had some (between the loss of the major part of the Second League in the Social War and the organization's final dissolution in 338). See generally e.g. Cargill (1981) 194; Rhodes (2010) 276–8.

[49] The link is explicit in 3.5.

industry, including the (slave) miners themselves. In addition to the workforce in private ownership, there should be a huge corps of publicly owned slaves available for leasing-out as miners. The risk entailed in cutting new mines (but finding nothing) can be offset by sharing it between the ten Athenian 'tribes'. Dangers of another kind, which might result from continuing mining operations during any enemy invasion, can be countered by strengthening the military defences of the mining district in southern Attica. And overall, the aim is to 'create adequate sustenance for every Athenian from public resources' (4.33).

Chapter 5 returns to the context implied (but not articulated) in 1.1, with post-Social-War peace as the backcloth. For Athens, the future will be a happy one if further war is avoided and peace proactively maintained. The Athenians can be leaders of the Greeks again, but this time in diplomacy—directed in the first instance at ensuring the autonomy of Delphi.

Chapter 6 concludes the work by briefly enumerating the benefits that Athens will reap if X.'s ideas are adopted, and urging that the advice and approval of the gods—specific ones—be sought.

The observations of Thiel 11–12 and, at greater length, Gauthier 88–9 (and 109) on 3.6 should be registered here. One way to look at the internal structure of *Poroi* is to divide it by subject-matter, as the six traditional Chapters do (above), competently enough: territory, metics, trade(rs), mines, peace, conclusion. But it is also possible that, for X. and his readers, there was only one fundamental internal division, at 3.6. Before it, all the proposals put forward are realizable without cash in hand; they are 'simply a matter of changing the rules' (Ober (2008) 251). After 3.6, all depends on capital—and X. must make that clear to his fellow-citizens, who might up to then have been hoping not to have to put their hands deep into their pockets. See further in the Comm. to 3.6.

5. GENRE

X.'s (?)Arkadian contemporary Aeneas 'the Tactician' (*OCD* 23) wrote a work called the *Poristikê* (*biblos*). It is lost. Even if it had survived, though, it would not have given us a true companion-piece to X.'s *Poroi*. Aeneas' topic, on whatever level or levels, was *military* provisioning—the polar opposite of X.'s peace-driven scenario.[50] *Poroi* belongs in a category of its own. It is a paradigm of what is meant by the phrase *sui generis*. But that is not to deny that it shares broad characteristics with other genres of prose literature recognized at the time. Its aim is to persuade, by argument and evidence. The type of writing to which it shows the closest affinity is oratory or rhetoric. The Comm. will point out the specifics of this as and when they arise.

So far so good—but the ancients distinguished between more than one branch of rhetoric. Classically (meaning: as articulated in the second half of the fourth century, by Aristotle and his contemporaries), there were three such branches: speeches 'for decision-making (demegoric), for display (epideictic), and for the courts (dikanic)'.[51]

The last of these has little bearing on *Poroi*. Neither internal nor external evidence hints at a court-room context for the work. At most, some of the specifics mentioned above present themselves in dikanic (a.k.a. forensic or judicial) oratory because that just happens to be the sub-genre which has been transmitted to us in the greatest quantity.[52] If we are seeking to identify in broad principle the species of rhetorical production to which *Poroi* owes most, the relevant categories are epideictic and demegoric (a.k.a. symbouleutic).

Jansen's discussion of this choice, favouring the symbouleutic subgenre over the epideictic, is comprehensive and convincing.[53] Thiel xxx had briefly made a case for the alternative, and the idea does have some merit, on several counts. The paean of praise for Attica and its products in 1.3–8, notably, is unmistakably epideictic in tone, i.e. comparable with such things as parts of the Periklean *Funeral Speech* in Thucydides, or Isocrates 4.42 (written in the 380s).[54] In this connection,

[50] Aen.Tact. 14.2; see Bettalli (1990) 11–12 and Whitehead (1990) 138. Another work sometimes suggested as a *Poroi* analogue is book 2 of [Aristotle's] *Economics*, with its collection of actual revenue-raising schemes adopted at various times and in diverse places (see the Appendix in this volume). But here too the putative correspondences diminish on close examination. [Aristotle's] topic is revenue-raising schemes designed to meet specific emergencies. Jansen (2007) 56, expanded at 406–14, is a fair-minded discussion, and dismissal, of both of these supposed comparanda.

[51] [Aristot.] *Rhetorica ad Alexandrum* 1.1421b7–10 = Anaximenes, *Ars Rhetorica* 1.1 Fuhrmann; more elaborately in Aristot. *Rhet.*1.3.1 (1358a36–b8), where the first type is 'symbouleutic'. See Whitehead (2000) 4.

[52] There are convenient catalogues in (e.g.) Ober (1989) 341–9; Edwards (1994) 74–9.

[53] Jansen (2007) 58–104.

[54] See Thuc. 2.38.2, compared with *Poroi* 1.7 by Loraux (1986) 86. One could add another *pre-Poroi* instance from the 'Old Oligarch': [X.] *Ath.Pol.*2.6–8, esp. 7. On the *Panathenaicus* of Aelius Aristides see Chap.1 intro. (end).

it is also relevant to recall that the mention of *Poroi* by Menander 'Rhetor' (above, section 2) occurs in one of his treatises on epideictic oratory; specifically, in a discussion of how to praise a place which has natural terrestrial and maritime assets. However, once we move into *Poroi* Chaps.2–6 the epideictic element retreats to the background and does not return.

Instead, and (in aggregate) overwhelmingly, the tone and methods of deliberative oratory come to the fore. To reiterate: this fact does not mean that *Poroi* is, pure and simple, a specimen of deliberative oratory. Apart from internal considerations, there is no reason whatsoever to suppose that X. stood and delivered it, verbally, to a deliberative body.

The absence of the formula 'o men of Athens' (or suchlike), noted by Jansen, is actually not a crucial matter. Isocrates' large body of deliberative 'speeches' (and one pseudo-dikanic one: Isoc. 15 *On the Antidosis*) makes hardly any use of it, either.[55] What *is* significant is *Poroi*'s concentration, and mix, of first-person and second-person plurals. X. shifts—just like an orator who can see his listeners before him (and vice versa)—between 'we'-statements and 'you'-statements.[56] An especially noteworthy instance of the latter occurs at 6.2, almost the work's end: 'if you do take a decision to do these things, my personal advice would be etc.'. In the Greek, the phrase 'take a decision' is the idiom used by real-life assemblies and other deliberative bodies when passing their resolutions.[57] And besides grammar and idiom there is rhetorical method in *Poroi*, some of it (according to the theorists) especially associated with deliberative oratory. Jansen highlights two excellent examples: X.'s use of the device of *prokatalepsis* (anticipating and answering a critic or opponent's objections)[58] and the attention he pays to assuring readers that his proposals meet the criteria of equality, resilience, and substance.[59]

[55] Jansen (2007) 62. In the relevant works of Isoc. see merely 14.1 & 6; the notional speaker is a Plataian.

[56] Noted by Thiel xxviii.

[57] In brief Woodhead (1981) 38 with 48; in full Rhodes with Lewis (1997) 19–20 and passim. See also Jansen (2007) 66–7.

[58] Jansen (2007) 70. For the ten instances of this trope see 4.40, 4.19, 4.22, 4.28, 4.34, 4.46, 4.48, 5.5, 5.11, 5.13; and contrast the single instance in *Hipp.* (5.4).

[59] Jansen (2007) 70–1. These criteria are the ones stipulated in [Aristot.] *Rhetorica ad Alexandrum* 2.1425b29–30 = Anaximenes, *Ars Rhetorica* 2.35 Fuhrmann. In *Poroi* see 2.7, 3.6, 3.10, 4.3, 4.26–7, 4.40, 5.2, 6.2–3. Jansen notes that 3.10 employs one of the very adjectives, *polychronios* ('long-lived'), used in the rhetorician's stipulations. A pleasing coincidence, but no more than that: this is a not uncommon word which X. also uses twice elsewhere (*Eq.*9.6, *Mem.*1.4.16).

In *Poroi*, then, X. directly and by definition addresses, in an Athenian version, a topic that Aristotle would later place first in his list of the five generic concerns of deliberative oratory, and in doing so he also brings in the other four. X. writes 'about *poroi*, and war and peace, and about the defence of the territory, imports and exports, and about legislation': Aristot. *Rhet.*1.4.7 (1359b19–21).

That list might call to mind another one. Section 43.4 of the Aristotelian *Ath.Pol.* enumerates various standing items which the Athenian assembly (*ekklêsia*) had to discuss at its 'master' meetings, i.e. ten times a year. They include discussion 'about grain and about the defence of the territory'. So are the 'we' and the 'you' of *Poroi* the Athenians as a whole, meeting on the Pnyx Hill (as in the putative scenario of Isoc. 8)?[60] The possibility cannot be ruled out. But there is a more plausible alternative. Marchant (Loeb edition xxvii) had stated that *Poroi* 'is addressed, apparently, to the Council of Five Hundred'.

The point was not elaborated there, but it can be. Germane to the issue is not the fact that X. twice (4.18, 6.1) mentions that very body, the Kleisthenic *boulê* (*OCD* 247–8; fully in Rhodes (1972); also Hansen (1991) 246–65). On neither occasion is the mention of it more than incidental. Nor[61] can the form of words in 6.2, quoted above, be regarded as that of a *probouleuma* (a preliminary determination by the *boulê*). That is because one key element of it, as we have noted already, evokes the enactment-formula of the assembly itself, *par excellence*. Besides, X.'s verb there, 'I would advise' (*symbouleusaimi*), in application to himself is paralleled in e.g. Demosthenes's *Fourth Philippic* (10.42), indubitably an address to the assembly.[62] Even so, it may be that Marchant's suggestion deserves more than Gauthier's brusque dismissal.[63]

The several supporting considerations mustered by Jansen need not be assessed in detail here. Most of them, in my opinion, would be convincing only to the convinced. More important, his overall conclusion is surely, anyway, the correct one: that *Poroi* as it stands is not a composition actually delivered to the *boulê*.[64] Rather, the Kleisthenic

[60] The opening of Isoc. 8 does make this explicit (in the kind of language nowhere used in *Poroi*): 'all those who are present here' (8.1) and esp. 'we have come for an *ekklêsia* about war and peace' (8.2).

[61] Despite Jansen (2007) 92.

[62] See also Demosth.19.14, addressed to a court but purporting to quote what Aeschines had said to the assembly.

[63] Gauthier 223.

[64] Jansen (2007) 94–8. Among the points he adduces, the one that seems most compelling to me (if not necessarily to him) is the striking similarity between the opening

council is relevant to *Poroi* in so far as it functioned as a forum, within the Athenian constitution, where ideas could be introduced, debated, and (preliminarily) finalized in an atmosphere of calm rationality, at least in theory. The council-house, *bouleutêrion*, was a place where the proposer of plans with complex financial implications might expect members of his audience to be assiduous in 'doing the calculations' (4.34) that he had done himself.

All that said, we return to the point that what the elderly X. composed here was something *sui generis*, certainly so in terms of an exact fit into any of the genres of prose literature recognized in his own time. In present-day terms, Jansen makes a good case for describing it as a 'pamphlet', while pointing out that any such term must not mislead us.[65] *Poroi* was not intended for mass-production, mass-circulation, and mass-consumption, all anachronistic concepts for this era. It was a contribution to a discussion—one that had already begun[66]—of the city's financial predicament at this time.

In the first instance this debate will have been conducted (no doubt mainly face-to-face) among serious, like-minded individuals. Nevertheless, because Athens was a democracy, X. made sure throughout his exposition, as Powell emphasizes, that Athenians of any and all backgrounds would see themselves and their concerns sympathetically reflected in the ideas put forward.[67]

6. 'VOTE EUBOULOS!'?

During the eighty-year period of the restored democracy, 403/2–322, the Athenians governed themselves and the other inhabitants of their polis by laws and by 'decrees'.[68] Any citizen was free to propose either,

of *Poroi* ('Personally, I always think that whatever kind of *prostatai* there are corresponds with the kind of civic communities they lead') and the opening of a *speech to the council* put into the mouth of Kritias in *Hell.*2.3.51 ('Personally, council, I think it the task of a true *prostatês*, when he sees his friends being deceived, not to allow it').

65 Jansen (2007) 57–8, 99–101—anticipated in this by e.g. Anderson (1974) 193.

66 The main reason to believe that *Poroi* was joining a debate already in progress comes in the compound verb 'I agree', *xymphêmi*, transmitted at 4.51. Attempts have been made to emend it to simple *phêmi*, 'I say', but they should be resisted. See further in Notes on the Text, and in the Comm. to the passage.

67 Powell (2015) 37–43.

68 Hansen (1991) 161–2.

though in doing so he ran the risk of prosecution for making a proposal that was unlawful (one of the weapons of the factional politics of the day).[69] In uncontroversial circumstances where that did not happen, a proposed 'decree'—a *psêphisma*: literally, matter for a vote—was, usually, first scrutinized in the *boulê*, amended there if necessary, and put to the *ekklêsia* of all (citizen) comers for a simple majority vote, by show of hands, either way.[70] Enacting a law, a *nomos*, was a procedure more complicated and, if the record does not grossly deceive us, very much rarer. Here, though the *boulê* and *ekklêsia* were involved at a preliminary stage, the actual voting body was a large group—running into hundreds, even thousands—of *nomothetai*, 'layers-down-of-the-law'. They were chosen, for one day's work of this kind, from the annual pool of sworn judge-jurors (*dikastai*), which meant that legislative as well as judicial decisions were vested in that 6,000-strong subset of the demos.[71]

This constitutional context is worth clarifying because it is sometimes misunderstood. For example, Jansen writes: 'Xenophon envisions that legislation will be necessary to implement most of, if not all, his proposals (3.6), and therefore the work evidences the first step in the legislative process. The legislative character is particularly conspicuous at the end of the work... The phrase ['take a decision to do these things' in 6.2] evokes the enactment formula of Athenian decrees and leaves the impression that Xenophon views his proposals as *probouleumata* [preliminary determinations by the *boulê*] to be enacted in the assembly.'[72] While most of this is correct, and significant for being so (see already section 5), the word 'legislation' is not. Decrees are what is at issue here: explicitly, indeed, in 3.6 (*psêphismata philanthrôpa*, 'beneficent decrees');[73] implicitly, still, in 6.2. In his own mind's eye, X.'s suggestions would *all*—individually, more probably than as a

69 Hansen (1991) 205–12, summarizing Hansen (1974).

70 Hansen (1991) 125–60 (*ekklêsia*) and 246–65 (*boulê*).

71 Hansen (1991) 165–77, esp. 168–9; cf. 151.

72 Jansen (2007) 66.

73 Besides Jansen (2007) 66 and 332, this mistranslation is also in Marchant's Loeb edition and Waterfield 172. Mention of Athenian *psêphismata* in earlier X.: *Hell.* 1.7.20–1 & 34, 2.1.32, 2.2.15, 3.5.16, 5.1.5, 6.5.2. For comparison, mention of Athenian *nomoi* in *Hell.*: 1.7.5, 1.7.14–15, 1.7.22 & 25–9, 2.3.2 & 11, 2.3.51–5, 2.4.42. However, these *nomoi* are broad, 'background' statutes. Given that X. was away from Athens when the more precise, Hansenian *nomos*/*psêphisma* distinction was first created and adopted, and for long afterwards, one suspects he might not have assigned it much importance (or even been fully aware of it).

totality—go to the full citizen assembly, and they would stand or fall in that arena.[74]

If the immediate audience for which X. intended *Poroi* was indeed 'serious, like-minded individuals' (so above: section 5, end), can someone among them be identified who might have sponsored its proposals before the assembled Athenian demos in this formal way?

First, there is no evidence that *X. himself*, although an Athenian citizen again, harboured any ambitions to step forward as one of the city's *rhêtores* (literally 'speakers'), that self-selected elite of fourth-century Athenians who influenced debates and framed proposals in the assembly and elsewhere; the nearest thing Athens had to present-day 'politicians'.[75] For X., the time for such things had long gone, even if his chequered past would not have been perceived as a handicap—whether for a full-blown career in the public eye or even as someone coming forward as a private citizen (*idiôtês*) with specific proposals.[76]

Second, Isocrates too can be eliminated from consideration under this head. The correspondences between *Poroi* and Isoc. 8 *On the peace*, written by X.'s slightly older fellow-demesman,[77] have already been noted. It is entirely possible that the writer of one of those works was familiar with the other.[78] Yet such a scenario, even if true, is not one which brings any direct consequences in the practical sphere. At no stage in his life was Isocrates active in the front line of Athenian politics, least of all in the mid-350s as an octogenarian pundit with more to write (and still almost two decades in which to write it).

[74] A possible complicating factor arises in the shape of the annual *merismos*, allocation of funds, to the various organs of government. (See ?Aristot. *Ath.Pol.*48.1–2, with Rhodes (2010) 299.) If the implementation of a decree breached part of the current allocation—by requiring any such organ *including the assembly* to exceed its budget—it seems that a law had to authorize this (Hansen (1991) 152, 173). However, we do know of instances where a decree of the assembly instructed the *nomothetai* to do precisely that (Rhodes (1972) 99–101). One way or another, it therefore seems, the *ekklêsia* kept the upper hand.

[75] On the *rhetores* see Hansen (1991) 143, 204, 268, 270–1. What Cartledge xiii means by labelling the X. of the 360s and 350s an 'ex-politician' is puzzling, as there is no evidence of his fulfilling that definition before he left Athens in his mid-twenties. (If it refers to the very broadly 'political' nature of his relationship with Agesilaos and the Spartans in the Skillous years, it has no bearing on the present topic.)

[76] On *idiôtai* see generally Hansen (1991) 266–8.

[77] Born in 436, Isocrates was perhaps seven or eight years older than X. The ancestral deme they had in common was Erchia (part of the tribe Aigeis), a large village or small town in eastern Attica beyond Mt. Hymettos. See generally Traill (1975) 41, 67; Whitehead (1986) 44 and passim.

[78] See above, section 3, at nn.33–5.

Instead, for connections between *Poroi* and practical politics, what is required is evidence of contact and influence between X. and one or more individuals who did belong to the category of authentic *rhêtores* or—to use his own preferred terminology, from 1.1—*prostatai*.

Here one man, above all others, is in the frame: **Euboulos of Probalinthos**, *c.* 405–*c.* 335 (*LGPN* s.v. no.61), 'probably the most important Athenian statesman of the period 355–342' (G. L. Cawkwell in *OCD* 543 s.v.1). A reputable source cited by Diog.Laert 2.59 names him as the man who proposed the decree reversing X.'s banishment, as we have seen, and only scepticism for its own sake would doubt it. Why Euboulos did X. this service is beyond conjecture. The mere fact that he did must (surely) guarantee at least one meeting between the two of them, for a grateful X. to express his thanks. But there needs to be more, much more, than that to justify Cawkwell's claim—a crystallization of one of the points argued in his classic article on the man (Cawkwell (1963))—that *Poroi* is 'an extravagant version of the sort of methods [Euboulos] probably followed'. So is there?

Given his prominence *after* 355, the first five decades of Euboulos' life are lamentably ill-documented. Before that watershed, in fact, only once (apart from proposing the decree about X.) is he known for certain to have been active in the public domain. This was in 370/69, when the accident of sortition brought him the office of *thesmothetês* (*OCD* 1466), one of the six lesser archons: *SEG* 19.133.4; *AO* 251. But *after* 355, with 'the imperialistic advocates of war... discredited and the state near bankruptcy' (*OCD* 543 again), Euboulos rose to power, or more exactly influence, of a very significant order, earning him a place in Theopompus' survey of the major 'demagogues' of classical Athens (*FGrH* 115 F(99–)100 = Athen. *Deipn.*4.166D–E).[79]

The constitutional vehicle for this was so-called theoric fund (*OCD* 1462), either created or enhanced by him and his associate Diophantos of Sphettos at or soon after this very time.[80] Its board of administrators was directly elected, rather than chosen by lot. Despite the fund's name (a reflection of just one of its tasks: paying small grants to needy citizens, to allow them to participate in religious festivals by attending theatre performances), the scope of its responsibilities, financed by

[79] Theopompus on Euboulos: Flower (1994) 72–3, 125–47. For Theopompus, Euboulos represented 'the culmination of a long succession of demagogues who had progressively weakened Athens through their corruption of the people': Pownall (2004) 156, with further bibliography.

[80] On Diophantos see, in brief, Rhodes (2010) 372.

regular annual income plus any surpluses, became almost all-embracing in the non-military sphere. And Euboulos' own stature matched it (Aeschin. 3.25) until, from the late 340s onwards, hawkish politicians such as Demosthenes gained the ascendancy.

Euboulos' support for the peace-treaty that had ended the Social War,[81] we may note, is merely implicit in the contemporary record, but an ancient scholiast (annotator) of Demosth. 3.28 names him as responsible (*aitios*) for it.

* * * *

It is against this backcloth that the links—in either direction—between Euboulos and *Poroi* need to be assessed. Starting from the Euboulan side, the discursive treatment in Cawkwell (1963) 63–6 is the prime statement of the view that they are clear and significant.[82] Starting from the *Poroi* side, Gauthier 223–31 addresses, in order of X.'s presentation, everything of relevance in Chaps.2–4; and he finds very lean pickings.

Gauthier's position is irrefutable, in my opinion.[83] His method is the one I will adopt here, while mentioning more of the content of *Poroi* than he did. In that way it is the absence of evidence for the political implementation of X.'s ideas—by Euboulos or, in most instances, by any contemporary of his—that can emerge with the cumulative force it ought to. (Besides any specific footnoting to the summary list which now follows,[84] see in all instances the Comm. for full discussion.)

2.2–4. Removal of the obligation for metics (of the appropriate income-level) to fight as hoplites alongside citizens. No evidence.

2.5. Granting of permission for metics (again, of the requisite income) to join the Athenian cavalry. No evidence.

2.6. Granting of permission for approved metic applicants to build and own houses inside the city walls. According to Cawkwell, 'it is a fact that, whereas before the Social War the conferment of *gês kai oikias egktêsis* [ownership-rights 'of land and house'] appears to have been very rare, after that war it is conferred, to judge by our epigraphic evidence, very freely indeed. This of course affected only privileged individuals, but suggests that Eubulus had taken Xenophon's advice, in

[81] See above, section 3, at n.31.

[82] Cawkwell (1963) 63–6. See also, before this, Thiel xxiii–xxv. After this see e.g. Burke (1984) 113–115; Burke (1985) 258–9; Meyer (2010) 48–50.

[83] As already stated, in part, in Whitehead (1977) 128–9.

[84] With which cf. Powell (2015) 19–20.

part, about how to attract metics'.[85] The frailty of this position has been pointed out by Gauthier and by Whitehead, independently of each other. In brief: the contrast, as claimed, between few *egktêsis* grants before the mid-350s but many directly afterwards is not borne out by the evidence. Likewise, X.'s stipulation of ownership-rights *for houses only* is hardly at all reflected in the grants actually given.[86] I would now add that his stipulation of intramural sites is never mentioned at all; also that none of the individual grants surviving on stone were made by a decree proposed by Euboulos. (For this caveat, equally applicable to the 'Periklean Athens' model in the fifth century, see again below.)

2.7. Creation of a board (of unspecified size) of *metoikophylakes*, 'metic-custodians'. No evidence.

3.3. Avoidance of delay in the settling of disputes involving non-resident foreign merchants (*emporoi*), by incentivizing 'the officials in change of the port'. A connection between this and practical Athenian politics and law has been routinely seen in the introduction (at some time before 347: Demosth. 21.176), of so-called *dikai emporikai*, 'mercantile suits'; lawsuits procedurally devised with *emporoi* in mind. The features which made them so included a provision for speedy resolution (though scholars have disagreed on exactly how this was achieved).[87] Cawkwell asserts that Euboulos 'may have been responsible...in response to Xenophon's demand'. Even Gauthier is content—I would not be—to attribute the measure, on no evidential basis, to Euboulos or 'un de ses amis'; however, he does point out the lack of evidence for achieving the avoidance of delay *by the means actually proposed by X.*[88]

3.4: Provision of rewards for the cream of foreign ship-owners and traders: *proedria* (front seats at the theatre) and invitations to 'hospitality' (*xenia*). As with **2.6** above, the (documentary) evidence for such honorific measures does not present itself until the 330s and 320s; and even then, these particular honours are hardly ever the ones given.

[85] Cawkwell (1963) 64. See also e.g. Herzog (1914) 480; Bodei Giglioni lvii–lviii (n.42), lxvii.

[86] Gauthier 223–5; Whitehead (1977) 128–9. At that time, all the relevant epigraphic evidence was collected in Pečírka (1966). More recent discoveries, and re-datings of old ones, have not altered the picture: see generally Lambert (2006), Engen (2010) 192–7.

[87] See e.g. Cohen (1973); Isager & Hansen (1975) 84–7; MacDowell (1978) 231–4; Todd (1993) 334–337.

[88] Cawkwell (1963) 64; Gauthier 225–6.

3.7:, with 9–11. Creation of special (?)*eisphorai* to create start-up capital (*aphormê*), and associated list of benefactors extending to foreigners and other states. No evidence.

3.12. Construction of hostels and other wholesale trading facilities in Peiraieus. A purple passage in the speech which Dinarchus (*OCD* 452) wrote, in 323, for one of the public prosecutors of Demosthenes in the so-called Harpalos Affair (*OCD* 646) contrasts the defendant unfavourably with Euboulos under several heads; one is that only the latter erected 'buildings', in Peiraieus, Athens itself, and elsewhere in Attica (Din. 1.96). A long-established orthodoxy relates this passage to 3.12.[89]

3.13. Construction of more retail premises, both in Peiraieus and the city-centre. See under the previous item.

3.14. Acquisition of a fleet (of unspecified size) of publicly owned merchant ships. No evidence.

4.1 (and passim). Reorganization of the mining industry, such as to produce a major increase in revenues. According to Cawkwell, 'Eubulus probably was interested: he prosecuted Moerocles in connection with mining contracts (Demosth. xix 293) and certainly after the Social War there was a new and considerable attempt to exploit the mines [on the footnote to this, see below]; by 341 Demosthenes could speak of them as a likely object for Philip to covet (viii 45). Indeed it is not inconceivable that some slaves were bought for hiring as Xenophon proposed [see **4.17**]. There is, however, nothing to suggest that Eubulus went in for large scale capital investment in the mines, and one may presume that he was suitably cautious.'[90] As we see, Cawkwell provides his own, overall caveat here. Subsidiary ones are also needed: the trial mentioned in Demosth. 19.293 is no proof at all of Eubulus' interest in the mines *per se*; and R. J. Hopper's guess (cited in Cawkwell's 64 n.99) that the tax-exemption for mining work that features in [Demosth.] 42.17 is gratuitous. See also the next four items.

4.17. Acquisition of a very large body of publicly owned slaves, for leasing as miners. No evidence relating to Euboulos; a passage in Aristotle's *Politics* might be relevant to his associate Diophantos.

4.30. Mitigation of the risk of cutting new mines, *kainotomiai*, by spreading it across the ten tribes. No evidence.

[89] Herzog (1914) 479; Thiel xxiv; Cawkwell (1963) 64; Bodei Giglioni lxxxii with n.57; Gauthier 226; Worthington (1993) 268; Garland (2001) 43 with 186 (cautiously).

[90] Cawkwell (1963) 64.

4.33. Provision (as an aim of the programme as a whole) of a certain level of sustenance (*trophê*) for every Athenian from the public purse. This is quantifiable by reference to 3.9 and its mention of three obols a day.[91] Loomis dismisses the figure as 'merely a projection by Xenophon of a scheme that never was realized'.[92] The theoric fund, whatever its other disbursements, did distribute *theôrika* (for the purchase of theatre-seats), but only to those who could not afford their own—and only, necessarily, on performance-days. The rate is attested as five obols in the 320s, otherwise two.[93] In any case a *theôrikon* could not properly be characterized as a dole, like the *diôbelia* of Kleophon (*OCD* 333 Cleophon (1); Loomis (1998) 222–3 no.7) in the late fifth century.

4.44. Construction of a central fortress (linking Anaphlystos and Thorikos) in the mining district, at Besa. No datable evidence.

4.52. Provision of sustenance-payments (*trophê*: cf. above, **4.33**) for military trainees. No evidence of such a thing before the Epikratean (post-335) ephebate as described in ?Aristot. *Ath.Pol.*42.2–5, at 42.3.

5.1. Creation of a board of *eirênophylakes* ('peace-custodians'). Cawkwell advances the proposition, startling at first sight, that 'Xenophon's demand for a board of *eirênophylakes* was met by the creation of the Theoric Commissioners'. This is in fact a provocative summary of an ingenious 'guess' expressed more carefully at its first appearance.[94]

5.9–10. Pursuance, by diplomatic means, of a Panhellenic policy of autonomy for Delphi. Here one could cite, *faute de mieux*, Demosth. 19.10 & 304: Euboulos' proposal of a decree of *c.* 347 to send envoys 'everywhere' and hold a conference in Athens about the threat of Macedon.

6.1. More lavish celebration of festivals, and refurbishment of shrines.[95] Again (cf. on **3.12**) Din. 1.96 is relevant: Euboulos, it seems, was responsible for some 'ornamentation for the goddess (Athena)' being taken up to the akropolis. No evidence otherwise.

6.1. Repairs to walls and dockyards. No evidence links Euboulos with Athens' walls. As regards dockyards (*neôria*), yet again—and much more importantly this time—Din. 1.96 is pertinent. The speaker there appears to claim that under Euboulos' administration 'ship-sheds'

[91] Gauthier 21, 168 (and already e.g. Marchant in the Loeb edition 203 n.1).

[92] Loomis (1998) 226–7, cf. 319.

[93] Loomis (1998) 227–31, cf. 319–20.

[94] Cawkwell (1963) 63, referring back to 56.

[95] This and the following two items, strictly speaking, are not proposals *per se* but assertions of how surplus money can and should be used (see the Comm. on 4.33).

(*neôsoikoi*) were built. This chimes in harmoniously enough with the statement in Aeschin. 3.25 that in Euboulos' heyday the administrators of the theoric fund also wore several other hats, including those of controllers of the dockyards (*neôria*—the word X. uses), and also with other evidence that associates the building of (more) ship-sheds with that of a new *skeuothêkê* (a.k.a. Philon's Arsenal), both beginning in 347.[96]

6.1. Restoration of traditional emoluments (and associated perquisites?) for priests, councillors, officials, cavalrymen. Evidence either non-existent or, concerning the cavalry, inconclusive.

6.2–3. Consultation of the oracles at Dodona and Delphi, to identify the deities whose goodwill is essential for the proposed measures overall. No evidence.

* * * *

It is plain to see that Cawkwell's phrase 'what Xenophon proposed, Eubulus enacted' inflates what little evidence we have into a misleading assessment overall.[97]

The temptation to conjoin, somehow, the man who wrote of the need to increase Athens' *prosodoi* and the man who, Plutarch comments, was praised for doing exactly that ('he increased the community's *prosodoi* and greatly benefited the state from them': *Precepts of Statecraft* 812D)[98] exerts a strong pull nonetheless. And in fact it would be foolish simply to discard it on the basis of the cold douche I have applied here. Some fundamental links remain: none more so than the commitment to peace (after a period of imperialism and war, and before another time when the second of these, at least, came to the fore again), and the concomitant idea that the state raises income *from* itself to spend *on* itself. As Gauthier expresses it, the 'application' of *Poroi* is

[96] Philochoros *FGrH* 328 F56a; *IG* II^2 505.11–17; Garland (2001) 96 (with 203), 156–8. On the Peiraieus *neôsoikoi* see B. Rankov in Blackman & Rankov (2014) part B chap.16.

[97] Cawkwell (1963) 56. One must add, of course, that its epigrammatic brevity could make it sound more misleading than intended. The investigation as a whole clarifies the argument, which is not that Euboulos enacted everything that X. proposed; rather, that if/when any of X.'s proposals was enacted, Euboulos was the enactor. For an even more guarded formulation see Rhodes (2010) 371: *Poroi* 'seems to reflect the thinking of Eubulus'; again in Rhodes (2013b) 122; and cf. also e.g. Worthington (2013) 90–1.

[98] By a slip Plutarch gives Euboulos' demotikon there as Anaphlystios ('of Anaphlystos'); he should have written Probalisios ('of Probalinthos'). For Euboulos and *prosodoi* see also Theopompus *FGrH* 115 F100, but a hostile view there: 'he continually spent the *prosodoi* of the Athenians on paying wages'.

hard to discern in the immediate post-*Poroi* years, but that still leaves 'influence'; 'la voie à suivre, sinon les moyens pour la suivre'.[99] Who did follow X. down this path is a question we must return to later (section 8).

7. *POROI* AND POLITICAL THOUGHT

The thrust of section 6 was largely destructive. Its title was framed as a rhetorical question, and the answer to the question turns out, after a search for supporting evidence, to be No. *Poroi* is not a political manifesto, if by that is meant a set of practical proposals that Euboulos (or anyone else connected with him) set about enacting and implementing in Athens in the immediate aftermath of the Social War. To turn the issue through 180°: we do find, unsurprisingly, emergency-style measures at this time to bring in money to the public purse, but they do not echo anything proposed in *Poroi*, and Euboulos is not their initiator. Notably, the venerable Aristophon of Azenia (*LGPN* s.v. no.19, *OCD* 159)—even older than X.—was the man behind the appointment of 'investigators' to find out whether any public money had been squirreled away by private individuals (Demosth. 24.11). As regards the major re-minting of Athenian silver coinage around this time, the meticulous study by Kroll (2011a) places it in 353 by reference to the partially numismatic content of an unpublished law, Agora Inv.7495; but whereas that law's proposer is named (Epikrates), responsibility for the blatantly revenue-raising currency ploy (the re-issued, so-called pi-style, coins were 'radically substandard': Kroll) is unattributable.

Whether X. himself intended the content of *Poroi* to be 'realistic' and, as such, a contribution to 'the art of the possible' (Otto von Bismarck's definition of politics) is of course a separate question again; one not readily susceptible to testing. But anyone who doubts the point has the task of explaining what, instead, X. supposed that he was writing, and his readers supposed that they were reading. Creative fiction? Satire? As soon as alternatives are stated, implausibility rules

[99] Gauthier 229–31; quotations from 229 and 231. I am not qualified to judge—others may be—the appositeness of the analogy that he briefly gives: the last years and immediate aftermath of Algerian War of Independence (1954–1962), when, it seems, some French commentators published programmes for Algeria's future that entailed (e.g.) Christian/Muslim partition. (Gauthier himself did military service in Algeria 1959–1962; he had by then already held an academic post in Tunis.)

them out. Yet even so the topic needs to be explored, if we are to assess the work as a contribution to political thought at the time.[100]

Any Athenian who looked at his city in the middle decades of the fourth century and wished that it were different—better—could turn to two main types of reading-matter (with discussion arising), *in established genres*, which addressed the problem.

Plato, writing sophisticated conversation-pieces (*dialogoi*) on a high philosophical level, devised an ideal polis: first (in *Republic*, 380s/370s) as precisely that, the very best polis imaginable; later (in *Laws*, 350s/340s) the best polis that was practically possible.[101] While his Cretan 'Magnesia', as detailed in *Laws*, does display certain Athenian and Athens-related features, it is emphatically not, overall, a sanitized Athens.[102] As far as Plato was concerned, the real Athens was incorrigible. It could continue going to the dogs. For X., by contrast, nothing whatsoever suggests that this was an approach, and a position, with any appeal. He and Plato are worlds apart.[103] If X. lived long enough to read *Laws* (it is impossible to know), he might have admired it as an abstract intellectual exercise, but not as any sort of contribution towards an improved Athens.

Isocrates, as we have seen already, did want a better Athens. Furthermore, most of his 'speeches' show that he shared with X. one of the key ideas for bringing this about, and had indeed been advocating long before him: external, Panhellenic peace. Already in the *Panegyrikos* of 380 this theme is announced, at its beginning (chap.3) and end (chaps.173–87)—albeit coupled there, and in later works, with an (un-Xenophontic) appeal to the united Hellenes to direct their unity militarily, against Persia.

Where X. has been linked with Euboulos (see the preceding section), Isocrates' influence has been claimed on Athenian leaders associated with the Second Athenian League.[104] But when it comes to the city's

[100] On this topic in general see most recently Ferrario (2017).

[101] Readers who are not Plato specialists will find no better summary of this than Saunders (1970) 17–28.

[102] See Morrow (1960); N. F. Jones (1990).

[103] For a radically different view, finding important resemblances between *Poroi* and *Republic* (*sic*), see Schorn (2011, 2012).

[104] Isocrates and Kallistratos: Mathieu (1925) 87, largely on the basis of perceived similarities between Isocrates 14 (the *Plataiikos*) and the speech put into the mouth of Kallistratos in *Hell.*6.3.10–17; but disputed by Jaeger (1938) appendix 1. Links between Isocrates and his pupil Timotheos of Anaphlystos (*LGPN* s.v. no.32, *OCD* 1484 s.v. Timotheus (2), *APF* 506–12) are self-evident in Isoc. 15.101–39 and elsewhere.

internal character and functioning, an even more significant contrast between X. and Isocrates presents itself. Implicitly in many of his writings, and most explicitly in the *Areopagitikos* (of the mid-350s), Isocrates looks to the past. His views are nostalgic, conservative. He wants to turn Athens' constitutional and political clock back. All would be well if the Athenians returned to their 'ancestral constitution' (*patrios politeia*), in which, among other things, the venerable Areopagos council—not to be confused with its upstart namesake the Kleisthenic *boulê* of Five Hundred—once again held sway. The result would be 'a democracy based on class as determined by birth, wealth and merit', with the Areopagos' restored powers enabling it 'to solve the city's economic and moral problems'.[105]

This did not happen. It is true that in the period *c.* 350–322 the Athenian constitution came to run on principles which were in part less egalitarian than had obtained in the high fifth century.[106] It is also true that the Areopagos, in particular, came to enjoy enhanced powers and 'ancestral' prestige—but mainly, according to the evidence, from the late 340s onwards.[107] On his death-bed in 338, even a man with Isocrates' degree of self-regard would have been hard put to it to assert (pre-echoing Cawkwell on X. and Euboulos) that in this sphere 'what I proposed, the Athenians enacted'.

From time to time, in *Poroi*, X. too explicitly makes a point about the past: so in 1.1, 3.7, 4.2–3, 4.13–15, 4.25, 4.28, 4.31, 4.40, 5.5–7, 5.12, 6.1. Most of these passages are neutral in tone. The last of them, 6.1, does heavily imply the view that the present would be better if it was more like the past. X.'s wish there to restore to priests, officials, and cavalrymen their *patria* is a sentiment—whatever exactly it means—which would not have been at all out of place in Isocrates. (Compare and contrast the very un-Isocratean rhetorical question in 4.16: 'But why speak of the past?') Nevertheless, no reader of X. can fail to see that, overall, the direction of his gaze is towards the future.

* * * *

George Cawkwell's attempt to establish both the connections between X. and Euboulos and the limits of those connections downplayed the

105 Wallace (1989) 145–73, at 146.

106 So Rhodes (2015) 60, summarizing Rhodes (1979–1980).

107 See Wallace (1989) 175–201, summarized at 210–12; also the summary in Hansen (1991) 291.

latter too much, I have argued (in the preceding section); yet Cawkwell too saw plenty of clear blue water between the thinker and the doer, and he expressed this by declaring that '[m]uch of the treatise is fantastic'.[108]

Cawkwell was endorsing there the scornful verdicts passed on *Poroi* by some of the greatest German historians of ancient Hellas, August Boeckh (1785–1867) and Karl Julius Beloch (1854–1929).[109] Nor was Cawkwell himself the last to take this view: it is also expressed in the standard general reference-article on X. (Breitenbach (1967) 1760) and, incidentally, by others.[110] Sometimes though, X.'s ideas are taken more seriously. Here is a notable example. Writing in 1990, the historical sociologist W. G. Runciman remarked that 'Xenophon was no Adam Smith. But he was perfectly well aware of the need for investment to show a profit (*to lysitelein*) and of the value of an economic surplus (*periousia chrêmatôn*). What is more, his ideas about expanding the output of the silver mines by employing state-owned slaves, building up a state-owned merchant fleet to be chartered out, and building good hostels in the Piraeus to attract more foreign traders are, whether or not politically practicable, eminently sensible in economic terms.'[111]

Dr (a.k.a. Viscount)[112] Runciman's final proviso/disclaimer there is crucial, of course, as we have seen. Considered as *probouleumata*

[108] Cawkwell (1963) 63.

[109] For Boeckh—whom Cawkwell cites—in this regard, see Boeckh (1886) 1.698 and esp. 703: 'Unklares est in dieser ganzsen Darstellung nichts, aber unbegründet beinahe alles' ('in the whole presentation nothing is unclear, but almost everything unfounded'). Beloch (1922) 452: 'sie enthält keinen einzigen Gedanken, der praktisch zu verwirklichen gewesen wäre' ('it does not contain a single idea that could be made to work in practice'). See generally Gauthier 257–60; Jansen (2007) 8–16, at 8–9.

[110] e.g. Meiggs (1972) 255: 'most of his proposals are very naïve'.

[111] Runciman (1990) 351. (A footnote there cites Gauthier, 'esp. pp. 107–8 on the merchant fleet proposal'; even so the index of the volume relates these comments to *Oeconomicus*—and thereby suppresses all mention of *Poroi*.) Runciman does not go as far as to call X.'s ideas Keynesian, but Davies (1993) 222 does; and cf. also the review of J. D. Lewis (2009) by Noreen Humble in *BMCR* 2011.05.33. On X. as no Adam Smith (but not, even so, a negligible thinker about economic matters) see also Figueira (2012).

[112] As the third Viscount Runciman of Doxford (Sunderland), his experience of the 'real world'—a pertinent point when charges of Utopianism have been made against X.—has come in public roles such as membership of the Bank of England's Securities and Investments Board (later the Financial Services Authority). Note also the remarks of Edward Cohen, banker and businessman as well as student of ancient Athens: 'fourth-century Attika possessed within its territory substantial reserves of unmined silver, whose exploitation could be accelerated to increase the amount of commodity money in circulation—a somewhat more laborious version of the printing-press used by some inflation-prone jurisdictions today. One fourth-century commentator insisted

set before the Athenian assembly, X.'s proposals would not, in my estimation, have been laughed to scorn, as fit only for Cloudcuckooland—least of all if it was made clear from the outset that everything was geared towards the universal three-obol provision (3.9 with 4.33), and that 'the rich' as well as the demos would see benefits (6.1). X. had even, on occasion, included an idea expressly aimed at appealing to the bigoted, visceral prejudices of his fellow-citizens: make life for metics more attractive, but keep them at arm's length within the infantry (2.1–7, at 2–4). Why then, among retrospective readers of *Poroi*, have such dismissive verdicts as Cawkwell's 'fantastic' been passed?

We can suitably begin with the three topics that Cawkwell himself broaches.[113]

(*a*) 'One leading idea seems to be that if the sources of revenue were fully developed it would be possible for every citizen to draw three obols a day, i.e. in a year a matter of 500 talents for 20,000 citizens.[114] No doubt Euboulos was more hard-headed, and there is no evidence that his [theoric] distributions were ever more than a small bonus; if *trophê* ['sustenance'] was to be got, it would have to be by work on the building programme as in the days of Pericles.' As can be seen, Cawkwell conflates two issues there: whether Euboulos implemented this scheme, and the viability of the scheme itself. With regard to the latter, X. himself addresses possible objections at length (4.34–48); and especially noteworthy is his common-sense realization that the capital fund needed, first mentioned in 3.6–10, could come into being gradually (4.34–8)—perhaps over two to three decades.[115]

(*b*) 'Nor is it likely that Euboulos shared Xenophon's optimism about the unlimited resources of the mines (4.1–3), even if he was unaware of the economic effects of flooding the market with silver.' As with *a*, Cawkwell's riposte slides into an opinion—

that Athens could increase its mining of silver exponentially, because its reserves were virtually inexhaustible [*Poroi* 4.11]. In fact, mining activity increased substantially during the fourth century, and almost 2,500 years later, silver was still being mined in Attika' (Cohen (2008) 67–8).

[113] Cawkwell (1963) 63–4.

[114] Two footnotes to this calculation should be added. (*i*) Regarding the figure of 500 talents, Cawkwell did not state the basis for his calculation, but it is simple enough to deduce. With three of its four elements stated, the only tacit one is the number of distribution-days per year: 300. But for X.'s own calculations, based on a 360-day year, see the Comm. to 3.9 and 4.14. (*ii*) At the time of *Poroi* the number of citizens is in fact likely to be higher than 20,000—perhaps 30,000 (Hansen (1985) 65–9).

[115] Two to three decades: Jansen (2007) 352, expanded at 400.

irrelevant in this context—about what Euboulos would have thought of X.'s view. If we confine our assessment to the idea itself, it is hard to exonerate X. from the charge of *some* dubious thinking here. First, the example of the island of Siphnos (*OCD* 1372, *IACP* no.519), if nothing else, ought to have given him pause before assuming that the deposits of Laureion silver were never-ending (4.3, cf. 4.26).[116] And second, while he concedes (4.10) that a glut of *gold* leads to a fall in its value, he does not see the same problem with silver. He merely says that more and cheaper gold means more expensive silver. But what if it were more *and cheaper* silver? Perhaps we could take comfort from Runciman's approval of the silver-mining scheme overall (cited above), and guess at the reasoning behind it. One point of relevance may be that the Laureion mines, after their first revival in the second half of the fourth century, were dormant in the third century but enjoyed a second revival in the second century, until the major slave revolt of *c.* 101.[117] A second and, in part, related consideration is that X. may have had the (perfectly rational) expectation that export markets for Attic silver, whether as bullion or especially as coinage, would not remain static, but increase.[118]

(*c*) 'Nor could the proposal that the State should keep merchant ships for hire (3.14) have much attracted anyone with practical experience of the difficulties of maintaining the [existing war-] fleet in good shape' (Cawkwell). As it happens, the only publicly owned merchant vessels attested in the record—the *dêmosia ploia* of third-century Olbia in the Black Sea (*OCD* 1035, *IACP* no.690)—are said in the relevant document to be 'in a poor state and having no tackle'.[119] But the point is hardly a

[116] On Siphnos see the Comm. on **1.5 though many**.

[117] Habicht (1997) 292–3, and cf. 242–5 on Athenian 'New Style' silver coinage as 'a spectacular success throughout mainland Greece and beyond'. Strab. 9.1.23 describes the Laureion mines themselves as exhausted in his own day, the first century, though superior furnaces were re-melting the old dross and extracting silver from it. John Ellis Jones in *OCD* s.v. refers to 'spasmodic attempts ... to reopen mines' in the fourth century CE and later still.

[118] Note Austin & Vidal-Naquet (1977) 313–19 n.4 on the international prestige enjoyed by Attic silver coinage—'hence the silver of Laurion cannot in fact be a commodity like any other'. They also comment that X. here 'makes allowance for a fundamental 'extra-economic' factor, the taste for hoarding' (in 4.7); see also Millett (1991) 169 and Jansen (2007) 376–7.

[119] *SIG* 495 (Austin (2006) no.115) lines 146–51. Gauthier 108 envisaged these *ploia* as warships, but see on this in the Comm. to the passage.

fatal blow where *Poroi* is concerned. Olbia was not Athens, a city with massive experience of maintaining ships in working order. In any case the fine detail of X.'s scheme could have made the lessees responsible; cf. Gauthier 107. (For a rough analogy see 4.14 on the slaves of Sosias.)

That, it turns out, exhausts Cawkwell's dossier of the 'fantastic' in *Poroi*—because he goes immediately on to balance these three adverse criticisms against the same number of 'sound' suggestions by X.: 'the increase of the total derived from the tax on metics,[120] the encouragement of trade and traders, and capital investment to stimulate the economy'. (I agree.)

Other scholars, though, have included under this head another of X.'s notions; more exactly, another facet of the ones we have considered already. A corollary of items *a* + *b*, above, is that public slaves (*dêmosia andrapoda*) for the mines will be acquired by the state. 4.23–4 envisages a modest start on this, with an initial 1,200; they rise to 'at least 6,000' during the first five or six years; and 10,000 is mentioned as a number that would bring in, annually, a hundred *talanta*. However, at its first appearance in 4.17, X.'s idea contemplates an eventual slave-force approaching 'three to each Athenian': that is, anything between *c*. 60,000 and *c*. 100,000 in total.[121] 'Xenophon's dream', Westermann dismissively called it. 'This seems too fanciful', is a more recent and more guarded response; 'the grander elements of [X.'s] scheme stretched credibility.'[122] Stretched it, yes indeed, but beyond breaking point? I would say no, provided we do remember that this is an aspiration for the distant future.[123]

* * * *

The prosecution's case for the *unworldliness* of *Poroi*, then, can be declared—at the very least—Not Proven.[124] But what of its *novelty*? X. himself fought shy of claiming any (see **4.17** with the Comm. on

[120] *Sic*: but in fact X. envisages a broader swathe of tax-take from metics than their *metoikion* poll-tax alone. See the Comm. on **2.1 this revenue**.

[121] For discussion see the Comm. on **4.17 the state** and on **4.25 In fact though**.

[122] Westermann (1941) 466; cf. Westermann (1955) 9. Whitby (1998) 110.

[123] *How far* distant has been variously estimated; most recently 30 years according to Jansen (2007) 372 n.269, but 125 (beyond the initial 5–6) in Powell (2015) 59 with n.300.

[124] Recent work on the historical substance of *Poroi* votes for Not Guilty: besides Jansen (2007), see especially Powell (2015). And from other perspectives one could add e.g. Dillery (1995), Gray (2011), Lu (2015) part II chap.4.

the only novelty). We in retrospect might nevertheless conclude that *Poroi* was a work ahead of its time, and such a conclusion would have some bearing on the reception of its ideas *at* the time. We would have an explanation, at any rate in part, of why some of them took a while before being reflected in practical politics, and some sank without trace.

On X.'s view that it would be good for metics to be granted some rights of landownership (2.6), Austin & Vidal-Naquet comment as follows: 'The proposal was not *of course* [my emphasis] adopted, but it is a fact that the majority of decrees granting to foreigners the right to own land date from the fourth century, and that some of them are in favour of traders, while others reward wealthy "benefactors" (*euergetai*) who contribute through their generosities to the enriching of Athens. From this point of view, as from many others, Xenophon is already a man of the Hellenistic age.'[125] And they say much the same about 3.4, where X. floats his idea 'to honour traders and ship-owners with front seats at the theatre, and to have periodic public receptions for those whose noteworthy vessels and merchandise seemed to make them a credit to Athens. If likely to be honoured in these ways they would hasten to us as to friends, with not only the profit but also the honour in mind.' Austin & Vidal-Naquet remark that on the matter of preferential theatre-seats (*proedria*) X. trespasses here into an area traditionally the preserve of civic dignitaries such as officials and priests; also that invitations to these public receptions in the *prytaneion*,[126] too, were jealously guarded, in X.'s day and for a generation afterwards; in any case that the whole idea is 'deeply subversive' because 'it is based on strictly commercial criteria'.[127] The description 'subversive' is one that Austin & Vidal-Naquet have already used a few pages earlier, when introducing their annotated translation of *Poroi* 2–3 as a whole: 'Xenophon is probably not well aware of the profoundly subversive aspects of some of his proposals, notably the proposal to extend for the benefit of the metics the right to own land in the city.'[128]

The notion that X. himself did not realize he was a revolutionary strikes me as unlikely and unhelpful. If we set that aside, here is one

[125] Austin & Vidal-Naquet (1977) 362–3.
[126] See generally S. G. Miller (1978), esp. 4–13 on this aspect of its function.
[127] Austin & Vidal-Naquet (1977) 367 n.14. (There are complications here, but this is not the place to go into them. See the Comm. on 3.4.)
[128] Austin & Vidal-Naquet (1977) 362.

answer to the question of *Poroi*'s novelty, and a bold one it is. Should it be accepted? My opinion is that it should, but only once a number of countervailing points have been made.

The most important, contextual one is made by Austin & Vidal-Naquet themselves, in fact, when they write that X.'s suggestions in *Poroi* Chaps.2–3 'remain, like those of Plato [in *Laws*], within the traditional framework of the city'. An authentic revolutionary would (or could) have advocated abandoning the entrenched hierarchy of legal statuses—chiefly citizen, metic, slave[129]—which provided a polis like Athens with one of its most important infrastructures. Admittedly in circumstances of dire military emergency, that is what the passionate *rhêtôr* Hyperides of Kollytos (*LGPN* s.v. no.3, *OCD* 716–17, *APF* 517–20) was to do in autumn 338, when he framed a decree enfranchising the metics, emancipating the slaves, and pardoning exiles and others. Hyperides survived a prosecution for having proposed something illegal, but his decree was overtaken by events and never implemented: Hansen (1974) 36–7 no.27. X. wants more 'and better' metics and more slaves, because, without that, his plans for improving the lot of *citizens* will have a very large financial hole in them.

M. I. Finley's dictum on this is famous, often quoted: 'Xenophon's ideas, bold in some respects, never really broke though the conventional limits.'[130] There, plainly, the emphasis is different from Austin & Vidal-Naquet's 'profoundly subversive' (above), but, to reiterate, theirs is a phrase which cannot stand without qualifications; and once the qualifications are made, the gap between the two positions becomes much narrower. Let us look again at landownership (2.6). Citizens had this right, metics did not; by definition, in both cases. X. proposes that metics have it too. Or does he? Yes and no. Yes in the sense that he does make a proposal on the subject. However: (*a*) his concern is solely with what nowadays would be called small brownfield sites, inside the city walls; (*b*) in accordance with that fact; grants of house-ownership rights only, *egktêsis oikias*, will be made; (*c*) further, the grants are not open-ended, i.e. allowing a house to be built anywhere 'inside the walls', but are instead grants of specific sites (*oikiôn erêma* and *oikopeda*); (*d*) those who want such a grant must apply for it; and (*e*) applicants will only be successful if they are adjudged to be (on unstated criteria) 'worthy'.[131]

[129] Kamen (2013) has a more complex model.
[130] Finley (1985) 163–4, at 163.
[131] Cf. Whitehead (1977) 127, and see further in the Comm. on **2.6 If the state**.

Realizing, then, that X. remained a man of the *pre*-Hellenistic age, with its clear lines of legal demarcation both within and between communities, is important—and not too difficult to accomplish, on a close enough reading. Yet that very reading also turns up items like 4.41–2. There, X. 'coolly envisages a systematic use of slaves in times of war', as Garlan puts it.[132] (In the context of discussing the silver-mines and his plan for large numbers of public slaves working in them, X. points out that the manpower involved would be a boon in wartime, both for manning ships *and deploying infantry*.) Garlan goes on to observe that this passage of *Poroi*, as far as he (an authority in the field) is aware, is unique in what it envisages, so that '[o]n this point, as on many others, [X.] displays a certain intellectual audacity in this work—though less than may at first sight appear. [*a*] These are public slaves, and [*b*] the only wars in which they are to take part are those of a defensive nature, in which the purpose is to repulse any enemy invasion. [*c*] Their being used as oarsmen is envisaged before the possibility of enlisting them in the army to fight on land. Finally [*d*], the author is careful not to disregard completely all the difficulties that could arise from putting such plans into practice. He… recognizes that, if good military use is to be made of these slaves, it will be necessary to "treat them with consideration".'[133] Garlan's caveat *c* is of no account, because the mere order of the two elements in X. conveys nothing about logistical priorities.[134] The three substantive ones, remaining, are correct as stated. Even so, in my estimation they do not *significantly* detract from the impact of X.'s casual remark.

To credit X. here with 'intellectual audacity'[135] is a far cry from condescension such as 'Xenophon [in *Poroi*] did not have an original or

[132] Garlan (1988) 176. (The reference applies to everything by Garlan quoted in this paragraph.) See also Finley (1985) 211 n.28; Hunt (1998) 175–7.

[133] On X.'s overall proposals for slaves see Jansen (2012) 734–40 and further in the Comm. on 4.17–50.

[134] Implicit in Garlan's point is the background circumstance that slave *rowers* were no novelty, even in Athens. (See generally Garlan (1988) 165–9.) X. himself recorded the preparations for the battle of Arginousai in 406, when the crews embraced 'all who were of military age, both slaves and free' (*Hell.* 1.6.24).

[135] I cannot refrain from noting that 1988's 'a certain intellectual audacity' was originally 'une *grande* audace intellectuelle' (Garlan (1972) 45; my emphasis). Of course, our view of the extent of X.'s audacity on this point depends on how rare we assess such slave deployment to have been in real life. The thrust of Hunt (1998) is that it was far less rare than the sources suggest, and thus more common than is assumed in the standard modern accounts, Welwei (1974, 1977) and Garlan (1988). Among reviewers, J. Hall (1999) is especially critical of Hunt's own assumptions and methodology. Hunt stands his ground in Hunt (2006).

distinctive mind'.[136] Yet it is a position that other scholars of sound judgement also take, including some who have subjected the work to particularly close scrutiny. Cartledge, for example, concludes his introduction to Waterfield's translation as follows: 'Xenophon's *Ways and Means* deserves more credit from us than his contemporaries were willing or able to accord it, as a bold and original intellectual construct.'[137] Jansen has to my mind comprehensively demonstrated that 'while Xenophon's political economy is . . . firmly rooted in the traditions of his native Athens, it also offers something radically new: a viable alternative to empire'.[138] Other experts in this period concur. Osborne hails *Poroi* as 'something new in Greek literature: a focused attempt to solve Athens' problems of underfunding', in an analysis of 'originality'.[139] 'Imaginative' and (as regards extended public ownership) 'remarkable' are the adjectives applied to X.'s ideas by Lambert.[140] And this sort of enthusiastic appreciation is now most fully to be seen in Powell.[141]

* * * *

Absent from this loud chorus of praise, it will be noticed, is the voice of Philippe Gauthier. When he claims—not without good cause—that 'few ancient writings offer the historian of Athens as many riches as does *Poroi*',[142] he is characterizing the work as the proverbial mine of information (for others to quarry) rather than applauding its inherent intellectual acumen. X. himself, Gauthier opines, 'did not pretend to be exceptional, either in intelligence or imagination'.[143] Again, I myself see no need to disagree. More to the point, though, is how far Gauthier's understanding of *Poroi* was shaped by what might be characterized as a minimizing conceptual framework, within which to view ancient Greek society and economy as a whole. Here the influential figure of M. I. Finley enters the picture again. In his Preface

[136] Sealey (1993) 114.

[137] Cartledge in Waterfield 167. Likewise Waterfield (2006) 195.

[138] Jansen (2007) vi–vii, 20–1, 281; Jansen (2012) 725. So also, in broad terms, Dillery (2017) 217: 'its underlying thinking [is] profoundly radical'.

[139] R. G. Osborne (2000) 38–9.

[140] Lambert (2010) 121, 122.

[141] Powell (2015) 11.

[142] Gauthier 238: 'Peu d'écrits antiques offrent à l'historien d'Athènes autant de richesses que les *Poroi*'.

[143] Gauthier 21: 'Xénophon ne passe pour avoir ni une intelligence ni une imagination exceptionelles'. Note also Gauthier 43 on X. as no powerful thinker: 'Ni X. ni Isocrate ne sont de puissants penseurs'.

Gauthier states that although he read *The Ancient Economy* (in its first edition, of 1973) only when his own labours had been almost completed, Finley's earlier works had often enabled him 'to understand or be able to understand' certain aspects of *Poroi* that were not immediately self-explanatory.

The contributory facets of Finley's picture (deriving from Max Weber, Johannes Hasebroek, and Karl Polanyi) of the ancient Greek economy are well set out in the introductory chapter of Austin & Vidal-Naquet (1977). Fundamental to everything is an insistence that the very concept of the (or an) economy in the present-day sense is anachronistic. Rather, economic activity was 'embedded' in society and politics. And major corollaries of this include the view that Greek poleis, even Athens, had no interest in promoting *ex*ports; their concerns focused on the supply and security of *im*ports.

The extent to which these are Gauthier's beliefs, too, can be left for users of the Commentary to discover for themselves; but two prefatory points are worth making here.

First, the idea of Athens' exports and imports as twin sides of the same coin is at least as old as Thucydides (1.120.2) and the 'Old Oligarch' ([X.] *Ath.Pol.*2.11–13) in the last quarter of the fifth century; cf. also e.g. Isoc. 4.42, from 380. Thus, unsurprisingly, it is a prominent theme in *Poroi* itself: incidental in 1.4 and 1.7, central throughout section 3. This fact enables us to perceive that X.'s wish (announced already in Chap.1) for Athens to be self-sufficient might be said to prefigure an Aristotelian notion of *autarkeia*, as explicated by Bresson: one which presupposed a trade in exports as well as imports.[144] And the crucial point where *Poroi* is concerned is that trading activity (and its by-products) is something to be actively monitored, fostered, and enlarged by the citizens themselves.

Second, all this means that X.'s aims and methods in *Poroi* cannot, nowadays, be fully and adequately understood through a Finleyite (or Gauthierian) lens. Sometimes we shall see their perspective, or kind of perspective, yielding valuable results, but not as comprehensively as an overarching model ought to. Another model is needed—and as of now, the prime contender is New Institutional Economics. Originated during the last quarter of the twentieth century by economic theorists such as Douglass North (1920–2015),[145] its leading exponent as far as

[144] Bresson (2000) chap.6; cf. Bresson (2016) 229.
[145] See esp. his trio of books North (1981), (1990), and (2005).

ancient Greece is concerned is the scholar mentioned in the preceding paragraph: Alain Bresson.[146] This successfully escapes from the false dichotomy, in this area, between 'primitivism' and 'modernism' (or *homo politicus* vs. *homo oeconomicus*) by means of a focus on relevant 'institutions', broadly defined to embrace legal rules and ethical constraints alike. And when Bresson writes that 'through both their private activities and their participation in the life of the city, citizens had a sense of their economic interests',[147] that is something vital to remember in any attempt to fathom the thinking of X. and his Athenian audience.

8. DELAYED IMPACT

The preceding section has sought to show that *Poroi* does make a worthwhile contribution to political thought within the context of mid-fourth-century Athens. X.'s proposals occupy various positions along a spectrum which runs between the judicious advocacy of policies already existing (and suitable for replication) through to ideas unprecedented at the time of writing. Section 6 has itemized them all, in the course of seeking to demonstrate (in Gauthier's footsteps) how little solid evidence there is that they were politically implemented there and then, whether by Euboulos himself or by anyone else in what might very loosely be called Euboulan Athens, 355–342. (The lower *terminus* is hardly precise, but cf. Cawkwell in *OCD* s.v.: his opponents gain 'full control' of Athens in 343–342.)

During the late 340s and on into the 330s, it was the continuing rise of Macedon under Philip II, and the appropriate Athenian response to it, which preoccupied the city's politicians and opinion-formers (and their counterparts elsewhere). A sense of impending crisis was exacerbated by Philip's siege of Byzantium in 340–339, which threatened Athens' grain imports from the Black Sea (Hammond & Griffith (1979) 575–80; Russell (2017) 65–9), and matters came finally to a head with his victory at Chaironeia in 338 and the establishment of the 'League of Corinth' in 337 (*OCD* 375; RO 76 (Harding (1985) no.99). Thereafter

[146] Besides a long sequence of articles, beginning in 1985, he too has set out his ideas most copiously in three books: the provocatively titled Bresson (2000), Bresson (2007–2008), and—adapted, expanded, updated, and translated from this—Bresson (2016). See also e.g. Ober (2015a), Ober (2015b), Harris et al. (2015).

[147] Bresson (2016) 24.

the Athenians again found themselves, perforce, at peace. Not only that, but in a mood, apparently, for a return to the sort of Euboulan policies which were predicated on spending its dividend. Enter—in the leading role: he seems to come out of next to nowhere, much as Euboulos had, almost two decades earlier—**Lykourgos of Boutadai** (*c.* 390–*c.* 325/4: *LGPN* s.v. no.4, *OCD* 872 Lycurgus (3), *APF* 350–3, *AO* 480).[148]

The office(s) which allowed Lykourgos to be in effective control of Athenian public expenditure for the dozen years before his death present long-standing problems which are not germane to our purposes here.[149] What *is* relevant is the fact that—in very sharp contradistinction to Euboulos—Lykourgos' role as a policy-maker in general, and as a proposer of specific laws and decrees in particular, is on display to a significant degree in the primary source-material.

Occasionally this means a contemporary allusion in a literary source, such as Demosthenes' mention of his responsibility for a decree awarding honours to Neoptolemos of Melite (*LGPN* s.v. no.8, *APF* 399–400), a rich cult-benefactor.[150] In greater bulk, it means summary references—especially to laws—in the Lykourgos *Life* in [Plut.] *Orat.*: see 841F–842A, 843F, 844A. And most valuably of all, by and large, it means the number of laws and (in particular) decrees *on stone* which were certainly, probably, or possibly proposed by Lykourgos. The synoptic study of this rich body of epigraphic material by Schwenk (1985) remains important, as do Tracy (1995) 7–16 and Habicht (1997) chap.1. State-of the-art access to these documents is now via *IG* II^3 and the translations on *AIO*, both the work of Stephen Lambert.

A link—delayed, at the time—between *Poroi* and the policies associated with Lykourgos did not wait until now, of course, to be made. On the contrary (and to be selective): Cawkwell, the modern champion of *Euboulos* as X.'s political executor, when mentioning the raising of capital from individuals by means other than conventional

[148] Before Chaironeia he is attested in public life only once, as one of a group of envoys (including Demosthenes) sent on anti-Macedonian missions to the Peloponnese—but even for that the evidence is suspect. His name does not appear in the best manuscripts of Demosth. 9.72, and [Plut.] *Orat.*841E seems to mistake the chronological context: 340–338 rather than 344–342. *AO* 329 registers Lykourgos as an envoy in 344/3.

[149] A very influential study, long before it was posthumously published, is D. M. Lewis (1997). See also Humphreys (1985).

[150] Demosth. 18.114, cf. [Plut.] *Orat.*843F; *APF* 399–400, *AO* 416.

eisphorai, writes that 'in the early years Eubulus may have begun to practise what Xenophon preached and Lycurgus subsequently carried out on so large a scale';[151] Gauthier cites him in connection with ephebes and *egktêsis*,[152] Bosworth in connection with the silver-mines,[153] Rhodes (like Cawkwell, above) in connection with capital.[154] (It is also relevant to mention Oliver's citation of *Poroi*, specifically on rewarding non-citizens, in connection with Athenian policy in *post*-Lykourgan Athens, the last quarter of the fourth century.[155]) However, rather than such individual, rod-and-line specimens, let us spread a net and haul in the catch as a whole.

'The funds that passed through Lycurgus' hands were colossal. Estimates in antiquity ranged from 14,000 to 18,900 talents, and it is hardly an exaggeration that the annual revenues amounted to 1,200 talents [so [Plut.] *Orat*.842F]. This huge increase must have been largely generated from commerce. There is no indication that domestic taxation, levies on land and property, were in any way increased, and the *eisphora*, the emergency levy upon the capital of the rich, was not invoked during this time of peace. It was the indirect taxation, harbour taxes and sales taxes, not to mention the leasing of mining concessions, which swelled the exchequer. If the commerce passing through Athens increased, so did the public revenues accruing from it. Since commerce at Athens was largely in the hands of non-citizens, it was a necessary corollary to encourage metics and foreign traders, who would generate income and, in the case of metics, pay additional levies, the twelve-drachma *metoikion* and the *eisphora* allocated to the arsenal and dockyards.'[156] (For this last see *IG* II^2 505 (Harding (1985) no.139, lines 14–18; Thomsen (1964) 241 with n.264.) Though Bosworth's mention of X. and the silver-mines, above, occurs in the paragraph which follows this quotation, his words might otherwise be describing the political realization, in Lykourgan Athens, of the programme set out in Chaps.2–5 of *Poroi*.

[151] Cawkwell (1963) 64–5. See also Cawkwell's entry on L. in *OCD* 872 (s.v. Lycurgus (3))—where however *Poroi* passes unmentioned.

[152] Gauthier 193 and 224, respectively.

[153] Bosworth (1988) 204–11, at 207.

[154] Rhodes (2010) 371.

[155] Oliver (2007) 96–7. See also Oliver (2011), a broader assessment of Lykourgos *and* (as his main forerunner) Euboulos, and also a reminder that neither man operated in isolation.

[156] Bosworth (1988) 206–7.

This can be best appreciated if we group the attested measures under three heads: (*A*) those of Lykourgos himself; (*B*) those of other men associated with him and (*C*) those which are unattributable.[157]

(*A*) Lykourgos' personal responsibility for practical policy is, inevitably, a criterion blurred at the edges but with a solid enough core. Witness for instance *IG* II³ 432/*AIO*. On Lykourgos' motion a certain Sopatros of Akragas (in Sicily: *OCD* 9, *IACP* no.9), evidently a merchant, is thanked for shipping in as much grain as he could, and rewarded accordingly. His rewards are headed by the honorific titles of hereditary *proxenos* and *euergetês* ('representative and benefactor'), but for present purposes it is the 'small print' which catches the attention. In lines 16–17 he is given 'ownership', *egktêsis*, uniquely without specification of whether it is to be 'of land and house' (*gês kai oikias*) or 'of house' (*oikias*) alone—the latter much rarer in the record *but advocated by X. in 2.6.*[158] Sopatros will also be invited to 'hospitality' (*xenia*) in the Prytaneion, and be assigned a 'view' of the forthcoming Dionysia performances. For both of these honours (albeit with the theatre-seat in perpetuity, *proedria*, not for a one-off event) see X. in 3.4.

There is also the much-cited RO 91 (Austin & Vidal-Naquet (1977) no.72, Harding (1985) no.111), now *IG* II³ 337/*AIO*, from summer 333. The first of the two decrees inscribed on this stele, proposed by the otherwise unknown Antidotos of Sypalettos, responds to an approach to the *boulê* by 'the Kitians', (i.e. men from Phoinikian Kition, in Cyprus) on the subject of their establishing a shrine of Aphrodite, by instructing the assembly to debate the matter. The second decree, a few weeks later, then records the assembly's determination. Proposed by Lykourgos, it reads: 'concerning the matters on which the Kitian merchants resolved to make a lawful supplication, asking the demos for ownership of a plot on which to establish a shrine of Aphrodite, be it resolved by the demos to grant to the merchants from Kition ownership of a plot on which to establish a shrine of Aphrodite—just as the Egyptians, too, established the shrine of Isis'. There is a connection of thought, in

[157] This differentiation should meet the objections voiced in Brun (2003) and Brun (2005), that Lykourgos is credited with more measures than were (or can be shown to be) his. In any case, for response to Brun's minimalism see Faraguna (2011), Lambert (2011b), De Martinis (2013).

[158] Camp (1974) 324 suggests that the stone's mention of unqualified 'ownership' might be explained by the (apparent) fact that the wording of the decree was done in the assembly, not in advance by the *boulê*. If so, the full 'land and house' grant is the more likely to have been meant, as indicated. (If on the other hand the anomaly is the mason's, not the drafter's, he might have missed out the single word *oikias*.)

broad terms at least, between X.'s idea that individual metics of worth could be conceded the right of intramural *house*-ownership (2.6, on which see already above) with this instance, citing its own precedent, of a *plot*-grant—the otherwise unattested locution *egktêsis chôriou*—for the building of a shrine. Responsibility for the Egyptians/Isis case is not stated,[159] but here is Lykourgos wanting to link his name with the Cypriot one.[160] And also, clearly, the measure is one of several which show him concerned—just like X. (see esp. 5.9–10, 6.1–3)—with religious matters.[161] For example: in [Plut.] *Orat.*841F & 842A Lykourgos is the instigator of laws which, respectively, revived performances of comedy on the third day, *Chytroi* ('Pots'), of the Anthesteria festival (*OCD* 97) and enhanced the 'Rural' Dionysia in Peiraieus.[162] (See also above on the honours for Neoptolemos of Melite.) In the epigraphic record there are summary allusions to decrees proposed by Lykourgos in *IG* II^2 1672 lines 302–3 (*re* a sacrifice and *re* a payment to *hieropoioi*) and *IG* II^2 1673 line 65 (*re* a payment for the Eleusinion); and honours for Eudemos of Plataiai who had given generously towards the making of the Panathenaic stadium and the theatre of Dionysos.[163]

There are also the tantalizing remains of *IG* II^2 333, now II^3 445/*AIO*. Dating from *c.* 335, it was entitled 'Lykourgos proposes a law to deal with the [*sic*] religious reforms' by Schwenk (1985) no.21. She was following there a long tradition which links this measure with a section of the posthumous (307/6) honorific decree, proposed by Stratokles of Diomeia (*LGPN* s.v. no.22, *OCD* 1406, *APF* 494–5), as quoted in [Plut.] *Orat.*851F–852E. Though the principal honorand is one of

[159] The phraseology itself offers no basis for believing that the Egyptians' grant, too, had been Lykourgos' doing; nonetheless, many (e.g. Mitchel (1973) 194) make that assumption.

[160] For Kition see in brief *IACP* p.1224.

[161] General studies of this include Parker (1996) 242–55; Humphreys (1985) 77–129.

[162] On both of these see Parker (1996) 246 n.100. What [Plut.] says about the Anthesteria is unproblematic (see Pickard-Cambridge (1988) 15–16 no.7), but Parker points out that the later passage must be faulty as transmitted ('that there should be a contest of Poseidon in Peiraieus', to include a dithyramb (*OCD* 469) competition). Parker endorses the emendation of this by Koerte (1902) to read 'in the month Poseideon', the month of the so-called Rural (as opposed to City) Dionysia. See generally Parke (1977) 103; Whitehead (1986) 212; Pickard-Cambridge (1988) 42; N. F. Jones (2004) 155. (Roisman & Worthington (2015) 56 with 198 retain the transmitted text, without discussion.)

[163] RO 94 (Harding (1985) no.118), *IG* II^2 351+624, now *IG* II^3 352/*AIO*. On these Lykourgan projects see also [Plut.] *Orat.*841D.

Lykourgos' three sons, Lykophron, who has asked for the hereditary free maintenance in the Prytaneion to which he is entitled, Stratokles also proposes a bronze statue of Lykourgos himself, for erection in the Agora, and backs up the idea with a review of the great man's career. 852B reads: 'and further, chosen by the demos, he brought together large sums of money into the akropolis, providing ornamentation for the goddess: solid gold Victories, gold and silver processional-vessels, and gold ornamentation for a hundred basket-carriers' (cf. Parker (1996) 244). Lambert in *AIO* entitles this stone, more cautiously, 'Laws about cult objects'. More than one enactment does seem to be inscribed here. Nevertheless, Lykourgos does propose something (Lambert's 'Law 2') in line 14, and later on, in material which may or may not still be part of Lykourgos' measure, there is reference to 'the surpluses of these sums of money' (line 25) and, twice (lines 26 and 28) the '*prodedaneismena*', i.e. the sums 'which have been loaned in advance'. This term recalls what is said about Lykourgos in [Plut.] *Orat*.841D and esp. 852B (and what Cawkwell and Rhodes had in mind: above). According to 841D Lykourgos 'took care of 250 *talanta* from private individuals entrusted to him on deposit'; and the version of that in Stratokles' decree (above) speaks of him 'having taken lots of money on trust from private individuals and loaned it in advance', *prodaneisas*.[164] As will be seen, *Poroi*'s principal idea for the accumulation of capital should not be characterized as a *loan*-scheme, strictly speaking.[165] Nevertheless, *Poroi* had blazed a trail in suggesting alternative ways of fund-raising than the much maligned *eisphora*, associated with war and waste.

Lower down on the same stone—and so, again, not necessarily in material emanating from Lykourgos himself—mention is made of 'asking the god' a series of questions about the cult items listed (lines 43–50). Compare generally *Poroi* 6.1–3.

(*B*) If we now broaden the perspective to take in *Poroi*-related activity in 'Lykourgan' Athens which cannot be directly attributed to Lykourgos himself, pride of place must go to items which have some claim to be indirectly linked with him, by being the work of known associates of his.

[164] The authenticity of the verb in a context of public financing is further supported by its two occurrences in Hyp. *Dem*.13 (in relation to Demosthenes), though there are many obscurities there; see Whitehead (2000) 400–2.

[165] See the Comm. on **3.9 Every contributor**.

In this category[166] one can place e.g. lines 165–271 of RO 100 (Harding (1985) no.121), *IG* II^2 1629, date 325/4: Kephisophon proposes a decree to carry forward a decision to found an Athenian military (or quasi-military) settlement in the Adriatic Sea. Its stated purpose is to bolster maritime and commercial security in that area, specifically against 'Tyrrhenian' (= Etruscan) pirates.

A decade earlier, Aristonikos had also sponsored measures against piracy, jointly with Lykourgos himself (*IG* II^2 1623 lines 280–82); and around the same time his was also the nominal responsibility for RO 81 (now *IG* II^3 447/*AIO*), a law and decree on the 'Little' (= annual) Panathenaia festival.

In the late 330s the antiquarian Phanodemos of Thymaitadai (*LGPN* s.v. no.7, *OCD* 1121, *FGrH* 325) preoccupied himself with the oracular cult and shrine of Amphiaraos in Oropos, at that time part of NE Attica.[167] Lines 9–10 of *IG* VII 4252 (Schwenk (1985) no.40), an honorific decree *for* him, mention a relevant decree proposed *by* him; and see also line 10 of *SIG* 287 (Schwenk (1985) no.41) for a relevant law of his, again resulting in honours.[168] X., we might note, is aware—as he could scarcely not have been—of the Amphiaraion (*Mem*.3.13.3 mentions the coldness of the water there, and cf. *Kyn*.1.2 & 8 for the heroic

[166] In [Plut.] *Orat*.842C it is claimed that, for decrees, Lykourgos 'used the great expertise of Eukleides the Olynthian'; whatever the truth of or behind that (see Roisman & Worthington (2015) 199–200), a non-citizen could not have addressed the assembly directly as Lykourgos' surrogate. (Cf. Perikles, in Plut. *Per*.7.7, reserving himself for special occasions like the state trireme *Salaminia*.) Fellow-Athenians whom Mitchel (1973) 190–214 identifies as Lykourgos' friends and associates are Aristonikos of Marathon, Kallias of Bate (Lykourgos' brother-in-law), Kephisophon of Cholargos, Neoptolemos of Melite, Phanodemos of Thymaitadai, and Xenokles of Sphettos. In addition, there were other 'celebrities' besides Lykourgos himself: see Mitchel (1973) 173–88, showcasing Aeschines of Kothokidai (*OCD* 24–5), Demades (*OCD* 429) and Demosthenes of Paiania (*OCD* 439–41), Hyperides of Kollytos (*OCD* 716–17), and Phokion of (?)Potamos (*OCD* 1139). Of these, Demades—a plebeian to Lykourgos' patrician—may have been the one most in tune with the *Zeitgeist*, or at least readiest to go along with it; cf. Bosworth (1988) 206, 210; Habicht (1997) 17 with n.20. See also Faraguna (1992) 211–43.

[167] Amphiaraos: *OCD* 73–74. Oropos (disputed between Athens and the Boiotians): *OCD* 1049, *IACP* no.214.

[168] Note also two other documents: *IG* VII 4254 (now *IG* II^3 355/*AIO*), from 329/8, crowning of the ten elected *epimelêtai* of the Amphiaraia festival (they include Lykourgos himself, alongside Phanodemos, Kephisophon, Demades, and others); and Schwenk (1985) no.56 (now *IG* II^3 360/*AIO*), contributors to a dedication at the Amphiaraion; they include Phanodemos, Demades, and Kephisophon. For general comment on Phanodemos in this regard see e.g. Bosworth (1988) 210; Parker (1996) 247; RO 133–4; and most fully Scafuro (2009).

exploits of Amphiaraos himself), but he lived a generation too late to see Philip restore Oropos to Athenian (from Boiotian) control, in either 338 or 335, and the subsequent eruption of Athenian activity surrounding the cult and festival of Amphiaraos: 'intense interest at the highest level, expressed most notably in the reorganisation of the Amphiaraia as a prestigious penteteric [i.e. four-yearly] festival'.[169] Had X. been writing in *that* context, he might well have suggested submitting his programme for the preliminary approval of not only Zeus and Apollo (6.2) but also this third divine authority, closer to home.

Finally under this head of measures attributable to Lykourgos' associates or fellow-travellers comes, in all likelihood, the law of (?)336/5 'about the ephebes' (*OCD* 508) authored by a man called Epikrates. It is not preserved on stone, nor even mentioned in contemporary literary sources, but the second-century CE lexicographer Harpocration alludes to it in his entry on the several men of that name, citing Lykourgos' lost speech *On the administration* as his authority. If (as argued in *APF* 182–3, following Lauffer) this Epikrates is the Epikrates of Pallene, *LGPN* s.v. no.106, who was unsuccessfully indicted during the first half of the 320s for illegal mine-working (Hyp. *Eux*.35–36, with Whitehead (2000) 247–51), it is possible that his moral fibre fell short of the high standards that Lykourgos demanded in his fellow-citizens. On the other hand, perhaps the prosecutor in that case, the otherwise unknown Lysandros, simply disliked Epikrates, and/or his enormous wealth. In any event, according to Harpocration, Epikrates' law earned him the honour of a bronze statue.[170] (The law's principal thrust, it is reckoned, was to make two years' service in the ephebate formal and compulsory for Athenian eighteen-year-old youths. The developed system, including ration-pay, is outlined in [Aristot.] *Ath. Pol*.42.2–5.)

Lykourgos' own interest in ephebes is revealed in his only speech extant in full, the *Against Leokrates*. There his lengthy sermon, to a court, on the obligations of citizenship includes a recitation of the oath sworn by enrolling ephebes, with comment thereon (chaps.76–78; RO 88.1 (Harding (1985) no.109). Given *Poroi* 4.51–52, all this would have elicited X.'s hearty approval.

[169] Parker (1996) 149 with documentation in n.109.

[170] For earlier (cult-related) measures authored by an Epikrates whom *LPGN* s.v. no.5 identifies with this one, see above, section 7, and further in the Comm. on **6.1 we will celebrate**.

(*C*) It remains to mention, briefly, two important phenomena which occurred during the Lykourgan years (and one further document which has been dated then) but which cannot be credited to any individual.

First and foremost, here, there is the rise in activity at, and production of, the Laureion silver-mines; see Chap.4 intro. Bosworth's view (above) that the sums of money which the Athenians had at their disposal to spend under Lykourgos' dispensation were 'largely' the result of increased commercial traffic through the city and port need not be disputed, provided it is added (as he himself did add) that '[t]he exploitation of the silver mines, which Xenophon (*Poroi* 4) had seen as the chief means of augmenting state income, continued and was carefully policed. A certain Diphilus was condemned to death for speculating on the sale of pit-props, and his confiscated estate, which amounted to 160 talents, was distributed among the demos.'[171]

Another unattributable policy pursued in this period is (and was) on display in the so-called *rationes centesimarum* ('accounts of 1% taxes') documents, the subject of Lambert (1997). This series of inscriptions records state-instigated sales, during the period, of plots of public land which were in corporate ownership, e.g. demes or phratries. Papazarkadas calls this 'a unique economic experiment, in fact the only recorded effort by Athens to make some profit out of her non-sacred landed resources'.[172] Nothing in *Poroi*, however, presents itself as the experiment's catalyst. X. had been eager to find income-generation in *leasing or renting* public property (3.12–14, 4.17–36, 4.49), but never does he advocate a once-and-for-all sale.[173]

Finally under this head, another fragmentary document: the law or decree *SEG* 16.55, now *IG* II^3 448/*AIO*. Its letter-forms suggest a date between *c.* 337 and *c.* 330. Sosin (2004) argues on general grounds for 335/4. Even if that is too precise, the measure does mention 'the *stêlê*

[171] Bosworth (1988) 207 with n.25, citing (and interpreting) the episode described in [Plut.] *Orat.*843D. On this Diphilos see *APF* 534. The name was common in Athens—*LGPN* lists 99 of them—and Roisman & Worthington (2015) 208 are surely wrong to identify the pit-prop man, without discussion, as the Diphilos awarded major honours on Demosthenes' proposal (Din. 1.43; *APF* 168–9.) Bosworth's note goes on to contrast Diphilos' fate with that of Epikrates (see above, main text, under *b*), but, as he comments, the account of this in Hyp. *Eux.*35–6 suggests that Epikrates' defence had convinced the court that an acquittal would be in the public interest.

[172] Papazarkadas (2011) 236.

[173] Papazarkadas' quotation continues: '[p]aradoxically, the principle of privatization meant that the project could never again be repeated'. In Lykourgan Athens, just in Thatcher's Britain, this thought induced no qualms.

concerning the peace'—evidently the Common Peace of 338/7 which had established the 'League of Corinth'. It seems that a festival to mark this is being (perhaps belatedly) inaugurated, with the hefty sum of five *talanta* devoted thereto, as (Sosin convincingly argues) an interest-generating endowment.

* * * *

Taken in the round, 'Lykourgan' Athens is a triumphant vindication of X.'s belief, for the future, that an Athens maintaining peace would be more prosperous than an Athens waging war (5.5–6.1).

Had he lived to see the age of Philip and Alexander, X. might not have disagreed with Lykourgos that some proportion of this new prosperity should be spent on the military. The list of Lykourgos' achievements in the 307/6 decree of Stratokles (above) includes the following. 'Voted by show of hands to be in charge of preparation for war[174] he brought up onto the akropolis many items of arms and armour, and fifty thousand artillery-projectiles; he also equipped four hundred triremes ready to sail, some of them refurbished, others built from scratch; and besides that, he took over half-completed works, the ship-sheds and the arsenal, and finished them' ([Plut.] *Orat.*852C). These claims might well have appeared extravagant if they had appeared in a law-court speech or a rhetorically inclined historian, but they are the unvarnished truth.[175]

[174] A problematic phrase. The decree has already mentioned Lykourgos' twelve years as 'steward of the communal revenue'; then we seem to have another post (as above: 'and further, chosen by the people'); then this one. Yet since the twelve years covers all the time available (336–324: D.M. Lewis (1997) 225–7) for his political and constitutional acme, the second and third items need to be subsumed under the first. (In the Greek, the two aorist passive participles which introduce these items, *hairetheis* and *cheirotonêtheis*, can just as well be causal in sense as temporal.) Lewis dismisses [Plut.]'s version of Stratokles' decree as 'not reliable evidence', in part because it diverges from what little is left of the actual inscribed version (*IG* II^2 457+3207: of no use for the present issue, but see generally Lambert (2015)). At any rate the view of Roisman & Worthington (2015) 276 n.11 that these military achievements of Lykourgos were chalked up during what they call Athens' second war against Philip, 340–338, seems to me inconceivable.

[175] (*i*) **Artillery (defensive)**: cf. generally Marsden (1969) 56–7, 68–9; more discursively in Rihll (2007) 63–71. (But the figure of 50,000 *bela*, if correctly transmitted, has to be taken on trust.) 'On the akropolis' means into the Chalkotheke, on which see Hurwit (1999) 215–16. (*ii*) **Triremes**: cf. the naval inventory of 330/329, which lists 392 of them (*IG* II^2 1627, line 266; Bosworth (1988) 208). Bosworth notes, *re* Lykourgos, that the vessels' state of readiness, as claimed, is even more impressive than their sheer number; also that larger warships, unmentioned by Stratokles, were gradually being

Equally tangible—because semi-preserved on stone (though not necessarily, in any sense, Lykourgan)—is the law of 337 which authorized a programme of building repairs to the Peiraieus and Long Walls, with specification of the work appended: *IG* II^2 244, now *IG* II^3 429/*AIO*.

Work, and outlay, of these kinds fulfilled to perfection two of X.'s three aspirations for the city, as expressed in 6.1: greater security, enhanced glory. The other one, becoming 'more appealing to the Hellenes', would be hard to connect plausibly with artillery-bolts, or even refurbished towers on Mounychia Hill (Garland (2001) 46 fig.10). But there is no need even to try to establish any such connection, when so much else in the domestic 'renaissance'[176] of Athens in these years—most of the reign of the absent young king Alexander—hits that target in the bull's-eye. The buildings, the festivals, the atmosphere of a great city once again 'highly favoured' (5.2, 6.2): everything transmitted the same beneficent message, to citizens and non-citizens alike. At the time, if looking for someone to thank for this, they will have thanked Lykourgos of Boutadai. On a longer-term view, some of the credit belongs to Xenophon of Erchia.

Appendix to section 8: the 'freedom bowls'

It will not have escaped attentive readers that, *vis-à-vis* non-citizens, more has been found in Lykourgos' measures which seems to concern non-resident foreigners than it does metics. Brian Bosworth reckoned it 'not surprising to find Lycurgus protecting the interests of resident aliens, repressing unpleasant officiousness on the part of fiscal authorities [...] and proposing legislation to grant merchants of Citium the right to acquire land for a temple of Aphrodite' (Bosworth (1988) 207). The second of these data, RO 91 (*IG* II^2 337/*AIO*), has been duly registered here; and such a measure was, clearly, a boon to Kitians both resident and visiting. Bosworth's other allusion, however, is to a story in [Plut.] *Orat.*842B–C: Lykourgos comes to the aid of the philosopher Xenokrates of Chalkedon (*OCD* 1580 Xenocrates (1)), Plato's

added to the fleet (fifty quadriremes and seven quinquiremes by 325/4: *IG* II^2 1629, lines 808–12; W. M. Murray (2012) 252, 261). (*iii*) **Arsenal and ship-sheds**—as projects 'taken over' by Lykourgos: cf. *IG* II^2 505 (Harding (1985) no.139); the pair of long-term foreign residents honoured there, in 301, had contributed to these works between 347/6 and 323/2. (The first of those dates is that of the arsenal's origins: the inaugural law and specifications, inviting tenders from contractors, is *SIG* 969, *IG* II^2 1668. The second is seven years after the building's actual completion. See generally Garland (2001) x, updating his first edition as regards 156–8 and 219–20.)

176 Habicht (1997) 16.

successor-but-one as head, between 339 and 314, of the Academy (*OCD* 2); Xenokrates had omitted, it appears, to pay his metic's poll-tax. Whitehead (1981) is a study of the six(!) versions of this incident, some of which have another person, Demades (*OCD* 429) or Demetrios of Phaleron (*OCD* 432 Demetrius (3)), playing the Lykourgos role (Whitehead (1981) 235–8). The anecdote might be unhistorical: so Roisman & Worthington (2015) 199. But if it is not, as I myself would judge, it is less likely to display the generic solicitude for metics seen in it by Bosworth than the individual recognition due from one member of an intellectual elite to another. Compare Plato's *Republic*. In 8.562E–563A Sokrates declares that one of the faults of a democratic polis is that 'metic and citizen are on a level of equality with each other, and foreigner too', yet this is a conversation set in the house, in Peiraieus, of a cultured and affluent family of Syracusan immigrants, including Lysias (1.328B–331D).

X.'s own tendency towards a degree of doublethink on this topic is in truth detectable throughout his Chap.2, as will be seen. Meanwhile, here, we must assess whether Bosworth's evidence for Lykourgan-era 'care' (X.'s word in 2.1: *epimeleia*) for metics—an even smaller haul if we discount the Xenokrates episode—should include another item, one of potentially much greater weight.

It arises from the fragmentary series of inscriptions from Lykourgan Athens which document more than four hundred instances of silver 'freedom bowls', *phialai exeleutherikai*. Orthodoxy (stretching well back into the nineteenth century) places them in an explanatory context of slave manumissions. The bowls are dedicated by ex-slaves—now metics (Whitehead (1977) 16–17)—whose acquittal in a legal procedure called the *dikê apostasiou* has freed them from ongoing obligations to their former masters. But Elizabeth Meyer's painstaking re-evaluation of this difficult material leads her to a different interpretation, one involving *any* metic (Meyer (2010)). In her scenario, metics lived at constant risk of finding themselves in the dock in a *public* prosecution, a *graphê*, if they failed to fulfil their two basic, status-defining obligations: paying metic-tax and/or registering with a sponsor (*prostatês*). Conviction in such a procedure, a *graphê aprostasiou* (the *pr* is crucial), would quite obviously be catastrophic for the defendant concerned, now condemned to slavery, but acquittal (Meyer argues) imposed a 1,000-drachma fine on the unsuccessful plaintiff, a 100-dr. tithe of which paid for the silver bowl.

Has any of this to do with Lykourgos himself? A great deal, on the assumption—taken over by Meyer from the pioneering study of these documents, in the 1950s and 1960s, by D. M. Lewis—that the heading on one of these broken slabs, *IG* II^2 1575 (apparently dating from 331/0), includes the phrase 'according to the law of Lyk]ourgos'. (What that law 'ordered' seems to have been set out in *IG* II^2 1560. Most of the detail has been lost, though there is mention of 'weight' and, apparently, 'destruction', *kataly*[-, translated by Meyer as 'melting'.) A new restoration by Meyer in another heading, that of *IG* II^2 1578, is what effects the shift from a mention of '*dikai apo*]*stasiou*' (private prosecutions of former slaves by their former masters: see above) to the phrase 'from the *graphai apro*]*stasiou*'. The ingredient of the 1,000-dr. fine for failure to pursue a *graphê aprostasiou* to a conclusion is based on general rules for *graphai* in this period. Such a fine was indeed imposed if the plaintiff either abandoned the case before its conclusion or failed so abjectly as to win less than 20% of the dikasts' votes; he also suffered *atimia*, a partial loss of civic rights (probably until the fine was paid); see Harrison (1971) 83, with the evidence in nn.2–3 there. Meyer's decimal link between the fine and the *phialai* is provided by the fact that many silver bowls listed in Athenian public inventories in the fifth century are of 100 drachmas *by weight*. Fourth-century lists mention fewer such bowls, but in the present, Lykourgan instance the (or a) reason for this is that his law, above, was all about melting them down for other purposes—a multi-stage process, largely in the period between 335/4 (or later) and 325/4, which it was the purpose of the *phialai*-inscriptions to place on record.

If the dates just given are correct, the melting-down policy does belong in the Lykourgan era. It can even be credited to Lykourgos himself with some degree of confidence, provided that the heading in *IG* II² 1575 is correctly restored. However, for our purposes here that is not the nub of the issue: X.'s recommended policy of 'care' of metics. To pursue *that*, the date(s) we need are not the one(s) when these shallow silver bowls were moved to the akropolis, inventoried, and melted down to create cult-vessels for Athena, but when they were first dedicated (to Zeus Eleutherios, 'Zeus of Freedom', Meyer argues).

Whether or not the 'law' of *IG* II² 1560 and the 'law of Lyk]ourgos mentioned in *IG* II² 1575 are the same, the former can be connected only with the Lykourgan-era afterlife of these *phialai*. The aspect of Meyer's model relevant here is the one she summarizes as '[a]t some point after 353, a financial penalty has been attached to failure in prosecuting [the *graphê aprostasiou*]: a regular fine (of 1,000 drachmas) is imposed' (Meyer (2010) 78, cf. 48). This dating is simply another way of saying after the Social War and *Poroi*. 'Euboulan' Athens, in other words, comes just as much into the picture as does 'Lykourgan'.

To Meyer herself, who several times couples the two men (Meyer (2010) 49, 59, 60 inc. n.179, 79), that fact is no problem; nor need it be. Where the problem arises is in the idea that the *graphê aprostasiou* was not armoured with its 1,000-dr. fine until as late as the 350s. The principle of the 20% vote threshold, with *atimia* as the penalty, goes back at least to 399, for the type of public prosecution known as *endeixis*. See Andoc. 1.33, with Hansen (1976) 65 n.37: '[t]his *atimia* can only be the result of failure to pay the fine of 1,000 dr. imposed on prosecutors who do not obtain the necessary votes at the hearing'. Specifically as regards *graphai* and the 1,000-dr. fine, Harpocration's entry (E1) which begins 'If someone bringing a *graphê* does not obtain a fifth of the votes, he owes a thousand (drachmas)' cites a lost speech by Lysias on the matter: (*In reply to Diokles*) *on the law against speakers*, no.XLI Carey. And even clearer is the direct quotation from Lysias preserved in another lexicon: 'look at what this Antigenes here did: having initiated a *graphê* against our mother he thinks that he can marry our sister as well as carrying on with the trial, in order to avoid paying the thousand drachmas which someone must pay if he initiates a *graphê* but does not pursue it' (*Lexicon Rhetoricum Cantabrigiense* 76.23–77.3). This is said to come from Lysias' lost speech *In reply to Antigenes on the abortion*, no.XI Carey, though the reconstruction in Kapparis (2002) 185–93 assigns it to another speech against a defendant of the same name. Be that as it may, Lysias' death is thought to have occurred in the 370s (cf. *APF* 589).

It would seem, then, that at some point in the *fifth* century the Athenians had decided to protect in this way (from frivolous or malicious misuse) *all* public prosecutions, and by extension *all* those liable to be defendants in them.

Meyer's model overrides this point. '[O]ne way of making metic status in Athens more attractive after 353 BC was the **imposition** of some controls and disincentives on the excessive legal harassment of metics, specifically in the form of a financial penalty for prosecutors in the *graphê aprostasiou* who failed to win their case. Starting with Xenophon's statement of the problem and ending with Lycurgus's wide-ranging legislation, this treatment of the changes in metic-status, in Athenian finances, and in the administration and adornment of Athenian religion will also find itself tracing the fate of those financial penalties as they are paid, tithed, dedicated, collected, inventoried, and melted down. For I argue that failed prosecutors in the *aprostasiou* paid to the polis the fine of the *graphê* that failed to receive one-fifth of the votes [...] It was this collection and melting that generated the lists of *phialai*; but it was the **increased** (indeed, very strong) protection afforded to metics facing a charge of *aprostasiou* that generated these *phialai* in the first place' (Meyer (2010) 48, with my emphasis in bold type). But we require proof—or much stronger circumstantial evidence—of that post-353 'imposition', which left protection for metics 'increased' in this area. Without it, a separate, special treatment of the *graphê aprostasiou* (initiated by Euboulos, Lykourgos, or anyone else) must be declared not proven.

Without it too, if I am not mistaken, the basis for Meyer's Xenophontic *terminus post quem* for the bowls evaporates. Some of them might have been dedicated earlier than that. Whether or not they were, supporters (who include myself) of her basic insight that the *phialai* were dedicated by immigrant-metics as well as by freedman-metics—all united by the experience of acquittal in a *graphê aprostasiou*—need another explanation of this aspect of the 'freedom bowl' phenomenon.

Notes on the Text

1. A second-century CE papyrus, published by U. Wilcken in 1901 (Thiel xxxiv–xxxv; R. A. Pack, *The Greek and Latin Literary Texts from Greco-Roman Egypt* (Ann Arbor 1965) no.1566), preserves 1.5–6. That apart, our texts of *Poroi* come from medieval Italian manuscripts—all thought to derive from a single, lost archetype—written between the twelfth and the fifteenth centuries: see Thiel xxx–xxxv, with a summary at xxxv. (Anyone comparing Thiel's summary with the one in Marchant's Loeb edition, xliii–xliv, should beware of differences in what the letters A and B designate, and also in some datings.) The first printed edition, undertaken by the Aldine press of Venice, was published in 1525.

2. The default Greek text for my translation and commentary here is E. C. Marchant's *OCT* of 1920. It is still in print, and it is also the (searchable) text available on the *TLG* website. Marchant's subsequent text and translation in the Loeb Classical Library does not reprint his *OCT* (presumably for copyright reasons) but bases itself on the 1865 edition by Gustav Albert Sauppe.

3. The starting-point of Gauthier's *Commentaire* is the text in Thiel (1922). Both of these scholars took the view that their predecessors had often been too quick to emend, rather than to understand, the transmitted text. I share their stance, subject always to the proviso—exemplified by them—that problems must be examined case by case. This has sometimes led me to support an emendation that Thiel and/or Gauthier do not, sometimes the reverse. (Schütrumpf 75–115 prints his own text. Like me he appends textual notes (117–29), more numerous but briefer than the ones below.)

4. I ignore textual issues if they make no material difference to a translation, but the following passages—collected here, so as to unclutter the

Commentary—do call for brief explanation. [Glossary: 'mss.' = the medieval manuscripts which contain *Poroi*; 'paradosis' = their reading(s) as transmitted.]

* * * *

1.7 imported items The mss. proffer what is evidently a neuter plural, ἐμπόρ(ε)ια. Marchant and Thiel, among others, adopt the emendation to dative singular ἐμπορίᾳ ('by importing') proposed by M. Schanz in an article of 1881, but I follow Gauthier 51 in retaining the paradosis. As he points out, ἐμπόρια occurs in precisely this sense in a fourth- or third-century inscription, regulating a 50th (2%) tax on imports, from Kyparissia in the Peloponnese (*SIG* 952). (Worthy of note, nevertheless, is the conjecture of Schütrumpf 82 with 121: ἐμπορε<ύματ>α, in line with 3.4.)

2.1 benefiting the state The unanimous paradosis here is 'the states', τὰς πόλεις. Though Marchant, Schütrumpf, and others accept this plural without comment, in context here it cannot be right. X.'s entire focus is on one city, Athens (irrespective of how many others also had metics, and derived benefit from that fact); and πολλὰ ὠφελοῦντες τὴν πόλιν here would be echoed by ὅσα μηδὲν ὠφελοῦντα τὴν πόλιν in the very next sentence. An emendation to that effect was proposed by U. von Wilamowitz-Moellendorff, in a note in Zuborg (1874), and was accepted by Thiel 7 and, tacitly, Gauthier 56. (For an actual manuscript discrepancy between τὴν πόλιν (correct) and τὰς πόλεις (incorrect) see Isoc. 15.309.)

2.2 indignities So the paradosis: ἀτιμίας, construed as an accusative plural. In his edition of 1804 B. Weiske proposed ἀτιμίας <τι>, i.e. genitive singular, 'a certain amount of indignity'. Wilamowitz (see 2.1 above) revived this. Marchant's Loeb printed and translated it. Nevertheless, in Greek as well as in English, using this noun in the plural is unexceptionable. (Plato's *Laws*, for instance, twice conjoins the opposites τιμάς τε καὶ ἀτιμίας, and Demosthenes twice links ἀτιμίας with ὕβρεις, 'outrages'.) See further Gauthier 57.

2.2 The absence of danger is an important consideration Some scholars have found fault with the reading of most mss., μέγας ... ὁ κίνδυνος ἀπών. Marchant's *OCT* chose the variant (from one manuscript) ἀπόντι, a dative which requires translation along the lines of 'It is very dangerous for one who is away'. Marchant's Loeb adopts αὐτῶν, from P. Wesseling via Sauppe: 'Their danger'. Thiel 8 lists other suggestions. He himself, however, declared that no change was needed, and Gauthier 62 agrees. The phrase κίνδυνος ἀπών (in the sense translated here) has a precedent in tragedy: Euripides *Hippolytos* 1019–20.

2.2 their crafts and their homes The unanimous paradosis for the first of this pair of nouns is τέκνων, 'children'. Marchant (*OCT*) retains it (hence the translation of Waterfield 170), but otherwise the simple, one-letter change to τεχνῶν that was seen to be desirable as early as the sixteenth century, by S. Castalio (1515–1563), has never been questioned.

The second noun here has occasioned more widespread disagreement. The mss. give οἰκιῶν, 'houses', and Marchant (*OCT*), Thiel, and Schütrumpf are among those who accept it. The alternative οἰκείων ('domestic affairs'), an emendation suggested by L. Dindorf in 1866, is hesitantly adopted in Marchant's Loeb as well as by Gauthier 62–3 (who points to the parallels in [Demosth.] 50.11 and—especially compelling, in his view—*Cyrop*.4.3.12, on matters which get in the way of military training: τοῖς μὲν γεωργίαι ἀσχολίαν παρέχουσι, τοῖς δὲ τέχναι, τοῖς δὲ ἄλλα οἰκεῖα, 'farming in some cases, crafts in others, domestic affairs in others'). Latterly the paradosis οἰκιῶν has been vigorously and convincingly defended by Jansen (2007) 298–302. See further in the Comm. to this passage.

2.6 Next, inside the walls there are many sites devoid of houses, and house-ruins too Within this sentence, some editors, including Marchant (*OCT*), Bodei Giglioni, and Schütrumpf have a comma after καὶ οἰκόπεδα, so that that phrase and the preceding πολλὰ οἰκιῶν ἐρημά are paired in the same clause, as above. Such indeed was the traditional, orthodox view, until an article by A. Brinkmann in 1912. Brinkmann placed the comma two words earlier (after ἐντὸς τῶν τειχῶν), so that καὶ οἰκόπεδα becomes part of the following 'If'-clause or sentence. Thiel 9 adopted this, and Gauthier 67 declares it preferable because otherwise a substantive difference between οἰκιῶν ἐρημά and οἰκόπεδα is hard to fathom. However, the Brinkmann punctuation makes the καὶ οἰκόπεδα εἰ clause even clumsier than it is already; and Gauthier's worry can be assuaged by a different, better, understanding of *oikopeda* here than his. See Daniel (2007), and further in the Comm. to this passage.

2.6 rights of ownership to those building houses for themselves Almost everyone agrees on what X. means here, but not on his means of expressing it. The crux is the dative plural participle, in the middle voice, from the verb οἰκοδομεῖν, transmitted as aorist: οἰκοδομησαμένοις. Among those content to accept this are Marchant (Loeb), Thiel 9, and Gauthier 66–8. Thiel mentions but expressly rejects the emendation to the corresponding future participle οἰκοδομησομένοις made by F. K. Hertlein in an article of 1874 and adopted by Marchant for the *OCT*; also by Schütrumpf. On the linguistic level, Thiel's parallel (for a future condition expressed retrospectively) of ἡ ὑπάρξασα πρόσοδος in 4.38—itself paralleled in Isoc. 8.19 and 140—seems enough to justify the paradosis. On what it means in substantive terms see the Comm. to the passage.

3.1 they can repose safely as far as winter is concerned The paradosis here is the Greek adverb, ἡδέως, 'agreeably/pleasantly'. Gauthier, following Dindorf (and Herzog (1914)), is satisfied with this, even though—or in fact, *because*—the agreeable conditions of Athens have just been mentioned (ἡδίστη τε καὶ κερδαλεωτάτη). Emendation by one letter, to ἀδεῶς ('in safety'), as advocated by two Dutch scholars (J. C. Van Deventer and C. G. Cobet) in the 1850s, is followed by the great majority of other editors; and cf. e.g. Jansen (2007) 318. In my view this is preferable. There seems no good reason why ship-moorings should be described as agreeable (as opposed to the *personal* responses evoked in 3.3); cf. Thiel 10–11. Also, it is easy to see ἀδεῶς being contaminated in transmission by ἡδίστη a few lines earlier. [So far so good—but there is perhaps another difficulty. If the final four words are as assumed here, ἀδεῶς ἕνεκα χειμῶνος ἀναπαύεσθαι, it seems to be universally assumed that ἕνεκα χειμῶνος is one element and ἀδεῶς... ἀναπαύεσθαι the other, i.e. with the verb used absolutely—as LSJ shows that it can be. However, LSJ also shows a common usage with a genitive, 'to take rest/relief from something', here obviously 'from winter'; and ἕνεκα-phrases in X. often place the noun *before* the preposition (as common usage allows); cf. 3.4, 4.11. If that were so here, ἀδεῶς (or ἡδέως) would have to be emended accordingly: ἀδείας ἕνεκα. Yet that is not an attested idiom anywhere, and X. does also have plenty of ἕνεκα-first phrases. Overall, then, I judge that the locution ἕνεκα χειμῶνος, an ungainly one in this context, must stand.]

3.5 purchases In the Greek, X.'s thought here is expressed by a string of verbs in the optative mood, but what comes after the first of them, εἰσάγοιτο καί ('imports and'), has been variously judged, as regards how many more verbs there are as well as what verbs they are. Between εἰσάγοιτο and the final pairing, Marchant's *OCT* printed three other verbs, but his ἐξάγοιτο and ἐκπέμποιτο seem tautologous. In his Loeb, that problem was 'solved' by eliminating ἐκπέμποιτο. The Thiel/Gauthier text, which I follow here, begins a list of six verbs in all with two mirror-image pairs: εἰσάγοιτο καὶ ἐξάγοιτο ('imports and exports') and then ἐμπολῷτο καὶ πωλοῖτο ('purchases and sales'). The final verb τελεσφοροῖτο is an emendation (to match the preceding μισθοφοροῖτο) in the posthumous 1596 edition by 'Leunclavius' (J. Löwenklau).

3.6 there is no necessity for additional expenditure The final three translated words here represent an aorist active infinitive in the Greek. The mss. proffer simple δαπανῆσαι or the compounds προδαπανῆσαι (to spend beforehand) and προσδαπανῆσαι (to spend in addition), with the context favouring either of the compounds. Marchant noted that G. A. Sauppe's edition had printed προσ-, from the *Vaticanus Graecus* 1335 ms. which seems to be the earliest of the group (tenth century?); otherwise προ- is the orthodox choice among editors, most recently Schütrumpf. I follow Sauppe. See further in the Comm. to the passage.

3.8 equipped at great expense The mss., most scholars think, do not preserve a satisfactory version of what immediately follows σὺν πολλῇ δαπάνῃ ('at great expense'): καὶ ταύτας γενομένας. Thiel 13 (tacitly followed by Gauthier 91) converted this into καὶ ταῦτα γενόμενα, thereby adopting a suggestion made by J. G. Schneider in his edition of 1838. Such an approach to the sentence differentiates between a first element which *ends* at ἐκπεμπομένας σὺν πολλῇ δαπάνῃ and a second element which *begins* with καὶ ταῦτα γενόμενα; and according to Thiel, the antecedent of ταῦτα is not the naval expeditions but the terrestrial ones (*expeditiones pedestres*) under Lysistratos and Hegesileos alluded to in the preceding sentence. I find this utterly unconvincing, even if the grammar fitted (which, as neuter, it does not). The best—or least worst—solution to this crux seems to be the one I translate here, as already by Waterfield 172 (with 235): τριήρεις πολλάκις ἐκπεμπομένας σὺν πολλῇ δαπάνῃ κατεσκευασμένας (so A. J. J. Bake in his edition of 1831).

4.2 the mines have been productive since very ancient times The paradosis here is the adjective παλαιά, which Marchant (both editions) retained. (Both he and, latterly, Waterfield, circumvent with their translations the issue of having two adjacent adjectives.) In defence of παλαιά, Herzog (1914) 474 pointed to the category of παλαιὰ ἀνασάξιμα in the mine-lease records, but Thiel 16 and Gauthier 115 justifiably protest that X. is referring here to *all* mines. One must adopt, with them and others, the emendation to the adverb πάλαι proposed by Aemilius Portus (Emilio Porto, 1550–1614) in the edition of 'Leunclavius' (see above, under 3.5). For cf. πάνυ πάλαι e.g. Isaeus 6.14.

4.5 in the silver-mining works everyone always claims Marchant (both editions) and others print here πάντας δή ('everyone claims, of course'), from a fifteenth-century supplement to a fourteenth-century manuscript. Other manuscripts of that time or earlier have readings that, in context, make no sense: πάντας δεῖ or πάντας δεῖν. Unusually for him, Thiel 17 adopted his own emendation, from δεῖ(ν) to ἀεί. Gauthier 120 and Schütrumpf 92 take this over without comment, and I accept it here also.

4.10 This I do not contradict Thus the paradosis, τοῦτο μὲν οὐκ ἀντιλέγω, accepted without comment by Thiel 19, Gauthier 131, and Schütrumpf 94. I mention the passage here because Marchant, in both of his editions, prints the emendation to τούτῳ, 'to him [the hypothetical objector] I make no contradiction': so L. F. Heindorf in J. G. Schneider's 1838 edition. The change is unnecessary: LSJ registers this verb's ubiquitous use with an accusative of thing as well as a dative of person. Note in any case the symmetry here between τοῦτο μὲν οὐκ ἀντιλέγω and ἐκεῖνο μέντοι οἶδα.

4.13 we hear the same from everyone Thus the (mss.-based) text printed by Thiel, Gauthier, and Schütrumpf: πάντων κατὰ ταὐτὰ ἀκούομεν. Marchant's Loeb adopts an adventurous emendation, by Wilamowitz (see under 2.1), of πάντων to παρὰ τῶν πατέρων, 'from our fathers'. But no change is needed.

4.19 lease precincts and shrines Bake (see under 3.8) deleted 'and shrines', on the basis that these two nouns, τέμενη and ἱερά, were synonyms and the phrase thus tautologous. Among those who have agreed with this are Marchant (both editions) and Thiel. Gauthier 147, following Wilhelm (1934) 50–1, cites documentary evidence which flatly disproves this, e.g. *SIG* 93, now *IG* I^3 84 (Athens, 418/17).

4.22 many, among those who are growing old in mine-work So the unanimous paradosis, with the participle in the genitive plural: γηρασκόντων. L. Dindorf (see under 2.2) emended it to nominative plural γηράσκοντες, which calls for a translation along the lines of 'many of those in mine-work are growing old'. Marchant (both editions) adopts this change. Thiel 23 sees no justification for it; likewise, tacitly, Gauthier 152, Schütrumpf 98 with 124–5.

4.31 more profitable still The paradosis simply has 'more profitable' (λυσιτελέστερα). This is accepted by Marchant for the Loeb edition, and by others, and indeed it might well be right. Nevertheless it is improved by the supplement <ἔτι> λυσιτελέστερα, suggested by Heindorf in Schneider's edition (see 4.10): so Marchant's *OCT*, Thiel 27, Gauthier 162, Schütrumpf 100.

4.37 would allow well-thought out ideas to be implemented again The paradosis is faulty: after τὰ καλῶς γνωσθέντα ('well-thought-out ideas') the mss. give καὶ αὖθις ἂν ἡμῖν οἰόμεθα, meaningless in this context. Suggestions, most of them plausible enough, for emending or replacing this are numerous. See Thiel 28, Gauthier 169, Schütrumpf 102, and latterly Waterfield 235, with his own idea: place ἡμῖν after καλῶς and emend οἰόμεθα to αἱρώμεθα. (The overall outcome, in his own translation, is 'we can repeat those aspects of our plans which were well conceived.') Marchant (both editions) admits defeat. Gauthier 169 is content with Thiel's own ψηφιζοίμεθα, 'vote'. At least the required sense is clear, if not the verbal way to achieve it.

4.42 We would be able to man many ships by public enrolment The unanimous paradosis for this verb is *third*-person plural εἶεν, followed by ἐν (δημοσίᾳ) in the Marcianus manuscript. Thiel 29 emends to first-person εἴημεν. Gauthier 176 accepts this, as do I. (Schütrumpf 104 demurs.) The essential point is that 'manning' a warship, πληροῦν, is something the state or an equivalent authority does.

4.42 many men too could fight for the community as foot-soldiers The problem here, as some have seen it, is the repetition of the adverbial dative δημοσίᾳ from the first clause of the sentence, concerning the manning of warships (see the preceding item). In an article of 1854 T. Bergk proposed deleting this second instance, and Marchant's *OCT* concurred; likewise Schütrumpf 104. Gauthier 176 explains why both instances are needed (because each means something different). See my translations here, and further in the Comm. to this passage.

4.43 at the sea to the south Bergk (see under the preceding item) deleted the noun 'sea'. Again Marchant agreed, this time in both editions. The deletion leaves τῇ, in this clause (ἐν τῇ πρὸς μεσημβρίαν) as well as the next one (ἐν τῇ πρὸς ἄρκτον), governing a feminine noun which is left unstated. (Marchant's Loeb translation renders this as 'side'; Waterfield 179 evades the issue.) Thiel 30, Gauthier 178 and Schütrumpf 104 accept the paradosis 'sea', I think rightly.

4.49 the income from the slaves So the mss.: *ἡ ἀπὸ τῶν ἀνδραπόδων εἰσφορά*. Other nouns have been suggested, notably *ἀποφορά*, 'rent' (by J. G. Schneider: see 3.8 above), and this is adopted by Marchant (both editions). Gauthier 186 supports Thiel 31 in retaining the paradosis, which derives a degree of support from a parallel within X.'s own oeuvre: *Oec*.7.40. (See also Schütrumpf 106 with 126, Jansen (2012) 735 n.41.) If this is correct, X. uses *eisphora* in a sense more generalized than the 'war-levy' one (of 4.40) not only in that *Oec.* passage (which is given its own classification in LSJ) but also twice here in *Poroi*: the present passage and already in 3.9 (*δέκα μναῖ εἰσφορά*).

4.49 from the market operating there The phrase which follows and qualifies 'market' is corrupted in the mss: *τῆς ἐκείνου* (or *ἐκεῖθεν*) *αὖ*. I translate *ἐκεῖ οὔσης* in Marchant (both editions), who followed Leunclavius (see under 3.5) on this. In any event the general sense is clear. See further in the Comm. to this passage.

4.51 I agree Thus the paradosis: the compound verb *ξύμφημι*. In the past it has sometimes been distrusted. Following an article of 1874 by Revd. Charles Badham, Marchant's *OCT* suppressed the preposition ([*ξύμ*]*φημι*), to produce simple *φημί*, 'I say', and Thiel 32 notes the emendation to *νῦν φημί*, 'I say here/now', suggested in H. Richards' monograph *Notes on Xenophon and Others* (London 1907). But the transmitted text should be accepted: so Thiel/Gauthier, and Waterfield 180 with 235. See already General Intro., section 5 n.66, and further in the Comm. to this passage.

4.52 an allowance higher than they would get in the torch-races Marchant (*OCT*) adopted the deletion of *πλείω* (after *τὴν τροφὴν ἀπολαμβάνοντες*) from J. J. Hartman's *Analecta Xenophontea nova* (1889). This would leave the *ἢ ἐν ταῖς λαμπάσι* clause as, simply, a second ('or in etc.') scenario to *ἐν τοῖς γυμνασίοις τὴν τροφὴν ἀπολαμβάνοντες*. Marchant's Loeb, however, retains *πλείω*, as also do (e.g.) Thiel 32, Wilhelm (1934) 36, Gauthier 191–2, Schütrumpf 108 (cf. 31 n.142), and latterly Waterfield 180 with 235. See further in the Comm. to this passage.

5.1 from the state itself Thus the unanimous paradosis: *ἐκ πόλεως*. Marchant (*OCT*) adopts the attractive emendation of the phrase—

advocated by both I. Pantazides and C. G. Cobet—to the adverbial dative ἔκπλεῳ, 'in full', which X. does use twice elsewhere (*Hier.*1.18, *Cyrop.* 6.2.7). Those who retain ἐκ πόλεως include Marchant (Loeb), Thiel 33, Gauthier 197, and Schütrumpf 108. On the general idea being conveyed Gauthier adduces 1.1, διατρέφεσθαι ἐκ τῆς ἑαυτῶν. One could add, for the baldness of ἐκ πόλεως without a definite article (yet meaning not 'a polis' but one polis in particular), *Cyrop.*1.4.17. (Compare also, for the omission of definite articles where others might have used them, 6.1: ἱερεῦσι δὲ καὶ βουλῇ καὶ ἀρχαῖς καὶ ἱππεῦσι.)

5.1 much more appealing to all people, and much more choc-a-bloc with them... The second of these comparative adjectives is given in the mss. as πυκνοτέραν, literally denser/thicker. Several attempts to improve this are registered in Thiel 33, and Marchant's *OCT* adopts one of his own: οἰκειοτέραν ('more amicable', essentially a variant on the προσφιλεστέραν already given). But the paradosis needs no change: besides Thiel, see Marchant's Loeb, Gauthier 198–9, Schütrumpf 108 with 128, and latterly Waterfield 235. Gauthier also notes that X. is compressing two ideas here: making Athens more appealing to everybody (προσφιλεστέραν... πᾶσιν ἀνθρώποις) and making the volume of visitors increase (πυκνοτέραν εἰσαφικνεῖσθαι). See further in the Comm. to this passage.

5.2 They too, in my opinion, are misjudging The paradosis here is faulty. While the parenthetical phrase ὡς ἐμῇ δόξῃ, though formally odd, can be accepted as transmitted—there is a close parallel in Sophocles *Women of Trachis* 718—rather than emended to ὡς ἐμοὶ δοκεῖ (as Marchant's Loeb, and cf. Waterfield 235), that is not the case with the garbled end of the sentence as transmitted: παραγγέλλω [!] σκοποῦσιν. Something to express the sense translated here is needed. Thiel 33 lists many suggestions. (Marchant's *OCT* spurns all of them; likewise Schütrumpf.) Thiel himself chooses (after K. G. Heiland and G. Kaibel) the compound verb παραγιγνώσκουσιν, which echoes γιγνώσκουσιν in the preceding sentence. (X. uses this verb in *Mem.*1.1.17.). Likewise, without comment, Gauthier 199. Marchant's Loeb adopts παραλόγως σκοποῦσιν, 'are looking at (the matter) unreasonably', from Leunclavius (see 3.5); likewise Waterfield 235. This has the advantage, plainly, of keeping the transmitted verb σκοποῦσιν, a common one in X.; on the other hand the adverb παραλόγως is one he does not otherwise use, and which indeed is extremely rare in pre-Hellenistic writers altogether.

5.3 men with bulk wine, men with premium wine All of the mss. do list *οἱ ἡδύοινοι* immediately after *οἱ πολύοινοι*—and indeed in a list which otherwise consists entirely of *πολυ*-compounds. Among those who, following the lead of Wilamowitz (see 2.1 above), delete *οἱ ἡδύοινοι* is Marchant, in both editions. Thiel 34 and Gauthier 200–1 both find good reasons for keeping it; likewise (tacitly) Schütrumpf 108. See further in the Comm. to this phrase.

5.9 any people who were trying to seize the shrine—once the Phokians had abandoned it For reasons already mentioned in the General Intro., section 2, this phrase has featured prominently in discussions of the date of *Poroi*. All manuscripts give the first verb as imperfect indicative *ἐπειρῶντο*—as translated here. A succession of scholars, beginning with J. N. Madvig (in his *Adversaria critica* I of 1871) and including Thiel xi–xii and Gauthier 4–5 and 210–11, has castigated this on grounds both linguistic (because, as Greek, it does not idiomatically describe a single past event) and historical/contextual. A scenario in which the Phokians *have* abandoned their control of Delphi and others *have* tried to seize it could only belong after 346, almost a decade later than is suggested by the strongest dating indications for the treatise. Accordingly, Madvig's emendation to present optative *πειρῷντο* has always been accepted by scholars, except those—in any era—bent on (re-)arguing the case for downdating *Poroi* to 347/6. We might note that X. had already used this form in *Anab.* 6.2.11; and compare Thuc. 1.143.1 (Perikles), which is also—coincidentally?—about high-handed treatment of Delphi. However, Jansen (2007) 52 n.63 insists that the paradosis *ἐπειρῶντο* can and should stand. The expression as a whole is an instance of a past general condition (protasis with optative, *λάβοιτε*; apodosis with imperfect, *ἐπειρῶντο*); its only unusual feature is that *οἵτινες* introduces the apodosis, but for that there is a precedent in *Anab.*1.1.5 (*ὅστις*).

Translation

(**1.1**) Personally, I always think that whatever kind of leaders there are corresponds with the kind of civic communities they lead. Some of those holding positions of leadership in Athens, though, used to say that they 'recognize what is just, no less than does the rest of mankind, but the poverty of the masses exerts a compulsion'—they maintained—'to be somewhat wrongful as regards the city-states'. So on the basis of this I set about examining whether there was any way the citizens could sustain themselves out of their own territory. That would be a *very* just system, I think, because if it existed they would be helped to escape their poverty and also, at the same time, the suspicion with which the Hellenes view them.

(**1.2**) Now, as I was indeed examining what I had in mind, I had an immediate realization: the natural condition of the territory provides very many revenues. I want it to be recognized that this is the truth I am speaking, so I will first describe the nature of Attica.

(**1.3**) Without doubt, the fact that the seasons are very mild here is something to which the actual products bear witness. At any rate, plants that in many places could not even grow bear fruit here. And what goes for the land is just as true of the sea that surrounds the territory: it produces everything in great quantity. Another point: the good things that the gods provide in their seasons all begin here very early and cease very late.

(**1.4**) And Attica is not only strong in the crops which bloom and age annually; she also possesses good things that are eternal. This is because there is a natural abundance of stone from which very beautiful temples and very beautiful altars are made, and very appropriately lovely statues for the gods. Hellenes and *barbaroi* alike, many have need of it. (**1.5**) There is land, too, which when sown does not bear a crop but when excavated supports many times the number of people than if it was bearing grain. Another point: land with silver beneath it is plainly determined by heavenly destiny. At any rate, though many city-states are nearby, both terrestrial and maritime, into none of them does even a tiny vein of silver-bearing earth extend.

(**1.6**) It would be no absurdity for anyone to think that Athens lies at the centre of Hellas—indeed, of the whole inhabited world. The more distant from it people are, the more difficult the cold or heat they encounter. Also, anyone who wishes to reach one extremity of Hellas from another must always do so, whether sailing or going by land, via Athens, as if it were a circle's hub. (**1.7**) Another point: although Athens is not 'flowed-around', nevertheless, just like an island, all the winds bring in whatever commodities are needed and send out whatever ones are wanted. This is because she is 'sea-girt'. She also receives many imported items by land—because she is on the mainland. (**1.8**) Furthermore, most states border on *barbaroi* who cause them trouble, but in Athens' case even the neighbouring states themselves are very far distant from the *barbaroi*.

(**2.1**) So, as I said, I think that the territory itself is responsible for all these things. But to the naturally-occurring advantages suppose we added, principally, care of the metics. I say so because, it seems to me anyway, this revenue is of the finest—the reason being that, supporting themselves and benefiting the state in many ways, they receive no wage but contribute a metic-tax. (**2.2**) It would be *sufficient* care, it seems to me, if we removed practices that without conferring any benefit on the state seem to bring indignities to the metics, and removed also the practice of metics fighting as hoplites alongside the city's men. The absence of danger is an important consideration, and so is being away from their crafts and their homes. (**2.3**) Another point: the state too would be benefited if the citizens served alongside each other, rather than if, as now, their comrades were Lydians and Phrygians and Syrians and other *barbaroi* from all over the place—as many of the metics are. (**2.4**) Besides the advantage of not having these men levied with the citizens, it would be a feather in the state's cap if Athenians, when going into battle, were seen to be relying on themselves rather than on 'outlanders'.

(**2.5**) Also, by giving the metics privileges that it is a fine thing to give, including cavalry service, it seems to me that we would make *them* more loyal and at the same time exhibit a stronger and greater Athens.

(**2.6**) Next, inside the walls there are many sites devoid of houses, and house-ruins too. If the state were to grant rights of ownership to those building houses for themselves on them—those who applied and seemed deserving—I reckon that that would create a larger and better class of people keen for residence in Athens.

(**2.7**) Also, suppose we established an official post of metic-custodians, just like orphan-custodians, and an honour of some kind went to those whose lists exhibited the most metics, this too would make the metics more loyal, and probably all stateless people would be keen for metic-status in Athens and would increase the revenues.

(**3.1**) My next topic is the import-and-export trade, and how Athens is so very agreeable and profitable to it.

Principally, of course, she has excellent and totally secure moorings for ships, where, once brought in and at anchor, they can repose safely as far as winter is concerned.

(**3.2**) Another point, too: in most states there is a degree of compulsion on the traders to take on a return cargo, because the currency they use there is not serviceable abroad. In Athens, they can export in return most things that human beings might have need of. And if they do not want to take a return cargo, they also export fine 'merchandise' by exporting silver—everywhere they sell it, they receive back more than the principal.

(**3.3**) Also, suppose that someone were to offer prizes to the officials in charge of the *emporion*, rewarding whichever one resolved matters of dispute most fairly and most speedily, so that whoever wanted to sail away was not prevented from doing so. These things too would greatly increase the number of traders, as well as making it more agreeable for them to do business.

(**3.4**) Another good and fine idea would be to honour merchants and ship-owners with grants of *proedria* and to invite them to public receptions periodically: those who seem to be of benefit to the state because of their noteworthy vessels and commodities. If likely to be honoured in these ways they would hasten to us as to friends, with not only the profit but also the honour in mind.

(**3.5**) As is plain, the more people came to live here and to visit, the higher, correspondingly, would be the volume of what is imported, what is exported, what is bought, what is sold, what generates fees, and what generates taxes.

(**3.6**) Now, to achieve such increases in revenues there is no necessity for additional expenditure. We need only pass beneficent decrees and be attentive. As to my other ideas for revenue-raising, I do recognize that they call for start-up capital. (**3.7**) However, the thought that the citizens would not contribute eagerly towards such things does not dishearten me. I bear in mind that the state made large contributions when, under the command of Lysistratos, it was helping the Arkadians, and large ones also when Hegesileos was in command. (**3.8**) I also understand that triremes are often sent out equipped at great expense. This happens on occasions when it is unclear whether the outcome will be good or bad—the only certainty being that payers will never get back what they contribute, or will even share in what they contribute. (**3.9**) But they would not earn so fine a return from anything as from the money they paid in advance into the capital fund. Every contributor of ten *mnai* receives almost a fifth, just as in a maritime loan, by taking three *oboloi* a day. For five-*mna* contributors the return will be more than a third. (**3.10**) The majority of Athenians, though, will take more each year than they contribute—because those whose advance payment is one *mna* will have a revenue of almost two *mnai*. And this will be based in a city-state, a context which seems to be the safest and most enduring of man-made institutions.

(**3.11**) I reckon, personally, that many foreigners would also contribute if by doing so they would have their names inscribed as 'benefactors for all time'. There are also some states which would be keen to join such a list. I expect too that certain kings and dynasts and satraps would wish to share in this display of gratitude.

(**3.12**) Once start-up capital was there, a fine and good project to spend it on is building hostels for ship-owners—besides the existing ones—round the harbours. It is also a fine idea to do the same for merchants, at places suitable for both buying and selling, and to have public hostels also for people who come here as visitors. (**3.13**) Also, both housing and shopping-centres should be organized for the retailers, in Peiraieus and also in the town. It would be a feather in the state's cap and, at the same time, generate many sources of revenue.

(**3.14**) Here is another good thing to try, in my opinion. The state already possesses publicly owned warships. Suppose it was also possible to have publicly owned *merchant*-ships, and to lease them out under guarantee, just like the other things in public ownership. If this too appeared feasible, there would be a large income from these vessels also.

(**4.1**) Now to the silver-mines. If they were organized as they ought to be, I think that massive sums of money would come in from them, even irrespective of the other revenues. I also want to show their potential to those unaware of it. Once this is realized, you will also deliberate better about how they should be treated.

(**4.2**) Without doubt, the mines have been productive since very ancient times; that is clear to everyone. At any rate, nobody even tries to put a date on when the ventures were first begun. But despite the antiquity of digging the silver-bearing ore and bringing it out, notice what proportion the *spoil heaps* are by comparison with the mounds that are natural and have silver under them. (**4.3**) In fact, the silver-producing area is in no way diminishing; on the contrary, one can see that its extent is always growing larger. At any rate, during the time when the maximum number of men was in mining, nobody was ever at a loss for a job. It was the opposite: the needs of the works always exceeded the number of the workers. (**4.4**) Even now, none of those who own slaves in the mines reduces his labour-force; he always acquires as many *more* as he possibly can. Presumably the reason is that when only a few men are digging and searching, the material found is correspondingly little, whereas when many do this, many times as much silver-bearing ore comes to light. Hence this is the only occupation, of the ones I myself know, where additional operators incur no spite.

(**4.5**) Furthermore, everyone who owns fields is in a position to say how many teams of oxen are enough for the plot, and how many labourers. If someone puts in more of them than is sufficient, they account it a loss. But in the silver-mining works everyone always claims to be short of labourers. (**4.6**) This is because mining is unlike what happens when there are numerous bronze-smiths, and bronze products become cheap, and bronze-smiths are rendered superfluous—and with iron-workers likewise. Also when there is a great deal of grain and wine: the crops are cheap, farming loses its profits, and the result is that many men give up working the land and turn to wholesaling and retailing and moneylending. When more silver-bearing ore is discovered, though, and more silver is available, there is a commensurate rise in the number of people entering this industry. (**4.7**) Take furnishings as an obvious example: when individuals have acquired enough for the house they do not go on buying more. But when it comes to money, nobody has ever yet acquired so much as to need no more of it. No, those who amass a huge amount derive no less pleasure from burying the surplus underground than from putting it to use.

(**4.8**) Another point: whenever states are faring well, assuredly the people have need of money. This is because the menfolk want to spend it on fine arms and armour and good horses; also magnificent houses and furniture. The women turn to expensive clothing and gold jewellery. (**4.9**) When, on the other hand, states are ailing because of crop-failures or war and the land is lying fallow, there is a much more urgent need of currency, to pay for supplies and for mercenaries.

(**4.10**) Someone might claim that gold is no less useful than silver. This I do not contradict. However, one thing I know is that when plenty of gold is being found, its value falls, but that of silver rises.

(**4.11**) So: the reason I explained these matters was in order that we should have the confidence to bring as many people as possible into the silver-mines, and have the confidence also to make arrangements in them—on the basis that silver-bearing ore will never run out and that silver itself will never lose its value. (**4.12**) Also, my impression is that the state acknowledged these facts before I did. At any rate, it provides the opportunity of working in the mines to any foreigners who wish to do so, too, on equal terms.

(**4.13**) In order to make myself even clearer on the subject of sustenance, I will now set out how the silver-mines, once organized, could be most useful to the state. Personally, I expect to be saying nothing on these matters that will cause surprise, as if I had discovered something difficult to discover. Some of what I shall say we all still see, now; as for the past, again we hear the same from everyone. (**4.14**) However, what *is* worth calling *very* surprising is the fact that the state notices many private individuals growing rich out of her and does not copy them. Long ago, of course, those of us with an interest in these matters have heard that Nikias the son of Nikeratos once owned a thousand men in the silver-mines. He contracted them out to Sosias the Thrakian, on condition that Sosias paid him back per man an *obolos* a day, net, and also maintained the same numbers. (**4.15**) Hipponikos had six hundred slaves let out in this same way, which brought him in a *mna* a day, net. Philemonides had three hundred, which netted him a half-*mna*; and there were others, I reckon, each operating at his own capacity. (**4.16**) But why is it necessary to speak of the old days? At the present time there are many men in the silver-mines let out similarly. (**4.17**) With my proposals progressing, the only novelty would be this: just as private individuals who acquired slaves have provided themselves with an everlasting income, so too the state would possess *public* slaves, up to a total of three per Athenian.

(**4.18**) Whether the things we are proposing are feasible, let anyone who wishes judge by examining them item by item.

Estimate of manpower: without doubt, the public treasury would be better able to provide it than private individuals; that is quite clear. At any rate the council could easily make a proclamation, for 'anyone who wishes to bring slaves', and then purchase the ones brought in. (**4.19**) And once they had been bought, why would anyone be less likely to lease them from the treasury than from private individuals, if he was going to have them on the same terms? At all events, people lease precincts and shrines and houses and buy tax-collecting rights from the state. (**4.20**) In order that the slaves it has bought are insured, the treasury can accept guarantors from those who are leasing them, just as it does from those who buy the tax-collecting rights. Wrongdoing, mind you, is easier for someone purchasing a tax-contract than for someone leasing slaves. (**4.21**) This is because, when public money looks the same as private, how could an exporter of it be caught? Slaves, on the other hand, would have been marked out by the public seal, and a penalty both for the seller and for the exporter of them would be laid down; the question thus becomes, how could anyone steal them?

Without doubt, then, it seems feasible, so far, for the state to *own* manpower and to *protect* it. (**4.22**) But suppose someone is concerned about how, once numerous workmen are available, numerous individuals too will come forward to lease them. Confidence on that score can rest on the reflection that many of the established operators will lease the public slaves *in addition*, so plentiful are the existing opportunities. Also to be remembered is that there are many, among those who are growing old in the mining industry, and many others, Athenians and foreigners alike, who either would not or could not do physical labour, but would gladly make their living in curatorial capacities, by brain-work.

(**4.23**) Assume, anyway, that the initial total of slaves is twelve hundred. In the course of five or six years that number could probably become, by using the revenue itself, not less than six thousand. Further, assume that each of this number brings in an *obolos* a day, net; the annual revenue is sixty *talanta*. (**4.24**) Out of this sum, assume that twenty *talanta* goes towards more slaves; the state will have the forty to use in whatever way it thinks necessary. When the slave total reaches *ten* thousand, the revenue will be a hundred *talanta*. (**4.25**) In fact though, receipts will be many times more than this. Those who could testify in my support are those who are still alive and can remember how much the tax on the slaves used to earn before the events at Dekeleia. And there is corroborative testimony, too, in this: although a countless number of people have worked in the silver-mines throughout their whole history, the silver-mines today are in no way different from what our ancestors used to recall them as being. (**4.26**) Everything that happens nowadays, too, is testimony to the fact that there could never be more slaves there than the operations require. Those who are digging find no limit, whether downwards or sideways.

(**4.27**) Another point: cutting *new* mines is no less possible now than in the past—and nobody could be in a position to state as a fact whether there is more silver-bearing ore in the well-worked ones than in those still uncut. (**4.28**) So why on earth is it, someone might say, that not many people do cut new mines today, as they did before? It is because the men who work in mining are poorer, as they are only recently operating again, and also because for someone who cuts a new mine there is a large risk. (**4.29**) He who finds a good working becomes rich; he who does not loses everything he will have spent. The consequence is that people nowadays are none too keen to embark on this risk. (**4.30**) Personally, though, I believe that this too—how new mines could be cut in a way as risk-free as possible—is something I am in a position to give advice on. There are, of course, ten tribes of Athenians. Assume that the state gave to each of them an equal number of slaves, and that the tribes took their chance collectively when cutting new mines. The result would be that if one tribe found silver it would be profitable for them all, (**4.31**) and if two, three, four, or half did so, these operations would obviously be more profitable still. That they would all miss out is a result like none from past history. (**4.32**) Of course, it is possible for private individuals also to combine in this way and reduce the risk by taking their chance collectively. But do not be fearful that the public enterprise operating in this way will cause private individuals extra grief—or be caused it by them. Rather, just as a military alliance makes its members mutually stronger as more of them join, so too in the silver-mines: the more people in the business, the larger the quantity of valuable things they will find and bring out.

(**4.33**) I have now stated what, as I conceive it, would create adequate sustenance for every Athenian—once the state was organized—from communal resources.

(**4.34**) Doing the calculations of so massive a sum of start-up capital might lead some people to think that not enough money for all these schemes would be contributed. But even so, let them not lose heart: (**4.35**) it is not the case that all these things must happen at the same time or no advantage arises. Rather, however many buildings are erected or ships constructed or slaves bought will be beneficial immediately. (**4.36**) In point of fact, proceeding in stages will in one respect be more advantageous than doing everything at the same time. This is because by building *en masse* we would pay more money for a worse result than in a stage-by-stage approach; and by looking for slaves in huge numbers we would be compelled to buy ones that were both inferior and too expensive. (**4.37**) Also, progressing on the basis of what was feasible would allow well-thought-out ideas to be implemented by us again, whereas if anything went wrong we could wash our hands of it. (**4.38**) What is more, with everything happening at the same time we would have to pay all the costs together, whereas if some things made progress but others were postponed, the revenue that had accrued would help to provide what is required.

(**4.39**) The aspect of this which perhaps seems most frightening to everyone is the thought that the state acquires *too many* slaves and the workings are crammed too full. But we could dispel this fear also, by not putting in more men than the workings themselves annually demand.

(**4.40**) Thus, it seems to me at any rate, the easiest way of doing these things is also the best.

If, on the other hand, because of the *eisphorai* which have been levied during the war just now, you think that there would be no possibility of further contributions, you yourselves have the solution. Administer the state next year, too, on the basis of the tax-yield before the peace; and invest the surpluses—the ones which would accrue from the fact that there *is* peace, and from metics and traders being looked after, and from the rise in import and exports because of the concentration of population, and from the harbour-dues and the market-revenues being augmented—so that the income from them is maximized.

(**4.41**) Another fear some might have is that this system would be pointless if a war broke out. But let them consider: if these schemes were in operation, the war would be much more frightening to those initiating it than to Athens. (**4.42**) After all, what possession is more useful for a war than manpower? We would be able to fill many ships by public enrolment. Many men too could fight for the community as foot-soldiers and put up hard opposition to the enemy, if someone looked after them.

(**4.43**) I calculate, personally, that it is feasible not to abandon the silver-mines even while a war is in progress. There is of course, near the mines at the sea to the south, a fortress in Anaphlystos, and there is also a fortress in Thorikos, at the one to the north. They are about eleven kilometres from each other. (**4.44**) So suppose there was a third stronghold in between them, on the highest point of Besa. The works would be unified into a single entity as a result of all the fortresses, and if any enemy activity was noticed, each man could retreat to a place of safety a short distance away. (**4.45**) Obviously, an enemy arriving in force would seize any grain or wine or livestock found outside—but after gaining control of silver-bearing ore, what would they have but stones to make use of? (**4.46**) Also, how could an enemy ever make a move in the direction of the mines? I say this because of course Megara, although the state closest to the silver-mines, is much more than ninety-three kilometres away, and the next closest, Thebes, much more than a hundred and eleven. (**4.47**) So assume that an enemy is marching against the silver-mines from some such point. They will be bound to pass Athens. If they are few, the likelihood is that they will be destroyed by cavalry and by patrollers. They might come in great strength, leaving their own possessions deserted, but that would be problematic for them: Athens town would be far closer to their own city-states than they would be, once they were at the mines. (**4.48**) Suppose that they came, even so: how could they *stay*, lacking supplies? For *part* of their force to go and find food would be hazardous, as regards both those making the search and the aims of their mission, while having everyone constantly making the search would mean their being blockaded rather than blockading.

(**4.49**) Note, however, that the income from the slaves would not be the only thing to enlarge the sustenance for the state. Rather, with a multitude of people gathering around the mines, many revenues would be generated: from the market operating there, from public 'houses' near the silver-mines, and from furnaces and all the rest of it. (**4.50**) Assuredly, a multitudinous *city* is what would come into being, if organized in the manner described; and the tracts of land would be no less valuable to the owners there than the ones near town are to theirs.

(**4.51**) Once the ideas I have expounded are acted on, I agree that Athens would become not only better-supplied with sources of income but also better in obedience, better in orderliness, and better in military effectiveness. (**4.52**) This is for two reasons. Those assigned to undergo physical exercise would do this much more diligently if receiving in the gymnasia a sustenance-allowance higher than in the torch-races, under gymnasiarchs; and those assigned to guard-duty in the guard-posts and those assigned to peltast-drill and to patrolling Attica would do all these things better with the sustenance-allowance being distributed in recognition of each of the tasks.

(**5.1**) To fulfil the intention that all revenues flow in from the state itself, there must be peace. If that seems clear, would it not be worthwhile to establish peace-custodians? Such a board of officials, if chosen, would make Athens much more appealing to all people and much more choc-a-bloc with them.

(**5.2**) Some might judge that by remaining at peace Athens will be both more powerless and more disesteemed; and of lesser renown in Hellas. They too, in my opinion, are *mis*judging. Surely the states that are spoken of as most highly favoured are the ones which remained at peace for the longest time; and of all states Athens has the best nature to grow in peacetime. (**5.3**) Would not everyone have need of Athens, if she was maintaining tranquility? The list starts from ship-owners and merchants, but also includes the men with abundant grain, men with bulk wine, men with premium wine, with lots of olive-oil, with lots of sheep; men able to use their brains and money in investments. (**5.4**) In addition, craftsmen, sophists and philosophers, the poets, their production staff; and those desirous of things worth seeing or things worth hearing, whether sacred or celebratory. Besides, for those needing to sell or buy lots of things quickly, where better to do so than at Athens?

(**5.5**) Perhaps nobody contradicts these points; but there *are* some who want Athens to take back the leadership, and they think that this objective would be achieved through war rather than through peace. So let them first consider the Persian wars. Was it by coercing the Hellenes or by benefiting them that we came by command of the navy and the office of treasurers of the Hellenes? (**5.6**) Furthermore, when Athens was deprived of the empire, having acquired the reputation of leading it too harshly, was it not the case that then too—when we refrained from injustice—we again, at the willing instigation of the island-communities, became leaders of the navy? (**5.7**) Without doubt, too, did the Thebans not grant the Athenians leadership over them because they were enjoying benefits? And then there are the Spartans. They conceded to the Athenians the right to make whatever decisions about the leadership they saw fit not because they had been coerced into this by us but because they were being well-treated.

(**5.8**) Now, at any rate, turmoil has arisen in Hellas—and it seems to me that, because of this, an opportunity has come Athens' way: to gain back the Hellenes without effort, without danger, and without expense. There is a possibility of trying to arbitrate between the city-states that are making war against one another, and a possibility, too, of bringing about reconciliation in any where people are engaged in factional strife. (**5.9**) Suppose also that you became conspicuous for striving to make the shrine in Delphi autonomous, as before, not by joining in a war but by going as envoys all over Hellas. Personally, I should not be surprised if you found all the Hellenes unanimous, bound together by oaths and a treaty of alliance, and ready to fight as allies against any people who were trying to seize the shrine—once the Phokians had abandoned it. (**5.10**) If you did become conspicuous for striving to bring about peace through the whole of land and sea, I personally reckon that the safety of Athens would take pride of place in everyone's prayers, second only to their own communities.

(**5.11**) Some may take a different approach and think that where money is concerned war is more profitable to the state than peace. Personally, I know of no better way this could be judged than to consider yet again what happened in past Athenian history. (**5.12**) Anyone who does this will find, in time past, a great deal of money carried up to the akropolis during peace, but all this spent up during war. And he will realize, if he looks into it, that this is true of the present time also. Because of the war, many sources of revenue were giving out and the ones that did come were spent up for purposes many and various; but ever since there has been peace at sea, the revenues are augmented and the citizens able to use them however they wish.

(**5.13**) 'Are you really saying', somebody might ask, 'that Athens should remain at peace even with someone who was doing us wrong?' Not at all. But what I do say is that we could punish them much more swiftly if *we* had taken the initiative in wronging no-one—because no-one would want to be *their* ally.

(**6.1**) So then: nothing of what I have suggested is impossible, or even difficult. By implementing these proposals we will become more appealing to the Hellenes, we will live in greater security, and we will enhance our glory. The common people will have plenty of sustenance, and the rich will be freed from the expense that goes into war.

Once a large surplus has accrued, we will celebrate festivals even more magnificently than we do now; shrines we will keep in good repair; walls and dockyards we will rebuild. To the priests, the council, the officials, and the cavalrymen we will restore their traditional emoluments. What better course than to take these matters in hand as soon as possible, to enable us to see *now*, in our own time, Athens secure and prospering?

(**6.2**) If you do take a decision to do these things, my personal advice would be to send representatives both to Dodona and to Delphi to ask the gods whether it would be 'preferable and better', 'both now and in time to come', for the polis to be organized on these lines. (**6.3**) And if they give their approval, I would then suggest a further question that ought to be asked: which of the gods are the ones we should win over, if we are to do these things in the finest and best way. Once the oracles had named these deities in response, and the sacrifices to them had resulted in good omens, the work could begin, undertaken with divine blessing; thus, in all probability, projects would continue in a manner always 'preferable and better' for the polis.

Commentary

CHAPTER ONE

In *Poroi*'s short Chap.1, X. announces the topic that the work will address: how the citizens of Athens, collectively impoverished by war and an overreaching foreign policy, can maximize their own domestic resources. He considers first the natural assets of their own territory, Attica itself. They are uniquely excellent, in his opinion, and under-exploited.

As Gauthier 52–3 remarks, Chap.1 has been the part of *Poroi* most ill-used ('maltraité') by modern scholars. Scorn has been poured on its allegedly naive idealization of rural Attica, which, if it had not appeared merely comic to his fellow-citizens, would have conjured up a rose-tinted tableau, of the kind painted by the chorus of elders in Sophocles' *Oedipus at Colonus* (lines 668–719). For such a criticism see e.g. Luccioni (1948) 284. Gauthier himself will have none of this. X's sole aim in Chap.1, he insists, is to tell (or remind) his readers which sources of state revenue come from the natural resources of Attica; cf. Jansen (2007) 214–15.

While true and important on one level, this leaves other points to be made. The rich, discursive exploration of Chap.1 by Jansen (2007) 212–37 makes many of them. Chap.1 is the 'linchpin' of the whole work; the place where X. must secure his readers' willingness to give a hearing to the vision of post-imperial Athens that he will be presenting. Jansen also makes a persuasive case for the importance of *autarkeia* (self-sufficiency) in Chap.1, and indeed in *Poroi* as a whole—even though it is a word X. never uses here. A self-sufficient (or self-reliant) Athens had in the past meant an imperial Athens, servicing its needs through direct or indirect use of military power; so e.g. Perikles in Thuc. 2.36.3–4. By the mid-fourth century Plato and (later) Aristotle were promoting an alternative kind of *autarkeia*. Sparta was now held up as the ideal: self-reliant and self-contained for largely moral reasons. In the earlier, Laconophile period of his life, that is a view of things that would have had great appeal for X.—but not now, when he believes it vital that Athens should be an open society (cf. Bodei Giglioni lv–lvi), with trade and commerce at the heart of her economic revival (cf. Dillery (1993) 4).

Given X.'s persuasive purposes in general, and particularly his view that the natural assets of Attica were under-appreciated, it has not gone unnoticed that he himself appears to under-exploit them. While his gaze is comprehensive enough otherwise, the man who had written *Oeconomicus* displays here an apparent blind-spot to agriculture and its potential.

The assessment in Gauthier 52–5 attempts to solve this puzzle. X.'s theme throughout is revenues, here in the form of the various taxes and dues, attaching to each of the assets to be mentioned, that individuals will incur (either by buying and selling them within Attica or by exporting them). The Athenian taxation system, according to Gauthier, left agriculture *per se* out of its scope. Though he takes this as axiomatic, it is in fact a polemical position enunciated, most obviously, by M. I. Finley in *The Ancient Economy* (first published in 1973) but also espoused over the years by, among others, D. M. Lewis, H. W. Pleket, and P. Roesch; see Isager & Skydsgaard (1992) 135–44 ('Taxes in agriculture'), at 135. Isager & Skydsgaard themselves open up the question and take a more nuanced view. On Athens their position is that 'there was a general purchase tax including tax on agricultural products; business was necessarily considerable. But comparatively few of the agricultural commodities sold on the market were actually grown in Athens.' This last point is well worth making: cf. [X.] *Ath.Pol.*2.7. Yet even if the productive capacity of Attica was lower than is generally argued nowadays, it did—on any view—grow things, and the more things grown (and, crucially, not consumed by their growers) the higher the tax-take when they were bought and sold locally or exported.

Thus, X.'s lack of interest in improving agricultural productivity does remain surprising. Could the explanation be, at least in part, that the contrast between *Oeconomicus* and *Poroi* has been exaggerated? Perhaps X.'s knowledge of farming in the first of them only appears to be 'hands-on', such that, on closer inspection, he is revealed as 'the gentleman farmer who knows agriculture primarily as a spectator' (Isager & Skydsgaard (1992) 7). Perhaps. But more probably, in my opinion, X. took it so much for granted that conscientious farmers wanted to maximize their yields *and knew how to do so* (*Oec*.15–20) that the matter went without saying. See also Jansen (2007) 214–16.

Thiel 40–2 (Excursus I) on X.'s '*prooemium*' addresses itself not to this aspect of Chap.1 but to the historical context. On this see the lemmata below, esp. **1.1 the poverty of the masses.**

X.'s picture of Attica here in Chap.1, as Brinkmann (1912) pointed out, was systematically drawn on by the second-century CE Mysian rhetorician Publius Aelius Aristides (*OCD* 154–5), for some of the opening material in his enormous *Panathenaicus* (ten times the length of the whole of *Poroi*); see also Thiel 4–5. Gauthier 53 terms this 'un magnifique exemple de plagiat littéraire' (while adding that Aristides had no understanding of *why* X. was apparently so eloquent in his praises). The relevant sections, in the edition by F. W. Lenz and C. A. Behr, are 14–23.

* * * *

1.1 Personally This word, in the Greek not an adverb but the first-person singular pronoun *egô*, does begin the whole work. X. will use it or its variant *egôge* ten more times: 3.11, 4.5, 4.13, 4.30, 4.43, 4.51, 5.9, 5.10, 5.11, 6.2. Since ancient Greek is a fully inflected language, such pronouns are not needed with verbs for them to make sense (witness e.g. the otherwise similar opening of *Ages.*). Their role, where used, is to add emphasis. Both here at the outset of *Poroi*, therefore, and by subsequent iteration, X. is making clear the personal nature of his views (if not their originality: see under the next lemma). *Lac.Pol.* had begun comparably—but, though a longer work, had deployed the pronoun only four more times.

On the echo of *Hell*.2.3.51 in this opening see General Intro., section 5, n.64; and further under the next lemma.

1.1 I always think that whatever kind of leaders etc. Dillery (2017) 216-217 identifies this opening as a 'favourite Xenophontean trope whereby the impression is created that the treatise is the outcome of a moment of reflection'. Dillery does not cite *egô* in this regard (see the preceding lemma) but he does adduce the word *pote*, attached here to 'always' (and sometimes hard, as here, to reflect in translation). It had featured in no fewer than five of X.'s other openings: *Cyrop*.1.1.1, *Hier*.1.1, *Lac.Pol*.1.1, *Mem*.1.1.1, *Oec*.1.1.

X.'s word here for leader, *prostatês* (plural *prostatai*), and two verbs cognate with it—one of which is used in the next sentence here—had been standard ones in this sense since the fifth century: witness Herodotus, Thucydides, and also Attic tragedy and comedy. Notable examples in X.'s earlier works include *Hell.*3.2.27, 5.2.4 & 6, *Hier.*11.5 & 7, *Mem.*1.1.8, 1.2.32, 1.2.40, 2.8.4, 3.6.1.

As regards this thought in full, X. had expressed it in almost exactly the same words—different only because he had not been considering democratic poleis—in *Cyrop.*8.8.5: 'the kind of *prostatai* there are is mostly mirrored in the kind of people under them'. (Gauthier 35 points out that this precedent is what justifies an understanding of *politeiai* in the present passage as 'civic communities' or suchlike, rather than the impersonal 'constitutions'. Cf. Jansen (2007) 106 n.183, citing in addition Cicero, *Ad familiares* (*Letters to intimates*) 1.9.12: whatever *principes* a state has, the rest of its *cives* will usually be the same.) Note also, more generally, *Cyrop.*8.1.8. The idea was not unique to X., however. Thiel 19 notes comparable instances, from the same period, in Isocrates' *Nicocles* (3.37), *Areopagiticus* (7.22 & 78), and *On the Peace* (8.53 & 133). Both Isocrates and X. himself, though, were offering variations on an existing theme or trope; in Greek a *topos*. See e.g. Euripides' tragedy *Orestes*, staged in Athens in 408: to Orestes' warning that 'It is a terrible thing when the masses have villains as *prostatai*', Pylades replies, 'But when they choose honest ones they always make honest decisions' (lines 772–3).

For the continuation of the *topos* beyond the fourth century, Gauthier 36 adduces two passages from the second-century historian Polybius. In 9.23.6–8, looking back to classical Hellas, the examples of Aristeides (*OCD* 154 s.v.1) and Perikles (*OCD* 1106–7 s.v.1) vs. Kleon (*OCD* 332 C-) and Chares (*OCD* 305 s.v.1) from Athens, and the Spartan kings Agesilaos (*OCD* 38–9) and his Agiad counterpart Kleombrotos, are named to prove the point that 'the character of poleis changes with the differences of their *prostatai*'. In 11.29.10–11, part of a speech put into the mouth of the elder Scipio Africanus, again the vocabulary includes *prostatai*.

1.1 Some of those holding positions of leadership in Athens On the verb here, see under the preceding lemma. This perfect participle of it is used simply as a variation of the noun; so already e.g. *Hell.*3.5.1 (on Persian gold ensuring that 'the *proestêkotes* in the city-states' will pursue anti-Spartan policies) and outside X. e.g. Lys. 13.7 ('the *proestêkotes* of the demos').

In the present context the phrase as a whole might come across as coy or evasive. X. probably did not intend it to be. He is not concerned with blame—or praise—*ad hominem*, whether retrospective or current. On the rare occasions, later, where individuals are mentioned by name, they are dating-fixes (two instances in 3.7) or past examples of successful entrepreneurial activity in the mines (three in 4.14–15).

That said, X. must in plain fact have had particular individuals in mind, at least by way of example. Thiel 3 suggested that the well-known, by now elderly, Aristophon of Azenia (*LGPN* s.v. no.19, *OCD* 159, *APF* 64–6) or his associate Leodamas of Acharnai (*LGPN* s.v. no.3, *APF* 523) might have said the sort of thing exemplified here—see the next lemma—in the assembly's debate in 366 about sending a cleruchy (military settlement) to the island of Samos. The proposal was opposed by one Kydias (*LGPN* s.v. no.4: identified there and already in *AO* 261 with a naval officer of that name in a fragment of comic drama, Eub. fr.67.11 Kassel-Austin), on grounds noted in a passage in Aristotle's *Rhetoric* (2.6.24 = 1384b32–5): 'imagine that the Hellenes are standing round you in a circle, not merely hearing but seeing what you are about to vote for'. (The decree was passed regardless: see e.g. Cargill (1981) 148–9; Shipley (1987) 138–43.) But Thiel's suggestion is far too specific, as regards personnel and date alike. From 377 onwards there were plenty of other Athenian opinion-formers, prominent among them Kallistratos of Aphidna (*LGPN* s.v. no.50, *OCD* 268 Callistratus (2), *APF* 277–82), whose fortunes rose and fell with the Second Athenian League: see generally Sealey (1956), Hochschultz (2007). In any case there may be grounds for extending the scope of X.'s remark, and memory, back into the fifth century: see below, **the poverty**.

An interpretation and contextualization of 'Some of those etc.' fundamentally different from this can be found in Jansen (2007) 21, expanded at 48–50. It is founded on the view that X. was back in Athens from 366 onwards, and honing his ideas for a full decade before they appeared in developed form as *Poroi*. On this model 'Some of those etc.' are some of his interlocutors in these years. Yet if this hypothetical debate was so current, would X. have written that these individuals 'used to say' (*elegon*) what they said? (This imperfect tense wrongly becomes a present in Tuplin (1993) 32, 'claim', an aorist in Gray (2007) 56, 'said', and a perfect in Powell (2015) 13, 'have stated'.)

1.1 'recognize what is just... exerts a compulsion' As Thiel 3 notes (and Marchant's Loeb acts on), X.'s Greek here, with everything between '(they) used to say' and 'they maintained' expressed in the present tense, does put this wording into direct speech. The phrase is a literary/rhetorical device intended to introduce immediacy and liveliness, rather than a quotation as nowadays we would understand it; nevertheless see below, **to be somewhat**.

Gauthier 37–8 registers the notion of 'what is just'—in Greek, *to dikaion*—in relation to leadership in the political thought of the period. (Within X.'s own oeuvre, note especially the exchanges between Sokrates and the would-be politician Euthydemos (*LGPN* s.v. no.5; *POP* 151) in *Mem*.4.2.1–40, its core 11–20.) An excursus then explores *to dikaion* with particular reference to imperialism (Gauthier 42–4). The speeches in Thucydides, such as the debate over the revolt of Mytilene (*OCD* 993, *IACP* no.798) in Thuc. 3.36–50, illustrate how hard it was for the fifth-century Athenians to administer their far-flung empire (as, in effect, it became) on the principles of equity and justice. It would have been remarkable if much the same moral dilemmas had not resurfaced in the fourth century, and in fact 5.6 here (to look no further) shows that they did. See also Isoc. 8.6.

1.1 the poverty of the masses This translation (or something akin to it) of the noun that X. uses to describe the economic position of the mass of Athenians is impossible to avoid, but needs explanation. *Penia* reappears at the end of the present chapter, likewise with a general application, and its cognate adjective *penês* (referring to men in the mining industry) in 4.28. There is mention of the *plousioi* in 4.29 and 6.1 (the latter passage contrasting them with the *demos*), and 4.14 uses a verb cognate with that adjective when describing individuals acquiring wealth. So the *plousioi*, plainly, are the rich, those with *ploutos*—but that does not require their opposite, the *penêtes*, people whose condition is *penia*, to be 'the poor' in the sense of the destitute, paupers (to whom other words, not relevant here, were applied). Essentially, *penêtes* needed to work for a living, *plousioi* did not. There are celebrated short statements to this effect, from divergent economic standpoints, in Finley (1985—originally 1973) 41 and Ste. Croix (1981) 431. See also e.g. *APF* xxi; Gauthier 38–9; Wood (1988) 176–7; Cecchet (2015) 25–7 and discursively in chaps.3–5. C. Taylor (2017) is the latest, model-driven study.

With that understood, what did these Athenian politicians mean by their admission that 'somewhat wrongful' behaviour towards the imperial allies (see the next lemma) was necessitated by the *penia* of the majority of their fellow-citizens? Gauthier 43–4 sketches a scenario in which the individuals whom X. has in mind, Socratically educated (see above, **recognize**), were in effect trapped in a fifth-century past where the enormous democracy did require hard-nosed imperialism—a policy inherently unjust—to sustain it. In my opinion it is right, and important, to recall the high fifth century: not only the sheer size of the Athenian citizen-body then but also its high degree of reliance on various types of public fees and allowances. A classic, if tendentious, statement of this is (retrospectively) made in chap.24 of the Aristotelian *Ath.Pol.*; and see also chaps.11–12 of Plutarch's *Perikles*.

Between 404 and the time of *Poroi* there were still, needless to say, plenty of 'poor' Athenians, and at least as many kinds of public pay for them to draw; crucially, however, this was now financed by *domestic*, not imperial, income (see Pritchard (2015), with ample bibliography). Consequently, if and when *fourth*-century Athenian politicians addressed the topics of imperialism and justice—whether before or after 377—we need to ask why should, and how could, 'the poverty of the masses' have featured in their arguments? One issue is indubitably relevant: cleruchies. Just as in the second half of the fifth century, some Athenians who were settled in overseas garrisons in the early (Imbros, Lemnos, Skyros) or the mid- (Samos, Poteidaia) fourth century will have escaped the grind of *penia* by going there; see generally Cargill (1995). X. might therefore have had in mind the proponents of this policy (cf. above, **Some of those**)—alongside their counterparts from the Perikles/Kleon era, and later the likes of Kleophon of Acharnai (*LGPN* s.v. no.5, *OCD* 333 Cleophon (1)), a man whom the young X. might have heard for himself during the closing years of the Peloponnesian War.

The discussion of 'the *penia* of the masses' in Jansen (2007) 135–41 would be a very good one indeed if the question needing elucidation was how such *penêtes* would benefit from X.'s central aspiration to give all Athenians three obols a day (4.17, with 3.9). Since it is in fact the question framed at the beginning of the preceding paragraph here, in my opinion something of a puzzle remains.

The puzzle would diminish, even vanish, for anyone prepared to go along with Jansen's 'hard', neo-traditional narrative of the Second Athenian League (Jansen (2007) 141–74). By neo-traditional I mean that Jansen rejects the view, ventured by Griffith (1978) and fully articulated by Cargill (1981), which differentiates this organization sharply from the Athenian Empire of 478–404. Instead he *in effect* returns—as have others—to the older, long-lived orthodoxy of Busolt (1874), Marshall (1905), and Accame (1941) in which, by and large, fifth-century history repeats itself. As there is neither scope nor need, here, to rehearse all the issues involved, it will suffice to say that Cargill goes too far (see the review by Simon Hornblower in *CR* 32 (1982) 235–9), as iconoclasts are prone to do, but his challenge has made it possible to take a more balanced, nuanced view: witness e.g. Seager in *CAH* 6.171 (and Rhodes (2010) 265–74). Jansen's balance is not struck quite where it should be, in my opinion. Importantly, the fourth-century allied 'contributions' (*syntaxeis*), levied by the allied synod, were not just a rebranded version of the exploitative, surplus-generating mechanism that the old *phoros* had been; cf. Rhodes (2010) 268. On the other hand, Jansen (2007) 174–205, esp. 187–200, persuasively identifies three types of Athenian 'imperial acquisition' that do characterize the fourth century no less than the fifth. Alongside cleruchies, these are 'tribute *and taxes*' (my emphasis) and 'depradation and extortion'; for the latter see e.g. *Hell.*6.2.38, Iphikrates of Rhamnous (*LGPN* s.v. no.4, *OCD* 743, *APF* 248–52) on the island of Kephallenia (*OCD* 299 C-, *IACP* nos.125, 132, 135–6) in 372.

X.'s own take on the Second Athenian League will emerge again in 5.5–8, esp. 6–7.

1.1 'to be somewhat wrongful as regards the city-states' The preceding lemmata should have made clear the particular identity of 'the city-states', the *poleis*. X. might have specified '*allied* city-states', just as (e.g.) Aeschin. 2.70 does when exaggerating the career-losses of the general Chares of Aggele (*LGPN* s.v. no.17, *OCD* 305 s.v.1, *APF* 568–9), but there was no need to do so. The usage had been entrenched since the fifth century. Evidence-in-chief (cited by Thiel 3, following Zuborg) is *Poleis*, a play written and staged, probably in the later 420s, by the comic dramatist Eupolis (*OCD* 550–1). It has not survived complete, but some of the many preserved quotations, and associated ancient commentary, show that the 'city-states' in question were those of the then Athenian Empire. Note also e.g. Thuc. 1.96.1, and how the 'Standards Decree' (*IG* I^3 1453; ML 45, now OR 155; Fornara (1983) no.97), enforcing the use of Athenian coins, weights, and measures throughout the Empire, refers to 'the (*sc.* Athenian) officials in the *poleis*'.

The phrase lemmatized above is one that I have made, in translation, as evasive as X. must have intended his Greek to be. (Waterfield 169 goes even further in that direction: 'to fall somewhat short of total equity towards the allied states'.) A comparison with 5.13 makes this clear. There (in X.'s own voice), the verb *adikein* is twice used transitively, i.e. with a direct object: to wrong someone. Here (in the voice of apologists for imperialism) we have a related adjective, in one of the functions served by its comparative degree—rather/somewhat *x*. By being an adjective, not a verb, it can only be followed by a more distancing prepositional phrase: '*peri* the city-states'. (The present-day (over-)use, by politicians and others in the public domain, of 'around' is an exact equivalent.)

The idea of just or upright conduct will be picked up near the end of the section, once the project of exploring 'whether there was any way the citizens could sustain themselves out of their own territory' has been announced. This, X. declares, best fulfils the aim of *to dikaion* (above, **recognize**).

1.1 I set about examining A commonplace-looking phrase, but there is perhaps more to it than meets the eye. In the first half of the 360s Isocrates' *Euagoras* had begun its closing section in this way ('these are the reasons I set about writing this treatise': Isoc. 9.76), and his *Philippos* of 346 would open similarly (Isoc. 5.1–2). X. seems to be adopting the language already established in this era for framing a rhetorical exposition.

1.1 whether there was any way the citizens could sustain themselves out of their own territory The concluding feminine noun here is in fact left unstated in the Greek. (Since it is a singular, Waterfield 169 is insufficiently precise with 'from their own resources'.) Gauthier 40 takes it to be, self-evidently, *polis* ('state'), stemming from 'the *politai*' who are the subject of the clause; likewise Schütrumpf 77. That is a possibility, and it could derive some extra support from the phrase 'revenues out of (the) polis' in 5.1. Nevertheless, I follow the lead of Dakyns ('from the soil of Attica itself') and Marchant ('from their own soil') in believing that the noun implicit here is *chôra*, about to be used in 1.2 (and again in 1.3–4; also 2.1 and 4.52). See generally now Jansen (2007) 254 n.112, with other references. Compare also 'Attica' at the end of 1.2 (and already *Apol.*23, *Hell.*1.7.22, 5.1.1, 9 & 23, 5.4.19, 6.2.14, *Mem.*2.8.1, 3.5.4); though functioning as a noun, in the original and in translations alike, 'Attica' is in fact a feminine adjective which on the orthodox view (see LSJ s.v.) presupposes the noun *gê*, land. If, here in 1.1, X. did mean to imply *chôra*, or even *gê*, he is referring to what is to come *within Chap.1*, rather than, at this stage, looking beyond that.

Gauthier 40 is insistent that 'the *politai*' here (and again 2.3, 3.7, 5.12; varied by *astoi* in 2.2) are the adult male Athenian citizens, in contradistinction not merely to non-citizens but also to the civic community more broadly defined. This is debatable. It is true that *Poroi* will not concern itself directly with women and children (and that metics, the city's resident non-citizens of free status, will be considered in their own right in Chap.2); but Gauthier's political conceptualization of 'the *politai*' may place too narrow a limit on what X. means. His own question about whether they could 'sustain themselves' uses the verb *diatrephesthai*. Though it does not appear again in the work, it is related to a word which does: the noun *trophê* (4.13, 4.33, 4.52, 6.1; see also *trephein* in 1.5 and, especially, 2.1). The provision of adequate *trophê*, in short, is a central object of X.'s. No questions would be begged at this stage by saying that, in itself, *trophê* means food, nourishment, sustenance; but on this issue see further under **4.33 I have now stated**.

1.1 they would be helped to escape their poverty and, also, at the same time, the suspicion with which the Hellenes view them The verb which X. uses here is *epikourein* (related to the noun *epikouros* in 4.9). It often takes the dative case: sometimes (*a*) for the persons helped, sometimes (*b*) for an aspect of their situation to which the help applies. Besides the present instance of *b*, see also *Lac.Pol.* 2.6, *Mem.*1.4.13. (*Lac.Pol.*10.2 has elements of both.) In translation, though not in the Greek, the addition of 'help to escape' or suchlike conveys the sense.

On 'their poverty' see already above, **the poverty**. As regards the other thing the Athenians can hope to escape if they take X.'s advice, Gauthier 41 reasonably comments that 'suspicion' seems an odd, punch-pulling word for the downright hostility felt towards Athens during the fourth-century League (Isoc. 7.8, 8.19 & 125, Demosth. 15.2) as well as its predecessor (5.6 with Comm.). Both in X. and elsewhere, those who strike others as *hypoptoi* are untrustworthy, suspected of saying one thing while doing (or wishing to do) another. In context here, therefore, it may be that the word came to X.'s mind because of allied perceptions that the Athenians had not abided by the various promises built in to the 'charter' decree of 377: RO 22 (Harding (1985) no.35) lines 15–46.

1.2 as I was indeed examining what I had in mind For 'what I had in mind' Gauthier 45 compares *Lac.Pol.*1.1, which uses a different compound form of the verb used here. But 'examining' is perhaps the more noteworthy element of the phrase. Not only has the concept been used already in 1.1 (see **I set about examining**), which the present passage picks up, but it will reappear, either two or three times, in the second half of the work, in reference not to X. himself but to putative readers: see 4.18, 5.2 (with Notes on the Text), 5.12.

1.2 I had an immediate realization Likewise Waterfield: '(As soon as I started to look into the project) I was struck by the realization'. Some translators render this phrase too flatly, e.g. 'one fact presented itself clearly to my mind' (Dakyns), or 'one thing seemed clear at once' (Marchant). X. had used the verb that he uses here in *Hell.*3.5.21, to describe the sudden and unexpected appearance of a Spartan army in northern Boiotia.

1.2 the natural condition of the territory provides very many revenues The concept (and idiom) of a natural resource reappears in 1.4, where one of these revenue-generating items is specified: marble. We may note in passing that X.'s claim ought, strictly speaking, to have been that Attica provided very many *poroi* of/for revenues. (For the distinction, underlined by Gauthier and by Schütrumpf 119–21, see General Intro., section 2.) As will emerge below, the revenues arise indirectly, by selling the marble etc.; cf. Jansen (2007) 223.

More generally, revenue(s) will be the keynote of *Poroi* from now on: cf. 2.1, 2.7, 3.6, 3.10, 3.14, 4.1, 4.17, 4.23, 4.25, 4.39–40, 4.50, 5.1, 5.12. Though X. had never been a front-line politician himself, he knew full well that a grasp of Athens' *prosodoi* and how to increase them were essential qualifications for the role. This is clear above all in the exchange between Sokrates and the late-teenage Glaukon of Kollytos (*LGPN* s.v. no.24, *APF* 332–3, *POP* 154–6), younger brother of Plato, in *Mem.*3.6—something we will return to more than once in this Comm. It begins by inducing the would-be statesman to agree that his main task is to make Athens richer, and that to do so he must be aware of its current revenues (*prosodoi*) and expenses (*dapanai*): *Mem.*3.6.4–6.

For the sort of expert introductions to Athenian public income (and expenditure) that Glaukon would have benefited from, see Rhodes (2013a) and Ober (2015a).

1.2 I want it to be recognized that this is the truth I am speaking, so I will first describe the nature of Attica For such first-person 'description' see again 4.13 (likewise with a stated purpose of it), and already e.g. *Ages.*1.6, *Hipp.*1.17, *Lac.Pol.* 13.1, More broadly, the trope—already established in the late fifth century, if not earlier still—comes from the narrative sections of court-room oratory: compare e.g. Isoc. 21.2 and 17.3, Andoc. 1.117, Lys. 3.3.

On 'Attica' see already **1.1 whether there was.**

1.3 the fact that the seasons are very mild here Gauthier 45 is surprisingly emphatic that X.'s field of comparison, here and in what follows ('... is something to which the actual products bear witness. At any rate, plants that in many places could not even grow bear fruit here'), is limited to Athens' neighbours in central and southern Greece, including the Peloponnese. However, in the light of 1.6 especially, there must be a possibility that X. has a wider area in view—as would be expected of someone who had traversed so much of it. My translation of *pollachou* as 'in many places' is non-committal; contrast Waterfield 169 ('many parts of the world').

Either way commentators, including now myself, are at a loss to give an example of the plants X. had in mind; ones which grow in Attica but not elsewhere. A less baffling claim is the one made two sentences later: that seasonal crops 'all begin here very early and cease very late'. We can take 'all' with a pinch of salt, but X. might reasonably have meant something like figs; cf. generally Athen. *Deipn.*3.77C–D, and L. Foxhall in *OCD* 575. Note also the quotation from Aristophanes' lost comedy *Seasons* (fr.581 Kassel-Austin), preserved in Athen. *Deipn.*9.372B–C: in Athens 'you will see, in the middle of winter, cucumbers, grapes, fruit... You might see baskets of figs and of myrtle-berries together, covered in snow, and because they sow cucumbers together with turnips the result is that nobody knows any longer what time of year it is. A great thing, if throughout the year one can have whatever one craves!' See also Braund (1994), Moreno (2007) 74–5. (Later in the speech this bounty is attributed to reverence for the gods.) Harmless fun, but not to be dismissed out of hand. At the very least it shows what the Athenians themselves enjoyed believing.

What scholars do cite when contemplating *Poroi* 1.3 are texts which appear to describe a less 'green and pleasant land' than X.'s: Thucydides (1.2.5, with Hornblower (1991–2008) 1.12) on the thinness of its soil; Plato's description (*Criti.*110E–111E) of a land impoverished since the profusion of early times; Theophrastus (*History of Plants* 8.8.2) on Attica as terrain best suited to barley (i.e. rather than the more prized wheat). Gauthier 46 notes that Plato's notorious verdict does not in fact contradict X.'s here, in that it is (or purports to be) relative. Plato too calls the Attica of his day 'unmatched anywhere for quantity and excellence of its crops and the suitability of its soil for all living creatures'. (As far as X. himself is concerned, Sallares (1991) 376 provides a bracing antidote from a present-day scientific standpoint: '[a] source such as Xenophon's *Poroi* obviously has an axe to grind and, in the absence of both a comparative perspective and a quantitative dimension, tells us nothing whatsoever'.)

1.3 what goes for the land is just as true of the sea that surrounds the territory: it produces everything in great quantity In 4.43 'the sea' will be divided into two, a southern and a northern: see the Comm. there.

My phrase 'produces everything in great quantity' is conveyed in the Greek by a single word, the adjective *pamphoros* in the superlative degree: *pamphorôtatê*. X. had applied it to the Thrakian Chersonese (*OCD* 308 Chersonesus (1), *IACP* no.695) in *Hell.*3.2.10. Applying it now to coastal waters is a novelty. For X.'s appreciation of the economic importance of the sea to Athens, see also the speech put into the mouth of the envoy Prokles, from Phleious (*IACP* no.355) in the Peloponnese, addressing the Athenian assembly in 370 (*Hell.*7.1.4): 'life, for most of you, comes from the sea'. (Despite its tacit endorsement by Pritchett (1971–1991) 4.468 and Jansen (2007) 178 n.189, I cannot share the view of Cartledge (1987) 274 that this refers to grain imports from the Black Sea and elsewhere.)

Talk of the bounty of the sea makes one think in the first instance of fish and other seafood. Thiel 42–3 (Excursus II) assembles a dossier of evidence, including some from X. himself (*Hell.*5.1.23: 'many fishing-boats' off the coast in 387), on the Athenian fishing industry and the consumption of its catches, especially tuna and anchovies. Much of this fish was salted, so Thiel (and cf. Gauthier 45) is also right to mention salt-works, memorialized in (e.g.) the names of three coastal demes: Halai Aixonides, Halai Araphenides, Halimous; cf. German Halle (Saale).

1.3 the good things that the gods provide in their seasons No empty banality this, as Gauthier (himself a devout Catholic, as noted in his obituary in *Le Monde*) was at pains to insist. Besides pointing out that the theme itself is as old as Hesiod (*Op.*320), Gauthier 46–7 cites Xenophontic precedents from *Mem.*4.3.3–6 (Sokrates' exposition of what the gods 'provide'—the present passage's verb is used four times), *Oec.*5.20 ('farm-work' needs the gods' blessing) and *Oec.*16.3 (useless 'to fight the gods', *theomachein*, when assessing what will grow where). One could add e.g. *Mem*.1.4.11, 2.2.3, *Symp*.6.7.

Within *Poroi* itself the gods and their affairs will feature several more times: twice more in this first Chapter (1.4, 1.5), and in an accumulation of instances in the closing two (5.4, 5.9, 5.10, 6.1, 6.2–3). See also 5.2 with the Comm. there on the adjective *eudaimôn*.

On Xenophon and various facets of religion: Anderson (1974) 34–40; Tuplin (1993) 215 (appendix VII); Bowden (2004); Parker (2004); Pownall (2004) 82–97; Bowden (2005) 77–9; Whitehead (2009) 327–30; Flower (2016); Haywood (2016).

1.4 This because there is a natural abundance of stone The connection 'because' flags up the fact that this is an expansion of '(Attica) also possesses good things that are everlasting'. Why Gauthier 47 insists that X.'s phrase *aidia agatha* carries no implications for the longevity of the supplies of stone (and silver—said to be inexhaustible in 4.2–3) is not clear. At all events, assets which are the result of nature (cf. 1.2 **the natural condition**), and thus eternal, evidently belong in a different category from the transitory gifts of the gods (see the preceding item), though the two overlap with the divine provision of silver (1.5). On Attica's 'stone' see generally Thiel 43–5 (Excursus III) and in full Wycherley (1978), esp. 267–77 ('Postscript: the stones'), who begins by citing this very passage of *Poroi*.

Though the Greek noun *lithos* can apply to stone(s) of any and every kind, a recognized sub-use signifies marble, 'a limestone miraculously metamorphosed by titanic heat and pressure into its characteristic crystalline structure... This has happened in many places, but in most the result consists of comparatively small lumps or thin veins; much rarer are the massive beds from which can be extracted the great blocks needed for the major architectural members of temples and other large buildings. In this... Attica is exceptionally favored. More than one huge layer runs through the fabric of both [Mt.] Pentelikon and [Mt.] Hymettos; and other extensive beds lie near the southern tip of Attica' (Wycherley (1978) 267). Note also Wycherley (1978) 275 on the 'hard blue-black limestone from Eleusis (sometimes inaccurately called marble)'.

One of the background implications of X.'s remarks here—see further under the next two lemmata—is that the Athenians of his day had no need to import building-stone from elsewhere. In fact we know that to some extent they did so, or at least had once done so. Some, brown in colour, came from nearby Aigina (Wycherley (1978) 269, 271, 272, cf. 35, 40, 43, 80), but for marble of a quality to rival Pentelic they had to look to a more distant island, Paros (*OCD* 1084, *IACP* no.509): Wycherley (1978) 274, 275, cf. 69, 73.

1.4 from which very beautiful temples and very beautiful altars are made, and very appropriately lovely statues for the gods Some might have mentioned 'secular' buildings also (as Thucydides did, in his famous imagining of a future, deserted Sparta, with only 'the shrines and the foundations of (other) constructions left': Thuc. 1.10.2); but not the pious X.

Here is the first instance in *Poroi* (for earlier works see e.g. *Ages.*5.5, *Lac.Pol.*5.8, *Mem.*1.2.12, 2.6.12, 4.3.6) of X.'s liking for items in trios. See also 4.6, 4.35, 4.51, 5.2, 5.3–4 (see **5.3 The list**), 5.8, 5.9, and 6.1. For the conjunction of temples and altars cf. already *Symp.*8.9; and *Hipp.*3.2 mentions 'the shrines and statues in the Agora'. All three items are mentioned together in chap.21 of Hyperides' *Funeral Speech* for the casualties in the Lamian War (of 323–322; *OCD* 790). See generally Mikalson (2016) 253–64, esp. 260–1.

X.'s reference to the statues (*agalmata*) as 'for', rather than 'of', the gods, contrasts with e.g. Isoc. 9.57 (on 'the *agalma* of Zeus' in the Agora) and Paus. 1.32.2 ('*agalmata* of gods' on the summits of two of Attica's major mountains: Athena on Pentelikon, Zeus on Hymettos). 'Appropriately lovely' is an adjective he applies elsewhere to women (*Anab.*4.1.14, and boys; *Mem.*2.1.22) and to the front legs of horses (*Eq.*1.7).

Examples of the domestic use of Attic marble (for external use, see the next lemma) in all three of these categories are legion; I confine myself to one specimen of each. Temple: the fifth-century Parthenon (*OCD* 1085, cf. 896). Altar (freestanding: see generally *OCD* 66): of/for Zeus Phratrios and Athena Phratria in the Agora (Wycherley (1978) 66). Statue of/for a deity (*agalma*; confusingly, *eikones*—icons—were statues of mortals): besides Paus. 1.32.2 (above), Apollo Patrôos a.k.a. the Kithara-player (Paus. 1.3.4; Wycherley (1978) 67).

1.4 Hellenes and *barbaroi* alike, many have need of it Jansen (2012) 733–4 draws attention to the prominence, in *Poroi*, of the notion of what people 'need'—and the associated (rather modern) idea that such need(s) should be met. Besides the present passage see also 3.2, 4.8, 4.10, 5.4.

This is the only instance in *Poroi* of the Hellenes/*barbaroi* dichotomy; the latter will reappear alone in 1.8 (twice) and 2.3. While 'non-Hellenes' would be a factually accurate translation of *barbaroi*, I retain the word itself, transliterated, for its more pungent flavour: those who speak not Greek but some unintelligible *barbar*-sounding language; cf. Strab. 14.2.28. (See in brief *OCD* 223; in full e.g. Diller (1937), E. Hall (1989); Vlassopoulos (2013).) Contempt was not always as overt as this might make it sound, but even here in *Poroi* the superiority of being Hellenic—and preferably Athenian—comes out: see for that 1.8 and, especially, 2.3 (with the Comm. to both).

The present passage's contention is that both Hellenes and *barbaroi* favour Attic stone. As the full study of this, Abraldes (1996), is extremely hard to find, it will be more helpful to adduce here a few examples which are not.

Gauthier 47 cites the lavishly documented instance of the use of Pentelic marble for the temple of Asklepios at Epidauros in the north-east Peloponnese (*OCD* 514–15, *IACP* no.348), constructed discontinuously between *c.* 370 and *c.* 330: Burford (1969); cf. Ober (1985) 30. On a smaller scale, one could note Paus. 9.11.6: 'colossal figures of Athena and Herakles in Pentelic stone', by Alkamenes (*OCD* 50–51), set up by Thrasyboulos of Steiria (*LGPN* s.v. no.22, *OCD* 1471–2) and other Athenians in the Theban Herakleion, to mark the starting-point of their liberation march on Athens in late 404 or early 403 (*Hell.*2.4.2).

For Attic stone admired and used by *barbaroi* in X.'s day, the obvious example is the Mausoleion (*OCD* 914) at Halikarnassos (*OCD* 643, *IACP* no.886), one of antiquity's Seven Wonders of the World. Parts of its structure, e.g. the 'Chariot Frieze', and some of its contents, e.g. the 'Artemisia' statue now in the British Museum, are of Pentelic marble.

1.5 There is land, too, which when sown does not bear a crop but when excavated supports many times the number of people than if it was bearing grain Compare generally Aristot. *Pol.*1.1258b29–31 on the type of money-making (*chrêmatistikê*) concerned with 'things from the earth and ones coming from the earth that, though bearing no crop, are useful; examples are tree-felling and any kind of mining'. X. here, as we very soon see, has mining in mind. Specifically, in the Athenian case, he is thinking of a hilly region in the southernmost part of Attica, about 12 km. wide (at its widest extent) and seventeen long, as it narrows to a point at Cape Sounion: Laureion (see Chap.3 intro.). X. never uses that toponym—contrast e.g. Herodotus (7.144.1) and Thucydides (2.55.1, 6.91.7)—but assumes that his readers will know what he means, here in 1.5 and again throughout Chap.4.

Gauthier 48 notes that the agricultural bleakness of the mining area is again implicit in '4.48' (actually 4.45, on fruitless enemy foraging there). Attempts, on our part, to visualize what life was like there must strike a balance between that kind of consideration and the ones adduced by R. G. Osborne (1987) 78: 'the landscape of the Laureion is scattered with small installations not directly connected with mining. These installations consist of or include a strong building or tower, isolated or attached to another building. Sherds of ceramic beehives have been found close to several of these [cf. Strab. 9.1.23 on Attic honey as best, and the sort produced 'in the (area of) the silver-mines' as best of the best: DW] and some are associated with threshing floors. All of this suggests that they are closely linked to the agricultural exploitation of the rather limited areas of viable soil in the region.' This provides some basis for the otherwise speculative suggestion in Jansen (2007) 244 that X.'s projected mining 'polis' in Laureion (4.49–50) might be fed in part, at least, from very local production.

The word I have translated as 'grain' is Greek *sitos*. While it has a range of attested applications, including the broad sense of food (of any kind) as opposed to drink, in a context such as the present one it obviously means a cereal crop. Gauthier 48 argues that its *de facto* meaning here is barley, and he cites Demosth. 42.2 & 20, where *krithai*, barley, is equated with *sitos*. However, given what we know about the cereals actually grown in fourth-century Attica (see Sallares (1991) 79, calculating 75% barley, 25% wheat), I think it more prudent to be non-committal, both here and when *sitos* reappears at 4.6 and 4.45.

1.5 land with silver beneath it is plainly determined by heavenly destiny The adjective X. uses here (with the noun 'land' understood from the preceding sentence), and again in 4.2 (plural), is rare enough to permit the conclusion that he has borrowed it from the dramatic stage. In Euripides' *Cyclops*, the only surviving example of the satyr-play genre (*OCD* 1322–3), Odysseus refers to 'Athena's rock of Sounion with silver beneath': lines 293–4. Its date of composition and staging is controversial, but an authoritative study argues for 409–408 (Seaford (1982)). If that is right, X. could have seen it for himself.

I have translated X.'s phrase *theia moira* as 'heavenly destiny' (cf. Marchant's 'divine providence'), but a more exact sense of *moira* is a process of allocation, assigning to people (or in this case, places) their proper due or function; what Jansen (2007) 247–52 calls X.'s 'providentialism.' X. had already used the phrase in *Mem*.2.3.18: Sokrates there applies it to a pair of feet not working together as they were designed to. It might in fact be Sokrates' own phrase given its appearance, also, in the works of two of his other pupils: Aeschines 'Socraticus' of Sphettos (*LGPN* s.v. no.84, *OCD* 26, *POP* 5–6) and, especially, Plato, who employs it more than a dozen times. (It does not otherwise occur in authors of this period.) Be that as it may, here is X. once again (cf. 1.3) stating his belief that Athens has advantages over other poleis because the gods wish it to be so. See further under the next lemma.

1.5 though many city-states are nearby, both terrestrial and maritime, into none of them does even a tiny vein of silver-bearing earth extend The tragedian Aeschylus had written of a 'spring' of (Attic) silver: *Persians* 238. X.'s different metaphor, a 'vein', seems to be his own invention. Either way, envisaging subterranean 'silver' or 'silver-bearing soil' was more pleasing than the principal geological reality: argentiferous lead ore.

X. here uses *argyritis*, the feminine form of the adjective *argyritês*, as a substantive (with *gê*, 'earth', implicit). Likewise in 4.2, 4.4, 4.6, 4.11, 4.28 and 4.45. The idiom is evidently his own, and he is proud of it. Its only other occurrences in classical Athens are in Demosth. 37.28 (in Pantainetos' charge against the speaker Nikoboulos, as read out to the court), from *c.* 346.

The claim made here, as commentators have observed, is quite true. Athens' immediate land-neighbours (Megara and Corinth to the south, Thebes and the other Boiotian poleis to the north) had no such ore, and had never had any. Nor indeed did *their* neighbours: the rest of the Peloponnese, and in the other direction the states of central and northern Greece as far as the ones which periodically gained access to the mines of Thrake's Mt. Pangaion (*OCD* 1074); by the time of *Poroi* they were coming under the control of Philip II of Macedon (Hammond & Griffith (1979) 358–61). As regards maritime states close to Athens, none, likewise, commanded silver-deposits in X.'s day, though he must have been well aware that until his own lifetime the Aegean island of Siphnos (*OCD* 1372, *IACP* no.519) had once done, very significantly.

If one may dare mention here the myth of Atlantis in Plato's *Timaeus* and the unfinished *Critias* (*OCD* 199–200): the school of thought which regards it as an allegory for, or avatar of, *Athens itself* equates the silver-mining at Laureion with the island's mining of the copper alloy *oreichalkon* (*Criti.*114E). See e.g. Dušanič (1982) 28–9.

1.6 It would be no absurdity for anyone to think that Athens lies at the centre of Hellas—indeed, of the whole inhabited world While I have translated the beginning of this sentence literally, X.'s words need carry no implication that he was saying something controversial, i.e. that some might consider his statement, precisely, absurd. To say, 'not *x*' (here 'not absurdly', *ouk alogôs*), where *y* is the opposite, often means 'decidedly *y*'. This is the rhetorical figure of speech called litotes, another possible instance of which will occur at 3.7. (For *ouk alogôs* cf. already *Ages*.1.26.) In any case commentators routinely adduce Aristot. *Pol*.7.1327b29–30 for the placing of Hellas as a whole in the middle of 'the whole inhabited world'. That at least looks like orthodoxy—among Hellenes.

The matter of Athens being, or occupying, the centre *of Hellas* is more striking. Thiel 5 and Gauthier 50 cite Isoc. 4.42 (Peiraieus as a trading-post 'in the middle of Hellas') and more generally X. himself (through the mouth of Prokles of Phleious) in *Hell*.7.1.3. I would add Isoc. 16.27 and 15.299. There, first in one of his early law-court speeches and decades later in a pseudo-forensic one, Isoc. mentions a view—one he shares—of Athens as the *asty* (town-centre, urban core) of Hellas. Cartledge in Waterfield 221 comments that, for many, Delphi (*OCD* 427–8, *IACP* no.177) would have been regarded as the centre of Hellas. That is true (Paus. 10.16.3, etc.), and in other contexts X.'s reverence for Delphi (5.9, 6.3) might well have seen him acknowledging it; but not here, where Athens needed to be kept in the spotlight.

Whereas Isocrates in 4.42 had felt no call to justify his assertion, X. here does, with four arguments that will occupy the remainder of 1.6.

1.6 The more distant from it people are, the more difficult the cold or heat they encounter Cf. generally a passage in the Hippocratic *Airs, Waters, Places* (12.4): the most fertile part of Asia is the one 'situated midway between the heat and the cold'. *Vis-à-vis* X. himself, note (with Gauthier 49) the discursive, and again non-Hellenic, version of this in *Cyrop*.8.6.21–2: after the subjugation of Egypt (there anachronistically attributed to Kyros rather than to his son Kambyses: for the latter see *OCD* 272 (Cam-)), the Persian Empire 'was bounded towards the east by the Gulf, towards the north by the Black Sea, towards the west by Cyprus and Egypt, and towards the south by Ethiopia. The extremes of these regions are hostile to habitation: some because of the heat, some because of the cold, some because of (too much) water, some because of too little. Kyros himself made his home in the centre of these places [cf. the preceding lemma]: in winter he spent seven months in Babylon, because the climate there is warm; in spring, three months in Sousa; and at the height of summer, two months in Ekbatana. They say that by doing this he spent all his time in the warmth and coolness of spring.' The young X. of *Anab.*, of course, could testify from personal experience to climatic conditions in the western and northern sectors of the Persian Empire.

As regards Attica, he has already (1.3) extolled the mild climate and the effects this has on plant growth.

1.6 anyone who wishes to reach one extremity of Hellas from another must always do so, whether sailing or going by land, via Athens, as if it were a circle's hub The earth as a circle is a concept found in early poetry: Hom. *Il.*18.607–8; [Hes.] *Sc.*314–17. It was also, on another level, developed in sixth-century Milesian cosmologies (with Egyptian and Near Eastern antecedents). See in brief *OCD* 83–4 on Anaximander and on Anaximenes (1). This had reached fifth-century Athens via Anaxagoras (*OCD* 82–3) and others, and by X.'s day it was a settled commonplace. (Plato's ultimately spherical model can be left aside for present purposes.)

My 'hub' translates the Greek noun *tornos*. According to Thiel 5, both *tornos* and *diabêtês* mean a pair of compasses; likewise Gauthier 50. The latter term, literally 'walker-across', appears twice in the comedies of Aristophanes (*Clouds* 178, *Birds* 1003), and an ancient annotator of the first of those passages comments that the tool was *Λ*-shaped. What X. was trying to convey here, therefore, is very close to what Herodotus had written about the foolishness of map-makers (Hdt. 4.36.2): 'I laugh when I see that not one of the many people who have drawn maps of the world has explained it intelligently. They draw Ocean as a river flowing round the perimeter of the earth, which is circular as (if) from a *tornos*, and they make Asia and Europe equal.' On this line of interpretation X.'s actual phrase, 'a circle's *tornos*', is rather clumsy because it conflates two things, the hub of a wheel and the 'pivot' (Waterfield 170) of a *tornos*. Matters would be improved somewhat, though not totally, if the *diabêtês* is set aside as irrelevant and X.'s *tornos*—and perhaps also the one in Herodotus—is visualized as a length of string with a pin at one end (= Athens, here) and chalk or suchlike at the other; see LSJ on the word. But either way we can grasp, broadly, what he means.

Juxtaposing 1.6 with 5.1–4, S. Lewis (1996) 26–7 notes that the Athenians will necessarily have maintained 'an open attitude towards news'; even so, she is right to add what little scraps of evidence there are for something similar in other places with a significant throughput of traders and other visitors, Rhodes (Lyk. *Leok.*18) and—*IACP* no.793—Tenedos (Aristot. *Pol.*4.1291b24–5).

1.7 although Athens is not 'flowed-around', nevertheless, just like an island, all the winds bring in etc. The adjective 'flowed-around' does merit quotation-marks. Even if X. is not quoting it from anywhere in particular, *perirrhytos* is the language of epic and other poetry. (Thucydides had also employed it on a single occasion: 4.64.3, in a patriotic speech by Hermokrates of Syracuse (*OCD* 670).) For similar language see below, **she is 'sea-girt'**.

Athens as an island had been a well-known analogy (or image) since the fifth century: see [X.] *Ath.Pol.*2.14–16; Perikles in Thuc. 1.143.5. After their enforced demolition in 404 (*Hell.*2.2.20–3), the Long Walls and the Peiraieus walls were rebuilt from early summer 394 onwards: RO 9 (Harding (1985) no.17) with *Hell.*4.8.9–10. This re-established the logistics of Athens' quasi-island condition. See generally Garland (2001) 37–41.

X.'s point here, though, does not have security in mind; cf. Gauthier 51. He is still (as in 1.6) thinking about geography and, on that count, the good fortune of Athens' position for commercial success. A terrestrial polis would hope to reap the benefits of overland trade; a true island, those of maritime trade; but Athens can do both.

1.7 all the winds bring in whatever commodities are needed and send out whatever ones are wanted The triple harbour-complex of Peiraieus (Chap.3 intro.) is undoubtedly what lies behind such vignettes of thriving Athenian commerce. Other harbours, in rural Attica, are occasionally mentioned but were very much subsidiary: Thorikos (Skylax 57) and Sounion (Thuc. 8.4; *Hell.*5.1.23).

On X.'s basic point see also 3.5, 4.40, 5.3–4. The same picture had often been painted elsewhere. See e.g.: [X.] *Ath.Pol.*2.7 & 11; Thuc. 1.81.2 (speech of King Archidamos II of Sparta, on whom see *OCD* 140), 2.38.2 (the Periklean *Funeral Speech*); Isoc. 4.42. This last passage (on which see already above, **1.6 It would be**) is linked with X.'s 3.2 by Isager & Hansen (1975) 62; and cf. Garland (2001) 87. Athen. *Deipn.*1.27E–28A preserves a lengthy quotation from a fifth-century comic dramatist, Hermippos (*OCD* 670), which consists of a mock-heroic catalogue of all the things that ships bring 'hither', i.e. to Athens (Hermippos fr.63 Kassel-Austin). The list is too long to reproduce in full here but alongside a few comic items (e.g. 'shipfuls of lies' from King Perdikkas of Macedon (*OCD* 1105 Perdiccas (2))) it includes such real ones as carpets (Carthage), cypress-wood (Crete), ivory (Libya), papyrus (Egypt), and *silphion* (Kyrene), the last a prized culinary and medicinal plant (see Dalby (2002) chap.1).

The distinction between what Athens *needs* and others merely *want* is probably not one that X. intended to lay any stress on; when the topic reappears at 3.2, the exports are of 'what is needed' (unless the shippers themselves 'want' to carry silver instead). We might note incidentally that when the fourth-century comic dramatist Antiphanes (*OCD* 108) lists the speciality products of nine states or areas, predictable ones such as Boiotian eels, Corinthian courtesans, and Sicilian cheese are joined by a surprising Athenian one: *perfume* (Antiph. fr.233 Kassel-Austin, in Athen. *Deipn.*1.27D).

1.7 she is 'sea-girt' This idea is expressed in the rare adjective *amphithalattos*. Like *perirrhytos* (see **1.6 although Athens**) it comes from poetry. Pindar (*OCD* 1148–50) had used it in his *Seventh Olympian* victory ode, composed in 464 to celebrate a win by the Rhodian boxer Diagoras. In line 33 there the foundation of Rhodes itself (*OCD* 1278–9, *IACP* no.1000) by Tlepolemos is described as taking place, by command of the Delphic Oracle, 'in a sea-girt pasturage'. That X. knew the poem is very likely. (On X. and Pindar cf. Phillips (2016) 136–40.)

Poetry aside, the only other instances of this adjective occur in the first-century geographer Strabo's comments on Attica and also on its northern neighbour Boiotia: both of them (in 9.1.3) he calls *amphithalattos*. The pairing is significant, because, from a modern perspective at least, the term cannot signify exactly the same in both instances. Boiotia has an eastern coastline on the Aegean Sea—albeit with the elongated island of Euboia occluding a direct view of it—and a western one on the Gulf of Corinth, giving access to the Ionian Sea and points west. Attica has no such western coastline. The Athenians enjoyed a means of entry to the Gulf only during periods when they were in control of one of their immediate neighbours, Megara and/or Boiotia (such as in the period *c.* 460–446/5: Thuc. 1.103.4–115.1). Both X. and Strabo, when referring to Attica, must therefore mean that the shape of Attica creates two 'seas' *out of the Aegean itself*. Strabo, indeed, implies as much; and X. himself will confirm that that is his meaning when he comes to write of southern Attica in 4.43. See the Comm. there.

1.7 She also receives many imported items by land—because she is on the mainland For the Greek here ('imported items'), see Notes on the Text.

From a substantive point of view Gauthier 51 challenges 'many' as an accurate description of the amount of terrestrial commerce between Attica and either Megara to the south or the poleis of Boiotia to the north. He does not mention possible trading partners either further south (especially Corinth) or further north than that, which is probably reasonable. I must disagree, though, with the idea that trading between Athens and her immediate neighbours was minimal. One should at least cite some of the evidence which does exist:

(1) MEGARA (*OCD* 924–5, *IACP* no.225). See, *par excellence*, Thuc. 1.67.4 (the 'Megarian Decree(s)' of the 430s, which among other things banned Megarians from the 'agora' of Athens), with Hornblower (1991–2008) 1.110–11. (Given that Gauthier himself published a short article on this (Gauthier (1975)), contesting the attempt by Ste. Croix (1972) 278–84 to limit the scope of 'agora' to a religious sanction, it is odd that he decided not to mention the Decree(s) here.) Amicable trading contacts doubtless took some while to re-establish themselves in the fourth century, and inter-polis relations more generally will not have been helped by such things as the long-running dispute over some 'sacred' land on the Attica/Megara border: RO 58 (Harding (1985) no.78), now *IG* II^3 292/*AIO* and *I.Eleusis* 144. Nevertheless, periodic returns, at least, to normality are suggested by such *aperçus* as the one in Lyk. *Leok.*58 (an expectation that during his six years living in Megara Leokrates would have exported Megarian goods into Attica).

(2) BOIOTIA (*OCD* 237–8, *IACP* pp.431–61). The equivalent—in Aristophanes' *Acharnians*, staged in 425—of the starving Megarian exchanging his piglet-daughters for garlic and salt (lines 729–835) is the Boiotian, possibly Theban, man with a dazzling array of items for sale, 'all the good things Boiotia has' (859–958, at 873). Some of them are included for comic surprise effect (doormats and lamp-wicks), but the majority are not, e.g. chickens, woodcocks, coots, hares, and the prized delicacy that Dikaiopolis actually buys—a large eel from Lake Kopais (*OCD* 372–3). Four years later, Aristophanes' *Peace* again coupled the two regions in the protagonist Trygaios' wish that 'our *agora* be

> filled with good things: from Megara garlics, early figs, apples, pomegranates, little woolly cloaks for slaves; and from Boiotia the carriers of geese, ducks, pigeons, plovers—and baskets of Kopaics' (lines 999–1005). In the real world, relations between the Athenians and their northern neighbours reached their nadir in 404, when the Thebans were among those pressing for Athens' annihilation (X. *Hell.*2.2.19), yet as early as 395 the Boiotian League and the Athenians became allies (RO 6 (Harding (1985) no.14A)). Almost immediately after that, in 394/3, one of the account-documents generated by the rebuilding of the Peiraieus walls (RO 9 (Harding (1985) no.17)), a project in which X. himself says that Boiotians were prominent (*Hell.*4.8.10), records that 'Demosthenes the Boiotian' was paid 790 drachmas 'for the actual bringing-up of the stones' needed for one (evidently lengthy) stretch; Garland (2001) 150. Other random pointers to economic intercourse in various forms include the presence of another 'Boiotian', Kephisodotos, as witness (twice over) to a disputed contract to send a merchant ship back and forth between Athens and the Black Sea in the mid-fourth century (Demosth. 35.13–14).

Overall, it will be better to take X. at his word—as, latterly, Fachard and Pirisino (2015) 145–6 do.

1.8 most states border on *barbaroi* who cause them trouble; but in Athens' case even the neighbouring states themselves are very far distant from the *barbaroi* While the second part of this statement is self-evidently true, the first has been differently assessed. At one extreme is Cartledge in Waterfield 221, who calls it 'numerically accurate—Xenophon is here taking an enlarged view of the Greek world with its well over 1,000 states'. *IACP*, in fact, puts a name to 1,035 communities which meet the definition of a polis, with 1,500 as a theoretical maximum; so Cartledge is making fair comment *if* X. was taking such a view. For Gauthier 51–2, on the other hand, X.'s phrase 'most states' means only Athens' great commercial rivals: the likes of Byzantium (harassed by her Thrakian neighbours: Polyb. 4.38 and 45; Russell (2017) 165–7, 194–5), or the Crimean cities (subject to Skythian incursions: Demosth. 34.8; J. G. F. Hind in *CAH* 6.500–1), or some of those on the coast of Asia Minor (such as Erythrai (*OCD* 537, *IACP* no.845), fearful of Persia in the 340s: RO 68 (Harding (1985) no.79)). Gauthier is obviously right to say that the idea of most poleis having *barbaroi* as neighbours is nonsense when applied to most of mainland Greece and the Aegean—but the Cartledge/*IACP* consideration meets that objection. So there is no middle ground here. Gauthier's position will be followed by those who agree with him that 1.8 is all of a piece with the rest of Chap.1: 'X. considère toujours l'aspect commercial'. (And even then X. would be stretching a point, given that e.g. Aigina, Corinth, Delos, and Megara were equally insulated from barbarian 'trouble'.)

Modern readers will note the casual assumption that non-Hellenes (for all their shared appreciation of fine marble: 1.4) are troublesome neighbours. Much the same view is expressed again, in another way, in 2.3; see the Comm. there.

CHAPTER TWO

Chap.2 turns from the 'naturally occurring' assets of Attica to a man-made one; indeed, in X.'s estimation the prime one (see **2.1 first**).

Athens' metics (*metoikoi*) in the classical period were her population of free-status immigrants. They were not necessarily free-*born*, for on the orthodox view of the matter it had been decided that this legal category should also embrace emancipated slaves, freedmen (the 'd' is crucial) and freedwomen. Rather, they were free at the moment of snapshot, so to speak, and as such, were appropriate people, in the Athenians' view, to be classified alongside men and women who had literally (im)migrated to Athens from elsewhere in Hellas or further afield in the Mediterranean world. (Challenges to this orthodoxy are Zelnick-Abramovitz (2005) 308–10 and Kamen (2013) 32–43. Kears (2013) 45–8 is a specific riposte to the former, Sosin (2016) to the latter.)

Metic-status had perhaps been given legal recognition as part of the Kleisthenic reforms in the late sixth century; alternatively, during the early decades of the fifth, or even (Watson (2010)) as late as the Periklean citizenship-law of 451/0. In any event, it developed over time into a judicious mix of rights and duties, concessions and responsibilities—all built around the central fact that residence *per se* bestowed no right to (and created no expectation of) Athenian citizenship by 'naturalization'.

The size of the metic community (or communities) was subject to fluctuation, in response to favourable or unfavourable circumstances. Four decades or so after *Poroi*, a census of the inhabitants of Attica, taken under the regime of the benevolent dictator Demetrios of Phaleron (*LGPN* s.v. no.448, *OCD* 432 Demetrius (3), *APF* 107–10), is said to have counted 10,000 metics: so 'Stesikleides (Ktesikles)' *FGrH* 245 F1, as cited in Athen. *Deipn.*6.272D; O'Sullivan (2009) 108–16. (The hypothesis of Van Wees (2011) 102–6, that Demetrios' '*metoikoi*' includes *c.* 5,000 men disqualified from citizenship by the regime's new property threshold(s) for that status, seems to me to leave insufficient room for the others. See also Ober (2017) 128 n.4, 130 n.8.) Indirect calculations based on the reported speech of Perikles in Thuc. 2.13.6–7 suggest that in 431, before the Peloponnesian War began, the figure had been twice, even three times, as high: Whitehead (1977) 97–8; Duncan-Jones (1980) 102, 106. (The view of Thür (1989) 118, taken over by Cohen (2000) 17, that in the early fourth century there were *c.* 100,000 metics, is aberrant.) In X.'s day the number will in my view have been somewhere between those extremities—and indeed too near the lower one, in *his* view, because he is keen to raise it. (Meyer (2010) 58 with n.168 envisages a vanishingly low point in X.'s day and therefore a *rise* to Demetrios' 10,000. This makes the mistake—see Meyer (2010) 48 with n.133—of taking literally the hyperbole of Isoc. 8.21: Athens in the mid-350s stands 'deserted' by 'merchants, foreigners and metics'.)

Evidence (circumstantial but strong) suggests that, whatever the case had been in the fifth century, fourth-century Athens operated procedures in the area of residence by non-citizens which converted a mere visitor into a *metoikos* automatically, and after a short period of time—perhaps as little as a month (Gauthier (1972) 122; Whitehead (1977) 7–9). If that is correct, it helps to explain why Chap.2 of *Poroi* on metics leads on so naturally to Chap.3 on foreign importers and other visitors (who are indeed paired with metics in 3.5; for that, compare again Isoc. 8.21).

Though Whitehead (1977) remains the only published monograph-length treatment of Athens' *metoikoi* in English (readers of German can profit from Adak (2003)), work, unsurprisingly, has continued. This is not the place to assemble a comprehensive bibliography covering four decades and more, but on various facets of the topic see e.g.: MacDowell (1978) 76–8; Ste. Croix (1981) 95–6, 228–9; Whitehead (1986) 81–5 and index s.v.; Sinclair (1988) 28–30; Hansen (1991) 116–20 and index s.v.; Millett (1991) 224–9 (appendix 2); Todd (1993) 194–9 and index s.v.; Hunter (2000); Patterson (2000); Nemeth (2001); Garland (2001) 58–72 with 191–4; Kapparis (2005); Watson (2010); Meyer (2010) 28–30 and index s.v.; Mansouri (2011); Kamen (2013) chaps.3–5; Bakewell (2013); Kears (2013); Kennedy (2014); Wijma (2014); Garland (2014) 155–66, 232–4; Akrigg (2015), on which see below, **2.6 I reckon**; Blok (2017) 265–76.

Cohen (2000) takes a view of metic-status radically different from that of most of these scholars (and from the one assumed here), believing for instance that metics were routinely regarded as *astoi*, 'city-folk'. Grave problems with this—above all, the fact that that would make metics Athenian citizens according to the definition of citizenship in and after the Periklean citizenship-law of 451/50 (?Aristot. *Ath. Pol.*26.4, 42.1)—are identified by (e.g.) Jansen (2007) 291 n.36 and Kears (2013) 39–43; and see also under **2.2 and removed.**

* * * *

2.1 principally, care of the metics The Greek two-part phrase *prôton men* ('first', 'firstly', 'in the first instance'), is often answered by a corresponding one such as *epeita de* or *eti de*, introducing a second element (and where necessary further ones) in a temporal sequence or hierarchy of importance. At 5.5 there is a temporal *prôton men* and an *eti de*. But nothing of the sort occurs here in 2.1. So we soon realize that X. is not presenting the topic of metics here as no.1 in what will be a summary list of others. It is the *only* illustration of man-made assets that he wants to give. (3.1, comparably, will begin the elaboration of 'the import-and-export trade, and how Athens is so very agreeable and profitable to it' with another unanswered *prôton men*.)

The term *epimeleia*, which I have rendered 'care' both here and when it recurs in 2.2 (the plural in 3.6 is rather different: see the Comm. there), is discussed by Gauthier 56. Common in X. and elsewhere, it can mean (*a*) an attitude of solicitousness or (*b*) supervision/surveillance. Here 'naturellement' it signifies *b*, according to Gauthier himself, who appeals to the kind of formulaic language often found in Athenian decrees of this period when they are thanking and rewarding non-citizens. If the honorand needs anything, officials such as the *boulê* and/or the generals are to take care of it. (The cognate verb *epimeleisthai* is used: table in Pečírka (1966) 152–7; discursively Henry (1983) 171–81. A representative instance is RO 77 (Harding (1985) no.100), where in 337 the Athenians are solicitous to exiles from Akarnania (*OCD* 2–3 Ac-, *IACP* pp.351–78).) However, Gauthier goes on to assert, surely correctly, that X. is envisaging here something more than a 'negative' kind of protection from harm. He adduces *Hier.*9.1–3, where a ruler's *epimeleiai* (i.e. type *b*, above) are said to be of two kinds: repressive ones which evoke hatred, and ones greeted with thanks because of their moral instruction and dispensing of praise and honour. X. here, as will be seen, is much concerned with honour, and with rewarding excellence. All that said, I do find 'care' a suitable translation of *epimeleia* both here and in 2.2, where X. hastens to add that this should not be unlimited: see **2.2 It would be**.

If our sources were fuller, they would showcase earlier occasions when an Athenian had contemplated the city's metics and advocated their *epimeleia* (in any nuance of the word). See e.g. Whitehead (1977) 148–9 on the far-sighted Themistokles of Phrearrhioi (*LGPN* s.v. no.39, *OCD* 1454–5, *APF* 211–20) in this regard. According to Diod.Sic. 11.43.3 he was interested in creating tax incentives for more metics to come to Athens, so as to build up the city's skills base and cement the foundations of naval power. These are also the twin areas of life highlighted by the 'Old Oligarch', when he declared in the (?)420s that Athens 'needs metics both for the multiplicity of skills and for the fleet' (so that it is reasonable that they are treated as the citizens' equals): [X.] *Ath.Pol.*1.12. (For warm feelings towards the metics see also e.g. Aristoph. *Ach.*507–8, with Whitehead (1977) 39, 41; Kears (2013) 25–6.) However, any generosity of spirit in the Oligarch's remark has to be offset against another, just two short sections earlier, where he had bemoaned the unruliness of both slaves and metics in Athens. He complains that they look too much like (poor) citizens; otherwise a gentleman impeded by one of them in the street could safely hit him ([X.] *Ath.Pol.*1.10). That self-same combination of economic realism and social elitism will be displayed by X. here, when specifying in detail what he means by *tôn metoikôn epimeleia*.

2.1 this revenue is of the finest—the reason being that, supporting themselves and benefiting the state in many ways, they receive no wage but contribute a metic-tax For the Greek here ('the state'—Athens—rather than 'the states') see Notes on the Text. (The plural, which is utterly out of place here, persists. Recent instances include Jansen (2007) 292, Rhodes (2007) 106, Meyer (2010) 48.)

If we were in any doubt on the point, the phrase 'this revenue is of the finest' (*tôn kallistôn*: seemingly a Platonic idiom) is a reminder of X.'s overall end, an end to which everything that fills the remainder of Chap.2 are means. (Thiel 6 rightly castigates Rühl's proposed deletion of 'revenue', which would leave the feminine antecedent of 'this' as *epimeleia*.)

The explanation appended to the principal statement expresses, in two ways, a cost vs. benefit or profit-and-loss assessment of the metics; one in which they come out as a clear benefit to the state. (The concept of benefit to the state remains prominent through 2.2–3; and see also 3.4, on traders, with the Comm. there.) The implicit comparandum, throughout, is the citizen-body. First and broadly, metics are economically self-supporting, *hautous trephontes*, by contrast with the Athenians themselves who, if X.'s ideas are implemented, will have *trophê* from the state (4.13, 4.33, 4.49, 6.1, all flowing from 1.1). Second and more specifically, only citizens—by definition—can draw a public wage (*misthos*; Hansen (1991) 98) for performing a constitutional function, whereas metics are net *contributors* to the exchequer. See generally Jansen (2007) 124–6.

On the Athenian 'metic-tax' (*metoikion* sc. *telos*) see generally Whitehead (1977) 75–7 and passim; Kears (2013) 57–70; Fawcett (2016) 154, 165. The view of (e.g.) Von der Lieck (1933) 20 & 29, Hasebroek (1933) 26, Cawkwell (1963) 64, Gauthier 57 & 73, and Schütrumpf 4–5 that X. is thinking of their fiscal contribution *solely* in terms of this metics' poll-tax is not plausible. So already Whitehead (1977) 125–6, at 126: X. means 'metic revenues in the widest sense, arising from both metic status itself (*metoikion*, *eisphorai*, liturgies) and metics' economic activities such as the "aliens" taxes' [Demosth. 57.34; Fawcett (2016) 154, 165–6] and not least the harbour dues from a revitalized Peiraieus'. (See also Thiel 6, and now, discursively, Jansen (2007) 295–317.) There must indeed be a high degree of irony in X.'s specification of the metic-tax. From the standpoint of revenue, quite obviously, *misthos* is a debit, *metoikion* a credit—and paid in by the very people who were already (in X.'s sentence, at any rate) in the black; so Whitehead (1977) 126, 152.

Be that as it may, X. does here single out for special mention the tax that represented one of the defining characteristics of metic-status in this era. The introduction of *metoikion* was not mentioned at the time, in any extant source, and its date cannot be fixed with precision; Whitehead (1977) 152–3 argues for the Peloponnesian War years. Once in place, the tax differentiated metics not only from Athenian citizens—who paid no sort of direct poll-tax—but also from those free foreigners who in the eyes of the law were merely visitors, with a home elsewhere. Anyone convicted of not paying the *metoikion* faced enslavement (Demosth. 25.57). Drawing on classical-period sources, the learned second-century CE lexicographer Harpocration (*OCD* 646) states that its rate was twelve drachmas a year for men, six for any women who did not have a (husband or) son who was a payer. This tariff was quite modest *per se*, and so (necessarily) was its aggregate contribution to the Athenian public purse—an unpredictably variable one (Gauthier 57). But that did not detract from its potency as a symbol. See further Whitehead (1977) 75–7 and index s.v.; Kears (2013) 57–70.

Notwithstanding the fact that the present passage relates to Athens alone (see the opening of this lemma), a *metoikion*—or at any rate what Athenian sources refer to as such—is independently attested for three of Athens' closest neighbours: Oropos (Lys. 31.9), Megara (Demosth. 29.3), and Aigina (Demosth. 23.211). In Plato's ideal state Magnesia, by contrast, the metics would pay 'not even a small *metoikion*—except good behaviour': Plat. *Leg.*9.850B.

2.2 It would be *sufficient* care, it seems to me, if we removed practices that without conferring any benefit on the state seem to bring indignities to the metics For the Greek here ('indignities') see Notes on the Text.

On this proviso '*sufficient* care' see under **2.1 principally**. (For the concept compare e.g. *Anab.*2.6.20 on Proxenos the Theban. In order to be, and to be thought, a good general Proxenos supposed it was sufficient to bestow praise on the good soldiers and to withhold it from the bad.)

It is frustrating that X. does not illustrate what he has in mind here, even by a single example. The clause immediately following does not provide one: quite apart from the syntax showing this, metic hoplite service makes a poor match with both of the stated criteria. (See further under the next lemma.)

Bodei Giglioni lxiii–lxv revives and expands a suggestion of Clerc (1893) 230, according to which 2.2–7 as a whole are structured as a chiasmus: A, B, B^1, A^1. In this, here, 'A' is what is lemmatized above, and the answering 'A^1' (after B and B^1 have ended at the end of 2.4) is *everything in 2.5–7*. In other words, the three proposals made in 2.5–7—admit metics to the cavalry (2.5), give them limited house-ownership rights (2.6), and create a new magistracy to protect them (2.7)—are all things which, by currently *not* existing, constitute the benefit-less 'indignities' of 2.2. However, besides being far-fetched as an interpretation of the structure of 2.2–7 (cf. Whitehead (1977) 126), this fails to take account of what X., here and elsewhere, meant by an *atimia* (clarified by Thiel 45–6 = Excursus IV): not a formal, legal exclusion but something insulting, causing offence.

Gauthier's discussion of this problem begins by declaring that X.'s *atimiai* are scarcely identifiable but ends by venturing a couple of brief suggestions (Gauthier 58–9): (*a*) the extent to which—according to him—judicial procedures such as *apagôgê* (summary arrest) fell disproportionately upon metics rather than citizens, and (*b*) the exclusion of metics from certain gymnasia or festivals. I am unconvinced. Concerning *a*: the catalogue of known *apagôgai* in Hansen (1976) registers more than twice as many with citizen defendants as with metics, so the evidential basis for Gauthier's idea appears to collapse. In any case it is hard to see how any putative disproportions that were detected could be procedurally rectified. Concerning *b*, the matter of gymnasia seems to me to fall foul of the very criterion that Gauthier himself stipulates for identifying these 'indignities': that they must affect *all* metics, not just an elite. Religious festivals, especially the long-established ones, seem a more fertile hunting-ground in that regard. (See Whitehead (1977) 86–9; Kears (2013) 76–81.) But an even better suggestion for one of X.'s *atimiai*, made by Austin & Vidal-Naquet (1977) 366 n.6, is 'the obligation of metics to have a personal patron or *prostatês*'. (On that enigmatic figure see Whitehead (1977) 89–92; MacDowell (1978) 77–8; Todd (1993) 197–9; Kears (2013) 51–7.) A consideration that provides support for this, I would suggest, is X.'s creation of new metic-custodians (2.7, q.v.); cf. Meyer (2010) 49.

2.2 and removed also the practice of metics fighting as hoplites alongside the city's men On hoplites, heavily armed infantry soldiers, see in brief *OCD* 704; in full e.g. Hanson (1989), Crowley (2012).

The compound verb that X. uses, *sysstrateuesthai*, means simply and literally to campaign (*strateuesthai*) in company with (*syn*-, here assimilated to *sys*-) somebody. For 'loose' instances of it cf. already e.g. *Anab*.6.2.15, 7.4.20, 7.5.9, 7.6.14, 7.7.25, *Hell*.2.4.36, *Symp*.2.14. So what exactly, in context here, is his proposal? In isolation it could bear either of two interpretations: the more radical, abolish metic hoplite service altogether; the less radical, create separate metic regiments. But two considerations tell against the second of these options, one internal and one external to the text. First, X.'s own expansion in 2.4 will soon make it clear that he does envisage citizen hoplites only. Second, the epigraphically attested privilege, for an individual non-citizen, of being allowed to fight 'with the Athenians' (Henry (1983) 249–50), though problematic (Whitehead (1977) 83–4), is best understood as implying that there were already separate units for the majority who were not thus favoured.

Gauthier 59 notes that X. is in fact the only writer of this era who makes mention of metic hoplites. (Thucydides had done so, but for the early Peloponnesian War years: Thuc. 2.13.7, 2.31.1–2.) The 'foreigners' (*xenoi*) as hoplites who appal Isoc. 8.48, contrary to what Bodei Giglioni lxvi supposes, are clearly mercenaries. Epigraphic evidence, however, fills the void. The prime specimen is *IG* II^2 505 (Harding (1985) no.139), from 301: two non-citizen honorands named as 'Nikandros Antiphanous of Ilion and Polyzelos Apollophanous of Ephesos' who have been 'residing in Athens'—as metics, in plain terms—are thanked and rewarded by the Athenians for decades of dutiful service which includes 'participating in all the campaigns, both naval and on foot' (lines 37–8); cf. Oliver (2007) 95–6.

Cartledge in Waterfield 222 comments that '[m]ost metics were probably below hoplite status, so Xenophon's proposal to exempt metics from the obligation to serve as hoplites would benefit only a minority'. Though it is a matter of nuance (Gauthier 60 and 62 likewise refers to 'une minorité'), I should prefer to say a *large* minority, so as to differentiate metics of hoplite-level wealth both from their few richer counterparts whom X. wanted to see in the cavalry (2.5) and from the many poorer ones who would have been classifiable, both economically and militarily, as *thêtes*. (On *hippeis*, *zeugitai*, and *thêtes* within the citizen-body see Hansen (1991) 43–6, 106–8.)

My translation 'city's men' recognizes the fact that X. uses here the word *astoi* (cf. *Mem*.1.2.60, *Oec*. 6.17), rather than the *politai* of 1.1, 2.3, 3.7, and 5.12; but he means the same thing by it.

2.2 The absence of danger is an important consideration, and so is being away from their crafts and their homes For the Greek here ('The absence of danger' and 'their crafts and their homes') see Notes on the Text.

The second crux is the important one from a substantive point of view, as is pointed out by Schütrumpf 122 and, especially, Jansen (2007) 298–302. For *oikiai* in X. as more than places of domestic residence see e.g. *Mem*.2.3.6, 'Kyrebos supports his whole *oikia* well and lives luxuriously from bread-making', and 3.11.4, where Sokrates asks Theodote (*LGPN* s.v. no.1, *POP* 282–3) whether she has an '*oikia* which has revenues', *oikia prosodous echousa*.

Given Theodote's profession, that of a courtesan, there may well be irony in Sokrates' question there. On the other hand, when conversing with Kritoboulos of Alopeke (*LGPN* s.v. nos.4 & 11, *APF* 335–7, *POP* 116–19) in *Oec*.4.2–4, Sokrates seems to state in terms that banausic crafts are rightly despised: they inflict physical harm on their practictioners, and they take up time which could be spent with friends or on public business. There is the voice of Colonel X. (retired), gentleman-farmer.

In the present passage, concerned as it is with military service, there can be no doubt that the noun *kindynos* does mean danger, a physical risk to life and limb. Likewise 5.8. Contrast 4.28–9 and 4.32; there the appropriate translation is (economic) 'risk'. Analogously, as regards the seven passages which refer to the criterion of safety, four do so in a literal sense (3.1, 4.44, 6.1 twice) but the other three in the sense of safe from risk (3.10, 4.30, 4.32). Cf. Powell (2015) 152–4.

2.3 the state too would be benefited if the citizens served alongside each other rather than if, as now, their comrades were Lydians and Phrygians and Syrians and other *barbaroi* from all over the place—as many of the metics are The first thirteen words here simply assert that exempting (eligible) metics from hoplite service would be a good idea not only for them but also from the community's side—for two reasons: an implicit one here in the remainder of 2.3 (the Athenian citizen hoplites would be glad to escape proximity to all these *barbaroi*); an explicit one in 2.4 (q.v. below).

Cartledge in Waterfield 222 observes, with some justification, that 'Xenophon's complaint about the non-Athenian-ness [in fact, non-Hellenicity altogether: DW] of the Athenian army might have been better addressed to Athens' increasing reliance on mercenaries'. (For that, see e.g. Isoc. 8.46; Demosth. 4.24–5 & 44–7.) Nevertheless, given that X.'s topic here is the metics, his assertion about their ethnicity is the striking point made. It has been much debated. Following Clerc (1893) 381–3, Thiel 8 was moved to declare it deliberate exaggeration, given the 1:9 proportion of Hellenes vs. non-Hellenes whose tombstones survive. (Other estimates are 1:5–7.) So also e.g. Breitenbach (1967) 1755. (The suggestion of Bodei Giglioni lxvi that X. was including mercenaries in his statement ignores the words X. uses.) Gauthier 63–4, reprising his earlier analysis in Gauthier (1972) 123–4, considers that X.'s picture should be accepted. Whitehead (1977) 109–11 contests this, arguing that the discussion needs de-polarizing. Anyone in mid-fourth-century Athens who saw—or thought they saw—that one in every five, even one in every nine, metics was non-Hellenic could reasonably say that there were 'many' of them, and could do so with or without distaste. (Apparently with it, in X.'s own case, even though the contempt is not as overt as in Andoc. 2.23. Using the same word as X. does here, *pantodapos*, Andoc. had outrageously asserted in *c.* 408 that one could see the Athenians 'often granting citizenship to slave fellows and foreigners from all over the place'.) For another 'many', one which can hardly mean more than 'quite a few', see **2.6 many abandoned house-sites.**

As regards the particular nationalities that X. singles out here, it seems to have been his standard illustrative trio. In *Mem.*2.1.10 Sokrates, speaking of Asia, calls the Persians the ruling race and 'Syrians and Phrygians and Lydians' the ruled. Nothing (of relevance to the metics of Athens) is deducible from the fact that he does not cite Egyptians, Karians, Kilikians, Phoinikians, or other peoples of the Near East. (Gauthier 64 is probably right to suggest that European non-Hellenes such as Skythians and Thrakians were less likely to strike X. as poor *soldiers*, specifically; cf. *Ages.*1.28.) We should note here the careful demonstration by D. Lewis (2011) that the number of Athens' *slaves* imported from Persian territories has been significantly underestimated; so, he remarks in passing (D. Lewis (2011) 100), X.'s observation in the present passage 'is no wonder'.

2.4 it would be a feather in the state's cap if Athenians, when going into battle, were seen to be relying on themselves rather than on 'outlanders' The point is largely self-explanatory. Metic-free regiments of heavy infantry would not only raise the morale of the citizen troops concerned (2.3) but also lower, or at least challenge, that of their opponents.

Two aspects of vocabulary call for comment. First, 'it would be a feather in the state's cap' will be repeated exactly in 3.13 (extra housing and shops, for traders, in both Athens and Peiraieus); cf. also *Mem.*11.9–10 on bringing credit to the polis (and *Mem.*1.2.61, Sokrates as a credit to Athens). My feather-in-the-cap image is, in the Greek, a single word: the multi-use noun *kosmos*, which in this semantic area implies decoration or adornment; cf. 4.8, woman's gold jewellery. Second, flagged up here in the same way as in the two instances in 1.7, the very last word of the sentence—always an emphatic place in ancient Greek, with the flexibility in word-order that a fully inflected language enjoys—is a poetic one: Homer, Theognis, Pindar, Sappho, Simonides, Aeschylus, Euripides; cf. Thiel xxiii, Gauthier 65. X. is unique among prose authors of the period in using *allodapos* here (and also at *Cyrop*.8.7.14). Doing so was doubtless prompted by the use, in the preceding sentence (2.3), of the similar but less high-flown *pantodapos* ('from all over the place': see **2.3 the state too**).

2.5 privileges that it is a fine thing to give, including This form of words, concerning positive things, mirrors the phraseology of 2.2 concerning negative ones (the *atimiai*), but with an important exception. Here, as indicated, the Greek idiom (literally 'both other privileges that it is a fine thing to give and *x*') means that an example is about to be cited: see the next lemma. Whereas what X. meant by the *atimiai* had been left obscure, here he does immediately elucidate, therefore; and the subject-matter of both 2.6 and 2.7 could be intended as further illustration.

2.5 cavalry service On the Athenian cavalry corps of this era see generally Bugh (1988) 143–58. (Spence (1993), differently organized, is not really relevant here; and *Poroi* is overlooked.) X. had already, in *Hipp*.9.3–6, proposed bringing the corps up to its full strength of one thousand by establishing a sub-unit of two hundred '*hippeis xenoi*'. The consensus view, surely correct, is that these are to be non-citizen *mercenary* cavalrymen: so e.g. Marchant in the Loeb edition (289 n.3, 291 n.1); Parke (1933) 147 n.3; Bugh (1988) 156; Waterfield 88. Nevertheless, 9.6 had added a comment about metics, and couched in language which anticipates the present passage: 'I also think that some of the metics would be proud to be enrolled in the cavalry—because I see that whatever other fine things the citizens give them, some willingly take pride in fulfilling the task assigned.' (X. the master of vagueness again. What can he mean? And what could he have 'seen', during decades away from Athens?)

In the past scholars have sometimes struggled with what they perceive as a contradiction between X.'s proposals for metics and army service. Infantry, no. Cavalry, yes. Gauthier 65–6 has a long note on this, starting from the essential fact that most of the contradiction vanishes if one keeps in mind that *metics of two different socioeconomic levels are involved here*; cf. above, **2.2 and removed.** (This point still eludes scholars such as Ferrario (2017) 67: metics 'should be released from mandatory military service... and at the same time should be allowed to increase the ranks of the cavalry'.) Gauthier also, and again correctly, dismisses any idea that hoplite service belongs in the real military world whereas the duties of cavalrymen were largely ceremonial (*Hipp*.2.1, 3.1–14; Spence (1993) 186–8), just like the plume-helmeted

Life Guards and Blues & Royals—together, the Household Cavalry—who nowadays impress the tourists in central London. Beyond that, he reprises the view stated in Gauthier (1972) 124–5 that X.'s cavalry proposal is something for the future, once 2.7's 'more and better metics' (essentially meaning more Hellenes) warrant it. Whitehead (1977) is unpersuaded, insisting that 2.2 and 2.5 can stand up to direct comparison. Each of the two plans, generated by this 'interplay of pride and prejudice' (Whitehead (1991) 149), makes sense in terms of *those metics whom it affects*. The hoplite metics would be glad of exemption for its own sake—and the citizens would be equally glad to see them go. The new cavalrymen metics, as stated here, would feel proud that the 'club' was admitting them—and many, even most, of its existing members would give them a warm welcome as socioeconomic and cultural equals. See further under the next lemma.

2.5 it seems to me that we would make *them* more loyal and at the same time exhibit a stronger and greater Athens Conventional-looking words to justify the proposal (and finish the section), but they repay scrutiny.

First, 'more loyal' (*eunousteroi*). X. seems especially concerned to devise ways of making metics 'more loyal', because he repeats the word in 2.7. His idea there of creating (citizen) metic-custodians would also, he avers, make the metics—and this time he means all of them—*eunousteroi* (more *eunous*, displaying more *eunoia*). On *eunoia* in X. see generally Dillery (1995) 57. Considered in isolation, the present passage might have suggested that he is thinking of *military* loyalty; predicting, that is, that these metics who are now fighting as hippeis (rather than, presumably, as hoplites) will be more amenable to obeying orders. However, the juxtaposition of 2.5 with 2.7 prompts a broader view. (So too do many instances of *eunous*—literally, well-minded—and its cognates elsewhere in X., e.g. *Apol.*27: Sokrates refers to 'my well-wishers'.) With recruitment must go retention. Athens needs more (and 'better') metics to come to Athens *and to stay there*; that is 'loyalty' in the present context. For *eunoia* as one of the canon of cardinal virtues recognized and rewarded by the Athenians during X.'s lifetime and beyond see Whitehead (1993), esp. 52–3, 67, and Cook (2009); more generally Hakkarainen (1997), Engen (2010) 119–39, Lambert (2011a), Meyer (2013), Liddel (2016). Broad-brush context: Domingo Gygax (2016) chaps.3–5.

Another vocabulary choice of note here is 'exhibit'. X. has already shown his sensitivity to what others think of Athens (see **2.4 it would**

be a credit); here it is again. Again too, 2.7 echoes the word: the metic-custodians are each to 'exhibit' their lists of metics. See also e.g. *Hipp*.1.21 (equestrian javelin-throwing) and several passages of *Cyrop*. on the Persian army: 1.6.18 (the best soldiers), 2.1.23 (the best units), 8.6.11 (the best cavalrymen). For X. there is an intimate connection between success in an aim or field and putting its results proudly on public view.

Finally there is the notion that enhancing metic-status, by the means specified (and unspecified), would make the state 'stronger and greater'. The first of these terms will recur in an analogy in 4.32: admitting new signatories to an alliance makes its members mutually stronger. That is the only other occurrence of the adjective in *Poroi*, suggesting that here in 2.5 also, *military* strength (and the perception of it) is the criterion. (For a polis, Babylon, that is 'stronger' by dint of its river than its walls see *Cyrop*.7.5.8.) 'Greater' occurs only here in this work, and is the comparative of an adjective just as ambiguous in Greek as it is in English. (For a perfect illustration of this within X., witness *Hell*.5.2.28: in 382 the Spartan Phoibidas, supposedly on his way north to Olynthos, is incited to capture Thebes, 'a polis much greater'.) In context here, a *larger* Athens is probably being forecast—but perhaps with overtones of a *better* one too, if it can muster the moral strength to do right by those metics who deserve it.

2.6 inside the walls there are many sites devoid of houses, and house-ruins too For the Greek here (the internal punctuation of the sentence beginning 'Next, there are...') see Notes on the Text, and further below.

The 'Themistoklean' (Thuc. 1.89–93) city-walls of Athens had been spared—unlike the Long Walls and the Peiraieus walls—in the treaty which ended the Peloponnesian War in 404 (*Hell*. 2.2.20, 2.3.11, with Krentz (1989) 187; Theocharaki (2011) 116–18). They encompassed an irregular circle of land approximately 1.5 km. in diameter. Plans: simple one in *WoA* (illustration 1.10); scholarly one in Theocharaki (2011) 104 fig.10. The five intra-mural demes (Koile, Kollytos, Kydathenaion, Melite, Skambonidai) are shown on Traill (1975) map 1, inset, reproduced in Whitehead (1986) xxiii and also as pl.1 at the end of Kellogg (2013). That X.'s phrase 'inside the walls' included the walls *of Peiraieus*, a deme where so many metics lived (Whitehead (1986) 83–4) is a theoretical possibility, but on balance I think it unlikely. Compare e.g. *Hell*.2.2.11: the Athenians in 405 negotiate to keep 'the walls and the

Peiraieus'. Here in *Poroi* 2.6, at any rate, X.'s 'inside the walls' cannot in my view (Rihll (1991) 107–8 appears to differ) have included the long, thin, deme-less, militarized corridor of ground *between* the pair of Long Walls (*c.* 6 km. by 183 m.; Conwell (2008) 4).

The walled centre of Athens will always have had its *erêma*: open spaces, vacant places. Thuc. 2.17.1 famously depicts the rural evacuees of 431 occupying some of them. Nevertheless X. here, if his words can be pressed, is alluding to something quite specific: spaces suitable only for houses (Timarchos' *oikêseis*, below), even spaces where houses had once stood but no longer did; see further below. The casual confidence of his statement suggests that he had either seen the phenomenon for himself or heard of it from someone who had.

Thiel 9 related the present passage to Aeschin. 1.81–4. It describes a meeting of the assembly, at the end of the year 347/6, where there was discussion of a proposal by the defendant Timarchos of Sphettos (*LGPN* s.v. no.36, *AO* no.3067) 'about the houses on the Pnyx (hill)' (*OCD* 1167). A speaker in the debate, the humourless Areopagite Autolykos (Fisher (2001) 219 disentangles him from homonyms), is reported as referring to the area in question as 'this *erêmia*', a noun related to X.'s *erêma* here, and he also uses the word *oikopeda*, which X. uses here. Gauthier 67 acknowledges the correspondences, while disagreeing that the passage proves what Thiel had claimed for it: a wholesale depopulation of Athens' city-centre (in favour of Peiraieus).

What then was an *oikopedon*? Gauthier (this time following Thiel to the letter) defines it as a plot upon which building is possible, either because a current building is dilapidated or because it is vacant—and where public or sacred space presents no obstacle to building. Likewise Fisher (2001) 220 (on the Aeschin. passage), whose definition of *oikopeda* as 'building-plots, or uncompleted, or partially ruined or abandoned, buildings on a site' is intended to reflect the varied dossier of (Athenian) evidence that he cites there, *Poroi* 2.6 included. It is instructive to compare this with the *twofold* definition in LSJ s.v.: (1) 'site of a house, place on which a house is or has been built... building-site'; also (2) 'the house itself, building'. For sense 2, two citations are given, Thuc. 4.90.2 and Plat. *Leg.*5.741C; cf. Finley (1952) 253 n.10, Hornblower (1991–2008) 2.288. Since we see other cases of Thucydides' vocabulary probably or possibly influencing X.'s, both inside and outside *Poroi*, this could be suggested as one of them, if the addendum 'and *oikopeda*' was taken to mean 'and (empty) houses too'. However, the possibility is not worth pursuing, because LSJ's sense 2 is an illusion.

Already ignored by Gauthier and by Fisher, it is expressly challenged and rejected by Daniel (2007). In the Thucydides passage an Athenian army in Boiotia is hastily fortifying the shrine of Delion (*IACP* 433; not a polis) in winter 424/3; its surrounding ditch, once dug, is filled with (vine-wood and) 'stones and brick from the nearby *oikopeda*, which they demolished'. Since the site was partially dilapidated at the time, LSJ's sense 1 is the one required. The Plato passage is not so clear-cut, on the face of it; the law promulgated there forbids Magnesians either to buy or to dispose of their allotted '*oikopeda* or *gêpeda*'. However, that distinction (there and in general) is elucidated by Nenci (1993)—noted by Daniel—in terms which rule out a 'house' meaning for *oikopedon*. Instead, within the general concept of a measured allotment of land, a *presella*, it is a matter of function: an *oikopedon* is for living on, a *gêpedon* for agriculture.

Both Nenci and Daniel, unsurprisingly, have something to say about *Poroi* 2.6—but their different approaches mean that only the latter places it in the correct context. Nenci expresses the difference between X.'s *oikiôn erêma* and *oikopeda* as, in the first case, areas of land to be divided into allotments in due course and, in the second, already measured-out allotments which either never had buildings on them or where buildings fell into ruin and were abandoned (Nenci (1993) 274). Though much of this squares with Gauthier and Fisher, above, Nenci's allotment model owes too much to the evidence concerning *newly constituted or reconstituted* cities. (Besides Plato on his Magnesia, here are three epigraphical instances. (*i*) The dossier of letters from King Antigonos I (*OCD* 102) to Teos (*OCD* 1440, *IACP* no.868) in the late fourth century, about a planned but never implemented merger between Teos and its neighbour Lebedos (*IACP* no.850): *RC* 3–4 (*SIG* 344; Austin (2006) no.48). Each Lebedian is to receive an *oikopedon* in Teos equivalent to the one he is leaving behind in Lebedos (lines 4–5), and all the Lebedians are to build on their *oikopeda* within three years (lines 14–15). (*ii*) A decree of Ilion (*OCD* 725–6, *IACP* no.779), *c.* 300, grants citizenship to a foreigner, with extra stated privileges which include an actual *oikopedon* for a house: Taşliklioğlu & Frisch (1975) no.3, with J. and L. Robert, *BE* 1976 no.564. (*iii*) A decree of Issa (*IACP* no.81) concerning its re-foundation of Kerkyra Melaina (*IACP* no.83) in either the fourth or the third century: *SIG* 141. Each of the settlers will receive 'an *oikopedon* within the walled city'.) Instead, *Poroi* 2.6 belongs with Thuc. 4.90.2 (properly understood: see above)—which I persist in thinking may have been

X.'s model. It also belongs with a second passage in Aeschin. 1, where the visible foundations or remains of a former house are referred to as its *oikopeda* (Aeschin. 1.182). Daniel's proposed translation of the present passage, 'not only are many sites devoid of houses but also occupied by ruins', is endorsed by Powell (2015) 201. (Papazarkadas (2011) 65 n.216 quotes Marchant's evasive Loeb translation, despite including Daniel's article in his bibliography.)

Daniel's core clarification of *oikopeda* in a literary context like this is impeccable, in my opinion, and it informs the translation of the word which I offer here; however, a facet of his larger argument seems open to challenge. He renders X.'s phrase as already quoted above: 'many sites devoid of houses *but* occupied by ruins' (my emphasis). X. actually writes 'and'. Though the point might seem small in itself, it has a bearing on whether *polla oikiôn erêma... kai oikopeda* is a description (using two neuter plurals) of *one category of site or two*. Daniel's belief that it is only one depends in turn on a novel hypothesis: that *oikopeda* here is an adjective, not a noun. Since the *erêma* are, in grammatical terms, adjectival (albeit functioning as a substantive), taking *oikopeda* to be one too makes X.'s phrase a single entity. This is what I doubt. According to Daniel (2007) 65–6, apart from an instance in a fourth-century CE patristic writer, *oikopedos* as an adjective ('in a ruined state') occurs in Diod.Sic. 5.66.1, concerning a Cretan myth about the Titans. 'Even to this day in the territory of Knossos', the historian writes, 'Rhea's *themelia oikopeda* can be seen.' One of those two words must be a noun (and the other its adjective)—but which? The orthodox view says *oikopeda*. Daniel points out, with perfect justification, that *themelia* is found as both noun ('foundations') and adjective ('foundational *x*'); however, determining which it is in Diod.Sic. 5.66.1 does not seem possible. Without the unequivocal support of that passage, *Poroi* 2.6 would be the sole attestation of an adjective *oikopedos* in classical literature. Such an idea is not intolerable, given X.'s inventiveness with other words; even so, on balance I judge that the orthodox understanding of it as a noun here can stand.

2.6 If the state were to grant rights of ownership to those building houses for themselves on them—those who applied and seemed deserving For the Greek here (the tense of the participle those building houses for themselves') see Notes on the Text, and further below.

In pre-classical Athens it was axiomatic that all the land of Attica not occupied by shrines (or otherwise the property of the gods) and not the possession of the community as a whole or any sub-group thereof was owned by its individual citizens, and passed by inheritance down within their families. By X.'s time the concept of the 'alienability' of land—an acceptance that its ownership could be transmitted by other means—had (in various forms) come into being, and was seemingly uncontroversial. Even so it remained true that the preponderance of Attic soil, with or without buildings on it, was in the hands of the *politai*: those born as such, plus any non-Athenian individuals or groups voted the privilege of becoming naturalized citizens (*dêmopoiêtoi*). Short of that, we see (from the 420s onwards) selected non-citizens, whether individuals or groups, being voted *egktêsis*: the right of land-ownership (*OCD* 506; Pečírka (1966); Henry (1983) 204–40).

Usually this was unrestricted *gês kai oikias*, 'of land and of house', allowing a recipient to acquire and own land as something separate from his residence. Much more rarely there was a restriction to a house only, *oikias*. MacDowell (1978) 134 realized that the existence of the restricted form posed a question: 'does that mean that [the recipient] could own a house without owning the land on which it stood, so that he would have to pay rent or feu duty to an Athenian citizen for the site? I think it is more likely that *egktêsis* of house implies the right to own enough land for a house to stand on, but not land for farming; I doubt whether it occurred to the Athenians that ownership of land underneath someone else's house could have any use or meaning.' Todd (1993) 199 concurs: '[t]here are no clearly attested grants "of land" only, from which we may perhaps (with MacDowell (1978) 134) infer that *egktêsis* "of a house" implied the grant of enough land to build on [or for a house already built: DW] but not enough for farming'. Latterly, Jansen (2012) 748 n.91 comments that MacDowell adduced no evidence for his view. That is quite true, because there is none to adduce. Instead, there is common sense, and Todd's supporting argument.

Whichever of the two forms of *egktêsis* was granted, some of the grants were hereditary, others were confined to the honorands themselves.

It is against this background, then, that X.'s proposal here must be evaluated. And the first thing to say is that the way he expresses it is unorthodox. Although familiar with the noun *egktêsis* (*Hell.*5.2.19, plural, in reference to the Chalkidian League), the epigraphic norm (above), he does not use it here. Instead, his form of words involves *egkektêsthai*, the perfect infinitive of the related verb *egktâsthai*. (This is otherwise unattested, though [Demosth.] 50.8 denotes Athenians who own land in demes other than their ancestral, Kleisthenic ones by the perfect participle *egkektêmenoi*.) Associated with this, here, is a plural participle from the verb *oikodomein*, 'to build'. Its middle voice, as Gauthier 68 points out, conveys the idea that these metic builders are erecting houses for themselves, not for anybody else. Its aorist tense, as transmitted, has appeared problematic to some, and an alternative is to emend it, by altering a single vowel, to a future. However, the change is not necessary—see Note on the Text—provided we understand that in this context it describes a future action as having already taken place (Thiel 9). And that in turn has to mean, in present-day terminology, that the deeds of the house are handed over once it has been built; cf. Gauthier 68. Jansen (2012) 746–8 appears to take a different position. Translating the proposal with a stress on the aorist participle, i.e. 'if the city were to grant the right of possession to those who have already built houses', he appears to envisage X.'s idea as one of retrospective legitimization. But is it credible that metics had been illegally building houses without this coming to the attention of the *astynomoi* (?Aristot. *Ath.Pol.*50.2), not to mention the demarchs of the relevant intramural demes? Besides, Jansen's belief in, and emphasis on, an aorist participle here leads him to a strange conclusion. 'Xenophon is offering *egktêsis* to metics who have already built and occupied houses in the city—a statement from which we must infer that metics in his day did not own the land connected to their domiciles, even if they had been granted *oikias egktêsis*. In other words, what Xenophon is specifically proposing here is not the right of possession of a house *per se* but of the land connected with the house, that is *gês egktêsis*' (Jansen (2012) 748). The grip of this chain of logic could have been broken via MacDowell's understanding of *egktêsis oikias* (see above).

So much for the words. As regards the resulting substance: on the basis of the source-material that we have, X. is proposing something new about *egktêsis* here—not least in the fact that the beneficiaries would be metics, as opposed to the typical recipient of the award in decrees preserved on stone, who is a *non-resident* foreigner. That said, the multiple constraints X. imposes seem to me very striking, both individually and in aggregate: so already General Intro., sections 6–8. For another view, expressly challenging Whitehead (1977) 125–9, see Lambert (1997) 281 with n.247; and cf. Papazarkadas (2011) 66 n.216.

If I adhere to my earlier view (which I do), it is largely because the expert work of Stephen Lambert and others on the primary evidence—the inscriptions—has made two points even clearer than they were before.

First, *egktêsis oikias*—the technical way of expressing X.'s suggestion here—was very much at the margins of land-ownership rights in general; Henry (1983) 205–7. An illustration of this is RO 77 (Harding (1985) no.100), now *IG* II³ 316/*AIO*: in 337 a group of Akarnanian exiles are granted '*egktêsis* of whatever houses they want while they live in Athens, *until they return home*'. *IG* II² 545, as conventionally restored, gives the same temporary concession to Thessalian exiles twenty years later. Other grants of *egktêsis oikias* are few and far between, whether before *Poroi* (*IG* II² 53, Philytos, before 387/6), contemporaneously (*IG* II² 130, [La]chares of Apollonia, 355) or—the crucial category—subsequently. Its sum total: *IG* II² 206, now *IG* II³ 294/*AIO* (Theogenes of Naukratis, 348); the Akarnanian exiles, as above; possibly—as suggested in the General Intro., section 8, at n.158—*IG* II³ 432/*AIO*, Sopatros of Akragas; *IG* II² 554, Euxenides of Phaselis, 306/5 or later; and cf., from 333, the unique instance of *egktêsis* of a plot for the Kitians' Aphrodite temple, RO 91 (Austin & Vidal-Naquet (1977) no.72, Harding (1985) no.111), now *IG* II³ 337/*AIO*).

The second fact, relevant to *Poroi*, which has emerged from the revised dating of several of these documents is this: a somewhat larger cluster of them than before occupies the third quarter of the fourth century now. This is partly because some have migrated earlier (*IG* II² 551, now II³ 473/*AIO*; *IG* II² 564, now II³474/*AIO*) but also because others have been moved later: so e.g. *IG* II² 285+414d, now *IG* II³ 405/*AIO*. To the degree—still a limited degree—that the Athenians did grant land-ownership rights *per se* more freely in the post-*Poroi* era, this is a phenomenon of 'Lykourgan' rather than 'Euboulan' Athens.

Jansen (2012) 746–53 argues strongly for X.'s *egktêsis* plan as the centrepiece of his vision of Athenian 'financial and economic growth', and his reminder that 'houses' can be more than dwelling-places is salutary; cf. already **2.2 The absence**, and further under the next lemma. Nevertheless, the flaw in his interpretation overall lies in the limited number of those involved, if applications are indeed to be restricted to a (?)few hundred 'abandoned house-sites inside the walls, and building-plots too'. (We should note in this connection that X.'s idea of making a formal application for a grant of *egktêsis* did make its appearance in Athenian practice—but not, it seems, until the first half of the second century. See Henry (1983) 215–16; Daly (2007) 545, who adds, to *IG* II² 907, only the second instance securely attested.)

From another angle of approach, Dillery (1993) 1 n.4 claims that D. M. Lewis (1990) 259 connected the present passage with 'the explosion of the leasing of sacred property in the 340s and 330s; however, as pointed out by Papazarkadas (2011) 66 n.216, Lewis did no such thing.

No light is shed on this set of issues—or indeed on anything else—by X's casual assertion (attributed to Sokrates) in *Mem*.3.6.14 that 'our polis consists of more than ten thousand *oikiai*': Davies (1981) 51 n.24.

2.6 I reckon that that would create a larger and better class of people keen for residence in Athens On the keenness X. wants to foster in these individuals, expressed in Greek by the verb *oregesthai*, see again 2.7 (and cf. 3.11 on other poleis eager to enrol in his proposed register of benefactors). It is also an attitude, in general terms, of which he has already shown his approval: see (e.g.) *Ages*.1.35, *Hell*.4.4.6, *Hier*.7.1 & 3, *Hipp*.1.23, *Mem*.3.1.1, 4.2.23.

Despite the circumscribed nature of the incentive that X. expects to bring it about (see the preceding lemma), his aim here might seem self-explanatory, until we ask what, in his eyes, made some metics 'better' (*beltious*) than others. Gauthier 63–4, 72–3 and Whitehead (1977) 126 both suggest, with 2.3 in mind, that he wants more *Hellenic* metics. Jansen (2007) 306 n.80 challenges this by claiming—on this view—a conflict between 2.3 and 2.5; but see already above, **2.5 cavalry service**. A point of considerable significance thus arises. Hellenic metics are 99% immigrant metics, not freed slaves, so the current state of affairs that X. finds unsatisfactory is one in which there are too many *barbaroi*; cf. above, **2.3 the state**. Such non-Hellenes are in part immigrants, in part ex-slaves—but in what proportions? Whitehead (1977) found it impossible to say. Latterly Akrigg has contended that the *metoikia* was 'substantially composed of freedmen and women' (Akrigg (2015) 162–73, at 168). The strength of the argument, at first sight, is that *Poroi* cannot be adduced against it. Here X. does, demonstrably, want more immigrants: see above 2.7 (end); also 3.5, which uses the verb *eisoikizesthai*, to *come into* Athens and settle there. And overall, Akrigg's warning that immigrant-metics should not be viewed as 'proper' (or typical) metics is salutary. But the opposite scenario (above) stems from assumptions also; they are simply different assumptions.

X.'s use of the phrase '*oikêsis* in Athens' seems to imply something grander than merely 'to live' there (Marchant, Waterfield); contrast

'Athens as a place of residence' (Dakyns). X.'s superior metics will not merely 'live' in Athens—which they could do already—but set up a secure home there; a home that could be bequeathed to descendants, as Jansen (2007) 309 is right to point out. Jansen also, with reference to 2.4, makes a good case for supposing that at least some of these new, owner-occupier metics would want to work productively from their own homes (Jansen (2007) 308–9, 311).

2.7 suppose we established an official post of metic-custodians, just like orphan-custodians One cannot help but notice X.'s liking for job descriptions of this kind. See also the 'peace-custodians' of 5.1, and (adduced by Gauthier 71) the 'law-custodians' characteristic of well-ordered states, according to *Oec.*9.14–15. Since Athens' own *nomophylakes* fulfilled a high constitutional role which cannot be relevant there (Pomeroy (1994) 302; O'Sullivan (2001), reprised in O'Sullivan (2009) 72–86), Gauthier and others might be right in supposing that X. has in mind—if they existed in his day—the *nomophylakes* of Sparta (Paus. 3.11.2, etc.; MacDowell (1986) 133; Cartledge & Spawforth (1989) 145–9), though the same obstacle might arise with them also.

As regards the present passage, commentators (and others) remark that what X. here must have intended as a helpful analogy is of no use to modern readers, because Athenian 'orphan-custodians' (*orphanophylakes*) are nowhere else mentioned. Gauthier 68 is right to add that X.'s Athenian readers must be being invited to contemplate, for comparison and enlightenment, a post that did exist *in Athens*, but it has left no trace in the record. (Instead, what we are told about is the responsibility for orphans, manifesting itself in various ways, of the eponymous archon each year. See especially ?Aristot. *Ath.Pol.*56.6–7; MacDowell (1978) 93–8.)

Following the lead set by Thiel 46–7 (Excursus V), Gauthier 68–72 assembles a dossier of epigraphic evidence from outside Athens: Chios (*OCD* 310–11, *IACP* no.840), Gortyn in Crete (*OCD* 623, *IACP* no.960), Gorgippia (*IACP* no.696) and (H)istria (*OCD* 749–50 Istria (1), *IACP* no.685) on the Black Sea, Naupaktos at the mouth of the Corinthian Gulf (*OCD* 1002, *IACP* no.165), Rhodes (*OCD* 1278–9, *IACP* no.1000). In these six states either *orphanophylakes* or putative equivalents thereof (*epimelêtai* of the *xenoi*, *orphanistai*, *orphanodikastai*, *xenophylakes*) are attested. However, most of this comparative material has enough obscurities of its own, without furnishing anything that sheds light on what X. is referring to here. The consensus view (Thiel,

Stroud (1971) 289–90, Gauthier, Rhodes (1981) 633) that Athens' orphan-custodians were, specifically, guardians of those whose fathers had died in military service is speculative, but hard to improve on.

In the broadest of terms, X.'s new 'official post' (*archê*) of metic-custodian—a multiple one: see the next lemma—must provide something not provided by the existing statutory arrangements for metics. These were centred on another of the major archons, the polemarch: ?Aristot. *Ath.Pol.*58.2–3; Whitehead (1977) 92–3. As Bodei Giglioni lxiv puts it, the metic-custodians must instil more confidence in the metics than the polemarch does—but we are not told how, and it is impossible to guess. (He changes annually, but surely they would too.)

See further under the next lemma.

2.7 an honour of some kind went to those whose lists exhibited the most metics Here X. discloses a few precious details about what he has in mind. First, the plural 'metic-custodians' of 2.6 is here confirmed as meaning not a succession of single office-holders, as (e.g.) Demosth. 6.20 refers to 'the kings of Macedonia', but a plurality serving at the same time. (See already under the preceding lemma.) Second, X. wants a spirit of rivalry between the incumbents—as again in 3.3 (q.v.), with an existing magistracy. There they compete for 'prizes'. Here 'an honour of some kind' looks vaguer but probably means much the same. If crowning is what X. was thinking of, an order of precedence—akin to present-day gold, silver, and bronze medals—would be simple to calibrate. In reference to 3.3 rather than the present passage (although in fact it could relate to either) Gauthier 83 adduces the instance of *SIG* 305 (RO 100; Harding (1985) no.121; now *IG* II^3 370/*AIO*), an Athenian decree of 325/4 to establish a colony at the top of the Adriatic. The first, second, and third trierarchs whose ships are ready to sail will be crowned in gold to the value of, respectively, five hundred, three hundred, and two hundred drachmas (lines 183–204). On crowning see generally Henry (1983) 22–62, at 23–8; Scafuro (2009) 61–4, 66–73. X. demonstrates in passages like this his belief that all Athenians love to win (*Hipp.*1.26, using one of his favourite terms, *philonikia*; Dover (1974) 233–4).

The great majority of Athenian *archai* came in Kleisthenic tens, a few in multiples of ten. Leaving aside the unique case of the Council of Five Hundred, forty is the maximum known (?Aristot. *Ath.Pol.*53.1–2). Gauthier 72 tentatively envisages the norm, ten *metoikophylakes*, though his associated suggestion of five of them located in the *asty* and five in Peiriaeus (like the *astynomoi*, the *agoranomoi*, the *metronomoi*, the former *sitophylakes*, and probably the *epimelêtai tou emporiou*: respectively ?Aristot. *Ath.Pol.*50.2, 51.1, 51.2, 51.3, 51.4) is a dubitable one, given the scattered residence-pattern of metics throughout Attica (Whitehead (1986) 83–4). At any rate, ten or—as I myself would imagine—more, of these men will somehow compete to sign up a total of between twenty and thirty thousand metics: see the Chapter intro. (The criterion for the honours (above) is purely quantitative, though X. perhaps hoped that 'most' would not be the enemy of best; cf. Isoc. 8.53, 'we think that metics are exactly the same sort of people as the *prostatai* they choose'.)

A clear irony here is that the winners of these honours would be hard-pressed to devote as much attention to each of 'their' metics as their colleagues who were less successful recruiters. In any event, the fact that the metic-custodians were to be public officials meant that they would be accountable to the public (through their end-of-service *euthynai*: *OCD* 557). Thus, and especially if it is correct to think that X. wanted to do away with the *prostatês* system for metics (**2.2 It would be**, end), his intention is that the mechanisms for protecting them will be more transparent. See further under the next lemma.

On 'exhibited' see **2.5 it seems** (end).

2.7 this too would make the metics more loyal, and probably all stateless people would be keen for metic-status in Athens and would increase the revenues On what X. means by loyalty see already 2.5 it seems to me. Here, in his view, is a second ('this too') idea that will contribute towards a *metoikia* (cf. [Lys.] 6.49, Plat. *Leg.*8.850C) that is not only larger but more stable. For 'stateless people' (*apolides*) see already *Hell.*6.3.1 on Boiotian Thespiai (*OCD* 1466, *IACP* no.222) and Plataiai (*OCD* 1154, *IACP* no.216); for the latter see also Isoc. 14.55; and cf. e.g. Antiph. 2.2.9 (the elderly defendant in a specimen prosecution for homicide contemplates exile and being *apolis*), [Lys.] 20.35 (an Athenian on trial fears this fate), and Isoc. 8.44 (a hostile perspective on them, as a source of *dis*loyal mercenaries). In the present context the advantage of '*polis*-less' people is that, in theory at least, they will not experience a pull to return to their places of origin.

Gauthier 72 takes it for granted that these *apolides*, literally 'men without a polis', must be Hellenes. It is by no means clear that Isoc. 8.44 (above) can bear that interpretation, however, and compare in any case lines 30–2 of RO 21 (Harding (1985) no.40), where a fourth-century

Athenian decree refers to Phoinikians from Sidon (*OCD* 1364) as '*oikôntes kai politeuomenoi*' ('living and having civic rights') in Sidon. Nevertheless I do believe in general terms that Gauthier is right; and cf. also Schütrumpf 85 n.6, 'heimatloser Griechen' (though Schütrumpf's principal argument there, against both Gauthier and Whitehead (1977) 72, that 2.7 should not be linked too closely with 2.6 because 2.7's argumentation is wholly 'quantitativ', seems off-target. *Everything* in Chap.2 works towards the same end.) It is helpful to cite Diod.Sic. 18.8.2–5, as Gauthier 73 does, on the scale of the *apolides* phenomenon in the fourth century: 'more than twenty thousand' exiles from Greek poleis congregate at Olympia in 323 to hear Alexander's edict about their restoration (*OCD* p.560, s.v. exile; Bosworth (1988) 220–8).

The final words of the chapter ensure that its overall aim is not lost sight of. Cf. 3.5–6.

CHAPTER THREE

Isocrates in *On the peace* expresses the hope that the end of the Social War (which had taken place largely in the Aegean) would see Athens once again 'full of *emporoi* and foreigners and metics' (Isoc. 8.21). X. here, likewise, moves smoothly from metics considered in isolation—free foreigners who, at least notionally, have settled down in Athens—to the more fluid group that he calls *emporoi* (3.2) and later envisages as foreign visitors (3.5, where they are coupled with foreign residents).

Some Athenian citizens, in point of fact, are known to have been active in mercantile trade, whether as *emporoi* or *nauklêroi*. (For this distinction see under **3.1 My next topic**.) Andocides in the late fifth century is the best-known example (see Andoc. 2.11–16, 20–1; [Lys.] 6.19 & 49), and fourth-century oratory mentions more than a dozen more, including the defendant in Lykourgos' speech *Against Leokrates*. (Isager & Hansen (1975) 72 n.78 gives a list.) The picture of this sector that we are invited to draw by Isocrates and X.—and by some modern scholars—is therefore not cut and dried in the matter of status. (So already Whitehead (1977) 117.) Nonetheless, the evidence in its totality, together with contextual considerations such as the 99% citizen monopoly on landownership in Athens and Attica, does suggest that goods and commodities were *predominantly* shipped in and out by non-Athenians; some based in Athens, some merely passing through. (Reed (2003) argues that visitors outnumbered residents. That may well be correct, though his recruitment of *Poroi* Chaps.2–3 in support of it is dubitable.)

The same citizen/non-citizen mix seems to characterize the loan-financing of these operations, especially the long-haul voyages which, for those prepared to take the risk, offered very high rates of interest; see 3.9 with Comm. Isager & Hansen (1975) 72–3 register non-citizens and citizens in approximately 2:1 proportions, while warning that these figures, most of them again drawn from courtroom oratory, are bound to ignore self-financed voyages which did not generate litigation.

Statistics aside, the mix of statuses (and ethnicities) in these walks of life seems rarely to have been contentious *per se*. 'The idea that the competition of foreigners might be damaging to the economic interests of citizens did not occur to any ancient writer': Hasebroek (1933) 24. Quoting this with approval, Ste. Croix (1972) singles out *Poroi* as a 'particularly illuminating' illustration (3.2, 3.3–5, 3.12–13, 4.40, 5.3–4), and notes that its assumptions are anticipated in earlier remarks such as the one in *Hipp*.4.7: 'all poleis always receive cordially those who are importing something'.

Though classical Athens would probably have become a major *entrepôt*, a hub of *emporia*, under other geological circumstances, the ones that actually obtained there represented another instance of X.'s view in *Poroi* that the Athenians enjoyed unrivalled natural advantages (Chap.1, esp. 1.4). As late as 490 (Hdt. 6.116) their principal harbour was their nearest access to the sea: Phaleron Bay with its exposed moorings and open sands (*OCD* 1120). However, already by then Themistokles (*LGPN* s.v. no.39, *OCD* 1454–5, *APF* 211–20) had seen and was extolling the superior advantages of Peiraieus. It was his fellow-citizens' agreement with him, in the 480s, that led them to 'attach themselves to the sea' (Thuc. 1.93.4).

Peiraieus (*OCD* 1150 Pir-), hiding in plain sight immediately to the west of Phaleron, is a hilly peninsula with three 'bites' taken out of it. There are two quite small ones, Mounychia and Zea, on the eastern side, and a much larger one, the so-called Kantharos ('Goblet') or Megas Limen ('Great Harbour'), facing west. Together they form one of the most naturally felicitous harbour-complexes anywhere in the Mediterranean. (Within the Aegean, only Rhodes—with no fewer than five harbours, including another 'Great' one (*IACP* p.1207)—could compete.) Once they had appreciated this, the fifth-century Athenians made up for lost time by giving Peiraieus man-made facilities to match (as well as the constitutional status of a 'super-deme' with e.g. a state-appointed demarch: Whitehead (1986) 394–6). These included a circuit-wall (and, later, Long Walls linking it with the Athenian *asty*: in brief *OCD* 859; in full Conwell (2008)) and, internally, a grid-plan of streets designed by the forward-looking Hippodamos of Miletos (*OCD* 688). Of especial importance for our purposes here was the *emporion*, a stoa-lined cluster of facilities for trade and exchange located along the eastern (innermost) perimeter of the Great Harbour: Garland (2001) 83–95, 152–4.

Athens' low point of defeat and despair in 404 was shared, necessarily, by Peiraieus, its circuit-wall and the Long Walls demolished (*Hell.*2.2.20–3). However, already during the second half of the 390s they were being rebuilt (RO 9, Harding (1985) no.17); and merchant vessels at the Great Harbour's *emporion* in 387, with *emporoi* and *nauklêroi* in attendance, are mentioned by X. in *Hell.*5.1.21–3—though only in the course of his narrative of how the audacious Spartan admiral Teleutias sailed right in and captured them. The gateless state of the Goblet, which helped to make Teleutias' feat possible, was put to rights nine years later (*Hell.*5.4.34). Even so, in 361 Alexandros the tyrant of Pherai (*OCD* 58 Alexander (5)) was able to mount an action replay, in miniature, of Teleutias' raid (Polyaen. *Strat.*6.2.2). Incidents like those will have done nothing to persuade shippers and ship-owners that Peiraieus was a safe place to transact their business. 'Though the port revived in the mid-fourth century, it never became more than the ghost of its former Periklean self' (*OCD* 1150). Nevertheless, as we see here, that was not for want of trying on X.'s part.

Basic information about Peiraieus: Robert Garland's entry in *OCD* 1150, already cited here. Garland (2001) is a comprehensive monograph. Demetriou (2012) 188–229 reflects work more recent (and more concept-driven, for which see also Von Reden (1995) and Roy (1998)).

* * * *

3.1 My next topic is the import-and-export trade, and how Athens is so very agreeable and profitable to it Similar transitions, noted by Thiel 10, occur in *Hipp.*3.1 and *Symp.*8.23. One could add e.g. *Anab.*2.5.10, *Hell.*5.4.1, *Mem.*4.5.1 and 4.7.1.

This trade is expressed here, and again in 3.3, by the verb *emporeuesthai* (cf. Thuc. 7.13.2, Demosth. 33.2); later, between 3.2 and 5.3, by nouns related to it, *emporos/-roi* for the personnel involved and, as a general concept, *emporia*. Associated with the *emporoi* are the *nauklêroi* mentioned in 3.4, 3.12, and 5.3. (For them, no associated verb or abstract noun here in X., though both do occur elsewhere.) The conventional distinction between an *emporos* and a *nauklêros* has been seen in the idea that the latter owns his own ship. Though I have adhered to this here for convenience's sake in translation, it should be noted that Mark Woolmer has sought to refine both definitions: initially in the first chapter of his 2008 Cardiff Ph.D. thesis *The Athenian Mercantile Community* and then in an article generated from it: Woolmer (2015).

'I shall now explain why maritime trade is a particularly agreeable and profitable pursuit for Athens' (Waterfield 171). X. could perfectly well have written that, as it would have been true—especially the 'profitable' part (for which cf. 5.11). But instead he puts it the other way round, as already in the translations of Dakyns ('the attractions and advantages of Athens as a centre of commercial enterprise') and Marchant ('the unrivalled amenities and advantages of our city as a commercial centre'); see also Schütrumpf 85, Jansen (2007) 317–18. The point is not merely one of translation; substance is at issue. The individuals concerned could ply their trade anywhere they liked, within the legal constraints that begin to be attested in this very era. (For their choice in action see e.g. Demosth. 56.8. The opponents in this mercantile suit had allegedly tried to manipulate grain prices on the Athenian market. If they rose, confederates in Egypt would ship grain to Athens; if they fell, the ships would go 'to some other *emporion*'.) Athens/Peiraieus therefore had to compete, to market itself, as the destination of choice; cf. Gauthier 75.

For 'agreeable' in this same context see again 3.3.

3.1 she has excellent and totally secure moorings for ships, where, once brought in and at anchor, they can repose safely as far as winter is concerned For the Greek of the concluding clause here see Notes on the Text.

X.'s description 'excellent and totally secure moorings' is susceptible to more than one interpretation, given the great rarity (in this sort of sense) of the noun he uses: *hypodochê*, literally a receiving-place. Waterfield 171 renders them 'havens', and Cartledge's note refers in general terms to the three harbours of Peiraieus (see above, Chapter intro.), 'of which the specially developed commercial harbour of

[Kantharos] is particularly in Xenophon's mind'. The point could be put more strongly, since Mounychia and Zea were *for the exclusive use of the military* (Garland (2001) 95–6); but that then creates the problem of why X. writes of *hypodochai* in the plural. I can only think that the scene in his mind's eye is microcosmic, i.e. at the level of a plurality of vessels at their moorings.

A problem of another kind is presented by the final six words lemmatized above: in Greek the two-word phrase *heneka cheimônos.* First, it seems to use the preposition *heneka* in what amounts to a temporal sense (during *x*) which is ignored in LSJ. (The same, in point of fact, applies to Marchant's 'in spite of', latterly in Brodersen (2010) 100. Here I adopt 'as far as *x* is concerned' from Dakyns.) Second, it employs a noun, *cheimôn*, which in the common usage of the period can mean either (*a*) a storm or (*b*) winter. In the present passage the overwhelming consensus among commentators, translators, and others opts for sense *a*, without discussion. However, Herzog (1914) 472, quoted by Thiel 11, believed that X. meant winter; and two considerations combine to suggest that that is correct. First, of the sixty-five other instances of the word *cheimôn* in X., a mere fifteen refer to storms (and more than half of that minority to a single, notorious storm, the one which hampered the rescue of drowning Athenian rowers after the battle of Arginousai in 406: *Hell.*1.6–7). Second, Peiraieus as shelter from storms would be of use only to ships near the beginning or the end of their voyages (for instance, a twenty-day one to the Black Sea, ten days with a following wind to return: Isager & Hansen (1975) 60). By contrast, all competent *emporoi* and *nauklêroi* knew that in normal circumstances the sea-lanes became perilous for several months between about October and March, so that they would probably want to find somewhere suitable to 'pass the winter' (the verb *paracheimazein* is used in Demosth. 34.8 and 56.6, in the latter case about doing so in Athens 'and waiting for spring').

Casson (1991) 99–100 sketches an evocative picture of merchant vessels docking in Peiraieus, unloading their wares, and paying their tolls—throughout spring and summer. 'With the coming of October, winds and weather put a close to the sailing season. Money changers folded their tables, shippers from abroad sailed for home, ship-owners hauled out their craft onto the beach or bedded them down at the quays, stevedores wandered off to the city. Like a summer resort, the harbor shut down to wait for spring.' But see now Beresford (2013) for a challenge to this traditional view of a clear-cut 'closed season' for sailing.

3.2 in most states there is a degree of compulsion on the traders to take on a return cargo, because the currency they use there is not serviceable abroad The compound verb 'to take on a return cargo' (*antiphortizesthai*), used twice in this section, is not extant in Attic authors before X., but occurs seven times in one of the mercantile speeches attributed to Demosthenes (probably correctly so in this instance, according to MacDowell (2009) 265–6), the *Against Lakritos*: chaps.11, 25–6, 31, 37–8. See further under the next lemma.

X's statement here, in combination with the one that immediately follows it (see the next lemma,) sets Athenian coinage on a pedestal of excellence, or at least of international utility, that other states cannot match.

As regards this first element of the comparison, Thiel 11 and others (including Hasebroek (1933) 84–5 and Bodei Giglioni lxx n.9) adduce Demosth. 24.214. Demosthenes' client there, the otherwise unidentifiable Diodoros (*LGPN* s.v. no.11) is speaking in court in (probably) the summer of 353; he credits the early Athenian lawgiver Solon (*OCD* 1380–81) with the doctrine that debasing laws is more heinous a crime than debasing coinage, 'because many states openly use silver alloyed with copper and lead' and get away with it. But Gauthier 77–8 is right to argue against any connection. Such as they are, the verbal echoes (underlined here) are banal. More important, the huge numbers of surviving Greek coins from the period falsify Demosthenes' assertion of widespread debasement by the issuing cities and mints. (Existing examples tend to be the work of later forgers.) So X. is considering non-Athenian coinages as legitimately issued. Gauthier points to the fact that none matched Athenian currency of the period, in terms of either consistent weight or purity of content. And even if they had done, there were the different weight-standards (on which see generally Melville-Jones (1986) 240–2) to take into account. Granted that X.'s 'most states' is probably hyperbole, coins with (e.g.) the winged pegasus of Corinth would need usually, sooner or later, to be changed into another currency—perhaps even Attic owls—and the money-changer's profit would be the trader's loss. (Thus, this 'degree of compulsion' is not exerted by the states themselves but simply experienced by the *emporoi*, when calculating their options.) See also e.g. Polyaen. *Strat.*4.10.2 on an episode in northern Greece in 364: fighting the Hellenes of Chalkidike (*OCD* 303–4, *IACP* 811–14), King Perdikkas III of Macedon exhausts his supply of silver coins and issues tin-plated bronze ones instead, to pay his troops; 'the *emporoi* would take the king's coinage, but since it was useless beyond the borders [= X.'s adverb *exô* here], they would exchange it for local produce'.

The phenomenon of city currencies being hard to use outside their home ports naturally calls to mind the Athenians' fifth-century 'Standards Decree' (*IG* I^3 1453; ML 45, now OR 155; Fornara (1983) no.97). Only a narrowly political/ideological view of the measure would deny that the practicalities of trade and commerce in the Aegean and beyond were much eased during the years it was in force. As illustration of the inconvenience, and sometimes expense, involved in cross-currency trading, Kallet (2001) 209 n.101 cites not only the present passage but also the honorific decree *IG* XII.5 817, from Tenos (*OCD* 1440, *IACP* no.525). There, in the late third or early second century, the 'League of the Islanders' (cf. Austin (2006) no.256) rewards a Syracusan banker called Timon for charging no rate-of-exchange fee when dealing with Tenian currency that had been spurned by the grain dealers of Delos.

3.2 In Athens, they can export in return most things that human beings might have need of. And if they do not want to take a return cargo, they also export fine 'merchandise' by exporting silver For 'things that human beings might have need of' cf. 1.4, on the need that both Hellenes and *barbaroi* do (rather than 'might') have for Attic marble.

The general line of thought here harks back to 1.3–5 and esp. 1.7; see the Comm. there for the sort of *foodstuffs* that departing merchants 'export in return' (*antexagein*, another first occurrence for the period). Isager & Hansen (1975) 34–8 demonstrate that olives and wine should not be included. But in another category it is clear that Athens exported *manufactured goods*, above all her fine red-figure painted pottery (Isager & Hansen (1975) 38–42).

For the international appeal of Athenian silver tetradrachms, Gauthier 78–9 quotes Bogaert (1968) 328: their purity—see under the preceding lemma—meant that their intrinsic value in silver was almost (*c.* 96%) equal to their face value, and as items of export in the fifth and fourth centuries they constituted one member of the top trio of 'international' currencies, alongside the Persians' gold darics and the electrum *statêres* of Kyzikos (*OCD* 408 Cy-, *IACP* no.747). It should be noted that the noun *argyrion* which X. uses here, and indeed throughout *Poroi*, embraces (*a*) the metal silver, (*b*) coinage made from it, and sometimes even (*c*) money that may or may not have any silver in it. That *b* is its sense in the present passage (as opposed, perhaps, to 4.8 and/or 4.21, q.v.) is almost universally assumed, though see below.

Fourth-century sources sometimes mention the hazards of transporting currency by sea: so Isoc. 17.36, [Demosth.] 50.28. Nevertheless Gauthier 76–80 never really puts forward any convincing arguments for his opinion that exporting Athenian currency in the way implied by X. was unprofitable and would only have been a last resort ('pis-aller'). In any case we should differentiate between different destinations. Coin hoards from the Black Sea region do not contain Athenian tetradrachms, presumably because Kyzikene *statêres* (see above) were the currency of choice there (Isager & Hansen (1975) 47 with 165–6). By sharp contrast, hoards from Egypt are completely dominated by Attic 'owl' tetradrachms, and also by local imitations of them (Isager & Hansen (1975) 48–9; cf. Howgego (1995) chap.5.3). The doubts of Gauthier (and of Melville Jones (2007) 79–80) concerning X.'s view of the profitability of exporting Athenian 'owls' are re-examined by Van Alfen (2012). While noting that X.'s use of the term 'silver' (*argyrion*) here might embrace bullion as well as coin (cf. generally Isager & Hansen (1975) 45; Kroll (2001)), he finds overall, as regards Egypt and the Near East, that 'the bulk export of owls for profit was not an unreasonable assertion'.

On the general matter of importing and exporting currency, *SIG* 218 (Austin & Vidal-Naquet (1977) no.103, Arnaoutoglou (1998) no.41) is a fourth-century decree from Olbia (*OCD* 1035; *IACP* no.690) which freely allows both; cf. J. K. Davies in *CAH* 7.1.281.

3.2 everywhere they sell it, they receive back more than the principal X.'s 'principal' (*archaion*) is often in the plural (so e.g. Aristoph. *Clouds* 1156; Isai. 6.38; Demosth. 1.15, 27.23, 28, 35, 38, 50, 59, 61, 62, 64, 34.26), but for the singular see also e.g. Demosth. 27.10, 17, 29, 56.35, [Demosth.] 53.20. Since Demosth. 27 does switch between singular and plural indiscriminately, there is clearly no question of a right vs. wrong usage. Rather, as Gauthier 77 points out, X. here deploys the term in a slightly transferred sense: not capital which is generating interest (cf. 3.9–10) but cash equated to a commodity or item of merchandise for 'sale' (= exchange).

3.3 suppose that someone were to offer prizes to the officials in charge of the *emporion* On the *emporion* see the Chapter intro., above.

Thiel 47–8 (Excursus VI) declared the identity of these officials a difficult question. This is because X.'s form of words makes it evident that he is not referring to them by their actual title, so our choice lies between two boards whose titles are on record elsewhere. One (*a*) is the *nautodikai*, 'naval-judges' (*OCD* 1002), mentioned in a fragmentary fifth-century inscription (*IG* I[3] 41, lines 90–1) about the Euboian city of Histiaia (*OCD* 690, *IACP* no.372), and also in Lys. 17.5 & 9 from the 390s (where, interestingly, the speaker mentions a delay in his case being heard). The other (*b*) is the *epimelêtai tou emporiou*, 'overseers of the *emporion*'. They are more copiously documented throughout the fourth century. See above all lines 20–2 of RO 25 (Stroud (1974), Austin & Vidal-Naquet (1977) no.102, Harding (1985) no.45), the currency law of 375/4; also, again, in oratory (Demosth. 35.51, [Demosth.] 58.8–9, Din. 2.10); and ?Aristot. *Ath.Pol.*51.4 (with Rhodes (1981) 579), giving their number as ten.

A long succession of scholars has identified X.'s officials here with *a*, the *nautodikai*: so Herzog (1914) 479; Von der Lieck (1933) 39–41; Gernet (1955) 180; Bodei Giglioni lxxix–lxxx; Harrison (1971) 24, cf. 27; Cohen (1973) 184; MacDowell (1978) 228–31, at 231. MacDowell also speculates that, since X.'s topic is visiting non-citizen merchants, he might also be thinking of the mysterious *xenodikai* who are mentioned in several fragmentary inscriptions from both the second half of the fifth century and the first half of the fourth (the latter are *IG* II[2] 46 and 144). Thiel himself, however, maintained that X. means *b*, the *epimelêtai tou emporiou*. Gauthier 80–1 (expanding Gauthier (1972) 154–5) concurs; likewise Schütrumpf 87 with n.8; and with the currency law extending their period of attestation well before *Poroi*, this is the preferable option (cf. Jansen (2007) 320–1 and Cartledge in Waterfield 223).

2.7 had included an example of giving officials an honour (*timê*); see the Comm. there. Now we have the related idea of incentivizing people, whether officials or not, with prizes (*athla*); a policy dear to X.'s heart. See especially *Hier.*9.3–11, and *Hipp.*1.25–6, and note also his accounts of others doing the same: Kyros the Great (*Cyrop.*2.1.22–4 and elsewhere), Derkylidas (*Hell.*3.2.10), and above all Agesilaos (*Ages.*1.25; *Hell.*3.4.16, 4.2.5–8). In the present instance the phraseology, 'suppose that someone were to offer prizes', is not what we would have expected if in fact (as was surely the case) what X. had in mind was the state itself offering them; however, *Hipp.*1.26 had already reproduced the exact wording of *Hier.*9.6 & 7 (a generalized discussion) in this regard, so for him it was a ready-made locution, slotted in again here without any constitutional implications.

See further under the next lemma.

3.3 rewarding whichever one resolved matters of dispute most fairly and most speedily, so that whoever wanted to sail away was not prevented from doing so This is how X. proposes that the *epimelêtai tou emporiou* will have the opportunity to win 'prizes' (see under the preceding lemma). These were probably, in practice, crowns (cf. Gauthier 83), as with the 'honour of some kind' suggested for successful *metoikophylakes* (2.7 with the Comm. there). For the 'crown'/'prize' connection see e.g. Perikles in Thuc. 2.46.1, Plat. *Rep*.10.613C, and frequently elsewhere (including *Ages*.1.25–7).

X.'s 'resolved' is a verb, *diairein*, with noteworthy fifth-century precedents when used in this somewhat uncommon sense. It occurs three times—lines 472, 488, 630—in Aeschylus' *Eumenides* (staged in 458), where Orestes, with the participation of Athena and Apollo, is tried for matricide before a prototype version of the Areopagos council (R. W. Wallace (1989) 87–93). If X. did not pick up the usage from Aeschylus, another possibility is Hdt. 4.23.5 on the dispute-resolving role of the Skythian Argippaioi.

The term 'matters of dispute' (*amphiloga*) had featured in two Peloponnesian War treaties transcribed by Thucydides: the one-year Sparta/Athens truce of 423 (Thuc. 4.118.8) and the fifty-year Sparta/Argos alliance of 418 (Thuc. 5.79.4). A Doricism, it had already been used by X. in other works, notably *Hell*.5.2.10 and 5.3.10 on the rights of returning exiles in Phleious (*IACP* no.355) in the mid-380s. In the present instance, plainly, he is applying it to commercial disputes involving *emporoi* and/or *nauklêroi*, some (at least) of them keen to 'sail away' (*apoplein*) quickly and get on with other business. 'Rather than Xenophon's favourite system of differential competitive rewards, the Athenians introduced special courts on an equal basis for all comers so that commercial lawsuits could be settled with particular dispatch' (Cartledge in Waterfield 233). On this—the creation (no later than 347) of the category of *dikai emporikai*—see already General Intro., section 6, at n.87. As Gauthier 81–2 (and 83) points out, X.'s proposal here does not concern court cases, given the language he uses, but summary justice dispensed by the *epimelêtai* in the *emporion*. (The general idea was not in itself new: on the summary powers of officials see Harrison (1971) 4; Hansen (1991) 190.) In any event it remains true that the Athenians themselves recognized the issue but adopted a different and more thoroughgoing solution to it.

3.3 These things too would greatly increase the number of traders, as well as making it more agreeable for them to do business With the first of these aims cf. 2.6 (and 2.7) on metics. With the second cf. the opening of 3.1.

In the latter connection Gauthier 84 aptly cites the advice of Isocrates to the young Cypriot dynast Nikokles (*OCD* 558, s.v. Evagoras, his father) in Isoc. 2.22: 'for all foreigners, provide a city that is safe and, where contracts are concerned, well-regulated'. (He goes on to recommend valuing most highly 'not the visitors who are bringing gifts but those who expect to receive them from you—because by honouring such men you will enhance your reputation with others'. Whether X. was familiar with Isoc. 2 is impossible to say, but this advice is certainly in substantive terms a precursor of what *Poroi* Chap.3 advocates, not only here in 3.3 but also, as will be seen, 3.4, 3.6, and 3.11.)

3.4 Another good and fine idea Again, but with the two elements reversed, in 3.12. (We have had a 'fine' idea at 2.5; another will appear in, again, 3.12; and for a 'good' one see 3.14.) In so far as their order matters, 'fine and good' (*kalon kai agathon*) has the louder resonance by virtue of its relation to the concept of *kalokagathia*: what a gentleman would do—or in this instance, would suggest. See e.g. *Ages.*11.6, *Anab.*4.1.19, *Cyrop.*2.1.17, 5.1.18, 8.4.34, *Hell.*5.3.9, *Lac.Pol.*10.2 & 4, *Mem.*1.2.23, 1.6.14, 2.1.20, 3.5.15 & 19, *Symp.*2.4, 3.4, 4.49, 8.3 & 11. Useful general analyses in Ste. Croix (1972) 371–6 and Dover (1974) 41–5. On X. specifically, readers of Italian can benefit from Roscalla (2004).

Engen (2010) 172 (followed by Powell (2015) 229–30) seizes upon, and objects to, Marchant's translation of this sentence-opening: 'It *would also be* an excellent plan' (my italics)—likewise in Dakyns, Schütrumpf, Waterfield, and elsewhere, in fact. Such a translation, the objection runs, masks the fact that X. is mentioning (and approving of) a practice that *already exists*; one that might be illustrated by *IG* II^2 81 (+ *SEG* 40.57), a fragmentary decree from sometime between *c.* 390 and 378/7 in honour of a (?)trader. This is a house of cards, on two counts.

First, the reason to think this unknown Megarian honorand a trader is the fact that he and his descendants seem to be awarded the privilege of 'inviolability' (*asylia*) of person and property, very rare in pre-Hellenistic Athens. Though the word is totally restored, in line 6, no other appropriate noun fits either the line-length or the remainder of the formula; and the same is true of line 19 of *IG* I^3 98 (ML 80, now OR 173; Fornara (1983) no.149), a second batch of honours, in 411, for a certain Pythophanes who more clearly *is* a trader. (For the formula cf. also the decree-fragment *IG* II^2 286, now joined with *IG* II^2 685 as *IG* II^3 393/*AIO*, honouring unknown Achaians at some time in the third quarter of the fourth century.) However, what must be kept in mind is that X.'s 'good and fine idea' concerns *two very specific privileges*: see the next lemma. It is therefore not cogent to claim—as both Engen and Powell do—that he was anticipated by awards such as the ones given to Pythophanes, or Lykon of Achaia (*IG* I^3 174, from 425–410), or the fourth-century Megarian. (Much the same objection must be entered against the view of Powell (2015) 234, reiterated 251, that the honours for non-citizens advocated in *Poroi* Chaps.2–3 are echoed to a high degree in the ones granted to Eudemos of Plataiai in 329: RO 94, Harding (1985) no.118, now *IG* II^3 352/*AIO*. X. says nothing about crowning, whether in gold or (as here) olive; and Eudemos does not get *proedria* or *xenia*—or the form of *egktêsis* restricted to housing, as per 2.6.)

The second point to make is more important but can be stated more briefly. Engen's reading of the present passage forces it into saying something that it does not. X. has a variety of ways of introducing any given idea of his. They include—not only here but again twice in 3.12—asserting that it is good, fine, or whatever, with 'is' suppressed. There is no implication that the idiom is reserved for instances where he is merely commending existing practice.

3.4 to honour merchants and ship-owners with grants of *proedria* and to invite them to public receptions periodically On 'ship-owners' (*nauklêroi*), coupled again with *emporoi* in 3.12 and 5.3, there is a monograph-length treatment in French (Vélissaropoulos (1980)). See also e.g. Hasebroek (1933) 1–6; Isager & Hansen (1975) 64–6; Casson (1995) 314–16; Garland (2001) 68, 95; and already under **3.1 My next topic.**

The punctuation in some translations (Dakyns, Waterfield) applies the proviso-clause—my next lemma here—solely to the second of these two proposals, but there is no justification for doing so. X. cannot be advocating preferential theatre-seats for *all* non-Athenian traders and ship-owners, even if that had been a logistical possibility. See rather Marchant's translation, and (e.g.) Gauthier 84; Jansen (2007) 323–4.

As with 2.6 and *egktêsis*, X. concerns himself here with two established privileges that were in the gift, and under the control, of the state. The first, *proedria* (cf. e.g. Aeschin. 2.80 & 110, 3.76 & 154, and the epigraphical evidence in Henry (1983) 291–4), meant specifically front-seats at the great theatre of Dionysos on the south-east slope of the akropolis (Hurwit (1999) figs.3 and 209). The second involved an invitation to Athens' equivalent of a City Hall, the Prytaneion (in brief *OCD* 1231; in full S. G. Miller (1978)). Such invitations were of two kinds, in this era. An invitation to 'dinner' (*deipnon*) would be issued if the guests were Athenian citizens, to 'hospitality' (*xenia*: literally, things suitable for a foreign guest) if they were not: Henry (1983) 262–75; Gauthier 84; Powell (2015) 198–9. (Schütrumpf 87 and Waterfield 172 efface this distinction with their translations 'zu einem Ehrenmahl einzuladen' and 'invite to state banquets', respectively.) Unless X. was oblivious to the convention, which does not seem at all probable (its technical language here is anticipated at *Hell.*6.4.20, a rebuff to a Theban herald in 371; cf. e.g. [Demosth.] 7.20), it is confirmation that in his view—despite the untidy truth of the matter (Chap.4 intro., above)—*emporoi* and *nauklêroi* were typically foreigners.

The epigraphic evidence collected and discussed in Engen (2010) 140–81 enables X.'s suggestions to be put into context. (See also, more briefly but with acute observations on the conceptual context, Jansen (2012) 742–5.)

The earliest surviving instance of a grant of *proedria* to a non-Athenian is *IG* II² 555, a decree passed in honour of Asklepiades of Byzantium, in the closing years of the fourth century. The beginning of the stone is missing, so if Asklepiades' actual services were mentioned, there is now no means of discovering what they were, and no reason to think that he himself was an *emporos* or a *nauklêros*. (Even worse preserved, by far, is *SEG* 21.343, from the same period. Not even the legal status of the honorand there is agreed.) Nevertheless, we should note *IG* II³ 432, now *IG* II³ 432/*AIO*, proposed by Lykourgos; it was carved by a mason active between 337 and 324 (so Tracy (1995) 107). This grant of proxeny (*OCD* 1231) to a Sicilian Greek, Sopatros of Akragas, adds extra awards which include one called *thea*. As distinct from *proedria*, this meant a once-only 'seat with a view', at a single festival performance (Henry (1983) 292).

Sopatros is also invited to *xenia* in the Prytaneion—and is in fact the only certain example of *xenia* being offered to an honorand for any kind of trade-related reasons. Sopatros had deserved his honours, we read, by assiduously shipping grain to Athens, in a 'bleak period for the Athenians, who suffered at least five food crises between 338/7 and 323/2' (Garnsey (1988) 150–63, at 162). In all, some twenty decrees from those years, passed for similar reasons, are extant. Most are incomplete and not available in translation, but an exception is RO 95, now *IG* II³ 367/*AIO*, the dossier in honour of Herakleides, a man from Cypriot Salamis (*OCD* 1309 s.v. 2, *IACP* no.1020). Tracy (1995) 30–4 has an overview comprehensive at the time of writing. (All the documents he lists there are now, like the decree for Sopatros, in *IG* II³ fasc.1. Its editor, Stephen Lambert, has full treatments in Lambert (2006) and Lambert (2007).)

Had X. been writing against *that* background, he would surely have been advocating honours for those foreign merchants and ship-owners who were helping to keep Athens from outright starvation, rather than ones who met the somewhat more rarefied criteria he actually suggests: see the next lemma.

3.4 those who seem to be of benefit to the state because of their noteworthy vessels and commodities X.'s criterion of benefit to the state has been invoked already at 2.1, 2.2, and 2.3. It will reappear in 4.13 and (implicitly) 4.35.

In the present instance of it, according to Austin & Vidal-Naquet (1977) 367 n.14, the honours he is proposing for *emporoi* and *nauklêroi* were 'simply in relation to the importance of their cargo'. Had that been true, it would have been readily understandable. His (?)Arkadian contemporary Aeneas the Tactician (*OCD* 23) advised that 'when the state is running short of grain or oil or anything else, incentives proportionate to the size of his cargo—and a crown in his honour—should be on offer to anyone who imports them, and the *nauklêros* should have beaching and re-launching facilities' (Aen.Tact. 10.12). Likewise, some of the decrees mentioned under the preceding lemma commend the honorands in quantitative terms for the grain they have shipped in, e.g. three thousand medimnoi (approx. 120,000 kg.) by Herakleides; and cf. Demosth. 34.39 ('more than ten thousand', allegedly, imported by the speaker there, Chrysippos). Cargoes such as that, as Gauthier 86 comments, would certainly have fulfilled X.'s requirement of 'noteworthy... commodities', *axiologa emporeumata*. (The noun had already been used in *Hier*.9.11, and is unique to X.)

A complication, though, is introduced by 'vessels'. Herzog (1914) 480 n.1, Thiel 12, and Gauthier 85 all adduce *Oec*.8.11–17. Ischomachos

(*LGPN* s.v. no.1, *APF* 265–8, *POP* 176–8) describes there 'the great Phoinikian vessel' which he had boarded and looked around; to him, its internal tidiness and order offered a model for how his young wife should manage their home. Pomeroy (1994) 288 supposes that Ischomachos 'must be referring to a particular well-known Phoenician cargo-ship'. That interpretation, in my opinion, places too much weight on the definite article X. uses ('the' *mega ploion to Phoinikikon*); more probably the allusion is to a recognizable *type* of merchant ship, not merely (in this instance at least) large but also, and especially, rounded. (See Casson (1995) 66 on the Phoinikian 'tubs', *gauloi*, mentioned by Herodotus, Aristophanes, and others.) Be that as it may, here in *Poroi* X. does—somehow—believe that the condition of a merchant vessel as well as the nature and quantity of its contents could be 'of benefit to the state'.

3.4 If likely to be honoured in these ways they would hasten to us as to friends, with not only the profit but also the honour in mind X.'s rather compressed Greek does not have 'If likely to be'; nevertheless we are presumably to envisage, in the main, traders who have not yet been so honoured (with perhaps just a few who have enjoyed the honorific experience and want more).

The reciprocatory relationship between benefit (to Athens) and honour here is noteworthy. He who craves the honour must provide the benefit (so Sokrates in *Mem*.3.6.3), and indeed, the more benefit provided, the greater the rewards merited (*Cyrop*.2.2.20); cf. Seager (2001) 385. The aspiration to receive honours, feeding back into the aspiration to perform the services that merit them, is something X. regards as admirable in its own right (cf. e.g. *Cyrop*.8.8.4), and not a mind-set confined to Athenian citizens. (*Hier*.7.3 calls it the point that differentiates men from animals—before adding that not *all* men feel it.)

LSJ s.v. register instances of the verb *epispeudein* used intransitively—i.e. as opposed to hurrying someone else along to do something—in Eurip. *Troad*.1275 (imperative) and in two occurrences in X.: *Symp*.7.5 ('these matters do not hasten into the same state as (in the case with) wine') and the present passage, summarized as hasten *to*. X.'s Greek, more compressed than translation can reflect, does not have (but does imply) 'to us'. The phrase 'as to friends' is taken over from *Cyrop*.1.6.4.

The description of the Phoinikian cargo-vessel—see under the preceding lemma—takes it for granted that its *nauklêros* was carrying his cargo 'for profit' (*kerdos*: *Oec*.8.13). Nothing indicates that X.'s attitude to it was one of disapproval. (Contrast Isoc. 21.6, which links *kerdos* with wrongdoing.) The furthest X. goes is to have Ischomachos declare that the difference between lovers of profit and lovers of honour is that only the latter—wishing to be praised and honoured (cf. above)—work hard, take risks, and avoid profit that is dishonest (*Oec*.14.10).

3.5 As is plain, the more people came to live here and to visit, the higher, correspondingly, would be the volume of what is imported, what is exported, what is bought, what is sold, what generates fees, and what generates taxes For the Greek here (from 'what is bought' onwards) see Notes on the Text.

By referring (albeit indirectly) to metics again, as well as to foreign visitors, X. makes it clear that this sentence is a summation of everything that has been put forward *in Chap.2 as well as Chap.3* (thus far: there is more to come in 3.11–14). So already Bodei Giglioni lxxviii–lxxxii, Gauthier 86, Whitehead (1977) 126, Jansen (2007) 296. (See also, retrospectively, 4.40.)

The corollaries, in X.'s view, of there being 'more immigrants and visitors' are presented as higher volumes of six types of transaction. The first four of them, at least, are grouped in pairs:

(*a–b*) IMPORTS AND EXPORTS. In broad terms this is self-explanatory: import- and export-taxes levied in the Peiraieus *emporion* (Gauthier 86); either equivalent to, or at least including, what 4.40 will call harbour-dues (*ellimenia*, on which see generally Powell (2015) 103–4, Fawcett (2016) 161). The 'Old Oligarch' mentions 'the *hekatostê* ['hundredth': in present-day terms a tax of 1%] in the Peiraieus' ([X.] *Ath.Pol.* 1.17), which in context might simply be a disembarkation tax on people landing there, with or without goods to sell. See Fawcett (2006) 47–53, citing also a stray line from the fifth-century comic dramatist Eupolis which mentions an *ellimenion* 'to be paid before embarkation'; also Fawcett (2016) 154, 159–60. Aristophanes in *Wasps*, staged in 422, refers to 'the *many* hundredths' (lines 657–9, at 658); the list of six things immediately after that phrase, which include 'harbours', could be an elaboration of it, but they might, alternatively, be new items added to this summary catalogue of the city's income. *IG* I^3 182, a fragmentary decree from the time of the Peloponnesian War, thanks and rewards two individuals who, it seems, have exemplified the Athenians' wish that timber for the oars of triremes be imported 'free of the hundredth tax' (lines 6–8). As it cannot be dated exactly within the period 430 to 405, this document could just as well be after as before *IG* I[3] 133, another fragmentary (but this time non-honorific) decree, which has a context-less mention of a *pentêkostê* (line 25), i.e. a 2% tax, of some unspecified kind.

Fortunately for our purposes here, Andoc. 1.133–4 (= Austin & Vidal-Naquet (1977) no.93) shows the 'fiftieth' firmly *in situ* in the late fifth century; and the fourth-century evidence is unproblematical in this regard (if not always in others). In Demosth. 35.28–30 the Athenian speaker, Androkles of Sphettos (Lambert (2001) 57–8 = Lambert (2012) 231–2), alleges that his opponent, the metic Lakritos from Phaselis in Lykia (*OCD* 1123–4), 'did not put in to your *emporion*, but anchored in Thieves' Cove, which is outside the boundary-signs of your *emporion*. Anchoring in Thieves' Cove is like anchoring in Aigina or Megara: anyone can sail away from that harbour to wherever he likes and whenever it suits him. The vessel lay at anchor there for more than twenty-five days, and these men were strolling around in your deigma ['display-area']... We were watching them to see whether they were unloading anything anywhere from the vessel or paying the fiftieth.' (They never did.) The 'fiftieth' is also mentioned in e.g. Demosth. 34.7, where it is levied on a shipload of goods being *exported* (to the Black Sea); in [Demosth.] 59.27, where it is called 'the fiftieth on (imported) grain'; and in RO 28, where the accounts of the Athenian amphiktyons of Delos (*OCD* 426–7, *IACP* no.478) for the years 377–373 include at one point a fiftieth apparently levied on oxen exported for sacrifice at a festival of Delian Apollo (line 38). Overall, then, Fawcett (2006) 97–9, at 97, seems justified in calling it 'the main ancient Athenian maritime import/export tax... payable on all goods, both imports and exports, whatever their place of origin'. See also Fawcett (2016) 159–63.

(Fawcett (2006) chaps.3 and 9 is a full study of Athenian 'maritime taxation'. Much of it, though, is not germane to our purposes here, as it does not concern traffic *through Peiraieus*.)

(*c–d*) PURCHASES AND SALES. Another mirror-image pairing. (In 4.40 they will merge into a single phrase, 'the increase in markets (*agorai*)'; see the Comm. there.) The 'purchase-taxes' (*epônia*: Pollux 7.15, Powell (2015) 102–3) mentioned occasionally in our epigraphical sources used to be assumed to have a limited scope, as taxes on the sale-price *of confiscated property*. And they may indeed have begun as such, as in the so-called Attic Stelai (*Agora* 19 P1, *IG* I[3] 421–30; extracts ML 79, now OR 172—Fornara (1983) no.147): the public sale, in 414, of the property of those convicted of having mutilated the Hermes-statues, and other religious offences. However, in the Athenian grain-tax law of 374/3 (Stroud (1998); RO 26), the successful bidders to collect that 'twelfth' (8⅓%) tax in the islands of Lemnos, Imbros, and Skyros must pay up-front '*epônia* and announcer's fees'—a phrase also found several times elsewhere—of *c.* 1% (lines 27–9). That fact might suggest that by X.'s day *epônia* had become general, or at any rate *more* general, in their application; cf. Fawcett (2006) 39–44, 52–53; Fawcett (2016) 166, 171–3. In any event, just as with *a*–*b*, the attested rate is different at different times. In this instance the higher one, 2%, appears to be the earlier.

The main frustration here is lack of evidence sufficient to establish whether X.'s apparent distinction between 'what is bought' and 'what is sold' can be pressed to mean that both of the parties in routine sale-and-purchase transactions were taxed.

(*e*) FEES. This is problematic. X.'s verb *misthophoroito* (passive) is otherwise unattested. More fundamentally still, the several meanings of its root noun *misthos* vex the issue. Gauthier 86–7 is adamant that here it means 'wage(s)'—as it had indubitably done in 2.1; and for that general sense of *misthophorein* and related terms he cites the 'Old Oligarch' ([X.] *Ath.Pol.*1.3), Thucydides (8.65.3, 8.67.3), Lysias (27.1), Plato (*Grg.*515E), and Demosthenes (24.96–7). A quite different interpretation is conveyed by the translation of 3.5 in Hasebroek (1933) 25: 'the public revenue from rents', glossed as 'from the state-owned lodging-houses'. (Likewise the translations of Dakyns, Marchant, and Waterfield.)

One large obstacle lies in the way of following Gauthier on this point: the fact that the substance of 3.5 is summed up at the beginning of 3.6 as 'increases *in revenues*' (my emphasis). Distributing more *misthoi* in the sense of wages is the opposite of increasing revenues.

Gauthier's argument against Hasebroek (and Von der Lieck (1933) 37) is three-fold: the topic of 'state-owned lodging houses' is not broached until 3.13, so X.'s readers could not be expected to anticipate it here; only very rarely does *misthos* have the sense of a 'rent' in fourth-century sources; and such rents would actually be taxes, and thus not worth distinguishing from element *f*. The third of these objections can be met by taking a different view of element *f* than Gauthier evidently did: see that item below. Nor (given the numerous ways in which X. in *Poroi* fashions his own vocabulary: see again *f*) can the second be a decisive counter-argument, at any rate as regards terminology. In

Isaeus 6.35 the property of the deceased Kiron (*APF* 312–16, *LGPN* s.v. no.2) includes a town-house 'bringing in rent', *misthophorousa*. Yet in cases like that the rent comes in to a private owner, not to the state, and only Dakyns, whose translation makes that explicit, is happy with it in the present context. Gauthier's first objection is thus very much to the point.

My solution to this impasse is to offer another interpretation altogether: public income from *fees* of various kinds. One example of such fees would be the *kêrykeia* (announcer's fees) mentioned above, under *c–d*. In that connection it is noteworthy that, according to the 'Old Oligarch', these functionaries 'do better' when there are plenty of overseas litigants in town ([X.] *Ath.Pol.*1.18). And that point in itself brings up the matter of court-fees, *prytaneia*. The Oligarch was surely exaggerating when he implied that these *prytaneia* funded the jurors' pay ([X.] *Ath.Pol.* 1.16). The suspension of private-suit hearings for two short periods in the mid-fourth century, because jurors could not be paid (Demosth. 45.4, several years in the 360s; Demosth. 39.17, in 348), is not something easy to connect with a drop in *prytaneia*-income. Nevertheless, the notion that *prytaneia* were fiscally significant is confirmed by their specific mention in Aristoph. *Wasps* 659 (see above, under *a–b*). Other allusions show that they operated not by a % mechanism but in fixed rate-bands: three drachmas if what was at issue in a case could be costed at less than a thousand, thirty drachmas if it exceeded that figure. Court-fees and fines of other kinds, called by other names (*parakatabolê*, *parastasis*), are also attested: Harrison (1971) 179–83.

Overall, this is an aspect of Athenian state income largely ignored in modern analysis, though Fawcett (2006) 343.5 does include it, unquantified, in his summary tabulations.

(*f*) TAXES. If elements *a–e* in X.'s list have been correctly identified here so far, it must follow that his sixth and final verb, *telesphoroito*, refers to something else. In itself it is every bit as unusual as item *e*'s *misthophoroito*. LSJ proffer the sense 'pay toll or custom' (likewise the translations of Dakyns, Marchant, and Waterfield), but *a–b* have covered that, and in any case the scope of the implicit *telê* here ought not to be constrained so, without good reason. On the contrary: these *telê* are taxes (as Gauthier 86–7)—and even excluding the ones which fall under *a–d* still leaves plenty for this final, catch-all category: the *metoikion* poll-tax (2.1 with Comm.), the *xenika telê* that allowed foreigners to work 'in the agora' (Demosth. 57.31 & 34), and the *pornikon* paid by brothel-keepers (Aeschin. 1.119), to name but three. (On brothels in Peiraieus see e.g. Aristoph. *Peace* 164–5 and Isaeus 6.19–21; Garland (2001) 143 with 214; and further below, **3.12 Once**.)

3.6 to achieve such increases in revenues there is no necessity for additional expenditure. We need only pass beneficent decrees and be attentive For the Greek here ('additional expenditure') see Notes on the Text. Besides the superior manuscript authority for *prosdapanêsai* over *pro-*, only the first of these verbs (both of them exceedingly rare in literary contexts) is attested in Attic epigraphy, albeit in the second century. See lines 10–11 of *IG* II^2 949 (*I.Eleusis* 229), a decree in honour of a demarch of Eleusis, and lines 8–10 of *IG* II^2 1227, a decree of 'the demos of the Salaminioi' (N. F. Jones (1987) 72) honouring a gymnasiarch; both men have spent their own money on cult-related matters in addition to the sums allocated.

Thiel 12–13 and Gauthier 88–9 (and 109) regard 3.6 as the crucial watershed in *Poroi*'s internal arrangement; see already General Intro., section 4 (end). This is because from now on, until the end of Chap.4, X.'s ideas *will* rely on additional expenditure (as well as income). Is their point overstated, if X. himself intended 3.6 to be merely the dividing-line *within Chap.3 itself*? One might be tempted to say so, but for Gauthier's expansion of the argument see under the next lemma. In any event, note that Schorn (2006) distorts *Poroi*'s internal balance by highlighting *only* its cost-free proposals, as both Gray (2006) and Powell (2015) 62 point out.

The phrase 'beneficent decrees' (*psêphismata philanthrôpa*) is without precise parallel in this period. Nonetheless Gauthier 88 must be right to see it as X.'s term for *ad hominem* decrees awarding honours; specifically the ones for foreign traders and others implied in 3.4. (Demosth. 18.209 describes the honorific decree proposed in his favour in 336 as his fellow-citizens showing him 'honour and *philanthrôpia*'.) Honorific inscriptions from the third century onwards commonly use the neuter-plural substantive *philanthrôpa* to encompass the very privileges they are bestowing. And X.'s actual form of words is attested in the 160s, when King Eumenes II of Pergamum (*OCD* 547–8) thanks the Ionian League for the *psêphisma philanthrôpon* that they have voted him, a decree bestowing a crown and a statue: *RC* 52 (Austin (2006) no.239, line 5). This means, Gauthier states, that 'principalement'—the proviso is used twice—such decrees in the present context concern the *xenoi*, while the needs of the metics are dealt with by what

X. calls here *epimeleiai*, literally 'attentions' (a characteristic idiom of his: cf. e.g. *Cyrop.*1.6.4, *Hier.*9.1 & 11, *Kyn.*13.13, *Mem.*2.1.20, *Oec.*7.41, 11.19). Yet even thus qualified, the distinction seems to me forced. True, an elite of the *emporoi* and *nauklêroi* will be the beneficiaries of honorific decrees (3.4)—but so will an elite of *metoikoi* (2.6). Otherwise, the general run of men in *both* categories (which overlap) will have to make do with generic 'attentions': the metics as explained in 2.2–5 and 2.7; the merchants and ship-owners as explained in 3.3.

3.6 As to my other ideas for revenue-raising, I do recognize that they call for start-up capital The noun X. uses here (and again in 3.9, 3.12, and 4.34) is *aphormê*. In broad terms it means a starting-point, as in e.g. Demosth. 18.156 ('the *aphormai* and the pretexts' of Philip's desire for the conquest of Greece), but commonly this takes on concrete form as the cash, resources, or something similar which allows spending to be undertaken. For this in X. see already *Hell.*4.8.32–3, *Mem.*2.7.11–12, *Oec.*1.16.

Gauthier 89 scolds those who translate *aphormê* here as 'capital' (he names Marchant and Bodei Giglioni; one could add Dakyns), on the basis that they are confusing it with *archaion* (as at the end of 3.2, q.v. above). According to Gauthier, a 'capital-*archaion*' is anything of worth—perhaps money, but equally well a house, slaves, etc.—which someone possesses and can sell or otherwise attempt to put to productive use. The resulting profit (theoretically an *ergon*, in practice a *prosodos*) is variable, given that e.g. a house for rent may or may not actually be rented. By contrast, in Gauthier's view, an *aphormê* consists solely and necessarily of cash, earmarked for particular expenditure. It is non-recoverable by the depositor except under certain conditions (and perhaps, in this era, it implied a fixed rate of interest; cf. Demosth. 36.11–14 and 45.5 & 47, and see below, 3.9–10). Thus, he concludes, the distinction between the two halves of *Poroi* is further underlined. So far everything—the Attic climate, the natural advantages of Peiraieus, the presence of metics—has been tantamount to a sort of available *archaion*, which (if properly used) produces good revenues naturally. From now on the topic will be *new* revenues. Some of them will come from the innovatory policies proposed (state-owned hostels and a state-owned merchant fleet here in Chap.3, and especially state-owned mining slaves in Chap.4), but to allow all this to begin there must be ready cash, up-front.

The crispness of this analysis must command respect, even if component parts of it are less clear-cut than they are made to seem. For instance, it is difficult to maintain that an *aphormê* is always, by definition, monetary, when we have cases like the one in Isoc. 19.6: Thrasyllos the Siphnian follows his deceased benefactor Polemainetos in the profession of divination, using as his *aphormai* (pl.) the latter's bequest of property to him and his books on the subject. However, if instances like that are set aside, as being at least quasi-figurative (alongside e.g. *Mem.*3.12.4), the concept works well enough for the four *Poroi* passages. As regards a translation of *aphormê*, I opt for 'start-up capital' on the three occasions where it lacks a definite article (3.6, 3.12, 4.34) and 'the capital fund' in 3.9.

3.7 the thought that the citizens would not contribute eagerly towards such things does not dishearten me Literally, I am not made *dyselpis* by it. This is perhaps litotes (for which see already **1.6 It would**), i.e. a downplayed way of expressing its opposite; thus, with X.'s 'not' suppressed, 'I venture to hope that . . . would' (Marchant), 'I am reasonably confident that . . . will' (Waterfield). In any event, *dyselpis* itself is apparently another of X.'s borrowings from the language of tragic drama: see Aesch. *Cho.*412 (and, in X., already *Hell.*5.4.31).

In reference to creating his start-up capital, X. uses the verb *eispherein* here and again five more times in 3.7–11. However, in 3.9 he employs its more precise cognate noun, and 3.7 applies the verb to two recent instances of what, almost certainly, was an *eisphora* in Athens: 'a proportional levy, imposed when the assembly chose and at a rate which the assembly chose, on all whose declared property exceeded a certain value' (*OCD* 494; cf. Thomsen (1964), Brun (1983) 3–73, Hansen (1991) 112–15); and see the next lemma. From this it might seem reasonable to deduce that the levying mechanism X. has in mind here is, simply, the same one that normal *eisphorai* adopted, but the point is contentious: see below, **3.11 There are also**.

X.'s adverb here, 'eagerly', is one of his favourites (59 instances elsewhere). It is also noteworthy in this particular context because the related noun *prothymia* was another of the cardinal virtues (cf. under **2.5 it seems**) that the Athenians had identified and decided to foster and reward during X.'s lifetime. (See generally Whitehead (1993) at 50, 65–7; fine detail, if required, in Veligianni-Terzi (1997) 195–8, 267–8, 287.) Rewards aside, there was also simple duty, as Demosthenes reminded his fellow-citizens in 349/8: make war (against Philip) wholeheartedly, paying *eisphorai* eagerly and serving in person (Demosth. 1.6; cf. 2.27, where the adverb migrates to the other element).

3.7 the state made large contributions when, under the command of Lysistratos, it was helping the Arkadians, and large ones also when Hegesileos was in command The significance of this passage in providing a *terminus post quem* for the date of *Poroi* has already been noted in the General Intro., section 3. It would be odd if X. was not citing the most recent illustrations he knew, of an *eisphora* levied for terrestrial campaigning. (He does use the verb rather than the noun—cf. under the preceding lemma—and Ste. Croix (1953) 52 believed that these particular 'contributions' had taken the form not of *eisphorai* but voluntary payments, *epidoseis*. For these see in summary Davies (1981) 91–5 and Pritchett (1971–1991) 5.473–85; at monograph length Kuenzi (1923), Migeotte (1992). But the orthodox view is re-stated, against Ste. Croix, by Thomsen (1964) 288–9, and see also e.g. Gauthier 91.

X.'s form of words here, that 'the state' made these contributions, is odd on any count, even if 4.49 offers a broad parallel. Waterfield 172 finesses it into 'how generous the citizenry was'. In any event it seems better suited to a levy across the board than to an aggregate of individual donations.

Lysistratos and Hegesileos, it is universally presumed, were each 'in command' *as generals*—i.e. one of the ten annually elected Athenian *stratêgoi* (*OCD* 1405–6)—on their respective ventures into the central Peloponnese. At first sight it is surprising that X. did not use that actual noun (or the verb related to it), when he had done so freely in earlier works. But for comparison/precedent see Thuc. 2.102.1 (in winter 429/8 Athenian forces mount an expedition from Naupaktos against Astakos 'with Phormion in command (*sc.* as general)'; *AO* 121), and within X. cf. similarly *Hell*.5.1.10 (Demainetos in 388/7; *AO* 217) and 5.4.61 (Chabrias in 376/5; *AO* 238).

Lysistratos (*LGPN* s.v. no.16) is attested only here; which is to say, he cannot be safely identified with any other bearer of this relatively common name. In *AO* 259 it is left open whether his year on the board of generals was 366/5 (so by equating this campaign with the one X. briefly mentions in *Hell*.7.4.6) or 364/3 (by reference to *Hell*.7.4.29 and Diod.Sic. 15.77.1–4). *LGPN* gives '?366/5', but 364/3 is the more orthodox choice.

Hegesileos—a very much rarer name—of (?)Probalinthos, *LGPN* s.v. no.5, is better-known. Besides the campaign X. refers to here, he went on to command the Athenian contingent on the right wing at the battle of Mantineia in 362: so Diog.Laert. 2.54, citing Ephorus *FGrH* 70 F85. (Diod.Sic. 15.84.2 mis-reports the name, as Hegelochos—a common failing of his: see Stylianou (1998) 138 for this and other instances.)

Some years later Hegesileos was to acquire political notoriety. Demosthenes, during his prosecution of Aeschines in 343 for misconduct as envoy to Philip, rhetorically berates the great Euboulos (General Intro., section 6) for his willingness to testify in Aeschines' support. That is contrasted with the fact, as alleged, that Euboulos had previously refused to do so for his 'cousin' (*anepsios*) Hegesileos when the latter was on trial. Given the rarity of the name, this man is sure to be the (ex-)general. As regards the trial, a learned scholiast (annotator) on the passage refers to events that can be placed in 349/8. A general again in that year, Hegesileos was in command of Athenian military operations on the nearby island of Euboia, designed to help Ploutarchos, the tyrant of Eretria (*OCD* 534–5, *IACP* no.370), but the pair somehow conspired to 'deceive the [Athenian] demos'. This sounds like one of the classic criteria that could justify a prosecution by impeachment, *eisangelia* (so, chiefly, [Demosth.] 49.67), though Hansen (1975) 62–3 with n.39 tentatively classifies Hegesileos' trial among those stemming from the mandatory audits, *euthynai*, at the end of an official's term of office.

3.8 I also understand that triremes are often sent out equipped at great expense For the Greek here ('equipped') see Notes on the Text.

The tone seems tentative, almost as if X. the former commander of cavalry and infantry is less sure of his ground when it comes to naval warfare. (This verb in the first person singular, *epistamai*, had been used by Thucydides only in speeches, never *in propria persona*. Likewise, in X., see *Anab*.1.3.15, *Cyrop*.1.5.11, 2.2.2, *Oec*.12.4, 15.8, 18.3, 19.1 & 14–16, *Symp*.4.6. The only parallels to the present instance of X. writing as himself are the two in *Lac.Pol*.14.4, on Sparta past and present.) At any rate it is curious that he names no names, to match those of Lysistratos and Hegesileos in 3.7. The general point is conveyed in brisker terms at 4.40: 'the *eisphorai* which have been levied during the current war' (also bemoaned by Isoc. 8.12 & 20); cf. *Hell*.6.2.1 on the mid-370s (with the table in Pritchard (2015) 111, calculating 927 and 998 *talanta* respectively for 376/5 and 375/4).

3.8 the only certainty being that payers will never get back what they contribute, or will even share in what they contribute Following Herzog (1914) 472–3, Gauthier 91–2 expands on the conceptual implications of this statement, particularly the idea of 'sharing in' (*metechein*) an *eisphora*-contribution one has made; in plain terms, getting a return on it. Citizens of present-day states never dream that paying their taxes is anything other than money exacted. At most they hope it will be well spent, in a generic, community-wide way. Athenian citizens in X.'s day might reasonably expect that an *eisphora* devoted to military expenditure would bring victories and accrue advantages to Athens—but beyond (or alongside) that, there was the older idea conveyed by the name *eisphora* itself. Taxes (*telê*) proper were tolerable because they taxed specific activities, which one had, or might have, the choice not to engage in. Citizens did not subject themselves to direct poll-taxation. (That was the mark of the metics: 2.1.) Citizens did—unless too poor—tolerate *eisphorai*, in theory and practice, but 'contributing' them could lead to self-praise (e.g. Lys. 7.31, 18.7, 19.29, 21.3, 25.12) of a kind rarely seen among clients of HMRC (or the IRS in the United States); and, as we are made aware by the present passage, it was also acceptable to allude to the fact that the only thing the payers shared was a farewell to their money. On this cluster of topics see also e.g. Austin & Vidal-Naquet (1977) 118–24; Fawcett (2006) 161–6; Fawcett (2016) 156–8.

Though it does not concern Athens, the anecdote from [Aristot.] *Oec.*2.1349a29–32, cited by Gauthier, serves to point out that the idea of *eisphora*-payers being reimbursed did exist in the period. Short of money for his fleet, the Syracusan tyrant Dionysios I (*OCD* 459–60) convenes the assembly, announces that a city is ripe for capture, and orders an *eisphora*. Two or three days later he declares himself mistaken and repays the money. Thus, on a later occasion the Syracusans pay a required *eisphora*, supposing 'that they would get it back' (*apolêpsesthai*: X.'s very word here)—but of course they never do.

3.9 But they would not earn so fine a return from anything as from the money they paid in advance into the capital fund X.'s Greek is more awkward than translations (including this one) make it sound: 'not acquire so fine an acquisition'. For paying in advance (already *Ages.*1.18, *Anab.*7.7.25) see again 3.10.

As Gauthier 93 comments, X. takes a short-cut here. After introducing the idea of his levy (3.7) he could have explained its use(s), what capital it will raise, how the capital will be managed, and *finally* what benefits of it the citizens will perceive (and when). Instead—and no doubt to prevent his readers, alarmed by the thought of a new *eisphora*, from immediately throwing his dissertation onto the fire (so Gauthier)—he loses no time in focusing on the glittering prizes: the profits that will result. This is not the organizational clumsiness that Thiel 49 saw here;

nor is it a justification for regarding 3.9-10 as misplaced (as Wilhelm (1934) 44–9 did, wanting to transfer it to the end of 4.33). It is, rather, good psychology; cf. Bodei Giglioni lxxxi.

3.9 Every contributor of ten *mnai* receives almost a fifth, just as in a maritime loan, by taking three *oboloi* a day X. now proceeds (in 3.9–10) to depict three specimen contributors, working from high to low: ten-*mna*, five-*mna*, one-*mna*. (Gauthier 94 searches for some intrinsic rationale in the figures chosen, but does not really find one.) First, the wealthiest. Such a man pays in a thousand drachmas (10 *mnai*) but takes out half a drachma (3 *oboloi*) per day, so on a 360-day year that makes 180 drachmas per annum; and as X. rightly says, 180 drachmas is 'almost a fifth' (almost 20%) of his original thousand.

The comparandum supplied here is 'just as in a *nautikon*', literally 'a maritime (something)', but the implied noun is not in doubt: loan, *daneion*. See in brief *OCD* 899; more fully e.g. Isager & Hansen (1975) 74–84, Millett (1991) 188–96; Bresson (2016) 280–5; at length Cohen (1992) 44–60, 121–83. 'To pay for a cargo, a merchant or ship-owner borrowed money for the duration of the voyage. Loan and interest were repaid out of proceeds of sale of the cargo only on condition that the ship arrived safely at its destination; loss was otherwise borne by the lender. High risks justified high interest' (*OCD*). Interest-rates calculable from the mention of such loans in the speeches generated by litigation in fourth-century Athens fall in a range between 12½%, for a one-way journey from Sestos (*OCD* 1356, *IACP* no.672) on the western side of the Hellespont down to Athens ([Demosth.] 50.17), and 22½-30% for an Athens/Crimea/Athens return trip (Demosth. 34.23, 35.30). The higher figure in the latter case reflects not only distance (much longer) but also timing (a voyage after mid-September, i.e. in more hazardous weather conditions). Here again, therefore, X. cannot be faulted. His highest-band contributor could indeed expect a return comparable with a typical *nautikon*. (From the same sources, attested sums invested in this way range between a thousand drachmas—X.'s figure here—and five thousand.)

Millett (1983) 42: '[t]he allusion to maritime credit in the *Poroi* is remarkable for its brevity. Xenophon's readers were expected to grasp the significance of a two-word comparison between his own money-making scheme, and the mechanism of maritime loans. And the same goes for all the other casual references to maritime credit in the literature. Writers apparently made the assumption that the general principles of maritime loans were familiar to all Athenians.' (In fact Millett himself had already sought to show, in Millett (1980), that this goes beyond Athens. Diog.Laert. 6.99, on the third-century Cynic writer Menippos of Gadara (*OCD* 933), attacks Menippos ostensibly for being a maritime lender; actually, on Millett's interpretation, for lending money at rates of interest *appropriate to* the returns on maritime loans.)

X.'s invocation of maritime loans here is one reason for the existence of a line of interpretation which characterizes *his entire scheme here in 3.9–11* as one of (compulsory) loans, to the state. So Thiel 48–50 (Excursus VII); Von der Lieck (1933) 41; Bodei Giglioni lxxxiv, citing the analogy of Lykourgos' investment of 'large sums of money belonging to private individuals' which generated 650 *talanta* (so the document transcribed in [Plut.] *Orat.*852B, cf. 841D). Gauthier 101–3 convincingly protests, on several counts; and see also Jansen (2007) 341–2. It is true that, besides the Lykourgos instance in Athens, such loans are nowadays quite well attested (by epigraphical documents) in other cities at various times during the late fourth century and on into the third. Léopold Migeotte is the expert in this field: his work was still in progress when Gauthier wrote, but see now Migeotte (1984). Two things are clear: loans were solicited more often from foreigners than from citizens, and there were often problems in repaying the capital and interest within the period(s) specified—a difficulty met by appealing to the generosity of rich citizens to advance the money necessary for repayment. Be that as it may, the basic point is that in loan-schemes the lenders could at some point expect their original capital back, with interest. But here in X.'s scheme the contributors will get neither (as in an *eisphora*: 3.8). Rather, their return is simply an allowance set at a universal three *oboloi* a day. See further below, **3.11 There are**.

3.9 For five-*mna* contributors the return will be more than a third Equally correct. These middle-band contributors pay 500 drachmas, and again take out 180, which at 35% is indeed fractionally more than a third of their outlay.

3.10 The majority of Athenians, though, will take more each year than they contribute—because those whose advance payment is one *mna* will have a revenue of almost two *mnai* Fair comment again, it would seem. Pay 100 drachmas (one *mna*); receive 180.

Cartledge in Waterfield 224 takes issue with X.'s phrase 'the majority of Athenians', implying as it does that the three contribution-bands have now covered, from top to bottom, the whole citizen-body. Not so, as already perceived by Gauthier 100. In sober truth, 'the majority of Athenians' were *penêtes* (see **1.1 the poverty**) or worse, many of them in no position whatsoever to lay hands on a lump sum of a hundred drachmas; the jurors, for example, whose daily *misthos* (as also X.'s *triôbolon* here) was half a drachma. Loomis (1998) 232–9 has demolished the old orthodoxy of a 'standard' Athenian daily wage of one drachma, but, without it, the norm appears to drop lower. Just as with the existing *eisphora*-system itself, therefore, X.'s scheme excludes the poor—*as contributors*. See further below, **3.11 There are.**

3.10 And this will be based in a city-state, a context which seems to be the safest and most enduring of man-made institutions X.'s words here echo what he had written in *Mem.*1.4.16: '*poleis* and *ethnê* are the most enduring and wisest of man-made institutions'; cf. Thiel xvi. (On *ethnê* defined as Hellenic states without developed urban centres see Austin & Vidal-Naquet (1977) 78–80.) More generally, Thiel 14 and Gauthier 95 cite Isoc. 8.120 on the 'deathlessness' (*athanasia*) of states, which should oblige them to act sensibly.

The phrase 'in a city-state' (*en polei*) here catches the attention. The standard interpretation of it is that X. is commending this form of 'investment' because participation in it did not entail leaving Athens. So e.g. Thiel 14; Von der Lieck (1933) 42, and the translation of Bodei Giglioni ('senza uscire dallo stato'). However, Gauthier 95–6 challenges this on grounds of both language (such a sense would need the definite article) and thought. If a *contributor*'s residence 'in a city-state' was the advantage being claimed, he could just as well move from Athens to another. Instead, what is 'in' a state—Athens in this case, since it is Athens X. is catering for—is *the 'investment' itself* (like gilt-edged stocks in the UK, or US treasury bonds), more secure than anything in what nowadays we would call the private sector. (Gauthier commends Marchant's Loeb translation for bringing this out strongly: 'an income...guaranteed by the state'. See also Schütrumpf 89 with n.16, and the translation of Waterfield 172 ('these returns are provided by a state').)

3.11 many foreigners would also contribute if by doing so they would have their names inscribed as 'benefactors for all time' Perhaps these 'foreigners' include metics, though by this stage in Chap.3 X. is concentrating on non-resident *xenoi*.

Whatever the case with that, it is unclear quite what he has in mind here by this procedure of inscribing (literally, writing up) their names.

What might be *consolidated lists*, of '*proxenoi* or benefactors or recipients of other honours', are mentioned in late fourth-century Lebedos and Teos (see under **2.6 If the state**): *RC* 3–4 (*SIG* 344; Austin (2006) no.48) lines 21–4. No such thing is attested in Athens, however. It is not until 243 that the Athenians are definitely known to have inscribed and set up a list of both citizens and non-citizens who had paid a voluntary *epidosis* (within a prescribed range of 50–200 drachmas): *IG* II^2 791, now *Agora* 16 243; Habicht (1997) 163. (Isaeus 5.37–8, referring to *epidoseis* invited in 392, mentions a 'naming and shaming' list of those who had promised to pay but did not. Rhodes (2010) 369 is not justified in stating that an associated list named those who did. For the same idea but as no more than a conjecture see Wyse (1904) 463.) X. is probably envisaging standard, individual *ad hominem* decrees, where this act of generosity would be mentioned; cf. Liddel (2007) 164.

I have suggested by quotation marks that the phrase 'benefactors for all time', as a totality, is what X. supposes these decrees will say. (The alternative is plain 'benefactors', *euergetai*.) He had used the phrase 'for all time' twice in *Hell.*: in 4.8.4 Derkylidas (*OCD* 442) urges the men of Abydos (*OCD* 1–2, *IACP* no.765) to become '*euergetai*' of the Spartans, which would be 'remembered for all time'; in 6.5.41 Prokles of Phleious similarly urges the Athenians to become 'friends' (*philoi*) of Sparta 'for all time'. See also e.g. Andoc. 3.29 on a treaty with Persia, Isoc. 8.142 on a putative Athenian hegemony. In documents on stone, this phrase (in its several variants) is in fact more characteristic of treaties etc. than of honorific decrees, though note RO 21 (Austin & Vidal-Naquet (1977) no.71, Harding (1985) no.40): in the (?)370s Straton I, king of Sidon (*OCD* 1364), is created '*proxenos* of the Athenian people, himself and his descendants' and he is assured that 'in time to come, as a good man towards the Athenian people, he will not fail to obtain from the Athenians whatever he needs'. See further under the next lemma.

3.11 There are also some states which would be keen to join such a list. I expect too that certain kings and dynasts and satraps would wish to share in this display of gratitude For 'I expect' cf. e.g. *Oec.*2.10, *Symp.*4.32–3.

Thiel 14–15 briefly considers each of these four categories in turn and endeavours to furnish them with specific names. (What follows here fleshes out Thiel's listings very considerably.)

(*a*) 'States' (*poleis*). Thiel takes this to mean, in particular, those member-states of the Second Athenian League which had not seceded either before or during the Social War, such as Karystos (see RO 48 (Harding (1985) no.65)), Mytilene, Thasos, and various Cycladic islands. See generally Rhodes (2010) 276–8. Of particular note in the present context are the inventory-documents *IG* II^2 1437, 1438, 1441, and 1443: they record crowns dedicated in Athens by more than a dozen states during the decade 354/3 to 345/4. Not quite all of them are imperial allies, e.g. Knossos (*OCD* 340 Cn-, *IACP* no.967) on Crete, but mostly they are.

Thiel also adds Sparta. This seems reasonable enough, given that both Sparta and Athens at this time were favourably disposed to Phokis, rather than to the Boiotians, over the matter of Delphi: see Diod.Sic. 16.27.5, and the Comm. to 5.9.

(*b*) 'Kings' (*basileis*). In the eastern Mediterranean, Thiel judges, this means the kings of Egypt (currently Nectanebo II: see e.g. Diod. Sic. 15.92.3–4, 16.41.3), of Cyprus (currently Euagoras II, who however soon turned pro-Persian), and of the several principalities that made up Phoinikia. (An instance of the latter, Sidon, has been cited under the preceding lemma, q.v. Straton I was by now dead; after the brief reign of Tennes, Straton II was now king. F. G. Maier in *CAH* 6.317–26 calls these Phoinikian communities 'city states'. Though they do display some civic features, in essence they are mini-kingdoms.)

As kingdoms abutting the northern Aegean, Thiel nominates those of the Thrakians, the Illyrians, and the Molossians. 'Thrakians' means primarily the Odrysians, who were allied with Athens during the Peloponnesian War but a nuisance during the Second League. See generally Z. H. Archibald in *CAH* 6.444–75 and Archibald (1998). Since the death of king Kotys I in 359, Berisades, Amadokos, and Kotys' son Kersebleptes (the last of these is *OCD* 301–2 Cerso-) were in theory joint rulers; RO 47 (Harding (1985) no.64) shows the Athenians making a treaty with all three of them in 357; but Berisades was soon dead, and another treaty (in 356: RO 53 (Harding (1985) no.70) saw his sons—'Ketriporis and his brothers'—becoming allies of Athens, alongside the then kings of Paionia (to the west of the Odrysians) and Grabaian Illyria (further west still). As regards the Molossians (*OCD* 966) of Epeiros, the relevant document is RO 70 (the Athenians grant sanctuary to their expelled king Arybbas), from 342; see the RO commentary there (pp.352–5).

Finally under this head Thiel adds Philip II of Macedon (*OCD* 1128), on the sort of calculations used in Isoc. 8.22–3.

(*c*) 'Dynasts' (*tyrannoi*). We should note first that the boundary between *tyrannoi* and *b*'s *basileis* is imprecise. Titulature could change, especially (though not solely) when hereditary succession had been accomplished. That said, according to Thiel this category would contain, first and foremost, the several dynasts in nearby Euboia. He adduces Aeschin. 3.85, where Euboia's two principal cities are singled out: Chalkis (*OCD* 304, *IACP* no.365) and Eretria (*OCD* 534–5, *IACP* no.370). The authors of these two *IACP* entries (K. Reber, M. H. Hansen, and P. Ducrey) point out that Aeschines' mention of the anti-Athenian actions of Mnesarchos and his sons Kallias and Taurosthenes in Chalkis falls short of proof that they were the tyrant family of the city (as opposed to prominent democratic leaders—a possibility positively suggested by the evidence for the brothers, who both became honorary Athenian citizens in the late 340s, if Aeschin. 3.85–92 is read in full). On the other hand Aeschines' 'Themison' at Eretria (also in Diod. Sic. 15.76.1) does fit into a context of other evidence for several Eretrian *tyrannoi*, perhaps discontinuously, between the early 360s and the early 340s.

Thiel also names Klearchos of Herakleia in the Black Sea (*OCD* 662–3 Heraclea (3) Pontica, *IACP* no.715; Burstein (1974), esp.47–65); Tisiphonos of Pherai in Thessaly (*OCD* 1124, *IACP* no.414; Diod.Sic. 16.14.1 on T.); and the—by now numerous—tyrants in Sicily (see generally H. D. Westlake in *CAH* 6.706–10).

(*d*) 'Satraps' (*satrapai*). Unless X. is using the term unusually loosely, he means Persian provincial governors: *OCD* 1321. (In X. cf. *Ages*.8.5, *Anab*.1.1.2 and passim, *Cyrop*.7.4.2 and passim, *Hell*.3.1.3 & 10–12, *Oec*.4.7 & 11.) The Athenians were formally at peace with Persia at this time (Diod.Sic. 16.44.1), after the turmoil of the so-called Satraps' Revolt which had come to a head in the late 360s: see in brief *OCD* 1321 (a separate entry from the above) and RO 42 (Harding (1985) no.57); more detail in *CAH* 6.84–90 (S. Hornblower). Consequently, X. must have in mind renegade western governors such as Orontes, of Armenia or Mysia—awarded Athenian citizenship in ?349/8 (M. J. Osborne (1981–1983) D12, now *IG* II^{3} 295/*AIO*)—and Artabazos (*OCD* 174), of Hellespontine Phrygia. Hornblower characterises the pair as, respectively, the Old and Young Pretenders of their era (*CAH* 6.90).

Thiel's lists are serviceable enough as the summary ones they were intended to be, and Gauthier 96 was happy enough to take them over—adding only, and tacitly, Thiel's single glaring omission: the Spartokid ruling dynasty (*OCD* 1392) in the grain-rich Crimea. They had been part of the Athenian honorific network since the 430s; see RO 64 (Harding (1985) no.82), now *IG* II^3 298/*AIO*, from 346. Nevertheless, it is fair comment (Gauthier 97) that the bigger picture must also be contemplated. Within it, he notes Hellenistic-era demonstrations of generosity by X.'s kings, dynasts, and states towards two communities that had been blighted by disaster: Thebes, finally rebuilt in 316 after Alexander's sack nearly two decades earlier (Diod.Sic. 19.53–4, etc.; Habicht (1997) 61–2); and Rhodes, devastated by an earthquake in 227 (Polybius 5.88–90 = Austin (2006) no.111). One could add, in a broadly similar vein, RO 96 (Harding (1985) no.116). There Kyrene, a successful outpost of Hellenism in present-day Libya (*OCD* 405–6 Cyr-, *IACP* no.1028), ships large quantities of grain north to Aegean Hellas during the region-wide shortages of the first half of the 320s; 12½% of it—some six million kg.—goes to Athens (Garnsey (1988) 159–61). However, as Gauthier remarks, X. the proud Athenian is not formulating his ideas on the basis that *his* city should be an object of pity (or proto-Hellenistic royal condescension). What he expects is what he says here: that these other states and other entities will be glad to be associated with such a great city as Athens. And cases like Orontes, the Spartokids, and king Arybbas of the Molossoi (RO 70, from 342) suggest that his expectations were not unrealistic.

Concerning 3.11 as a whole, X.'s thinking begs obvious comparison with a declaration made in Demosthenes' speech 20 *Against Leptines*, written (and delivered in court) at almost exactly the same time. Participating for the first time in his career in a 'public' prosecution, one which maintained that Leptines' law to abolish exemptions from liturgies was 'not expedient' (see Hansen (1974) 44–8, at 47 n.21), the thirty-something Demosthenes devotes a substantial part of this speech to named examples of honorands who (and/or whose descendants) would allegedly be disadvantaged by the law, if passed. Two of these individuals are Athenian generals: Konon of Anaphlystos (*LGPN* s.v. no.21, *OCD* 361 s.v. Conon (1), *APF* 506–9) and Chabrias of Aixone (*LGPN* s.v. no.2, *OCD* 302, *APF* 560–1); see Demosth. 20.68–87. The bulk, though, are non-resident non-citizens; foreign VIPs, in short. After chap.63, when the clerk of the court has read out decrees in honour of two groups of men for political services in their native Thasos (Ekphantos et al; partially preserved as *IG* II^2 33) and Byzantium (Herakleides et al.; cf. *IG* II^2 8), Demosthenes underlines the issue as follows: 'the proper thing to do is to allow these *stelai* to hold good for all time, so that, as long as any of the men are alive, they suffer no injustice at your hands, and when they die, those *stelai* may be a memorial of our city's character, and may stand as examples (*paradeigmata*) to those who wish to do us a benefit, recording how many benefactors the city has benefited in return' (Demosth. 20.64). More broadly, many honorific decrees from the third quarter of the fourth century onwards include a clause (in several variant forms) exhorting others to emulate the behaviour of the honorand, and promising rewards like his if they do so—a virtuous upward spiral of reciprocation. See in brief Whitehead (1983) 62–4; more fully, on the formulaic language, Henry (1996); fullest, on content and context, Cook (2009), Lambert (2011a), and J. Miller (2016).

* * * *

Before following X. into 3.12–14, on how the capital fund once established might be used, the nature of his proposed *means* of establishing it must again be addressed. Under **3.9 Every contributor**, the idea (held by Thiel and others) that contributors to it were making *loans* was examined, and it proved easy enough to discard. Put simply, this is not a loan-scheme because no contributor gets his money back. But two possibilities are still left. One—prompted not solely but especially by the present section with its expectation that non-resident non-citizens and even other states (etc.) will participate—is that what X. is proposing here is a matter of donations; the so-called *epidoseis* to which I have alluded already (**3.7 the state** and **3.11 many foreigners**); so e.g. Ste. Croix (1953) 52. The other option, championed by Gauthier, is that this is a special kind of *eisphora*.

The vocabulary of the issue, first, is not quite as clear-cut as Gauthier 98 makes it sound. For the verb *eispherein* used of contributions in circumstances other than that of an *eisphora* proper, he cites only, and as examples, the *eranos* (*OCD* 532) contributions mentioned in [Demosth.] 53.8 and 59.32 and the interest-free loans made to the city of Erythrai (*OCD* 537, *IACP* no.845) by one of its rich citizens called Phanes (*SIG* 285; now *I.Erythrai* 21, with a dating of (?)334–332). In fact such instances can be multiplied, without going outside Athens during X.'s lifetime, *and with reference only to epidoseis*. Besides claims in court (Lys. 30.26 and 31.15; Demosth. 45.69) which might be treating language in unorthodox ways, the published list of those who had not paid the *epidoseis* of 392 that they had promised, as quoted in Isaeus 5.38, twice uses the verb *eispherein*. (Gauthier 98 n.27 is justified in pointing out that Isaeus' own language in 5.37 might be purposely conflating the vocabulary of *eisphorai* and of *epidoseis* in order to blacken the opponent, but 5.38 comes from an official document.) Yet on the other side of the argument, within the microcosm of *Poroi* itself 4.40 is key to understanding X.'s own position on the matter; cf. Gauthier 100. During the span of a single sentence there he glides from 'the *eisphorai* which have been levied during the current war' to 'no possibility of further contributions'—*eisenegkein*, the irregular aorist infinitive of *eispherein*, already in 3.11, and cf. e.g. (explicitly applied to *eisphorai*) Lys. 22.13, Isoc. 15.108 & 156, *IG* II^2 554 (*SIG* 329), lines 8–11 (honours for the metic Euxenides of Phaselis, late fourth century; Oliver (2007) 96).

As mentioned above, the participation of non-resident foreigners et al.—the qualifier 'non-resident' is needed because *metics*, of an eligible property-level, were liable to *eisphora* (Demosth. 22.61, etc.; Whitehead (1977) 78–80)—might seem a strong indication that X.'s scheme here is founded on *epidoseis*. Gauthier's rejoinder is to point out that in 3.7 X. has envisaged 'the citizens' as the contributors. Only here in 3.11, as a species of afterthought, does he surmise that *xenoi* too would be keen to join in, for the sheer kudos of it (Gauthier 99–100).

Arguing expressly against Gauthier, Jansen (2007) 342–6, summarized in Jansen (2012) 740–1, ably restates the view that X's idea was for *epidoseis*, i.e. voluntary contributions by anyone who made them. Even so, I remain unconvinced that 3.6–10 visualizes the payments made by Athenian citizens as optional. If they were not, this was to be an *eisphora*—but an *eisphora* of an unprecedented kind. It would be a 'peace' *eisphora* as opposed to a 'war' *eisphora* (Gauthier 99, 101), and it would entail twin novelties: a relatively tangential novelty of method, and a crucial novelty of aim (Gauthier 97 and 100–1). The procedural innovation is to invite voluntary contributions from outside the community, as an augmentation of the compulsory ones coming from inside it. The innovation in aim is to pay all Athenian citizens a daily *triôbolon*. (The sum is quantified only in 3.9, but it relates to two other passages: 4.17, where it takes the form of three slaves per citizen who each bring in an *obolos* a day, and 4.33, on which see below.) Gauthier 104–5 calculates that there might be a delay of five or six years before the *triôbolon* could be distributed, and he considers this something that X. would not have wished his readers to realize. Be that as it may, Gauthier follows Herzog (1914) 473 and Wilhelm (1934) 32–4 and 46 in insisting that the payments, when ultimately payable, would go to all citizens (4.33), whether they had been contributors or not. (There had been no need to mention non-contributors in 3.9–10 because their gain had no payment offsetting it.)

As should be clear, it is hard to decide categorically between these two options, *eisphora* or *epidosis*. And perhaps it is not essential to do so, if we keep in mind the novelties of X.'s plan. Neither pigeonhole is an exact fit (cf. Pritchett (1971–1991) 474 n.708).

3.12 Once start-up capital was there, a fine and good project to spend it on is building hostels for ship-owners—besides the existing ones—around the harbours On 'fine and good' see **3.4 Another**.

X. writes 'hostels' (*katagôgia*) here and 'public hostels' (*dêmosia katagôgia*) at the end of the sentence: see the next lemma. Though I have translated what he wrote, Gauthier 105 is surely right to think that 'public' applies to both. X. is not saying that some are 'public' whereas others—these first ones—are not. In adding a category of people to their clientele it simply occurs to him to specify that they are in public ownership (and as such would be leased by the *pôlêtai* to private landlords; see further below, **3.14 to lease**).

The term *katagôgion* itself is uncommon, even though Thuc. 3.68.3 had used it of the large, two-storey structure built in 427, for festival pilgrims, on the site of the destroyed Plataiai (*OCD* 1154, *IACP* no.216). As regards Peiraieus, X. here reveals that some existed already (and indeed one would be surprised to learn otherwise), but perhaps they were not always salubrious, or in salubrious surroundings; Garland (2001) 143 cites Aristoph. *Frogs* 112–15 on the underworld's succession of 'harbours, bread-shops, brothels, resting-up places... accommodations, landladies where there are fewest bugs'. (X.'s own *katagôgia* will not be brothels, unless clandestinely: see under **4.49 from state-owned houses.**)

For 'ship-owners' (*nauklêroi*) see already 3.4 and again 5.3 (and under **3.1 My next topic**). Here in 3.12, uniquely, they are mentioned outside the *nauklêroi*-and-*emporoi* pairing, but for the latter see under the next lemma.

3.12 It is also a fine idea to do the same for merchants, at places suitable for both buying and selling, and to have public hostels also for people who come here as visitors Thiel 15 observes that if hostels are to be built for *nauklêroi* (see the preceding lemma) and also for visitors, it would make no sense not to have them for *emporoi* also. Likewise, implicitly, Gauthier 105. Most translators (Dakyns, Marchant, Waterfield) ignore the issue, seeing here only X's 'places suitable for both buying and selling' being provided for the merchants—which they would surely have already. The Thiel/Gauthier position is unassailable, and I follow it here. The point is that whereas the ship-owners' accommodation will be 'around the harbours', near their vessels, that of the *emporoi* will be closer to places like the 'display-area', *deigma* (Garland (2001) 84, 86, 154).

By contrast, it is not important to specify a location for the hostels for visitors, especially since not all of their customers would be visiting for commercial reasons; cf. Thuc. 3.68.3, cited under the preceding lemma.

3.13 both housing and shopping-centres should be organized for the retailers, in Peiraieus and also in the town. It would be a feather in the state's cap and, at the same time, generate many sources of revenue Besides the wholesale sector (*emporoi* and *nauklêroi*), X. also wants better facilities for retailers. Here again there is a background assumption that they are non-citizens; and here again (cf. Chap.3 intro.) this seems to be true as a broad generalization with a sizeable minority of exceptions. In any event, they could have been referred to here by the term *kapêloi*; see 4.6 for the related abstract noun. 'The *kapêlos* is the local dealer—the man who in general does not leave his own place of residence for the purpose of either importing or exporting, but confines himself to selling on the home market' (Hasebroek (1933) 1). That definition works equally well for the term X. does use here: *agoraios*, literally market-man. See already *Cyrop*.1.2.3 (on the tranquil and cultured Persian 'free agora', which excludes 'sales and the *agoraioi* and their noises and shouts and vulgarities'), and the equally disparaging periphrasis in *Mem*.3.7.6 ('those trafficking in the *agora* and thinking of what they can buy cheap and sell dear'). Here in *Poroi* there is no place for such snobbery if Peiraieus, and Athens at large, is to be revitalized.

'Housing' for them is a different concept from the owner-occupied town-houses for selected metics proposed in 2.6. This is accommodation for rent. Most probably, as Gauthier 106 envisages, it involves the kind of multiple dwellings referred to elsewhere as *synoikiai*. See e.g. [X.] *Ath.Pol*.1.18, Isae. 5.27 and 6.21, Demosth. 36.6 and 45.28, [Demosth.] 53.13, Aeschin. 1.124; Finley (1952) 64–5; Cohen (1992) 212.

As regards the business premises X. wants for the retailers, some translators render it 'shops' (Marchant, Bodei Giglioni, Waterfield). However, not merely does the very rare noun *pôlêtêria* (literally 'selleries') suggest that he has in mind something grander than that, like Schütrumpf's 'Verkaufshallen', but also (Gauthier 106–7) it is something that, as he adds, would be a *kosmos* to the state; cf. already **2.4 it would be.** (Saliou (2015) 133, taking the present passage in isolation, juxtaposes it with Plat. *Leg.*6.779B and Aristot. *Pol.*7.1330b on walls, as illustration of the beauty some saw in utilitarian buildings. Though the point need not be rejected outright, evaluating 3.13 with 2.4 does suggest that for X. himself the *kosmos* was primarily an ethical matter: the adoption of ideas that would do Athens credit.)

3.14 The state already possesses publicly owned warships The surrender-treaty of 404 had reduced Athens' fleet of triremes to a token dozen (*Hell.*2.2.20), and the ensuing regime of the Thirty—ideologically opposed to sea-power and its intimate connection with democracy—had made sure to destroy the Peiraieus dockyards and ship-sheds (Lys. 12.99, Isoc. 7.66). But regeneration had begun within a decade and continued until X.'s day (and beyond). A naval inventory for 378/7 shows 106 vessels (*IG* II^{2} 1604, corroborating Polyb. 2.62.6 against Diod.Sic. 15.29.6–7), overwhelmingly triremes. Later lists give totals of 283 in 357/6 and 349 (seven of them unseaworthy) in 353/2; Garland (2001) 97.

The vessels themselves were indeed *dêmosiai*, as X. says, and the state also supplied their basic equipment and (usually) the pay for the crews; but the trierarchy liturgy performed by the richest citizens (*OCD* 1507) furnished the costs of maintenance and repair. By the time of *Poroi* the burden of this had had to be progressively shared out: first (before 406) by the introduction of co-trierarchies, men in pairs; then (in 357) by resort to *symmoriai*, syndicates of contributors. See generally Gabrielsen (1994), esp. chap.8.

3.14 Suppose it was also possible to have publicly owned *merchant* ships On merchant ships see already under **3.4 those who seem.** X. uses here, for once, quite a commonplace term, *holkades* (already *Anab.*1.4.6, *Hell.*5.1.23). The name literally meant a vessel that had to be towed (from the verb *helkein*), but the concept should not mislead; it meant in practice a vessel powered only by sail, not oars (Casson (1995) 169 with n.2).

X. presents this idea of publicly owned *holkades* as a 'good thing *to try*': a novelty. And novel it would have been—across the Greek world as a whole, if the evidence can be trusted; cf. generally Ste. Croix (1972) 393–6 (but see further below). As regards Athens in particular, Gauthier 108 cites the apposite document, almost contemporary with *Poroi*. In RO 40 (partially in Austin & Vidal-Naquet (1977) no.86 and Crawford & Whitehead (1983) no.282) Athens sought, at some time around the mid-fourth century, to secure a monopoly on the export of ochre, *miltos*, from three of the cities on the nearest of the Cycladic islands, Keos (*OCD* 299, *IACP* nos.491–4); among the matters regulated is the ships that can be used, which must be ones that the Athenians designate. Going that far was one thing; going as far as X.'s suggestion entailed another (Gauthier 108).

While no scheme of this kind is attested earlier than X., a third-century instance has been noted in the General Intro., section 7 (at n.119): the *dêmosia ploia* of Olbia in the Black Sea (*OCD* 1035; *IACP* no.690). Gauthier 108 took them to be 'évidemment' warships, here given the task of transporting heavy stone building-blocks. To D. M. Lewis (1990) 254 with n.25 it was equally obvious that this was a recourse to private merchant vessels while the public ones were in disrepair; likewise in the translation of the document as Austin (2006) no.115, 'public (transport) ships'. (Müller (2011) does not address the point.)

As a medieval comparandum, Bresson (2003) 158 (again Bresson (2016) 385) cites the instance of the Republic of Venice, studied by Lane (1973) 126–34. From 1314 onwards La Serenissima maintained a state-owned merchant fleet, which traded with ports in both the eastern Mediterranean and north-west Europe (though private commerce remained predominant).

3.14 to lease them out under guarantee, just like the other things in public ownership Including, we must presume, the other new *dêmosia* proposed here in 3.12–14 (Gauthier 105, 108). See also 4.19–20 for the role of leasing (and guarantees) in X.'s proposal for a large body of publicly owned slaves.

The system in general, leasing-out by the *pôlêtai*, is summarily described in ?Aristot. *Ath.Pol.* 47.2–3; Hansen (1991) 260–2. X.'s phrase which I have translated 'under guarantee' is more precisely, in the Greek, 'on condition of guarantors'. Such a guarantor (*eggyêtês*)—not of course confined to the present type of transaction: cf. Todd (1993) 212–14—would put up collateral as guarantee for a lessee's performance of whatever he had contracted to do, and was liable to forfeit if he defaulted. The 'Catalogue of lessees and guarantors of polis-controlled *temenê* [tracts of land belonging to a deity]' in Papazarkadas (2011) 299–325 lists by name more than forty *eggyêtai*. (As a rule they serve individually, though a couple of pairs are attested.)

In the case, here, of X.'s *dêmosiai holkades*, Gauthier 106 envisages a leasing of one vessel per lessee-plus-guarantor. Why he rules out less cumbersome procedures is not made clear.

CHAPTER FOUR

Chap.1 has already given a brief survey of the natural assets of Attica. Most of them are not mentioned again. But here in Chap.4 X. returns to the silver-deposits (1.5), doing so because he has a great deal more to say of them.

Desultory mining of the argentiferous lead ore of the Laureion region dates back to the early Bronze Age. It had continued sporadically from then until the 480s (after the stimulus, from the mid-sixth century onwards, of the issuing of silver coinage), but its great age fell in the seventy years between 483 and 413. These *termini* are set by the discovery of the rich 'third contact' seams at Maroneia, which financed the triremes that would fight and win at Salamis (Hdt. 7.144 and ?Aristot. *Ath.Pol.*22.7: a story perhaps more dramatic than the reality), and the Spartan military occupation of Dekeleia, referred to by X. in 4.25 here. This paralyzed eastern and southern Attica (Thuc. 7.27–8) and, evidently, the silver-mining industry with it.

After 404 the situation was slow to improve (and Athenian silver coinage was not minted again for a decade). When, why, and how it ultimately began to do so is not a process that can be traced in detail. Nevertheless, evidence of various kinds reveals that during the second quarter of the fourth century regeneration was under way. Therippides of Paiania (*LGPN* s.v. no.3), known to readers of Demosthenes 27–9 as one of the young man's dastardly guardians, is the lessee of a mine whose location-marker has been found (*SEG* 28.205); and lines 40–83 of the perfectly preserved records of the *pôlêtai* from the year 367/6 show others in the same role (RO 36, Austin & Vidal-Naquet (1977) no.95, *Agora* 19 P5). They include some seriously rich individuals, men of liturgical capacity (on which see generally *APF* xvii–xxxi; Davies (1981) 9–37). Two of them, Nikias (II) of Kydantidai (*LGPN* s.v. no.96, *APF* 406) and Kallias (III) of Alopeke (*LGPN* s.v. no.84, *APF* 263), are descendants of men singled out by X. here (4.14–15) as prominent fifth-century mining entrepreneurs. Orthodoxy holds that even in 367/6 'mining was not happening on a very large scale' (RO pp. 181–2), though Kroll (2011b) posits a much higher volume of minting—and thus of mining—than previous estimates. Garlan (1988) 67 has a hypothetical graph, taken from Lauffer (1955-1956), of the numbers of slave-workers in the mines—as an index of the health of the sector overall. If correct, it shows that pre-Dekeleia levels had not been reached again before X. wrote, as indeed would be generally agreed from other perspectives. (In the 340s they did, before reaching their 'Lykourgan' peak and then falling again.)

Associated with the mines themselves (which were networks of horizontal galleries and vertical shafts: 4.26) were the several mine-related operations above ground. Once extracted, the silver-bearing ore had to be processed: by successive crushing, washing, sorting, smelting, and refining. (The washeries: Ellis Jones (1982) 176–9 figs.2–5, 182–4 figs.8–10; Fisher (1995) 48–9 figs.5–6.) X. himself does not have a lot to say about these ancillary activities, though 4.49 mentions the furnaces (Ellis Jones (1982) 180 fig.6), and 4.49–50 as a whole briefly conjures up an image of a large, thriving Metallopolis with urban amenities which will take shape if X.'s plans are successfully implemented.

Readers of *Poroi* cannot help but notice that Chap.4 is very much longer than any of the other five. Why so? The answer begins to emerge as early as 4.2. Before it, the introductory 4.1 has restated the theme of the need for revenues, and has asserted that the mines possess the potential for 'huge sums of money' to be raised. However, 4.13 is reached before X. begins properly to explain how this can happen. The delay is caused by the need he feels to give, first, some history of and background to the topic. Ostensibly this is to inform those readers who do not already know it (4.1); in truth, we may suspect that he has done 'research' for his own benefit. Even when the exposition is under way he reverts to the past (4.14–15), before calling himself to order (4.16). There ensues a core section largely free of such distractions, 4.17–33—but just as lengthy is what follows it, a catalogue of possible objections to his scheme with rejoinders to them (4.34–48). Sections 49–52 then round off a chapter which has turned out to be not merely longer than any of the others, but almost as long as all of them put together; cf. Gauthier 110–11, with praise for its tight logical construction.

Bibliography on some specific aspects of the Laureion mines will be marshalled under the relevant Comm. lemmata, but the basics can be laid down here. The *OCD* entries on 'Laurium' (800) and 'mines and mining: Greek' (957–8) by John Ellis Jones distil material set out in full in Ellis Jones (1982). See also Isager & Hansen (1975) 99–106 and Hopper (1979) 170–89. Still useful are MacDonald (1961), Hopper (1961), and Cunningham (1967). Geological, mineralogical, and technological aspects are covered in depth by Ardaillon (1897)—reflected in Isager & Hansen (1975) 99–103—and by Conophagos (1980). The classic study of the mining leases is Crosby (1950), though see also Aperghis (1997–1998); that of the slave labour-force in the mines is Lauffer

(1955-1956, second edn. 1979), cited already above. On Athenian law in this area see Hopper (1953) and Hopper (1968); summarily MacDowell (1978) 137–8. More recent work: Bissa (2009) 49–66, Rihll (2010a, 2010b), Davis (2014), Powell (2015) 73–143.

* * * *

4.1 Now to the silver-mines. If they were organized as they ought to be This neuter plural *argyreia*, an adjective in which the noun 'mines' is implicit, will recur in 4.5 (with another noun, 'works'), 4.11, 4.13, 4.14, 4.17, 4.25 twice, 4.32, 4.43, 4.46, and 4.47. It is X.'s term of choice for the topic he is addressing, though for another prominent one see below, **4.3 At any rate**.

The verb X. uses here, *kataskeuazesthai*, is repeated from 3.13, where it had referred to the establishment of housing and shopping-centres for retailers. In that context, presumably, it had meant building them from scratch; and a broadly similar meaning will attach to it in 4.32 (on a newly created, publicly owned body of slaves) and 4.50 (on the creation of a *de facto* sub-polis in the mining-area). However, throughout the rest of Chap.4—where it occurs a further six times, including the present passage—and also in 6.2, the sense is that of organizing or re-organizing something that already exists (but needs improvement). Gauthier 112 notes that this is the verb employed by philosophers in reference to the construction of an ideal polis (Plat. *Rep*.8.557D; Aristot. *Pol*.2.1267b30, on Hippodamos of Miletos (*OCD* 688)). While true, that fact is perhaps less important than X.'s own resort to the word—in *Poroi* above all (*pro rata* it is more common here than in any earlier work)—as his language of choice when describing the conversion of rational planning into tangible results.

4.1 I think that massive sums of money would come in from them, even irrespective of the other revenues The phrase 'massive sums of money' (*pampolla chrêmata*), unremarkable in translation, uses a locution characteristic of X.; see already *Cyrop*.6.2.9, *Hell*. 6.2.36; and cf. 4.34 here.

What did he expect his readers (and listeners) to understand by 'the other revenues'? It seems to me conceivable that he meant the other sources of new and/or increased revenue *which he had been proposing here*: see esp. 2.7, 3.6, 3.14. More probably, though, Thiel 16 and Gauthier 112 are right to assert that the reference is to Athens' existing income from the mines, i.e. principally from leasing them out.

For such leases see already above, Chapter intro.; in general Isager & Hansen (1975) 105–6; the commentary in RO to their no.36; Powell (2015) 84–91. Whereas the land *above* mines could be, and usually was, in private ownership, long-established modern orthodoxy holds that a mine (*metallon*) itself was and always remained state-owned. (I note, but cannot pursue here, the challenge to this orthodoxy in Davis (2014) 263–6.) The *pôlêtai* leased the mine—despite the word 'sold' as the routine description of the transaction—to an individual applicant. This would be for a three-year period if the mine was *ergasimon* (meaning either working or workable: see below); for a seven-year or ten-year period if it was 'given up'. So, at any rate, the binary language of ?Aristot. *Ath.Pol.*47.2. (Its second figure is indistinct in the papyrus; both 'seven' [ζ] and 'ten' [ι] have their advocates.) The lease-inscriptions themselves differentiate, eventually, between four categories of mine: *kainotomiai*, 'new cuttings', i.e. not yet in operation; the *ergasima*; the *anasaxima*, literally 'loaded-up'; and the 'old' *anasaxima*. Orthodoxy since Crosby (1950) and Hopper (1953) has understood the *ergasima* to be mines actively working, though if so there seem to be surprisingly few of them (and, equally surprisingly, they are all leased at a fixed price of 150 drachmas). Perhaps, therefore, the term means 'deemed to be potentially work*able*' (so Aperghis (1997–1998) 5, 7; Bissa (2009) 52). Alternatively, an *ergasimon* is what Crosby envisaged, a mine whose existing lessee is renewing his lease, as opposed to an *anasaximon* where it is changing hands (and a *palaion anasaximon* where it is doing so after a period of closure); cf. Shipton (1998) 59 n.14.

Clarifying these contentious terms is not imperative in a commentary on *Poroi*—where X. uses none of this vocabulary except *kainotomia* (see 4.27–31). More to the point for present purposes is another obscurity presented by the leases. The prices which they record are predominantly 20 drachmas and 150 drachmas, with only very occasional leaps (perhaps the outcome of auctions) to much higher ones. Since such prices can hardly be what was paid *per lease* (quite apart from the indication in Demosth. 37.22 that payment was by instalment), what was the frequency of the payments? Per prytany, i.e. ten times a year, or annually? As regards the 367/6 leases: though yearly payment is the option favoured by some (e.g. Crosby (1950) 203–4; Aperghis (1997–1998) 16–17), its upshot here would be only 3,690 drachmas, seemingly a paltry sum (even in the light of X.'s view here that 'masses of money' was still there for the state's taking). The same year's leases calculated by payment per prytany (as favoured by e.g. Hopper (1953) 237–9 and Isager &

Hansen (1975) 106) would total 6 *talanta* and 900 drachmas—still quite modest, but at least not derisory. To be sure, each lease-document is a snapshot of the leases *initiated in that year*, so that alongside the income accruing from them is income from leases that were at intermediate stages of their three-year or seven-year terms. Working on the assumption of a ten-year lease for the majority of mines (see above) and thus an income from ten different 'accounts' each year, Bissa (2009) 53–4 arrives at a hypothetical total, for the year 367/6, of 61.5 *talanta*. Yet given the number of unknowns, caution is required. Adjudication between seven-year and ten-year leases (for those which were not three-year ones) does not seem to me possible. As to the frequency of payments: 'the large size of the largest rent suggests that the output of the most productive mines must have been very considerable indeed if payment once a prytany is involved. Recording the prytany in which the mine is leased makes most sense if *annual* payments which become due in different prytanies are at issue' (RO p. 181; my emphasis).

Lease-income, furthermore, is unlikely to be the only thing encompassed by X.'s 'other revenues from the mining industry—even though, here again, there are more questions than answers. For example: in the 430s the building accounts for two high-prestige projects on the akropolis, the Parthenon (*OCD* 1085) and the Propylaia (*OCD* 1222–3), seem to show occasional contributions by a named Laureion mine (or fund?); Powell (2015) 106. Also in respect of that period, X. himself refers to something significant when he recalls 'how much the tax of the slaves [*to telos tôn andrapodôn*] brought in before the events at Dekeleia'. (See 4.25 with the Comm. there.) And relevant evidence pertaining to X.'s own day comes in an allusion, in one of the leasing-lists, to 'the five-drachma in the workings', but its nature is opaque; contrast e.g. Shipton (1998) 62 ('5-drachma prytany charge') with RO p.181 ('fiftieth tax'), and see generally Powell (2015) 94–5. An entry in the late-Byzantine Suda lexicon (*OCD* 1408), 'prosecution for an unregistered mine' (alpha 345 Adler; see http://stoa.org/sol), asserts that 'when those operating the (Athenian) silver mines wanted to begin a new working, they would make this plain to the (officials) assigned by the people to the workings and would register a twenty-fourth part of the new mine as a tax payable to the people'. (Failure to do so could lead to prosecution.) This, however, it is orthodox to suppose (e.g. Hopper (1953) 224–39, esp. 230; Isager & Hansen (1975) 106; Rhodes (1981) 554; RO p.181), was a development—perhaps replacing the fixed price of a lease—from a time much later than X. See now Powell (2015) 95–7.

4.1 I also want to show their potential to those unaware of it. Once this is realized, you will also deliberate better about how they should be treated For 'potential' (*dynamis*, in this sense) cf. *Oec*.16.3–5, relating to land, and more generally *Cyrop*.8.8.14 on plants.

In the gentle tutorial given to young Glaukon of Kollytos (*LGPN* s.v. no.24, *POP* 154–6) by Sokrates in *Mem*.3.6, it is noteworthy that a grasp of 'the silver-mines...(and) why less comes in from them now than before' features among the topics which a would-be politician should have mastered (*Mem*.3.6.12). In any event X. is more tactful here than Thucydides had been, when beginning his account of the Athenians' decision to invade Sicily in 415: 'most of them were unacquainted with the size of the island and the number of its inhabitants, both Hellenes and non-Hellenes' (Thuc. 6.1.1). That aside, X.'s decision to give so much 'background' (above, Chap.4 intro.) is only explicable if, in the mid-350s, it was needed; cf. Gauthier 115.

For the way to deliberate well see also *Cyrop*.8.7.24.

4.2 the mines have been productive since very ancient times For the Greek here see Notes on the Text. With the Portus emendation, the implicit subject is 'they' of the preceding clause (see above), and *energa* can be the adjective, not noun, that it is in *Hier*.11.4 and *Mem*.1.4.4; also e.g. Isoc. 7.35 and Demosth. 27.10.

Given our present-day knowledge that the beginnings of mine-working in Laureion stretch back to the Bronze Age (above, Chap.4 intro.), it would have been instructive to know what X. meant, and what his readers understood, by 'very ancient times'. The 'very' shows him keen to display his knowledge (or belief) that these origins belonged in a period further distant than the merely 'ancient' times inhabited by Nikias and others in the later fifth century (4.14 & 16). Even so, he might not be thinking of anything beyond the sixth.

4.2 nobody even attempts to put a date on when the ventures were first begun Compare Waterfield 173: 'when the enterprise was first undertaken'. X. has employed the verb *epicheirein* (here at the end of the clause) already in 1.6, and it is commonplace enough. Even so, this particular form of it, the aorist passive, is a great rarity. Perhaps he was influenced by its two occurrences (the only pre-X. ones we know of) in book 6 of Thucydides: on the extravagant hopes that surrounded the departure of the Athenian forces to Sicily (6.31.6) and on the daring plan of Harmodios and Aristogeiton to assassinate the Peisistratid tyrants (6.54.1; *OCD* 156–7). All three contexts have a sense of risk about them. (See Isager & Hansen (1975) 99–101 and 104 on the hazardous conditions below ground.)

4.2 despite the antiquity of digging the silver-bearing ore and bringing it out For the adjective 'silver-bearing' (*argyritis*), with the noun implicit, see already **1.5 though many**. (4.3 will apply the variant *argyrôdês* to an ore-rich area.)

For 'digging'—not, of course, a task confined to the mines: *Oec.*19.1–13—see already 1.5 and again 4.4 and 4.24. 'Bringing out' the ore is mentioned again in 4.32. Lauffer (1955-1956) 25 and 34 assembles the texts which pertain to these two fundamental stages of a mining operation (corresponding to 'underground' and 'above ground' in Isager & Hansen (1975) 99–103); cf. Gauthier 116.

4.2 notice what proportion the *spoil heaps* are by comparison with the mounds that are natural and have silver under them Theramenes of Steiria (*LGPN* s.v. no.7, *OCD* 1463, *APF* 227–8) in *Hell.*2.3.45, accused by his enemy Kritias (*LGPN* s.v. no.7, *OCD* 394 Cr-, *APF* 326–7, *POP* 108–11) of constantly switching sides, had asked his audience to 'notice' (and, as here, grasp the significance of) things that would counter this.

What *Poroi* readers are being asked to notice is what a *small* proportion of the landscape these man-made slag heaps make up. X. here calls them, literally, thrown-out heaps. As Thiel 16 points out, they are what Strab. 9.1.23, when writing of Laureion, calls 'the old *ekbolas* and *skôria*'. In present-day mining terminology this means the *overburden* and the *gangue*, and it must actually be the latter to which Strabo is referring when he writes that in post-classical times it was re-smelted, more efficiently, to extract more of the ore. See also Gauthier 116, Lauffer (1955–1956) 35 and 42 n.4.

Waterfield 173 misrepresents X.'s meaning here by reducing his 'heaps' to a single one in the mind's eye ('how small a pile what has been removed so far would make'). As Gauthier 116 comments, X. is encouraging a purely visual comparison between the *sôroi* that mining has produced and the natural *lophoi* of the region. (Furthermore, Gauthier argues, the 'mounds that are natural and still have silver under them' means not the as-yet-untouched, virgin terrain envisaged by Marchant and Bodei Giglioni (and now Waterfield)—which is evoked in the next sentence—but the natural hills with working mines below them. If Gauthier is right, X. is asking the reader to 'notice' two phenomena very close to one another.)

4.3 At any rate, during the time when the maximum number of men was in mining, nobody was ever at a loss for a job. It was the opposite: the needs of the works always exceeded the number of the workers This claim about the past—evidently the pre-Dekeleia (4.25, cf. 4.14–15) decades: Thiel 16, Gauthier 116–17—is offered as proof of the preceding assertion, timeless and unverifiable: 'the silver-producing area is in no way diminishing; on the contrary, one can see that its extent is always growing larger'. (4.4 will base the same argument on the situation current at the time of writing.) Modern scholars who castigate X.'s view as naive begin with Boeckh (1886). Defenders of his position, with varying degrees of conviction, include Thiel 16, Von der Lieck (1933) 44, Bodei Giglioni xcix–c, and Gauthier 119.

X.'s form of words here is actually 'when the maximum number of men was in *them*'. The grammatical antecedent for that pronoun is 'the silver-mines', at the very outset of 4.1, since when there have been only other such pronouns (as in the remainder of 4.1) and implicit subjects (as at the beginning of 4.2). Translating the present phrase as 'in mining' leaves open the possibility that, by now if not before, X. has in mind the mining industry at large. Another reason for seeing a macrocosmic picture here is his use of the word 'men', *anthrôpoi*. Does he mean slaves? We would have been left in no doubt on the point if he had referred to *andrapoda*, as he does sixteen times in the rest of Chap.4: 4.4, 4.15, 4.17 twice, 4.18, 4.21 twice, 4.23, 4.24, 4.25, 4.26, 4.30, 4.35, 4.36, 4.39, 4.49. That brutal neuter noun, clearly, is his term of choice for what Gauthier 151 calls the anonymous, disposable mass of slaves without masters. In fact '*anthrôpoi*' too will reappear, seven times (4.11, 4.14, 4.16, 4.18, 4.21, 4.25, 4.39), but in contexts where the natural assumption is usually that they are slave *miners*. The present passage stands apart as broader, in Gauthier's view. I agree; and I would say the same of 4.11 (q.v.).

Between here and 4.44 there will be copious further references to 'the works' (*ta erga*) and to 'those working' (*ergazomenoi*, a participle) in them. In context here, both terms have special reference to the Laureion silver-mines.

'The works', as Gauthier 117 notes, denote both the operations themselves and the place(s) where they occur. (For this outside *Poroi* see e.g. Isae. 3.22; Demosth. 37.4, 42.3, 17–21, 23, 31; Hyp. *Lyk*.2.1.) The same is true of the other, more precise, plural that X. uses throughout Chap.4 (beginning in 4.4): *ta metalla*, 'the mines'. Harpocration M25 Keaney reports that in the lost Lysianic speech *In reply to Diochares* 'those working the *metalla*' were denoted by the noun *metalleis* (Lys. fr.99); and upper-case *Metalleis* (Miners) was the title of a comic drama of the (?)420s (by or attributed to Pherecrates, *OCD* 1124; surviving fragments suggest that in the play the chorus of miners broke through into the Underworld, returning with vivid accounts of its abundance). X. himself never uses this noun. In some writers, though again not X. (and none as early as X.), those working in *ta metalla* are referred to, again participially, as the *metalleuontes*. For *ta argyreia*—more precise still—see already **4.1 Now to the silver-mines**. If X. intended any consistent and precise differentiation between these various words, it is impossible to discern; and with the *ergazomenoi* least of all. The term was all-embracing. It covered, as Gauthier 117 puts it, everyone who worked in or for the silver-mines, i.e. from the affluent individuals who took out the leases (mainly citizens, though see 4.12) to the labourers at the rock-face and elsewhere.

The one item of vocabulary conspicuous by its absence here is a mine-related *ergastêrion*, 'workshop'. For that see Isae. 3.22 and Demosth. 37.4, above; also e.g. the leases in RO 36 (Austin & Vidal-Naquet (1977) no.95; *Agora* 19 P5) lines 55 & 75.

4.4 Even now, none of those who own slaves in the mines reduces his labour-force; he always acquires as many *more* as he possibly can For 'owning/acquiring' *andrapoda* cf. 4.14 on Nikias, with the Comm. there. Gauthier 118 states as a fact what I should prefer to call a reasonable supposition: that X. intended the verb used in both of these passages, *ktâsthai*, to encompass owners like Nikias and sub-contractors such as the Thrakian Sosias also mentioned in 4.14 (q.v. Comm. there).

4.4 Hence this is the only occupation, of the ones I myself know, where additional operators incur no spite X.'s comment here is a thought that would nowadays be an impersonal, economic one: intensifying the operations does not create competition between the operators; cf. Gauthier 119 with 129–31. More interesting than that, though, are the moral (and personal) terms in which he himself expresses it. Following up a hint by Gauthier 130, Cartledge in Waterfield 225 speculates that X. might have in mind a famous passage of the early Boiotian poet Hesiod (*OCD* 678). In Hesiod's *Works and Days* a good, productive kind of Strife (*eris*), Cartledge writes, 'encourages "potter to be angry with potter and carpenter with carpenter" (line 25) in the interests of economic self-improvement'. X.'s point would then be that 'so abundant is mining wealth that economic advantage accrues even without expenditure of anger'. As we see, X. here has nothing to say about anger, but he does mention *phthonos*, envious or jealous spite—and so, in fact, did Hesiod, in the very next line (26): 'and beggar to be spiteful to beggar, and minstrel to minstrel'.

For the Xenophontic Sokrates' definition of *phthonos* as pain at a friend's success (cf. Gore Vidal: 'whenever a friend succeeds, a little something in me dies') see *Mem*.3.9.8. As regards X. himself, one wonders how many other *erga* he did know. Since agriculture must be among them, the comments of someone who is a present-day (fruit) farmer as well as a scholar are illuminating. 'Envy is instinctual. It wars daily with rationality, reflecting the farmer's own ground-eye view of the immediate results of his own labor; success for him, failure for the man across the road…Warily, farmers watch the land of kindred. Keenly they note a new barn, a vineyard's fresh stakes, a heavy grape crop, all seen as potential symbols of their own demise' (Hanson (1999) 99).

4.5 Furthermore, everyone who owns fields is in a position to say how many teams of oxen are enough for the plot, and how many labourers. If someone puts in more of them than is sufficient, they account it a loss Thiel 17 objects to any conjunction of the 'Furthermore' kind here on the grounds that 4.5 merely rephrases 4.4. Gauthier 120 counters that 4.5 does introduce an authentically new argument, not for the wealth of Laureion but—with that as a given—for the intensification of operations there. (Sales, ultimately, are in mind: see 4.6–7.)

Oec. had made no direct statement of the kind made here, but something of the sort is implicit, arguably, in a section such as 20.16–29. For 'putting in labour' cf. *Oec*.17.12 & 15 (hoers), and again 4.39 here. For *zêmia* as an economic loss (rather than a legal penalty, its meaning in 4.21), see already *Mem*.2.3.2, an anecdote about two brothers quarrelling over their property.

On 'teams' (literally, yokes) of draught-animals see generally Isager & Skydsgaard (1992) 104–6. The beasts involved are mules or, more usually, oxen. Where neither animal is expressly mentioned (for oxen see *Cyrop*.6.1.52), the latter can be assumed.

4.5 in the silver-mining works everyone always claims to be short of labourers For the Greek here ('always') see Notes on the Text.

4.6 This is because mining is unlike what happens when there are numerous bronze-smiths, and bronze products become cheap, and bronze-smiths are rendered superfluous—and with iron-workers

likewise Both 'bronze-smiths' (*chalkotypoi*) and 'iron-workers' (*sidêreis*) had featured in X.'s memorable description of Ephesos (*OCD* 509, *IACP* no.844) in 395, bustling with the preparations for Agesilaos' expedition against the Persians. (So *Ages*.1.26. Instead of *sidêreis*, the version in *Hell*.3.4.17 has *chalkeis*—which looks like a mistake caused by the preceding *chalkotypoi*.)

Using the examples of these two metallurgical industries in an Athenian context, and also the occurrence of a glut of grain or wine (see the next lemma), X. expresses the common-sense ancient view of supply and demand. Thiel 17 expresses brief approval of it. Gauthier 120, with expansion at 129–31, subjects it to a rigorous analysis designed to bring out its supposedly 'primitive' character—one which does not consider the sort of questions a modern reader might have (such as: why not solve these gluts of production by exporting the commodities concerned?). In sharp contrast, 4.6 is a passage cited no fewer than four times by Bresson (2016)—14–15, 110, 395, 432—in order to emphasize that, contrary to the Polanyi/Finley model of a pre-modern economy 'embedded' in society, it was price fluctuation which determined economic activity and productivity.

4.6 Also when there is a great deal of grain and wine: the crops are cheap, farming loses its profits An example of the first of these situations, from the 320s, is furnished by Demosth. 56.9: 'when the ships from Sicily had arrived and the prices of grain were falling'. Unsurprisingly, its opposite is also attested. In Demosth. 42.20 & 31 the defendant, the wealthy Phainippos of Kolonai (*LGPN* s.v. no.18, *APF* 552–4), has allegedly sold the barley and wine from his estate at three times their former price. Fluctuations of that order in *grain*-prices, at any rate, find corroboration in other evidence from a period somewhat later than *Poroi*. See e.g. Demosth. 34.38–9; RO 95 (now *IG* II^3 367/*AIO*) lines 10–11, 56–7, 68–9, with their commentary p. 485.

Gauthier 122–3 poses a question: why did X. single out—in the category of agricultural products—grain and wine, when other evidence shows the great importance of, notably, olives (Demosth. 43.69–70)? More exactly perhaps: since grain is self-selecting as the first example, why is wine the second? Gauthier's answer is that in *Oec*. wine, second only to grain (chaps.16–18 there), had taken up most space (more than half of chap.19), with olives and figs a cursory addendum. Both works highlight the two most labour-intensive crops.

4.6 the result is that many men give up working the land and turn to wholesaling and retailing and moneylending On wholesaling and retailing see under **3.13 both housing**. Associated with them here is 'moneylending', an activity which X. describes with an abstract noun related to *tokos*, 'interest'. It occurs again in Aristot. *Pol.*1.1258b25, applied to one of the three branches of money-making (*chrêmatistikê*: Austin & Vidal-Naquet (1977) 162–8), but is otherwise unattested in writers of this era.

A point lost in translation (if the English is to be idiomatic) is that X. gives all three of these nouns in the plural: *emporiai*, *kapêleiai*, *tokismoi*. (The last of these nouns is a great rarity, but cf. Aristot. *Pol.*1.1258b25, singular.) Noting this choice of plurals, Gauthier 121–2 finds its explanation in X.'s wish to say not that superfluous farmers will turn their backs definitively on the land (as Thiel 18 and others suppose) and actually *become* wholesalers, retailers, and money-lenders; rather, that they will put their disposable money to work in these areas temporarily, as long as it is shrewd to do so, and perhaps revert to 'working the land' later. In my opinion this is plausible in part, though there seems no good reason why X.'s scenario should be restricted to agricultural *investment*; those who 'give up working the land' might include subsistence farmers, and indeed landless farm-labourers. Also, Gauthier has overlooked the way in which writers of X.'s background can sometimes use plurals as a distancing device. An instance relevant to the present passage is Plat. *Leg.*1.643E, on (relatively) uneducated men finding their niche in such areas as *kapêleiai* and *nauklêriai*. Note also Plato again on *daneismos* (another word for lending and borrowing money) in *Republic* 9.573E and *Laws* 8.842D: both passages actually use the plural *daneismoi*.

4.6 When more silver-bearing ore is discovered, though, and more silver is available, there is a commensurate rise in the number of people entering this industry This Silver Rush phenomenon sounds dramatic—and sometimes it can be: as in the two *Berggeschreien* in medieval Saxony (Ball (2006) 30) and their later equivalents in British Columbia, Chile, Colorado, Mexico, Ontario, and elsewhere. Here, doubtless, X. has in mind quite modest upturns in interest and activity, contingent upon word spreading of increased production in a specific locale.

In any event, underpinning X.'s scenario here—and on throughout 4.7–10—are his two firm convictions on the matter: the *supply* itself is inexhaustible (4.3–4, 4.11, 4.25–7); the *price* can only go up, never down (cf. Gauthier 129–31), exempt from the normal laws of supply and demand illustrated already (and again in 4.11 and 4.36).

4.7 Take furnishings as an obvious example: when individuals have acquired enough for the house they do not go on buying more This illustrative example, linked (by the retrospective Greek conjunction *gar*) to the immediately preceding sentence, in reality connects with the material between 'Furthermore' at the beginning of 4.5 and 'money-lending' in 4.6. The remainder of 4.7 then expands 4.2–4 and the final sentence (= the lemma immediately above) of 4.6. So Gauthier 123.

Most translators render the neuter plural *epipla* here as 'furniture' (Dakyns, Marchant, Waterfield). However, as Gauthier 123–4 points out, the term for that is *kataskeuê*, which will feature in the very next section, 4.8 (and cf. e.g. *Ages*.8.7, *Cyrop*.3.1.2, *Hier*.2.2). For *epipla* see already *Mem*.2.7.2; *Oec*.3.2, 9.6 & 8. I have borrowed 'furnishings' from Finley (1952) 53, where he translates and comments on Aristot. *Pol*.2.1267b9–12: the legislator Phaleas (N. F. Jones (2004) 234–5) made the mistake of attempting to create equality among the citizens of Chalkedon (*OCD* 303, *IACP* no.743) as regards land only, i.e. ignoring wealth in slaves, livestock, money, and *epipla*. Finley's definition of furnishings/*epipla* there (endorsed by Gauthier) is 'wealth as objects of use and display, not in the productive sense of capital goods', and the present passage is cited. In fact, definitive on the matter (at least as far as X. is concerned) is *Oec*.9.6–8. Ischomachos describes there how he and his young wife had sorted their *epipla*—meaning their entire household contents—'by tribes' (e.g. bedding, men's clothing, women's clothing, shoes, best dinner-service, kitchen equipment, foodstuffs, weapons). See also Pritchett (1979–1991) 5.179–80.

The central assertion here that one acquires 'enough' *epipla* and then stops—apart from replacement and replenishment where required—had already appeared in tangential form in *Oec*.3.2. To X., clearly, it was a self-evident truth.

4.7 But when it comes to money, nobody has ever acquired so much as to need no more of it. No, those who amass a huge amount derive no less pleasure from burying the surplus underground than from putting it to use Again (cf. under the preceding lemma, end) X. states here first, and very directly, an idea that in an earlier work he had expressed in a more roundabout way; *Symp*.4.35–6 in this instance. It is not, of course, peculiar to him. As Gauthier 124 comments, if we leave aside particular philosophical doctrines which prescribed austerity or frugality (such as those of the Cynics: *OCD* 402–3), most Hellenes wanted to be rich, and the rich ones to be richer. A much-quoted line from one of the elegies of Solon (*OCD* 1380–1) had declared that 'of wealth, no limit for men is fated and fixed' (Solon fr.13.71 West). X.'s contemporaries agreed: see e.g. Aristoph. *Plut.*193–7, Isoc. 8.7.

The second sentence here, the final one of 4.7, relies on a differentiation between what is essential/necessary (*anagkaion*) and what is merely superfluous/surplus (here the participle *peritteuon*, more usually the related adjective *periton*); so e.g. in *Hier.*2.2, *Oec.*20.1. If a surplus remains, after all necessary expenditure has been attended to, people either spend it (see further in 4.8) or, according to X., are equally happy to bury it.

Thiel 50–1 (Excursus IX) addresses the latter phenomenon. Diagnosing it as symptomatic of a mistrust of banks and bankers, he offers three explanations: fear that the bank(er) would risk the money on maritime loans (on which see **3.9 Every contributor**); a broader moral aversion to lending and borrowing at interest; and a view held by those who wanted to conceal their wealth (to avoid liability for liturgies etc.) that they could better do so by burying it than depositing it in a bank. Gauthier 125–6 finds none of this convincing, or necessary. As background we simply need to keep in mind that in the ancient Greek world there were few *secure* opportunities for investment (outside agriculture); that banks were not treated as routine depositaries for money in the way we find so natural nowadays; and that hiding/hoarding was a perfectly sensible option. Even kings (*Cyrop.*3.3.3) and gods (Hdt. 8.35–6, on Delphi in 480) did it. On burying and hoarding in general see Millett (1991) 169–71; Johnstone (2003) 255–6.

4.8 whenever states are faring well, assuredly the people have need of money For 'assuredly' see again 4.50 (and cf. *Oec.*1.15, 'most assuredly' as an answer).

This statement and the explanatory expansion of it which immediately follows (see the next two lemmata) contain a prime example of the difference between the two words for 'man' in ancient Greek. First, here, *anthrôpoi* means humankind in general (as opposed to animals or gods); then the next sentence elaborates on how men (*andres*) and women like to spend money.

Taking issue with the basic contention here in 4.8, Thiel 18 insists that X. has matters back to front. People do not desire money in order to buy expensive things; rather, they buy them because the money is there. Be that as it may, Gauthier 126 draws attention to the logical structure of 4.8–9 as a whole. Apart from the overt differentiation (in the remainder of 4.8) between male and female priorities in expenditure 'whenever states are prospering', X. interposes the larger point—or claim—that in hard times the state's financial needs are the important ones. See further below, **4.9 When.**

4.8 the menfolk want to spend it on fine arms and armour and good horses; also magnificent houses and furniture On 'furniture' see above, **4.7 Take furnishings.**

The coupling of 'fine arms and armour [*hopla*] and good horses' had occurred already in *Hipp*.1.7. (In practice a 'good' horse meant an expensive one, though aptitude and obedience were also relevant; cf. 'good' dogs, as breeding stock, in *Kyn*.7.2.) The phrase *hopla kala* is repeated by Aelian (*OCD* 18) when describing the appeal they exerted on X. himself: see *VH* 3.24, partly deriving from *Anab*.3.2.7. Naturally, they could be also purchased and used by the generals (and other officers) of infantry troops. Plutarch gives two instances of exceptional shields: Nikias' gold-and-purple one, fine enough to be kept and displayed in a Syracusan temple after his death (*Nik*.28.6), and Alkibiades' golden one emblazoned with a thunderbolt-wielding Eros (*Alk*.16.1–2). In the present passage, nevertheless, the *Hipp*. precedent does suggest that what X. has at the centre of his mind's eye is again the *hopla* of a cavalryman, particularly the breastplate; note X.'s own in *Anab*.3.4.47–8, and see generally *Eq*.12.1–7. (Presumably armour for the horse itself, as mentioned in *Anab*.1.8.7 and *Eq*.12.8–9, might also be costly if the owner wished it to be.) Spence (1993) 49–65 is a survey of the topic.

Both this shopping-list and what the women will buy (next lemma) fall into the category of 4.7's 'surplus' (or luxury) expenditure; the sociologist Thorstein Veblen's celebrated concept of conspicuous consumption. Also, the two lists taken together echo the very similar one already in *Hier*.2.2: 'you (despots) have so many *peritta*—you own horses of outstanding excellence, arms and armour of outstanding beauty, superb jewellery for women, and the most magnificent houses equipped with the most expensive furniture'. (In applying this, wholesale, to the *andres* of a democratic polis like Athens, X. at least remembers to omit the superlatives.)

4.8 The women turn to expensive clothing and gold jewellery The only explicit mention of women in *Poroi*. (For a possible implicit one see 4.49.) In *Mem*.3.11.4 Sokrates notices that both Theodote and her mother are wearing opulent clothing and jewellery, but there is no suggestion that this characterizes Theodote's profession (of *hetaira*: *OCD* 679–80).

Men too have ostentatious clothing in *Oec*.9.6. In that same passage X. classifies women's jewellery as appropriate for festival days, outdoors; however, Polemarchos' wife in Lys. 12.20. is wearing her spiral gold earrings (which the oligarch Melobios removes from her ears) inside the house.

Another late fifth-century mention of earrings occurs in a long list of women's accoutrements recited by a character in the second (lost) version of Aristoph. *Thesm*. The passage was striking enough to be quoted in two later writers, one of them Pollux (7.95–6).

4.9 When, on the other hand, states are ailing because of crop failures or war and the land is lying fallow, there is a much more urgent need of currency, to pay for supplies and for mercenaries The first of these contrasting situations had been described at the beginning of 4.8 in colourless terms ('whenever states are faring well'). Now its opposite uses medical language. The personified image of a polis that 'is sick' is first attested in tragedy: Soph. *Antig*.1015. See also e.g. Aesch. *Eum*.941–2 (a fear of 'crop-less eternal sickness' setting in to Athens); [X.] *Ath. Pol*.2.6 on 'sicknesses of the crops', and the observation that 'the whole earth is not sick at the same time'.

In X.'s scenario the land is fallow (*argos*) for either of the two reasons given. Gauthier 127 cites the instance of the people of Phleious in the north-east Peloponnese (*IACP* no.355) in the first half of the 360s, denied the normal use of their territory by the Argives and others (*Hell*.7.2.1 & 17–19). For X.'s phraseology here cf. already *Cyrop*.3.2.2 (Kyros sees that much of Armenia was 'deserted and *argos* because of the war'); and Gauthier adduces an Athenian honorific decree of *c*. 215 (*SIG* 497, Austin (2006) no.74) where the honorand's c.v. mentions his services at a time when 'the territory during] the wars had been *argos* and unsown' (lines 7–8).

The example of Phleious, above, well illustrates X.'s point about the need to buy in supplies in such circumstances. As regards its other stated use here, paying for *epikouroi*, Gauthier 127 flatly rejects the usual translation of that noun here as mercenaries (Thiel, Marchant, Bodei Giglioni) on the basis that in X. mercenaries are never *epikouroi* but always *xenoi* or *misthophoroi*, and *epikouroi* are instead allies/

auxiliaries/helpers whose rations and pay (as the custom was) the benefiting city ultimately had to provide. But Gauthier's categorical 'jamais' overlooks *Hell.*7.1.23: 'mercenaries' is the inescapable translation of the Arkadian *epikouroi* mentioned there. It is also the natural meaning here.

4.10 This I do not contradict For the Greek here ('this') see Notes on the Text.

The answering clause which follows (and fills the remainder of 4.10) expresses a view that has attracted ridicule in many modern readers, from Boeckh to Cawkwell and beyond. Why should the value of gold fluctuate up and down, if that of silver only stays the same or rises? Among others, Thiel 19, Andreades (1933) 387–8, Von der Lieck (1933) 46–9, Bodei Giglioni lxxiv and lxxvii–lxxviii, and Gauthier 132–3 tackle this inconsistency head-on. It can be put in context and proportion by the fact that in the fourth century the overwhelming majority of Hellenic states—excepting only those like Kyzikos (*OCD* 408, *IACP* no.747) and Lampsakos (*OCD* 791, *IACP* no.748) which coined in the gold-and-silver alloy called electrum—used and *thought in* a monometallic standard: silver. Also relevant to the intrinsic validity of X.'s view of silver is something that he and his contemporaries would have been hard-pressed to discern as early as the 350s: the extent to which Attic silver was beginning to create expanding markets, and apparently ever-increasing demand, in the eastern Mediterranean.

As regards gold itself, the Athenians had none that was naturally available to them. The Macedonian kings, on the other hand, did; specifically, in this era, Philip II, from the mid-century onwards. See Hammond & Griffith (1979) 662–70, noting there (663) that in the years after Philip's dissolution of the Chalkidian League (*OCD* 303) in 348 his gold coinage would become 'the strongest currency in Europe'. Scholarly work on gold-to-silver ratios prevailing in Athens in the period has shown that from a norm of roughly 1:12 in the years 406/5 to 355/4 it shifted to 1:10 after about 330: so D. M. Lewis (1968); cf. Gauthier 133–4. But again, these were developments that X. could scarcely have foreseen. (As Gauthier 134 points out, his attitude to gold will have been formed by, above all else, the Persian 'darics' that he first encountered in Asia Minor and later recalled arriving in Hellas—*Hell.*3.5.1, etc.)

4.11 we should have the confidence to bring as many people as possible into the silver-mines This phrase 'have the confidence' is repeated later in the sentence: see the next lemma (and cf. 4.22). Beyond that, the language is carefully chosen for the context's needs. 'People' (cf. above, **4.8 whenever**) is broad enough to embrace the slaves who will be the principal labour-force underground (4.17), but it does not have to be confined to them (as it effectively is in 4.14); and men coming 'into' the mines can likewise include the workers above ground, and indeed, surely, everyone in the mining industry, including the lessees. See further under the next lemma.

4.11 and have the confidence also to make arrangements in them—on the basis that that silver-bearing ore will never run out and that silver itself will never lose its value Here, as X. nears the end of this part of his exposition (4.1–12), he restates the two fundamental assumptions that have underpinned it.

Can anything more be learned from his words? Gauthier 134 and 137 (and already 113) sees here and elsewhere in Chap.4 signs of the bipartite differentiation argued for by Hopper (1968) 296–302: (*a*) the ongoing provision of above-ground facilities by the owners of the land in question; (*b*) the short-term, speculative aspect of leasing a mine and discovering what might or might not lie underneath. Hopper discerned this (more exactly, the first half of it) from the material remains. Gauthier's claim is that it is reflected in language: (*a*) the *kataskeuazomenoi* and (*b*) the *ergazomenoi*—the latter term embracing the workmen proper as well as the lessees. In my opinion this is unproblematic as regards *b*, but, concerning *a*, too restrictive an application of the verb *kataskeuazesthai* in *Poroi*; see already above, **4.1 Now to the silver-mines.** The two first-person plurals here in 4.11 are not naturally understandable as two different subsets of those Athenians who will actually enter the mining industry. Rather, they are twin steps which the Athenians as a whole, *qua* decision-makers, should be confident in taking if they follow X.'s advice.

4.12 my impression is that the state acknowledged these facts before I did Another clear-cut case (cf. 3.7) of 'the state' standing for its citizens. So again in 4.14, where the state 'notices' something.

The verb which X. uses, *gignôskein* (here its perfect infinitive), is sometimes found in the official language of city assemblies and other decision-making bodies. For this in the singular, as here, see *SIG* 443 (Austin (2006) no.64), lines 9–10: in the mid-third century the 'demos of the Chians' (*OCD* 310–11, *IACP* no.840) 'acknowledged', *egnô*, that the Aitolians should have priority of access to their council and assembly.

Note also the plural *egnôsan* in line 38 of RO 54 (Mylasa: *OCD* 988–9, *IACP* no.913), 355/4, and in lines [11] and 24 of RO 87 (the Chian (?) tribe Klytidai), 330s. In *SIG* 368 (Burstein (1985) no.8), from 289/8, the Ionian League honour and reward their general Hippostratos of Miletos; the document twice (lines 15, 10) refers to the Ionians' decisions as *ta egnôsmena*. I am not aware of any exact Athenian counterparts of this formula—if we set aside, as a different phenomenon, *gignôskein* as expressing the verdict of a court: so e.g. in the republished version of Drakon's homicide law (*IG* I^3 104, ML 86; Fornara (1983) no.15), lines 16–18. Nevertheless, it may still be that X.'s phraseology here is intended to convey the idea that what he goes on to say (see the next lemma) represented a formal decision on the Athenians' part—as indeed it surely did.

4.12 it provides the opportunity of working in the mines to any foreigners who wish to do so, too, on equal terms Here, without doubt, 'to work in the mines' means to take out a mining-lease; so e.g. Lauffer (1955–1956) 14–15, Gauthier 135, and cf. e.g. Hyp. *Eux.*35. Contrast 4.4, and cf. e.g. Demosth. 37.38 (slave workers).

The other words translated here are problematic. Following Thiel 19 (who had himself tacitly revived an idea from Wilamowitz-Möllendorff (1887) 116 with n.1) and Wilhelm (1934) 21–2, Gauthier 135–6 seizes on the phrase which—in line with most other translations (Dakyns, Marchant, Waterfield)—I have rendered here as 'on equal terms': ἐπ' ἰσοτελείᾳ. This, Wilamowitz and his adherents assert, is an allusion to *isoteleia* (literally, tax-equality), the legal status of an *isotelês*: an honour/privilege that we find voted, to named foreigners, in extant Athenian decrees from the fourth century, *c.* 370 onwards. (See Henry (1983) 246–9. The wholly restored instance in RO 4 (Harding (1985) no.3, main part), from 401/0, is controversial.) What 'normal' *isoteleia* entailed is hard to grasp from the epigraphical and lexicographical evidence extant (Whitehead (1977) 11–13). In the present context Gauthier envisages the possibility of temporary respite from taxation for non-Athenian entrepreneurs, i.e. for the duration of their being *ergazomenoi*. Be that as it may, there is only a handful of individuals in the leasing-documents who might fall into this category (all of them designated 'Siphnian': *OCD* 1372, and see under **1.5 though many**; on Sosias the Thrakian see the Comm. to 4.14).

Whitehead (1978) challenges the view that the present passage has anything to do with *isoteleia* in the technical sense assumed by

Wilamowitz et al. In point of fact, the only two instances of the noun in fourth-century literary (as opposed to epigraphical) sources both occur in X. The earlier one is *Hell.*2.4.25. There, the troops of Thrasyboulos of Steiria (*LGPN* s.v. no.22, *OCD* 1471–2) who are about to free Athens from repressive oligarchy, swear oaths among themselves that once success is achieved there will be *isoteleia* for all the participants, even if they are *xenoi*. Krentz (1989) 47 renders this *xenoi* as 'mercenaries'. That is probably too narrow, but whoever these 'foreigners' are, it seems that they are being promised the same treatment as the citizen freedom-fighters *on a general level*—the only sense of the word likely to be used by Thrasyboulos (if he did use it) at that time and/or by X. himself not long afterwards. So that is the background against which to judge what X. meant by 'on *isoteleia* terms' in the present passage—one written after decades away from the city which, in his absence, had devised and awarded *isoteleia* as a closely guarded privilege for individual 'foreigners' (as *xenoi* is bound to mean in this second instance).

With access to a pre-publication copy of Whitehead (1978), Gauthier 267–8 responds to it in his Addenda. He adheres there to his original position, and adduces a fresh argument to support it. It is this: *isoteleia* was above all, according to the lexicographers, a privilege which had metics in mind; consequently, when X. writes 'even if they were foreigners' here [and already in *Hell.*2.4.25, above: DW], the implicit element is 'rather than *metics*', not—as Whitehead's case requires—'rather than *citizens*'. I am unconvinced, and for the simplest of reasons. The epigraphic evidence shows that the lexicographers' focus on metics is misplaced. More precisely: while Pollux and the rest were right to attempt to define *isotelês*-status by the extent to which it constituted an improvement on basic metic-status, they were wrong to imply that metics would be typical *recipients* of it. I do, accordingly, continue to believe that *isoteleia* in these two passages of X. was a verbal idiosyncracy of his own, by which (for different reasons in each of the two contexts) he was endeavouring to express the idea that his fellow-citizens were offering non-citizens, as today's cliché has it, a level playing-field. (Compare in that regard Demosth. 42.31, from *c.* 330: 'you (Athenians) have given public help to all the *ergazomenoi* in the *erga*'.)

Whether or not users of this Comm. accept my arguments that honorific *isoteleia* is a distraction in the understanding of the present passage, the view that its meaning here is confined to equality in 'l'exploitation minière' (Gauthier 135) is adopted by e.g. Calhoun (1931)

361, Schwahn (1931) 265, Bodei Giglioni cvi n.77, Lauffer (1975) 209 n.2, and Schütrumpf 95.

4.13 In order to make myself even clearer on the subject of sustenance This central topic, *trophê*, had been broached at the very outset of the work: 'I set about examining whether there was any way the citizens could sustain themselves out of their own territory' (1.1). That full formulation meant that the present passage could be telegraphic. 4.33 will merit another full version; see the Comm. there. See also, retrospectively, 6.1.

4.13 Personally, I expect to be saying nothing on these matters that will cause surprise, as if I had discovered something difficult to discover Things that are 'difficult to discover' had also been disavowed (by Sokrates) in *Mem.*3.14.7, a passage perhaps unconsciously recalled by X. here. The adjective in this sense is rare (and, in origin, poetic). At all events, X. is at pains in this section to stress that he has done nothing out of the ordinary, but simply observed what is in plain sight. *Oec.*15.10–11 (Ischomachos to Sokrates) had articulated much the same position as regards agriculture. See further under the next lemma (and **4.17 the only novelty**).

4.13 Some of what I shall say we all still see, now; as for the past, again we hear the same from everyone For the Greek here ('from everyone') see Notes on the Text.

This, as Gauthier 137 notes, is X. wanting to emphasize that he is proceeding not on the basis of personal argumentation, proffered by him, but communal testimony—on which present (again briefly in 4.16) and past (again 4.14–15) alike are unanimous. This conjunction is also invoked by Isocrates (8.21) and Lykourgos (*Leok.*93), among others.

4.14 the state notices many private individuals growing rich out of her and does not copy them For 'private individuals' (*idiôtai*), as a counterpoise to the community acting collectively, see again 4.17–19 and 4.32 (and already e.g. *Cyrop.*1.6.45, *Hell.*3.4.28, 6.5.40, *Mem.*2.6.18).

Usually, in X. just as elsewhere, growing rich and/or (especially) enriching others are morally admirable: so in e.g. *Ages.*4.6, *Cyrop.*5.1.28, 5.5.27, 8.2.22, *Hier.*11.13, *Mem.*2.1.28, 4.2.9, *Oec.*14.9. But they can sometimes be equivocal phenomena: witness *Ages.*1.17–18 and *Mem.*1.5.3. In the present context no blame attaches to the *idiôtai* who are acquiring wealth 'out of' the state (cf. 5.1; Waterfield's 'out of the mines' is too narrow). X. simply wants to emphasize that their means of making this happen could also increase the riches of the polis itself (for which cf. *Mem*.3.6.6–7).

4.14 Long ago, of course, those of us with an interest in these matters have heard X.'s phraseology here catches the attention, and some translators press it hard: 'It is an old story, trite enough to those of us who have cared to attend to it, how once on a time' (Dakyns); 'For instance, those of us who have bothered to pay attention to these matters have of course known for a long time by hearsay' (Waterfield). In my view there are just two elements here that call for—slight—emphasis. One is that, by contrast with his fellow-citizens (invoked in 4.1) who know little or nothing of the mines, X. himself has studied the topic. (The Greek idiom he uses here had been applied in *Mem*.3.6.10 to the young Glaukon of Kollytos (*LGPN* s.v. no.24, *POP* 154–6), who needs to acquire some knowledge of the matters on which he is keen to address the assembly. See also e.g. Plat. *Cra*.428B, [Demosth.] 59.15.) Additionally, X. is picking up on 4.14 with its appeal to what 'we hear' from the older generation, and quietly pointing out that that is *his* generation; cf. again 4.25.

Thomas (1989) 3 with n.3 gives *Poroi* 4.14–15 as a prime example of the wide range (not confined to historians) of 'oral tradition or memory in the preservation of the past'.

4.14 Nikias the son of Nikeratos once owned a thousand men in the silver-mines A famous (and ultimately tragic) fifth-century figure: *LGPN* s.v. no.95, *OCD* 1013 Nicias (1), *APF* 403–7, *POP* 212–15. Alongside his public career as politician and general (summarized at *AO* 487) between the death of Perikles in 429 and his own demise in 413, Nikias (I) Nikeratou of Kydantidai was notable for great wealth and for the lavish liturgical and related expenditure which it financed: see *APF* 403–4. Identifying him as 'the son of Nikeratos', and so differentiating him from numerous classical-period homonyms, is something X. had already done in *Mem*.2.5.2 (cf. under the next lemma), but Thucydides had led the way (with ten instances beginning in 3.51.1); see also Andoc. 3.8, Plat. *Gorg*.472A.

On the proportion of Nikias' wealth—'not less than a hundred *talanta*', according to Lys. 19.47—which came from Laureion, Plutarch writes as follows: 'in one of the dialogues of Pasiphon it is written that Nikias used to sacrifice to the gods every day and kept a seer at the house, ostensibly for his constant enquiries about public affairs but in fact, mostly, about private matters, and especially about the silver-mines. This was because he had many holdings in the Laureion region, bringing in a large income but worked at great risk. He maintained a mass of slaves there, and the preponderance of his property was in silver' (Plut. *Nik*.4.2). Perrin (1902) argued that everything here—and indeed much else in Plut.'s chaps.4–5—derives from this Pasiphon (thought to be a pupil of the early Hellenistic philosopher Menedemos of Eretria: *OCD* 931 Menedemus (1)). If one rejects or questions this, the issue becomes where Pasiphon's material ends and comment by Plutarch himself takes over. In any event Davies (at *APF* 403) is content to accept as fact that final assertion, and also X.'s quantification here of the 'mass of *andrapoda*' as a thousand. Likewise (on the number) Thiel 20, Lauffer (1955-1956) 154, Bodei Giglioni cx-cxi, Gauthier 142, Garlan (1988) 66, Fisher (1995) 49–50, and generally elsewhere. (The scepticism voiced by Westermann (1941) 460–61 (again in Westermann (1955) 8) and endorsed by Gomme (1946) 129 is not so much heard nowadays, though see Harris (2012) 14–15. Gauthier does credit Westermann with asking a pertinent question, why X. chose a figure from the past to illustrate his argument, but the answer is not difficult to fathom: Nikias' was the most arresting case in living memory. Note that 4.14 as a whole is paraphrased in Athen. *Deipn*.6.272C.)

See further under the next lemma.

4.14 He contracted them out to Sosias the Thrakian, on condition that Sosias paid him back per man an *obolos* a day, net, and also maintained the same numbers This Sosias, *FRA* no.2586, is universally taken to be the unnamed individual who had been mentioned in *Mem*.2.5.2 (see Gauthier 140–1): 'Nikias the son of Nikeratos is said to have bought a manager (*epistatês*) for the silver-mines at a price of one *talanton*'. At the time when that statement was true, therefore, Sosias was a slave. His price was extraordinarily high (compare the other figures, none of them higher than one-fifth of a *talanton*, in that same passage, and the Comm. on 4.23 below), and it evidently reflected his credentials. (Gauthier 141 guesses that a 'Thrakian' origin might hint at a connection with the mines of Mt. Pangaion: *OCD* 1074.) 'One can only assume that Sosias kept any marginal income earned by the slaves he managed. His job required skill and care—he was supervising others and did not need supervision himself—so he would have been motivated by reward' (Rihll (2011) 69). How long Sosias remained a slave, though, is another matter. In the past it has sometimes been deemed possible (by e.g. Herzog (1914) 475–6) that what Sosias 'paid back' to Nikias was in fact the slave's so-called *apophora* due in such circumstances (as in Andoc. 1.37–8; cf. generally [X.] *Ath.Pol.*1.11, Aeschin. 1.97; Kamen (2016), esp. 414–419). However, following Thiel and Wilhelm, Gauthier 141–2 argues that Sosias was by now a freedman(-metic), because both the language and the context here demand it. The language does so in that *misthôsis* (the procedure presupposed by X.'s verb 'contracted…out' needs both parties to the contract to be persons of free status (cf. Demosth. 36.4 for Pasion contracting his bank and shield-workshop to his freedman Phormion). And the context likewise calls for this conclusion because X.'s whole argument here is that the state itself should do what individuals have successfully done: own slave-miners and contract them out to concession-holders. Beginning as Nikias' *epistatês*, the manumitted Sosias has become an *ergazomenos*—in this sense—in his own right (so already Ardaillon (1897) 183).

Whether or not that is correct, the certain fact remains that the one thousand slaves (or 'men'; cf. 4.16) belonged to Nikias. He received a financial return from allowing Sosias to use them—and indeed, as we are told, to replenish any losses. (In asserting that it was Nikias who undertook to do this, Acton (2014) 261 turns the provision on its head.) Obviously, some slaves would die or suffer incapacitating injury at work. Others would abscond, even before (and after) the inducement to do so presented by the Spartan presence at Dekeleia between 413 and 404 (see 4.25 with Comm.). Others still will have fallen victim to the 'oppressive' atmosphere of the region, mentioned in *Mem.*3.6.12; cf. Plut. *Comp.Nik.Crass.*1.2, 'some perishing in unhealthy, underground places'.

Nikias' return of an *obolos* per slave per a day—which on a 360-day year would have brought him in a hefty ten *talanta* per annum (*APF* 403; Gauthier 141 with 139–40)—can be assumed to be a standard one in this area. Besides applying in all three of the cases here in *Poroi* 4.14–15 (note 'let out in this same way' in 4.15), it also features in a court case from the year 333: Hyp. *Lyk.*1–2. Ariston, the plaintiff in this impeachment trial (Hansen (1975) 106–7 no.119; Whitehead (2000) 75–149), is said to have *andrapoda* (of unstated numbers) in the *erga*, an asset which furnishes him—via a certain Theomnestos—with food-money at the rate of an *obolos* a day per slave. (This is said to enable Ariston to pursue his career as an 'eternal sykophant'—meaning blackmailer and vexatious prosecutor. Gauthier 139 attractively suggests that the adjective *athanatos* might well be ironic in that context, if a commitment to maintain the numbers of mining slaves at a stated total, as here, was in fact a standard feature of such arrangements. Following Wilhelm (1934) 26, Gauthier adduces contracts from Ptolemaic Egypt which require a signatory to maintain a herd of animals as *athanatos*; LSJ s.v., III.2, has examples. One could add the elite of the Persian army—the ten thousand *athanatoi*: never fewer—mentioned in Hdt. 7.83.)

For the term 'net' (*atelê*) here, and again 4.15 and 4.23, cf. e.g. Demosth. 27.9 (twice), 28.12; per year, in those cases. Though the word literally means 'free of tax(es)', Gauthier 138 is doubtless right to suppose that Sosias and other men in his position were undertaking to meet any and every kind of expense (including food, clothing, and accommodation: all, no doubt, minimal) entailed in paying the owner his *obolos* per slave per day.

4.15 Hipponikos had six hundred slaves let out in this same way, which brought him in a *mna* a day, net Despite his lack of a patronymic or other identifier (to match 'Nikias the son of Nikeratos' in 4.14), X.'s second example is again an identifiable figure from the second half of the fifth century. Hipponikos being a much less common name than Nikias, this has to be *LGPN* s.v. no.13, Hipponikos (II) Kalliou (II) of Alopeke in *APF* 260 and 262, *POP* 172–3. Andocides (1.130), Isocrates (16.31: mentioned there because Alkibiades married his daughter Hipparete), and Lysias (19.48) all refer to him as, reputedly, the richest man in the whole of Hellas. Confirmation, were it needed, that much of the family's riches came from the mines is provided by Cornelius Nepos, *Cim.*1.3 on Kallias (II): *magnas pecunias ex metallis fecerat*. Hipponikos' income from the six hundred slaves attributed to him here—most unlikely to have been all the slaves that he owned, and perhaps not even all the ones he owned in the mines—would have been six *talanta* a year.

Gauthier 143–4 draws attention to the fact that whereas Nikias (according to X.) had 'contracted out' his slaves to Sosias, a different verb is used here in 4.15 and again in 4.16, in reference to the slaves of Hipponikos, and many others at the time of writing (including, implicitly, those of Philemonides: see the next lemma). They are 'let out', *ekdedomena* (*andrapoda*) or *ekdedomenoi* (*anthrôpoi*). The different terminology should be respected. Nikias and Sosias, to reiterate, were entering into a contract with each other. In these other cases—more normal cases, one may suspect, *in this respect*—it was simply a matter of an owner supplying his own slaves to people who were not, in themselves, lessees (and who pass unmentioned here).

4.15 Philemonides had three hundred, which netted him a half-*mna* After two celebrities, a much more unknown quantity, at least as far as we are concerned. X.'s Philemonides, *LGPN* s.v. no.2, claimed an entry in *APF* (535) on the strength of this datum alone: three hundred slaves in the mines, and annual income of three *talanta* from them.

In fact there is more to be said; cf. Gauthier 143. Since the name is so very rare (with only five instances in *LGPN*), suggestions of prosopographical links that would otherwise be rash become more persuasive.

First, we should note *SIG* 1203 (*IG* II^2 2638), cited by Wilhelm (1934) 24. This is the marker-stone of a mine (sold to the otherwise unknown Polymelos of Lamptrai) called the *Philemoniakon*: 'Philemon's'. Following Wilhelm, Gauthier asks whether the Philemon after whom the mine was named could be X.'s 'Philemonides'; likewise R. G. Osborne (1985) 117. (Another possibility is that Philemon was the father, or son, of Philemonides. In the short dialogue *Theages* attributed to Plato there is a fifth-century Philemonides son of Philemon: 129B = *LGPN* s.v. no.1, *POP* 238.)

Second, there are no fewer than three possibilities for a homonymous descendant of X.'s Philemonides. Gauthier brings up only the one mentioned, without (patronymic or) demotic, as one of the generals of the year 330/29 (Reinmuth 42–50 no.12, right side, line 3): *LGPN* s.v. no.3, Davies (1981) 165, *AO* 413. He might be the grandson of X.'s man, Gauthier hazards. But the same applies to Philemonides of Alopeke, a councillor in *c.* 330 (*AO* 424); *LGPN* s.v. no.5. And note also *LGPN* s.v. no.4, Philemonides of Aixone, father of the ephebe Amphistratos in line 15 of RO 89 (*IG* II^2 1156), Harding (1985) no.108, from 332.

4.15 and there were others, I reckon, each operating at his own capacity Thiel 21 cites Andoc. 1.38 (see already under **4.14 He contracted them out**): the informer Diokleides there (*LGPN* s.v. no.3), it would appear, had *one* slave working at Laureion. A less extreme instance, no doubt, is Pantainetos in Demosth. 37.4 (*LGPN* s.v. no.1), with thirty slaves in a rented *ergastêrion*.

4.16 But why is it necessary to speak of the old days? At the present time there are many men in the silver-mines let out similarly This rhetorical question is a trope perhaps indebted to Thucydides. 'And why is it necessary to speak of the very old days', the Athenian spokesmen at Sparta in 432 declare, 'where the testimony is verbal hearsay, not eye-witness of what the listeners will hear?': Thuc. 1.73.2 (itself, Gomme suggested, perhaps influenced by Hdt. 9.27.2–4). In any event cf. also e.g. Isoc. 5.43, Demosth. 22.15, [Demosth.] 26.7.

As we see, X. here refers to 'men' (*anthrôpoi*, as in 4.14 and again 4.18 and 4.21), not 'slaves' (*andrapoda*), but no substantive distinction can be intended. LSJ s.v. registers 'slave' as a simple, one-to-one meaning of *anthrôpos* (I.7 there) as a post-classical phenomenon. Before it, as here, the word is chosen to suggest a generally low grade of humankind. Laureion miners who were not slaves did exist but only, by X.'s day, in almost invisibly small numbers. Sometimes adduced in this connection is the celebrated verse epitaph on marble, *IG* II^2 10051 (now lost): 'Atotas, miner. From the Euxine Pontos, Atotas, great-hearted Paphlagonian, put to rest from toils his body, far from home. Nobody rivalled me in my craft; I am from the stock of Pylaimenes, who died subdued by Achilles' hand.' (For Pylaimenes' death—actually in combat with Menelaus—and for 'great-hearted' Paphlagonians see Hom. *Il*.5.576–9. On this stone see also (e.g.) Vlassopoulos (2013) 130–1, Hunt (2015) 136–9, C. Taylor (2017) 223-4. Linguistic and stylistic considerations, I gather, would assign it a date much later than the orthodox one of the mid-fourth century, but the matter cannot be pursued here.) While the expense and the cultural sophistication of Atotas' monument does indicate that he died a free man, his life as a *metalleus* had probably begun as an imported slave; cf. Ste. Croix (1981) 274 with n.14. In support of their statement that '[f]ree men undertook only with reluctance the hard work in the mines', Isager & Hansen (1975) 103 with n.20 cite (without further discussion) 4.22 here and Demosth. 42.20. *Poroi* 4.22 does support the position expressed (see further in the Comm. there), but Demosth. 42.20 is irrelevant. (The unnamed speaker there says that he had 'formerly amassed large sums out of the *argyreia erga*, labouring with my own body and *ergazomenos*'. Since by his own account he was at the time one of the richest three hundred citizens (42.3–5, cf. 25), this pen-portrait cannot be taken seriously, except as that of someone who paid occasional visits to inspect in person the value of his investments.) Overall, it seems safe to say that the only men of free status who did work as miners, in the manner envisaged by Austin & Vidal-Naquet (1977) 102–3, were any who chose—or 'chose', if we allow for economic compulsion—to do so; cf. Powell (2015)

115. Note that the Athenian judicial system did not include condemnation to the mines among the penalties it employed; nor is there evidence for POWs in the Laureion mines.

For 'let out' see already under **4.15 Hipponikos.**

4.17 With my proposals progressing A favourite verb of X.'s: see also 4.37, 4.38 (and already e.g. *Hier.*9.5 & 7, *Hipp.*1.9, *Oec.*11.8).

The *present* participle here, and again (of another verb) in 6.1, contrasts with the aorist in 4.51, but this seems to be nothing more than stylistic variation. The basic idea is one that X. can express on a spectrum that ranges between total assurance (4.51) and polite conditionality (6.2–3).

4.17 the only novelty would be this Maximizing novelty, or claims to it, would be likely to characterize any modern equivalents of *Poroi.* X. was not averse to novelty on principle, as can be judged from *Hipp.*3.13 (on his own suggestions for the most realistic manoeuvres in cavalry displays in the Hippodrome; Kyle (1993) 95–7); see generally Godin (2015) 19–22. Even so, like many of the ancients, he did instinctively tend to equate the novel with the strange and suspicious. See e.g. *Cyrop.*4.4.10, 7.5.85, 8.8.16, *Lac.Pol.*10.8, *Mem.*2.3.10, 4.4.6–7.

In this instance the nature of 'the only novelty' is spelled out in the remainder of the sentence: see the next two lemmata. There was no novelty *as such* in the Athenian state's ownership of slaves. Hansen (1991) 122–3 estimates at 'at least several hundred' the *dêmosioi* who are attested as clerks, cleaners, labourers, and other functionaries. See also Fisher (1995) 55–6, Hunter (2006), and below under **the state.** Even so, X. is in a position to present his idea as a novelty in twin respects (Gauthier 144): the fact that 'his' *dêmosia andrapoda* are to be leased out to private individuals, and the sheer number of them.

4.17 just as private individuals who acquired slaves have provided themselves with an everlasting income More precisely, slave miners, as with Nikias and the other cases cited in 4.14–15.

The adjective 'everlasting' here (for which cf. already e.g. *Ages.*1.20, on cultivated land providing an everlasting food-supply) is poetic, often applied to ever-flowing rivers or the like, and by extension such phenomena as the everlasting power of Zeus (Eurip. *Orest.*1299). Against that background its application here to monetary income might at first sight seem banal, but we should recollect 1.4–5 on the 'eternal' assets of Attica that include its deposits of silver.

4.17 the state would possess *public* slaves, up to a total of three per Athenian Here at last, as Thiel 22 comments, some light is shed on the *triôbolon* of 3.9 (and the *obolos*-income per slave of 4.14–15 and 4.23).

Thiel went on to assert, without discussion, that three such slaves per citizen would mean 60,000 of them. Gauthier 144 notes that the basis of the calculation, the number of citizens at this time actually appears to lie somewhere between 20,000 and 30,000. The higher figure has been strenuously advocated by M. H. Hansen, among others: see Hansen (1985), summarized in Hansen (1991) 92–3. If X. himself had any means of knowing the number—which should not automatically be assumed—he will have built in to his scheme the idea of, *ultimately* (see 4.23–5), some 90,000 of these publicly owned slave miners. (NB: A figure of 10,000 crops up in the secondary literature from time to time: see e.g. Michell (1940) 109; French (1964) 138–9; R. G. Osborne (1985) 111, repeated in R. G. Osborne (1995) 31 and R. G. Osborne (2004) 91; Millett (2001) 37. One can only think that it stems from a misunderstanding of a later passage, 4.23 (q.v. Comm. there), and also—to avoid a supposed conflict with that—construes the present passage as referring to three *oboloi*, not three *andrapoda*, per citizen. That is not what the transmitted text says, and forcing it to do so by emendation would be no simple matter when the two nouns are of different genders. See also below, **4.25 In fact though**.)

Since these slaves are explicitly to be in public ownership (4.17–22), there is no necessity for the view of Bodei Giglioni cxxii, endorsed by Jansen (2012) 735 (and 738–9), that they would be an example of 'the *chôris oikountes*' (Demosth. 4.36), the kind of slaves 'living apart' from their owners—and regarded, to that extent, as privileged. (On the *chôris oikountes* see in brief Garlan (1988); in full Kamen (2013) chap.2; most recently Sosin (2015), urging however a novel and dubitable interpretation of the phrase, as mercenaries.) Perhaps attested as early as the sixth century (Hdt. 6.121.2), Athens' *dêmosioi* lived neither with nor apart from their only master (or mistress), the state; cf. Ismard (2015) 103–6 (whose estimate of their number is *c.* 1,000–1,200).

Aristotle, at the end of his critique of the constitutional measures of Phaleas of Chalkedon (cf. under **4.7 Take furnishings**), infers that Phaleas wanted 'the city'—meaning its citizen-body—to be small, because all the craftsmen (*technitai*) were to be public slaves (*dêmosioi*). Aristotle then comments: 'however, if there are to be *dêmosioi*, they ought to be *ta koina ergazomenoi*—just as in Epidamnos, and also as Diophantos once tried to organize at Athens' (Aristot. *Pol.*2.1267b16–19).

Of the public slaves of Epidamnos, in north-west Hellas (*OCD* 514, *IACP* no.79), nothing whatever is otherwise known, but with Diophantos it is possible to make some headway. His name is not rare: *LGPN* has 81 instances. However, 75% of them post-date Aristotle, and of the twenty or so who do not, the one that stands out as a public figure is no.921 in *AO* 457: Diophantos of Sphettos (*LGPN* s.v. no.54). First attested as the proposer of two honorific decrees in the early 360s (*IG* II^2 106–7, the second of them RO 31 (Harding (1985) no.53) decree I), Diophantos' principal claim to fame is having been, seemingly, co-creator of the theoric fund in the second half of the 350s, with Euboulos of Probalinthos (General Intro., section 6), and more generally a prominent member of the Euboulan political faction. See e.g. Isae. 3.22, Demosth. 19.86 & 198, 20.137, 35.6. Diophantos' interest in mining is guaranteed by two appearances in one of the more fragmentary mining-lease records (*Agora* 19 P9 (*SEG* 16.123), lines 10–13), thought to date from the 350s.

As regards what Aristotle says about Diophantos (above), Cawkwell (1963) 58 n.67 ignores '*tried to* organize' and so poses a misconceived question: when *did* Diophantos 'provide the city with these *dêmosioi technitai*'? His answer: later than *Poroi*—which is silent on the matter—and perhaps because of it. X.'s conative imperfect means that Diophantos tried *but failed* to bring in his plan; cf. D. M. Lewis (1990) 257–8. In practice, presumably, the assembly rejected it. With that understood (cf. Gauthier 229), it is still worthwhile to attempt to fathom what Diophantos' idea would have entailed. Here Aristotle's words (above) are crucial. The point of certainty is that in *Phaleas*' system all craftsmen were public slaves, but then (as Gauthier 228 notes) ambiguity arises with the *ta koina ergazomenoi*. Gauthier points out that that phrase can theoretically be interpreted in two ways (between which he himself refuses to choose): they are either (*a*) a subset of the *technitai,* i.e. those who work for the community, or (*b*) the entire labour-force (not purely the *technitai*) employed in public works. Even if we presume (with e.g. Barker (1946) 68 n.1) that option *a* is what Aristotle meant, the scope of *ta koina* remains unclear. In another passage Aristotle himself refers to officials who begin their term of office by 'offering magnificent sacrifices and organizing some aspect of the *koina*' (Aristot. *Pol.*6.1321a35–6), which seems to apply to the domain of religion and cult. On the other hand, as we have seen, *ergazomenoi* is a term often encountered (including here in *Poroi*: see **4.3 At any rate**) in the context of mining etc. Again Gauthier is reluctant to discard either of these avenues of interpretation for *Pol.*2.1267b16–19 and Diophantos. His caution is salutary. He does, though, venture a final set of observations which are worth our attention (Gauthier 229). Building-inscriptions of the late 330s and early 320s from Eleusis (*OCD* 500, *IACP* no.362), such as *IG* II² 1672 (now *I.Eleusis* 177; Papazarkadas (2011) 24–41), reveal a group of *dêmosioi*—preserved figures range between seventeen and thirty-three—and their manager (*epistatês*) maintained daily at the state's expense. Aristotle, resident in Athens between 335 and 323, surely knew of this practice, but does not mention it in the passage on Phaleas. Instead, by mentioning something that Diophantos had unsuccessfully tried to bring in, he invites the inference that Diophantos' scheme was significantly different from what the Athenian state actually did, twenty years or so later. But different in nature, or scale, or both? It is impossible to tell. Gauthier allows himself the hypothesis that Diophantos' plan took its inspiration 'more or less faithfully' from *Poroi*. Whether or not that is true, his fellow-citizens spurned it—perhaps because objections to it were not dealt with as studiously as X. does in what follows here.

4.18 Whether the things we are proposing are feasible, let anyone who wishes judge by examining them item by item This first-person plural stands out, amid the singulars elsewhere in the work, but what can be deduced from it? Perhaps X. is speaking for a consortium of like-minded reformers (including Diophantos?—see under the preceding lemma). Alternatively, this is simply his version of the 'royal' we.

Later in this sentence, as Gauthier 145 points out, there is an echo of the language of officialdom. Compare e.g. the Standards Decree *IG* I³ 1453 (ML 45, now OR 155; Fornara (1983) no.97), clause 14: 'the *epistatai*... are to set up [a stone stele in front of the mint] for examination by anyone who wishes'. See also e.g. Andoc. 1.83–4, Demosth. 24.18; and cf. again below, **At any rate**.

The idiom 'item by item' (already *Apol.*15, *Cyrop.*3.1.12, 5.5.15, 6.4.5, *Kyn.*1.13, 6.24, *Oec.*19.14) is perhaps a borrowing from Thucydides: see his 6.15.4 and 7.70.6.

4.18 Estimate of manpower: without doubt, the public treasury would be better able to prepare it than private individuals; that is quite clear For 'the public treasury' (*to dêmosion*) cf. e.g. *Ages.*1.18 (the Spartan one, in that instance). LSJ s.v. *dêmosios* gives examples from Thucydides (6.31.3) and other authors: see III.c there. This sense is of course very closely related to *to dêmosion* in its larger connotation of 'the state' (literally, the people's thing), and there are many instances where either translation would serve equally well. Here, for consistency's sake, 'state' is my usual rendering of polis and 'treasury' that of *to dêmosion* (so again 4.19 and 4.20).

Schütrumpf 97 n.25 points out that this criterion of what is *dynaton* ('realisierbar') for the state, again in 4.21 and 6.1, was a recognized trope in political theory when something out of the ordinary was being proposed: cf. e.g. Plat. *Rep*.5.466D, 5.471C, 5.472B; Aristot. *Pol*.7.1325b38.

Because this sentence is syntactically paired and contrasted with the one after next ('And once they have been bought', etc.), it has seemed natural to translators to understand its opening phrase as '*Cost/price* of manpower' (so Dakyns, Marchant, Bodei Giglioni, and Waterfield, among others) and thereby to presume that X.'s point is that the state can *afford* these slaves more easily than private individuals could. Gauthier 145–6 protests, I think rightly so (despite the objections of Schütrumpf 97 n.26). On the usual view, the sentence which comes between the two contrasting ones—see the next lemma—has to be adding a new consideration ('Moreover': Marchant). However, it is introduced by one of X.'s most characteristic phrases (in this work and earlier ones), *ge mên*, for restating a point already made, but in a more concessive, qualified way. Gauthier adduces the parallels of 4.3, 4.31, and 4.37; one could add 2.2, 3.1, 3.5, 3.12, 4.1, 4.17, 4.20, 4.23, 4.47, 4.48, 4.51, 6.1, and 6.2.

4.18 At any rate the council could easily make a proclamation, for 'anyone who wishes to bring slaves', and then purchase the ones brought in For the Athenian council of 500 see again 6.1 with Comm., and generally Rhodes (1972), Hansen (1991) 246–65.

I have marked the words indicated (four of them, in the Greek) as a quotation because of the strong possibility that they are the ones used in the proclamation. In particular, the phrase 'anyone who wishes' is a staple formula in classical Athenian law and legal procedure. Here are three examples out of many: lines 33–5 of *IG* I^3 34 (ML 46, now OR 154; Fornara (1983) no.98), Kleinias' decree of the (?)mid-420s for tightening up imperial tribute collection; lines 32–4 of RO 25 (Austin & Vidal-Naquet (1977) no.102, Harding (1985) no.45), the coinage law of 375/4; and the citizenship law quoted in [Demosth.] 59.16. It was indeed a fundamental democratic principle. See generally Hansen (1991) 71–2, 266–8.

In the present context, the proclamation itself would be made by the public crier/herald (*kêryx*) Philokles, who had succeeded his father Eukles in the post (*IG* II^2 145; Rhodes (1972) 84-85; M. J. Osborne (1981–1983) 3.39–41 (T20)). Purchasing would then, no doubt, be the task of the fifty executive *prytaneis* in office (*OCD* 1231–2); cf. Gauthier 146. In 4.23 a normal price of 180 drachmas appears to be presupposed (see the Comm. there); and 4.36 will envisage the purchasing process as a gradual one, to keep the asking-prices within reasonable bounds.

4.19 why would anyone be less likely to lease them from the treasury than from private individuals, if he was going to have them on the same terms? Namely, an *obolos* a day per man, and keeping up the numbers (4.14–15).

4.19 people lease precincts and shrines and houses and buy tax-collecting rights from the state For the Greek here ('precincts and shrines') see Notes on the Text.

X.'s point is simple enough: there would be nothing novel (and hence alarming: see **4.17 the only novelty**) in itself about leasing slaves from the state. Two subsets of the existing activities of the *pôlêtai* are cited in support of this (cf. ?Aristot. *Ath.Pol.*47.2–5). They (*a*) already do issue leases, of named sacred properties, and analogously they (*b*) sell the rights—farm out is the traditional term—to collect specific indirect taxes, *telê*, on the state's behalf (and, implicitly, to make a profit from doing so).

Concerning *a*, Papazarkadas (2011), esp. 51–75, is comprehensive and authoritative; 56–7 there briefly discuss *Poroi* 4.19 (and 4.20, q.v. below). X.'s 'houses' (*oikiai*) in this list had already been glossed by Gauthier 147 as *sacred* houses, i.e. ones belonging to a deity and leased out for that deity's profit. (The confiscated houses of ?Aristot. *Ath.Pol.*47.3 are entirely different, therefore.) Gauthier cited the example of a particularly profitable one, attested in the 430s, belonging to the community's patron goddess Athena Polias; for that, see also Papazarkadas (2011) 18–19, with further discussion and illustration at 195–6 and throughout appendix VII.

Concerning *b*, Andoc. 1.133–4 (= Austin & Vidal-Naquet (1977) no.93), on two rival consortia vying for the *pentêkostê* contract (cf. under **3.3 As is plain**), provides a detailed vignette of what was involved. See also the anecdote in Plut. *Alk.*5.2–5: ostensibly about *all* 'the public taxes', it is in fact, surely, about a single unnamed one.

4.20 In order that the slaves it has bought are insured, the treasury can accept guarantors from those who are leasing them, just as it does from those who buy the tax-collecting rights See also 3.14 (a closer parallel, in fact, though only a hypothetical one). X.'s noun here for guarantors (*eggyoi*) is an unusual one, not otherwise attested before the Hellenistic period, but there is no reason to suppose that he means anything different by it than the *eggyêtai* of 3.14 (and other works). I take this opportunity to note that the translation of 'the treasury can etc.' in Marchant's Loeb edition ('can insure the slaves purchased by requiring some of the lessees to become guarantors') factually misrepresents the procedure involved; cf. Papazarkadas (2011) 56–9.

In the opening clause I have followed other translators in rendering the verb as 'insured', but the verb changes (to 'protected') in the retrospective 4.21. The senses of keeping safe and (financially and legally) insuring are combined; and 4.14's idea of maintaining numbers is probably implicit as well.

Gauthier 148–9 considers that X. presents his idea here as a new one, and he finds this surprising, when such well-established parallels were available. (The one that X. cites himself, guarantors in tax-collecting contracts, is illustrated by Plut. *Alk.*5.1–5. For the same in leasing sacred property see Papazarkadas (2011) appendix VII.) In my opinion X.'s form of words does not, in point of fact, justify Gauthier's premise. Rather, X. is simply continuing to express himself as fully as he can for the benefit of those to whom the whole topic is unfamiliar (4.1).

4.20 Wrongdoing, mind you, is easier for someone purchasing a tax-contract than for someone leasing slaves. (4.21) This is because, when public money looks the same as private, how could an exporter of it be caught? Having brought in, himself, the parallel of tax-farming (4.20), X. here persists with it in a rather laboured comparison (continued under the next lemma); cf. Gauthier 149.

Andoc. 1.92–3 illustrates the simplest sort of 'wrongdoing' that could be attempted by those who entered into contracts with the Athenian state (to collect rents from some men farming public lands, in this instance). As alleged there, Andocides' accuser Kephisios (*LGPN* s.v. nos.1 & 2) simply defaulted on the sum he had undertaken to give the exchequer, and left town. See generally Rhodes (1972) 149–51, with comment on the penalties attested—different at different times—for defaulting contractors, and also (if to a lesser degree of severity) for their guarantors. 'The fourth-century law governing public contracts',

Rhodes writes, 'should perhaps be reconstructed as follows: *Those who became public debtors by undertaking to collect a tax, or by some other form of contract, had to provide guarantors when the contract was made. If they fell behind with their payments, they incurred a multiple debt and lost their civic rights until that debt was discharged; and to ensure that the debt was discharged the* boulê *had the right to order their imprisonment until payment was made, and the confiscation of their guarantors' property*.'

None of this, however, really bears in a direct way on what X. is saying (or claiming) here. As Gauthier 149 puts it, he has tried to make into a qualitative matter (one sort of money vs. another) what is in fact a purely quantitative one: the state demands the sum of money it was promised, and is bent on getting it. (X.'s point—essentially that one coin looks like another whereas one branded slave does not—has been unduly influenced by the second half of the comparison. See under the next lemma.)

4.21 Slaves, on the other hand, would have been marked out by the public seal The general phenomenon of 'marking out' slaves among the ancient Hellenes—generally by tattooing (not branding; cf. Stadter (1989) 249)—was less widespread than might be supposed from Near Eastern (and, later, Roman) practice. One of its purposes was punishment, for slaves who ran away but were caught again; *Hell.* 5.3.24 mentions one. On another level, this was a possible fate for the losers in military conflict. An extreme instance is said to have occurred during the revolt of Samos (*OCD* 1313–14, *IACP* nos.864–5) from Athens in 441–439: the Athenians tattoo Samian POWs on the forehead with the Athenian owl; the Samians retaliate by disfiguring captive Athenians with the Samian city-mark, the pig-like prow of a *samaina* galley. Plut. *Per.*26.3–4 gets the two marks the wrong way round, but other versions of the story—ignored in Shipley (1987) 116–17—tacitly correct him. Compare Plut. *Nik.*29.2: the Athenian POWs at Syracuse (*OCD* 1420–1, *IACP* no.47) in 413 are tattooed, again on the forehead, with the Syracusans' horse-symbol. This and other evidence is collected at Stadter (1989) 249–50; and more broadly see C. P. Jones (1987).

A taunt which invokes slave-tattooing is said to have been levelled at Hyperbolos of Perithoidai (*LGPN* s.v. no.5, *OCD* 716, *APF* 517) by Andocides: 'of Hyperbolos I am ashamed to speak—his father [Antiphanes] was a marked slave, and still works in the public mint'; Andoc. fr.5, preserved by an ancient scholiast (annotator) of

Aristophanes. (Cartledge in Waterfield 26 misattributes the jibe to Demosthenes, on his adversary Aeschines. On the latter's father Atrometos of Kothokidai, *LGPN* s.v. no.3, see rather Demosth. 18.129: 'your father Tromes was a slave in Elpias' primary school near the Theseion, and wore stout shackles and a wooden collar'.) Even though what Andocides alleges about Antiphanes is nonsense (see *APF* 517), it creates a significant connection with RO 25 (Austin & Vidal-Naquet (1977) no.102, Harding (1985) no.45), the 375/4 Athenian coinage law mentioned above (under **4.18 At any rate**). Much of it concerns the 'public approver' (*dokimastês dêmosios*), who evidently exists already; he will be 'sitting' daily (either in the agora or in the council-house), and will receive fifty strokes of the lash if he fails in his duties. He is without question a slave. In addition lines 36–44 ordain the appointment (by the council) of a new, separate *dokimastês* in the Peiraieus, 'for the *nauklêroi* and the *emporoi* and everyone else'. He will come 'from the public slaves if (a suitable one is) available, or will be bought'.

In connection with the city *dokimastês* in that law there is mention of 'the public *charaktêr*', a die or stamp—but rather than this slave *bearing* it he *looks for* it, on the coins he is examining. From this it follows that 'the' public *charaktêr*, applied in the mint, was whatever was stamped on the Athenian silver coins of the era: on a tetradrachm, for example, an Athena-head on the obverse and an owl (and small olive-twig) with the legend *AΘE* on the reverse. Smaller denominations have the same obverse but sometimes a different reverse (e.g. a double-bodied owl on the diobol); see generally Head (1911) 374. Gauthier 150 adduces the symbols stamped on the bronze allotment-plates (*pinakia*) that belonged to individual Athenian jurors in this period (Demosth. 39.10–12, etc.). The comprehensive study of the *pinakia* by Kroll (1972) chaps.2–3 differentiates between their 'primary' and 'secondary' seals. The former (stamped at the time of manufacture) are two-fold: a *triôbolon* numeral (indicating the dikast's entitlement to his pay), and a gorgon's head (associated with Athena: *OCD* 622–3 Gorgo/Medusa). The latter—where they exist—are an owl in a square, a double-bodied owl, or occasionally a (?)sphinx. If we leave Kroll's secondary seals out of account, the link with fourth-century Athenian currency is weakened by the fact that gorgon's heads had not been used since the Peisistratids (Melville Jones (1986) 97 has a photograph); on the other hand, the triobol seals on most of the *pinakia* 'precisely duplicate the reverse type of fourth century Athenian triobol coins and could have been struck with dies engraved and originally used for the minting of coins' (Kroll (1972) 41).

Terminologically speaking, the picture becomes more complicated still when the public 'seal' (*sphragis*) is brought in. On this there are short general studies by W. P. Wallace (1949) and D. M. Lewis (1955), the latter drawing attention to its earliest attestation, in an inventory-document of 397 (*IG* II² 1408, lines 12–13). See also RO 58 (Harding (1985) no.78), now *IG* II³ 292/*AIO* (and *I.Eleusis* 144), a decree of 352/1 where the chairman of the *prytaneis* must use it to seal two water-jugs containing messages for the Delphic oracle to choose between (lines 23–42, at 39–40); and ?Aristot. *Ath.Pol.*44.1, the basic text which lists holding the public seal as one of the duties of such a chairman (*epistatês*) during the twenty-four hours in which he functions as Athens' head of state (Hansen (1991) 250). In his commentary on that passage Rhodes (1981) 532 quotes the present one, *Poroi* 4.21, and indeed the *sphragis* must be identical with what X. calls here 'the public *sêmantron*'; so Thiel xxii n.1 and others. (For *sêmantra* in X. see already *Lac.Pol.*6.4: private Spartan ones. He might have borrowed the word from Eurip. *Iph.Taur.* 325 and 1372, but see also Hdt. 2.121.β1, in an Egyptian story. X. mentions a *sphragis* twice, both times referring to letters bearing the seal of the King of Persia: *Hell.*1.4.3, 7.1.39.) What symbol this Athenian *sphragis*/*sêmantron* bore is impossible to say for certain, but an Athena head would be a plausible guess.

4.21 a penalty both for the seller and for the exporter of them would be laid down X.'s words do show that he has in mind a single penalty for the two offences likely to arise: selling these slaves (by the lessee) and exporting them (by their purchaser, who knows that he cannot use them within Athens); cf. Gauthier 150–1. He does not suggest what that penalty should be. For possible analogies see above under **4.20 Wrongdoing**.

4.21 the question thus becomes, how could anyone steal them? Translations have 'steal' because that is the verb X. uses. Nevertheless (as Thiel 23 and Gauthier 151 remark), the fraudulence envisaged here would in practice be *substitution*. Granted that some of the cohort might have absconded or died, requiring good-faith replacement (cf. 4.14–15), the Athenian state wanted to receive back at the end of a contractual period not the same *number* of slaves, merely, but *the same slaves*, rather than inferior surrogates; cf. Gauthier 149.

4.22 suppose someone is concerned about how, once numerous workmen are available, numerous individuals too will come forward to lease them This opening verb has already been used in 3.7. It does not necessarily imply concern in the sense of anxiety; rather, paying rational attention to a question and working out answers to it; cf. e.g. *Cyrop.*4.1.5, 4.2.3. In this instance, X.'s two-fold response to his own question fills the remainder of 4.22: see the next two lemmata.

4.22 many of the established operators will lease the public slaves *in addition*, so plentiful are the existing opportunities This statement (using the compound verb *prosmisthousthai*) together with 4.32 make it a certainty that X.'s publicly owned slave miners will work alongside privately owned ones, not replace them. Dillery (2017) 217 is wrong to state that the plan would see Athens 'turning the extraction of ore over' to the *dêmosia andrapoda.*

Gauthier 151 repeats here his view (see under **4.11 and also**) that X. designates as *kataskeuazomenoi*—rather than *ergazomenoi*—those who provide the above-ground facilities. I find that interpretation no more cogent in the present passage than in the earlier one. In any case, here as already in 4.17, the perfect tense of the participle must have been chosen for a reason; cf. Dakyns ('those who have already embarked on mining operations') and Waterfield ('those who are already established in the mines').

Gauthier 151–2 must be right, on the other hand, in how he understands the explanatory clause, which in the Greek simply adds 'for the existing (things) are many'. Some translators (Dakyns, Marchant, Bodei Giglioni, Waterfield) take this as referring to the deep pockets of the operators themselves, but that seems unsatisfactory because of the conflict it would create with 4.28's (unambiguous) statement that 'the men who work in mining are *poorer*' than they used to be. (One could add—a point overlooked by Jansen (2007) 377–8 in his rejection of Gauthier's position—that if that is what X. meant to say here, it is very odd that he chose an impersonal construction, rather than linking the point grammatically with 'many of the established operators'.) Following Thiel 23 and others, Gauthier adduces 4.3, which lays emphasis on the potential of the deposits themselves; cf. also 4.26 (and 4.39).

4.22 there are many, among those who are growing old in the mining industry, and many others, Athenians and foreigners alike, who either would not or could not do physical labour, but would gladly make their living in curatorial capacities, by brain-work For the

Greek here ('many, among those who are growing old in the mining industry') see Notes on the Text. If the view taken there is correct, some translations (Dakyns, Marchant, Waterfield) have X. making *three* points, not two, in 4.22 as a whole.

'Brain-work', literally using judgement, will feature again in 5.3 (and see already *Oec.*2.18); and for a brains vs. brawn distinction, as here, cf. *Symp.*2.26. As noted under **4.14 He contracted**, X. in *Mem.*2.5.2 gives the job description of Nikias' man Sosias as that of *epistatês*. Here he is vaguer, using the verb *epimeleisthai* (cognate with the *epimeleia* of 2.1–2). Its related concrete noun would be *epimelêtês*, a term we have encountered in connection with 3.3 and the *emporion* (q.v.). No actual post in the mining industry is known to have borne such a title, but that is not a problem. X. is thinking in generic terms, of how these two categories of people—one of them in the industry already, the other (he presumes) wishing to be—could fill the ancient equivalent of white-collar jobs. (Bodei Giglioni cxiv–cxv understands 'those who are growing old in the mining industry' to be ageing *slaves*, but Gauthier 153—following Ardaillon (1897) 90 and Thiel 23–4—insists that they are free men, as is required by the structure of this whole clause which pairs them with the 'many others, Athenians and foreigners alike'.)

This passage as a whole, as has long been recognized, echoes one in *Mem.*2.8.1–6. There X. recalls Sokrates, in or after 404, meeting (after a long absence) an old comrade of his, Eutheros: *LGPN* s.v. no.1, *POP* 150–1. Financially ruined by the Peloponnesian War, Eutheros says that he must brace himself for 'physical labour', since the only alternative would be begging. Sokrates wonders how long Eutheros thinks he would have the strength to 'make his living' in that way, and suggests that he would do better to approach a more affluent individual who needs someone 'to join him in a curatorial role', managing his *erga* and helping to bring in his crops and assisting him to safeguard his property. Eutheros is aghast. He calls this slavery; it would bring him reproaches. Sokrates' advice is that he should make provision for 'growing old' by trying to find an uncensorious employer. (The context indicates that '*erga*' there is unlikely to refer to mining.)

Cartledge in Waterfield 226 finds the present passage 'verging…on the utopian'. To be kinder to X. one might call it somewhat naive. (He might have done better to leave this issue and move on after 'the existing opportunities', q.v. above.)

4.23 Assume, anyway, that the initial total of slaves is twelve hundred. In the course of five or six years that number could probably become, by using the revenue itself, not less than six thousand Gauthier 155 asks why this initial figure of 1,200 is chosen, and offers what he calls a 'fragile conjecture'; in truth, an ingenious one. At a price per slave of 180 drachmas (see the next paragraph), buying 1,200 would cost 36 *talanta*. Given that in 4.40 X. will say, in effect, that implementing his proposals in Chap.2 (metics) and Chap.3 (traders) would be possible without imposing an *eisphora*, it seems to follow that proceeding with the proposals made in Chap.4 *would* require one; so Gauthier's surmise is that 36 *talanta* is all that could realistically be raised by it. Demosth. 14.27 supplies an exactly contemporary context. In his earliest surviving address to the assembly, Demosthenes says that a 1% *eisphora* would raise 60 *talanta*, a 2% one 120 *talanta* (neither sum, he insists, enough to fight the Persians); the calculation presupposes an overall valuation of 6,000 *talanta* (Demosth. 14.19; cf. Polyb. 2.62.6–7 for 5,750 *talanta* in 378/7). Accordingly, Gauthier's conjecture is that X. has in mind a 0.5% levy, which would bring in 30 *talanta* from those citizens who were liable, and 6 more from the wealthier metics (who paid 'the sixth part'; Whitehead (1977) 78–80).

Be all that as it may, Gauthier 155–6 follows Thiel 52–4 (Excursus X), Lauffer (1955-1956) 68, and others in noting that these figures enable the *price* of the slaves envisaged by X. to be calculated. To reach 6,000 from 1,200 in *five* years implies a price of 158 drachmas each; to reach it in *six* years, 195 drachmas; The resulting median figure of 180 fits well enough with slave-prices in classical Athens known from other sources, notably the 'Attic Stelai' confiscations of 414: *IG* I^3 421–30 (*Agora* 19 P1; ML 79, with comment p.247; OR 172; Fornara (1983) no.147).

See further under the next lemma.

4.23 Further, assume that each of this number brings in an *obolos* a day, net; the annual revenue is sixty *talanta*. (4.24) Out of this sum, assume that twenty *talanta* goes towards more slaves; the state will still have the forty to use in whatever way it thinks necessary. When the slave total reaches *ten* thousand, the revenue will be a hundred *talanta* For the *obolos* a day per slave see already 4.14–15 (with 4.15 He contracted on the meaning of 'net'). On this basis X.'s calculations are irreproachable. The fact that he stops illustrating them at a figure of 10,000 slaves does not of course mean he was under the misapprehension that there were fewer than 3,500 citizens (cf. under 4.17 the state), as 4.25 will show.

In the opinion of Gauthier 156, the use of two-thirds of the revenue for purposes other than purchasing more slave miners means stepping up the distributions of a *triôbolon*. But why restrict X.'s phrase so?

4.25 In fact though, receipts will be many times more than this X. actually writes here '(implicit subject) will receive etc.' So what is the verb's subject? Thiel 24–5, Lauffer (1955–1956) 144, Gauthier 156, and latterly Jansen (2007) 361 all take the view that it must be 'the silver-mines'. Thiel even goes so far as to transpose *ta argyreia* into this sentence from its transmitted place in the following one. Gauthier supplies it here and leaves the later sentence unchanged. All this is justified, in their view, by X.'s use of the verb *dechesthai*, rather than more usual verbs for a state (or suchlike) deriving revenues, such as *apolambanein* or *komizesthai*. Mines, on the other hand, might properly be said to 'receive' *slaves*.

There is a problem here, without doubt, but this solution to it seems to me a remedy worse than the disease. At the heart of the difficulty is the inherent ambiguity, taken in isolation, of X.'s phrase *pollaplasia toutôn*: 'many times more than these', plural (though idiomatic English requires the singular). The scholars cited above evidently regard the antecedent of 'these' as the 10,000 slaves just mentioned. Grammatically, though, it could be the 100 talents just mentioned. And that alternative looks preferable in the light of the fact that X. has been writing of the income/revenue that *the state* will have at its disposal (4.24); cf. Schütrumpf 125. It would be confusing if, without warning, he switched here to something the mines themselves will receive. In my opinion we must accept, here, another example of the older X.'s often idiosyncratic lexicon.

A less troublesome matter is the sense of *pollaplasia* itself. Dakyns translates 'much more'; Marchant, Waterfield, and Powell (2015) 100 'far more'; A. H. M. Jones (1969) 'much more'—all wrongly. This adjective (already in 1.5 and 4.4) is a *multiplier*. Thus, in context here, anything less than *c.* 300 talents/*c.* 30,000 slaves would be a travesty of the word.

4.25 Those who could testify in my support are those who are still alive and can remember how much the tax on the slaves used to earn before the events at Dekeleia X. employs here—knowingly, one would assume—a rhetorical device from the courtroom (where actual testimony was presented as a matter of routine, but litigants and other speakers could try to influence juries by claiming that other witnesses were available but would not in fact be heard). Examples of this occur in the early forensic speeches of Isocrates (19.36, cf. 21.14) and also in e.g. Isae. 9.18, from (perhaps) the late 360s. See also below, **And there is**.

This passage as a whole, as we have seen in General Intro., section 3, has played a modest role in the process whereby *Poroi* is assigned its orthodox date of 355/4. 'The events at Dekeleia' is a coy allusion to what Thucydides (7.19.1–2) describes as happening in spring and summer 413, on the original advice of Alkibiades (6.91.6–92.1, with 6.93.2 and 7.18.1). The Spartans and their allies invaded Attica and established a permanent fortress at Dekeleia (*OCD* 419), a village in the foothills of Mt. Parnes, some 18 km. north of Athens itself (and with an unimpeded view of it). Alkibiades in Thuc. 6.91.7 mentions 'the silver-mines of Laureion' as one of the revenue-streams that would be lost to the Athenians by this move, and Thuc. 7.27–8 has a celebrated description of the logistical and psychological after-effects overall. They include the desertion of 'more than twenty thousand *andrapoda*, the majority of whom were handicraftsmen' (7.27.5). Despite the attempts of scholars to argue the case either way, there is no means of telling whether Thucydides supposed—let alone whether he knew—that more of them were in mining than in agriculture or *vice versa*; cf. Hornblower (1991–2008) 3.591–2.

Cartledge in Waterfield 226 remarks that readers old enough to remember for themselves a fact that had obtained *before* this catastrophic development would have to have been 'at least 75'. Gauthier 157 attempts to raise that to >80, with a parallel from Plut. *Per.*7.1. 'Very old men' who heard the young Perikles (*c.* 494–428: *LGPN* s.v. no.3) were reminded of the young Peisistratos (*c.* 600–527: *LGPN* s.v. no.3); so they were octogenarians when Perikles' public career began. The calculation does work in the Peisistratos/Perikles case; cf. Stadter (1989) 89. In the present instance, however, there is no good reason to stipulate that the men in question had to have been old enough to attend the assembly, so as to absorb there such facts at first hand. Here, in my view, it is enough to say that X. is marshalling his own (dwindling) generation.

For describing a tax as 'earning' (literally 'finding') income see again 4.40, and cf. already *Hell.*3.4.24 (by defeating Tissaphernes, Agesilaos 'earned' more than seventy talents); elsewhere e.g. Isae. 8.35 (a house 'earning' a thousand drachmas in rent), *Agora* 19 L13 (*IG* II^2 1176+), leasing of the Peiraieus deme theatre, 324/3; Whitehead (1986) 385, and more in Wyse (1904) 615.

As regards precisely what tax 'of' (= on) *andrapoda* X. was referring to here, Gauthier 157–8 notes the two possibilities that have been championed. One (advocated by Boeckh (1886) 402 and Thiel 24, among others) is a direct capitation tax on slaves, paid annually by a master (Boeckh) or contractor (Thiel) to the tax-collector authorized to receive it. The other (urged by, among others, Andreades (1933) 281–2 and Lauffer (1955–1956) 72 and 144) is that X. is thinking of the indirect tax(es) incurred by the provision of slave miners, i.e. the 2% levy on entry to and exit from the Peiriaeus *emporion* (see under **3.5 As is plain**) or a relevant sales tax. Gauthier himself supports the second of these options. He stresses that such a capitation tax is unattested in the Greek world at large and that, within that macrocosm, the relatively copious evidence for Athens shows no trace of it or of the legal consequences of enforcing it—which would have been considerable. (One could comment that the rich evidence of oratory would be irrelevant if this was a tax *only levied before 413*, but that is not the natural interpretation of what X. says.) By contrast, a tax on the *sale* of slaves has parallels in e.g. late sixth-century Kyzikos (*SIG* 4; Fawcett (2006) 193–4) and late third-century Akarnania (*IG* IX.1^2 583); and, as indicated above, the Athenians' own *pentêkostê* is independently attested. What is more, one of the late antique lexicographers states in terms that it covered slaves as well as other commodities: 'the *emporoi* used to pay a fiftieth of cargoes and *andrapoda* being brought in to the Peiraieus from a foreign land' (Bekker, *Anecdota Graeca, Glossae Rhetoricae* 1.297.21–6—almost certainly an entry generated by Demosth. 35.29). If X.'s reference here to 'the' tax can be pressed (cf. Fawcett (2016) 154, 167), this is the likeliest. Gauthier also notes the evidence suggesting that, in periods of prosperity at least, revenues from the *pentêkostê* were so substantial that it was sub-divided. 'The fiftieth of grain (*sitos*)' is mentioned in [Demosth.] 59.27, relating to the year 369. (One can now add lines 7–8 and 56–7 of RO 26, the grain law of 374/3.) Also, a law of *c.* 335 on the Little (= annual) Panathenaia festival orders the *pôlêtai* 'to sell the fiftieth in the [Nea] separately from the other (taxes)': RO 81 (now *IG* II^3 447/*AIO*) lines 11–13. (The identification of 'the Nea', mentioned throughout this law and the accompanying decree, is controversial, but for present purposes the only relevant point is that it was a large tract of land.) Accordingly, a discrete *pentêkostê tôn andrapodôn* seems entirely within the bounds of possibility.

4.25 And there is corroborative testimony, too, in this: In general terms the idiom (with Greek *kakeino hoti* prompting a colon in translation) is one that X. had already used in *Ages.*8.4–5 and *Mem.*2.6.27. More specifically, the notion of impersonal testimony (contrast **Those who**, above), already in 1.3, now reappears with greater emphasis in 4.25–6, first invoking the past, then the present.

4.25 although a countless number of people have worked in the silver-mines throughout their whole history, the silver-mines today are in no way different from what our ancestors used to recall them as being A second appeal (cf. 4.13) to the authority of oral tradition, stretching even further back than what the living could recall (see the preceding lemma).

4.26 there could never be more slaves there than the operations require. Those who are digging find no limit, whether downwards or sideways More exactly, they 'find a limit neither of (= to) depth nor of underground passages', *hyponomoi* a.k.a. galleries (always horizontal: Thiel 25). LSJ s.v. unnecessarily assigns the sense 'vein' to the noun in the present context. Paired as it is with *bathos*, depth, the clause as a whole has an antecedent in *Hell.*3.1.7: the Spartan commander in Asia Minor in 399, Thibron (*OCD* 1469 s.v.1), cuts off a town's water-supply by sinking a vertical *phreatia* (shaft, well) and extending a horizontal *hyponomos* from it. For *hyponomoi* as siege 'mines' see also Thuc. 2.76.2 (the Plataians in their own defence, 429).

Fisher (1995) 48 fig.4 is a photograph of one of the deep shafts at Laureion (which range between 25 and 105 m. in depth); Ellis Jones (1982) 179 figs.7a&b show galleries cut horizontally into a hillside. See generally on the topic Ardaillon (1897) 24–33, Wilsdorf (1952) 113–17, Lauffer (1955–1956) 21–2; Morin et al. (2012).

4.27 cutting *new* mines is no less possible now than in the past—and nobody could be in a position to state as a fact whether there is more silver-bearing ore in the well-worked ones than in those still uncut X. uses here and throughout 4.27–30 the technical language of this operation: the verb *kainotomein* (which can also have figurative applications, not relevant here: see LSJ). Its cognate noun *kainotomia* (of which the same is true) is generally found in the plural, describing newly cut mines: so, six times, in mining-leases on stone from the last quarter of the fourth century, and also in Hyp. *Eux.*35–6 (with Whitehead (2000) 250–4) from the first half of the 320s. See further under the next lemma.

It is noteworthy that in the first instance a silver-mine is 'cut' rather than dug (though see 4.2 & 4 and 4.26—and 1.5—for the digging that takes place thereafter). Besides *kainotomein* itself, the *tem*- root is also present here in the perfect participle of the verb *katatemnein* (here 'well-worked') and the adjective *atmêtos*, and cf. *temnein* in Hyp. *Eux*.35 (above), a mine that had been 'cut inside the limits'. (Aristot. *Meteor*.378a19–21 differentiates between two categories of thing that occur in the ground: *ta orykta*, those one gets by digging, and *ta metalleuta*, those one gets by mining.)

4.28 not many people do cut new mines today, as they did before Hyperides' assertion in the 320s that 'newly cut mines, previously neglected through fear, are now active' (Hyp. *Eux*.36: see under the preceding lemma) makes a good fit with this. Citing 'fear' (*phobos*) might seem hyperbolic, but it is really no more than a one-word summary of what X. goes on to say here about the risks that *kainotomiai* entailed (4.28–32).

I note here *faute de mieux* the unparalleled and tantalizing decree *IG* II^2 411. Dating probably from the Lykourgan period, though possibly the 340s, a certain Sokles—perhaps a freedman—is to have control of something from which he claims there will be 'revenue' (X.'s *prosodos*) to the demos. He and the polis are to share the proceeds for twenty-five years, each party in alternate years. Orthodoxy since 1935 holds that the context here is the mining industry, and (within that) possibly the area of *kainotomiai* or similarly exploratory ventures; however, the most recent study, Lambert (2010), urges that that is not a certainty. (If it is wrong, the earlier view that this concerns agricultural land is a worse idea, not a better. Lambert himself very tentatively suggests salt-pans, as in line 17 of RO 37 (the Salaminioi *genos* own one), or other dispersed minerals or natural resources; cf. X.'s bullish view in 1.2.)

4.28 It is because the men who work in mining are poorer, as they are only recently operating again The scope of Greek adverbs which mean 'recently' (*arti* or, as here, *neôsti*) can sometimes surprise present-day readers. An extreme example is when Thucydides writes that in 432 the rural Athenians, obliged to evacuate their homes and take refuge inside the walls, had 'only just' re-established themselves after the Persian War evacuation of 480 (Thuc. 2.16.1). What did X. intend to convey by it here? Since this was a process, not an event, there is little point in trying to pin X. down to a date, even if he knew one to give. Gauthier 161 is confident that the period of time (before 355/4) in question can only be fifteen to twenty years, rather than the four decades that would take us back to the beginnings of the Athenian naval and psychological renaissance in the late 390s. Jansen (2007) 366 n.254 notes that on the rare occasions when X.'s use of *neôsti* can be quantified (*Cyrop*.3.3.36, *Hell*.4.7.5) it does refer to only a few years. If that is so in the present passage, even Gauthier's focus on the 370s would be too early; the 360s, rather. Jansen (2007) 364–6 actually makes a not implausible case for the *late* 360s as the key period. Against that, however, we must set the scenario presented in Kroll (2011b), mentioned already in Chap.4 intro. The sheer volume of Athenian tetradrachms he envisages as produced and circulating during decades before the re-mining of 353 (Kroll (2011a) presupposes a significant level—or upward curve—of silver-mining. 'One may then ask why Xenophon expressed concern about the state of Athens' silver mining industry… His statement (4.28) that investors in the industry had only recently begun to explore for new mine workings does not mean that the industry was just recovering from the Peloponnesian War; rather, his point was that, even though the old mines were operating successfully, exploration for new veins of silver needed to be undertaken if the industry were to expand and return to its full, fifth-century potential' (Kroll (2011b) 17).

The assertion that *because* 'they are only recently operating again' the men who work in mining are characterized by too much *penia* (cf. 1.1 with Comm.) to allow them to take a risk on an untried mine is dissected by Gauthier 160–1. Here just as elsewhere he strives to pinpoint those to whom X.'s various locutions apply. In this instance, he contends, 'those concerned with *ta metalla*' are (*a*) the same individuals as those who 'are only recently operating again', and (*b*) in either case the people X. means are 'sans doute' first and foremost those who own the land and associated facilities above the mines themselves. Proposition *a*, as I have indicated, seems cogent on grammatical grounds. The verb in the explanatory clause, in other words, is in the middle voice—as throughout *Poroi*—with 'the men' as its subject, rather than the (identical) passive assumed in translations such as Marchant's ('For operations have only lately been resumed'). Proposition *b* cannot stand or fall by the same test, and it is not a form of words otherwise attested. In common-sense terms the idea has merit, in as much as the damaged and dilapidated structures above ground required capital for their refurbishment; but some of the underground workings too will have fallen into disrepair. As Gauthier effectively concedes, owners and (potential) lessees alike—some of them the same people, in fact—were in much the same boat.

4.29 He who finds a good working becomes rich; he who does not loses everything he will have spent. The consequence is that people nowadays are none too keen to embark on this risk As Thiel 26 notes, this use of the noun *ergasia*, 'working', has a precedent in Thuc. 4.105.1 (on the historian's own ancestral right of gold-mining *ergasia* in Thrake) and a later parallel in—again—Hyp. *Eux.*36 ('the remaining *ergasia* of the mine'). The term embraces not merely the operation itself but the legal right to profit from it; cf. Hornblower (1991–2008) 2.335.

These two sentences are offered in expansion/explanation of what has immediately preceded them ('for someone who cuts a new mine there is a large risk'). Readers who have been following the argument did (and do) not really need 4.29 at all. Perhaps X. has remembered once again his promise (4.1) to cater for those who know nothing of mining. What, in any event, arguably saves these comments from banality is the vividness of X.'s pair of all-or-nothing scenarios. As Gauthier 162 remarks, he simply suppresses the dull middle ground: the likelihood that the outcome for many would be neither riches nor rags, but managing to break even.

4.30 Personally, though, I believe that this too—how new mines could be cut in a way as risk-free as possible—is something I am in a position to give advice on For X. giving advice (the verb is *symbouleuein*) see again 6.2, and already e.g. *Hipp.*5.14.

On the matter of minimizing the risk entailed in cutting new mines (which 4.27–9 have stressed) his advice is *group*-speculation. In 4.32 this will take the form of voluntary consortia of private individuals who lease a *kainotomia*; but here first (4.30–1) he envisages Athens' own constitutional infrastructure meeting the need. See under the next three lemmata.

In other circumstances, 'risk-free' mining could have been a description of the conditions experienced by the miners themselves—but not, in context, here. ('The first place to look for entrepreneurial spirit in the Athenian economy is the mining industry, which by its very nature requires constant attention and risk taking': Thompson (1982) 59.) This financial sense of 'as risk-free as possible', *asphalestata*, has a parallel in Demosth. 33.8 (on a loan taken out in someone else's name); and see Powell (2015) 144–88 for a comprehensive assessment of X.'s 'understanding of risk' in *Poroi*.

4.30 There are, of course, ten tribes of Athenians On tribes (*phylai*) cf. *Hier.*9.5 (generic), *Hipp.*2.2 (Athenian cavalry).

In one sense there were '*four* tribes of Athenians', this because Athens was an Ionian Greek community and all Athenians *qua* Ionians were ancestral members of the tribes Geleontes, Argadeis, Aigokoreis, and Hopletes. These entities are still mentioned in documents as late as the beginning of the fourth century: N. F. Jones (1987) 28–31. However, in 508/7 the constitutional reforms of Kleisthenes (*LGPN* s.v. no.1, *OCD* 330 Cleisthenes (2), *APF* 375–6) had allocated all Athenians, via their demes (*OCD* 430), into one of ten new so-called *phylai*, and these are the ones to which X. refers here. They bore names commemorating the community's very early history and mythology: Erechtheis, Aigeis, Pandionis, Leontis, Akamantis, Oineis, Kekropis, Hippothontis, Aiantis, Antiochis. (This list is in the official tribal order which solidified during the fifth century.) Tribe-membership was hereditary, because deme-membership was, so that X. himself, for instance, was a tribesman of Aigeis, by virtue of being a demesman of Erchia, just as his forebears had been.

Besides their own internal functioning (N. F. Jones (1987) 58–72; N. F. Jones (1995)), the ten *phylai* formed the regiments of the Athenian army; not only cavalry, as above. They also supplied, fifty each, the annual complement of city-councillors (cf. 4.18, 6.6.1), and fulfilled a wide variety of other important constitutional functions for the state (N. F. Jones (1987) 31–60)—functions to which X. is here proposing to make an addition. See further under the next lemma.

4.30 Assume that the state gave to each of them an equal number of slaves, and that the tribes took their chance collectively when cutting new mines. The result would be that if one tribe found silver it would be profitable for them all, (4.31) and if two, three, four, or half did so, these operations would obviously be more profitable still For the Greek here ('more profitable still') see Notes on the Text.

No role of this precise kind for the tribes is attested, either before or after *Poroi*. Thiel 54 (Excursus XII) saw evidence in the episode described in Hyp. *Eux.*15–17 (first half of the 320s) that X.'s advice was, to some extent, followed: *Xenophontis consilium... aliquatenus peractum*. Gauthier 162–3 insists that the differences are greater than the similarities. Who is right?

Hyperides describes there the circumstances which led to Hansen (1974) 40 no.35: a public prosecution, by Euxenippos of Lamptrai (*LGPN* s.v. no.2), of the prominent politician Polyeuktos of Kydantidai (*LGPN* s.v. no.35), for a proposal that breached the constitution.

Polyeuktos had proposed that the tribes Akamantis and Hippothontis should relinquish to the ownership of the oracular deity Amphiaraos (*OCD* 72–3) their portion(s) of the territory of Oropos (*OCD* 1049, *IACP* no.214); this had been transferred from Theban to Athenian control by Philip II of Macedon, at some time between 338 and 335, and given to the ten tribes grouped into such pairs. Polyeuktos' proposal would mean the Akamantis-Hippothontis pair losing the income from the sale of its land's produce, but the other four pairs of tribes would indemnify them. (See generally Whitehead (2000) 206–13; Parker (2005) 107–8; Jansen (2007) 381 with n.292; Papazarkadas (2011) 102–6.) We know from Hyperides' account that the court found in favour of the plaintiff Euxenippos and thereby overruled Polyeuktos' proposal; however, the latter retaliated with an impeachment (*eisaggelia*) against Euxenippos, essentially on a charge of fabricating the solemn report that he and two others had made about what Amphiaraos himself wanted. It is in the *eisaggelia* hearing that Hyperides is speaking (Hansen (1975) 109 no.124; Whitehead (2000) 157–8); this time the outcome is unknown.

There are significant differences here from the scheme sketched out in *Poroi* 4.30–1, and Thiel should not have suppressed them. That said, an important element they do share is the basic idea of fairness, among tribes, across the board. And there is also something more specific. According to Hyp. *Eux*.16 the Athenian demos 'gave' the Oropian land to the ten tribes. The same verb, *didonai*, is used by X. here (4.30). Thiel 26 and Gauthier 163 both assert that X. is talking about *leasing*, but Jansen (2007) 381 n.292 protests, with every justification, that their view has no basis.

4.31 That they would all miss out is a result like none from past history Though the verb *apotygchanein* does derive from the noun *tychê*, chance or luck (cf. 'took their chance collectively' in 4.30 and again 4.32), its specific implication is having an aim but not achieving it. Compare e.g. *Hell*.7.5.14: before the battle of Mantineia in 362 the Theban general Epameinondas (*OCD* 507–8) was reluctant to face the enemy, because their troops had won (literally, had had good *tychê* in) the preliminary engagement, while his own had lost, *apotetychêkotôn*.

The remainder of this short sentence re-works an idiom from *Kyn*.9.10: the speed of young fawns is *oudeni eoikos* ('like (to) none other').

4.32 Of course, it is possible for private individuals also to combine in this way and reduce the risk by taking their chance collectively Without emendation of the text (as some editors in the past have advocated, including Rühl in the Teubner edition—to the disapproval of Thiel 27 and Gauthier 163), X. here is not supporting his idea about the tribes by drawing attention to what *idiôtai* already do. He is adding a supplementary suggestion of his own: about what they could, simultaneously, do.

It is certainly the case that the evidence for syndicates of mining entrepreneurs at Laureion all dates to the third quarter of the fourth century. In the orators the relevant passages are Demosth. 37.38 (probably from 346) and 42.3 (from around 330), and Hyp. *Eux*.35 (first half of the 320s). See also lines 13–15 of *Agora* 19 P21 (not long after 350), where three named men, one of them Hyperides (*LGPN* s.v. no.3, *OCD* 716–17, *APF* 518), 'buy' the same mine, in Besa (4.44 below); and generally Shipton (1998) 61–2. Herzog (1914) 480 anticipated Thiel and Gauthier in the suggestion—it can be no more—that the present passage of *Poroi* paved the way for this practice to be authorized, even encouraged.

4.32 do not be fearful that the public enterprise operating in this way will cause private individuals extra grief—or be caused it by them Fear (*phobos*) has not featured in the work so far, and even here means little more than anxiety or worry. Contrast the cluster of four instances in 4.39–41.

Thiel 27 asserts that 'operating in this way' refers back not simply to what has been said about the tribes in 4.30–1 but to the entirety of the public slaves project. Gauthier 164 concurs. Nothing less than 4.13–32 is the relevant antecedent material, with the phrase 'operating in this way' here an echo of 'the silver-mines, once organized' in 4.13. (The verb is the same in both passages, even if it does not lend itself to quite the same translation in both.)

At the end of the sentence my translation 'cause...*extra* grief' reflects the compound verb X. uses there (*para*lypein), ignored by other translators. His train of thought is that taking on a *kainotomia* is already worrisome enough, so he must give reassurance that this will not make it even more so.

4.32 just as a military alliance makes its members mutually stronger as more of them join, so too in the silver-mines: the more people in

the business, the larger the quantity of valuable things they will find and bring out For the verb 'bring out' (*ekphorein*) see already 4.2.

X.'s analogy does not bear close scrutiny. No matter. As he approaches the end of the exposition of his plan (and before turning to possible objections to it: 4.34–48) he relaxes the tight logical grip that has characterized the argument thus far (Gauthier 164) and indulges in an old soldier's piece of morale-boosting exhortation.

4.33 I have now stated what, as I conceive it, would create adequate sustenance for every Athenian—once the state was organized—from communal resources This pivotal statement connects explicitly—via *treph*-vocabulary—with 1.1 ('I set about examining whether there was any way the citizens could sustain themselves out of their own territory'), 4.13 ('In order to make myself even clearer on the subject of sustenance'), 4.49 ('enlarging the state's means of sustenance'), and 6.1 ('The common people will have plenty of sustenance'); cf. also the more specific 4.52 (on which see further below). It also connects *im*plicitly with 3.9–10, 4.14–15, 4.17, and 4.23, which, between them, quantify the present passage's 'adequate' (and 6.1's 'plenty') at three *oboloi* a day. All well and good. But what, in conceptual and practical terms, was the payment's rationale?

In a preliminary discussion entitled '*Trophê* et *misthos*', Gauthier 20–32 addressed the question at some length. His starting-point is the very different answers to it given by three scholars of generations past for whom he had particular respect: Herzog, Thiel, and Wilhelm. (The missing name, we may note, is M. I. Finley's. Gauthier acknowledged his intellectual debt to Finley at the outset of the *Commentaire* (p.xi), and despite their being scholars of such different kinds, it was a significant one. See General Intro., section 7 (final part); also Thonemann (2012).)

On the one hand Herzog (1914) 473–4 and Wilhelm (1934) 38–40 characterize X.'s *triôbolon* as a constitutional-cum-political payment, a *misthos* (cf. 2.1), and thus see his aim as ensuring that the already existing *misthoi*—notably for attendance at the assembly and for jurors—could be paid as frequently and as reliably as possible. (Jury pay was a *triôbolon* a day in itself; Demosth. 45.4 reveals difficulties in paying it in the 360s, with war-related expenses competing. Assembly pay at the time of *Poroi* was probably still the *triôbolon* attested in the late 390s.)

On the other hand Thiel 55 (Excursus XIII), responding to Herzog, found 3.9–10 and the present passage incompatible with that position.

A *misthos*, proper, was paid only to someone who performed a particular function, and only as and when he performed it; X.'s scheme makes a payment to *every* Athenian *every* day. (For this view cf. also Andreades (1933) 389 n.7; Cawkwell (1963) 63 n.92.)

The arguments Gauthier deployed in 1976 are too intricate to be reproduced here, but the thrust of them is plain: he himself strongly upheld the Herzog/Wilhelm position. The *trophê* of *Poroi* is to be identified with *misthos*, pay—and indeed, specifically, pay earned by attendance at the assembly and/or council and by serving as jurors. Yes, X.'s payment is ultimately to be a daily one, but it will also be an authentic *misthos*; no 'neutral' subsistence allowance or welfare handout but a reflection of activity in the public domain. X.'s *euporia trophês* is the same as the *euporia misthou* of Aristot. *Pol*.7.1317b31–4. Aristotle describes it, quite dispassionately, as one of the bulwarks of radical democracy. X. *wants to see it in place in his own city*.

This last matter, it is relevant to note here, enables us to fix on a key difference between Gauthier's position and the one formulated by a later commentator on *Poroi*, Schütrumpf. Besides pp.45–72 there, see Schütrumpf (1995) 293–300; also the summary in Schütrumpf (2010) 829. Two main points emerge. First, in Schütrumpf's view, X.'s *triôbolon* is to be an actual replacement for, not an augmentation of, political *misthos*, with its (to some) distasteful associations. (Pay for the council and (other) officials will stay; assembly and jury pay will go.) Second and arising, Schütrumpf sees X.'s whole mentality as oligarchic. All in all then, as Jansen (2007) 16 puts it: Gauthier's X. wants to promote the political activity of the common people; Schütrumpf's X. wants to retard it. And expressed in those terms, Gauthier's X.—a portrayal presented even more directly in Gauthier (1984)—is the one, in my view, that an unbiased reading of *Poroi* exhibits; cf. also now Farrell (2012). (Did X.'s views on democracy mellow during the course of his life? Some studies of that question by e.g. Kroeker (2009) and, more briefly, Ferrario (2017) 66–72 suggest that the evidence is equivocal. The evidence of *Poroi* itself, though, is not; cf. Powell (2015) 39.)

Whether Gauthier was right to equate *trophê* with *misthos* is another question. The past tense (in reference to his discussion in the *Commentaire*), as in my paragraph before last, is appropriate because he himself subsequently revisited the topic and—partly in response to Schütrumpf's critique—engaged in some soft-pedalling on this very point (Gauthier (1984 [2010] 122–5). There is also, now, a penetrating treatment of the question in Jansen (2007) 120–35. As with Gauthier's own analysis, above, more issues are adduced than need to be comprehensively aired here: the relationship between the two terms in the military sphere, in particular. (Pritchett (1971–1991) 1.3–52 is a classic study; see also Loomis (1998) 32–61.) However, X.'s own usage in his earlier works provides scant evidence that he regarded the two terms as interchangeable. On the contrary, witness e.g. *Cyrop.*8.5.23, where Kyros' father praises what he has done for those who shared his campaigns: 'the best men he has made rich, and for the many he has provided *misthos* and *trophê*'. (The distinction is also made in *Hell.*2.1.1 and 5.1.17.) It is true that in X. just as elsewhere *trophê* seems sometimes to denote money, which does or will purchase food (so in e.g. *Anab.*1.1.9; Gauthier 23), but much more commonly there is no involvement of money at all—as indeed in 1.1 here, quoted at the beginning of this lemma. 6.1, likewise, returns to the wish stated later in 1.1, to alleviate the citizens' *penia*. (For other issues in 6.1 and 4.52 see the Comm. there.) Overall, Jansen makes a strong case for the view that in *Poroi* '*trophê* refers strictly to food and/or money for food' (Jansen (2007) 119); and my translation of it, throughout, as 'sustenance' seeks to convey that.

More broadly, the analysis of *Poroi*'s aims in Bresson (2000) 253-257 finds elements of cogency in all three of the most recent published interpretations: Bodei Giglioni (stimulation of the economy), Gauthier (maximization of *misthoi* in the context of restoring public finances), Schütrumpf (amelioration of the lot of the poor without 'soaking' the rich). This Bresson does by juxtaposing *Poroi* with what survives of a grain law from Samos (*SIG* 976, Austin (2006) no.135) passed in *c.* 200 or earlier. It created a permanent fund to enable the free monthly distribution of grain to all Samian citizens; the money came in the first instance from public subscription (a list of contributors, most of whom contribute 100 drachmas, is appended; cf. 3.11 here), which was then let out at interest.

4.34 Doing the calculations of so massive a sum of start-up capital This capital fund has not been mentioned since Chap.3 (3.6, 3.9, 3.12), where relatively modest inroads into it had been envisaged. But the cost of Chap.4's slave miners should have made X.'s readers realise now, if not before, the sheer scale of what he is proposing. (The *aphormê*—viewed as a theoretical totality—will be 'massive' but so will the income: see already 4.1 for this adjective.)

Just as in 4.5, doing calculations (the Greek verb is *logizesthai*) is meant literally; contrast 4.43.

4.34 But even so, let them not lose heart The concern of an old soldier (and commander) that morale be kept up in the face of adversity, whether real or apparent. Compare generally *Anab*.1.4.9, 3.1.36 & 40, 3.2.8 & 18, 4.8.10, 5.4.19, 6.6.36.

4.35 it is not the case that all these things must happen at the same time or no advantage arises Indeed not. 4.23–4 has already assumed that the ultimate total of slave miners will be reached by slow degrees. This is now repeated, and the same point made about two of the ideas from Chap.3: 'however many buildings are erected [3.12–13] or ships constructed [3.14] or slaves bought will be beneficial immediately'.

4.36 In point of fact, proceeding in stages will in one respect be more advantageous than doing everything at the same time This advantage 'in one respect' is explained clearly enough in the remainder of 4.36 (see further below)—but in fact X. is not satisfied (or presumes that the hypothetical 'calculators' of 4.34 will not be satisfied) to leave it at that. More attempts at reassurance are added in 4.37–9, and added so piecemeal that their number is not self-evident. For Gauthier 169, 4.37 is a second point, 4.38 a third and final one, because 4.39 addresses a different issue. By contrast, Thiel 27 seems to imply that 4.39 belongs with 4.36–8, and I would concur. See also the translation of Waterfield 178, who however appears to consider 4.36–7 a single point, not Gauthier's two; there I agree with Gauthier. The issue is of no great moment except in showing that X.'s otherwise tight organization of Chap.4 (Gauthier 110) does temporarily loosen in these sections.

As now formulated, the wisdom of proceeding slowly with the three projects summarily listed in 4.35 (q.v. above) is that it is the (only?) way to prevent exploitative behaviour on the part of those whom the state must pay for their goods and/or services. X. does not even consider the idea that market forces could be legally constrained in these areas.

4.37 Also, progressing on the basis of what was feasible would allow well-thought-out ideas to be implemented again For the Greek here ('to be implemented again') see Notes on the Text.

4.38 if some things made progress but others were postponed A shift in ground from 4.37, where the opposite of carrying a scheme forward had been abandoning it, as misconceived.

The Greek here is a modified echo of *Anab*.3.1.47. After speaking, the Spartan Cheirisophos is immediately in action, to show that what is necessary will *not* be postponed but will make progress.

4.38 the revenue that had accrued would help to provide what is required The verb 'help to provide' (the doubly compound *sygkataskeuein*) is rare enough in this era to be, perhaps, borrowed from Thucydides. In 479, with his visionary work on Peiraieus, Themistokles 'helped to make provision for the empire' (Thuc. 1.93.3–4, with Hornblower (1991–2008) 1.140). X. had already used the verb in *Lac. Pol.*8.3.

4.39 The aspect of this that perhaps seems most frightening to everyone is the thought that the state acquires *too many* slaves and the workings are crammed too full After the quite bland material in 4.34–8, couched in terms of what *some* people *might* see as problematic in his ideas, X. finishes this point (or turns to another: Gauthier 170–1, cf. 111) with something more attention-catching. True, 'perhaps' and 'seems' soften its edges, but the picture otherwise becomes more categorical. *Everyone* has the thought in question, and it is 'the most [or: a very] alarming' one, *phoberôtaton*. Translations such as 'the chief worry' (Waterfield 178) fail to convey the force of the adjective *phoberos*; cf. 4.41, where it describes an outbreak of war, and elsewhere e.g. *Anab.*2.5.9, *Hier.*6.9, *Hipp.*4.11 and 8.21. So what exactly is X. saying here?

The commentary in Gauthier 170–1 begins well by pointing out that 4.39 seems to be addressed to readers unconvinced by the optimistic statements of 4.22 and, especially, 4.26 ('there could never be more slaves there than the operations require'). But thereafter his note pursues a conceptual distinction between the Athenians as *homines politici* (who must decide whether to vote for X.'s proposals) and as *homines oeconomici* (who must actually make the mining industry work if they are adopted) which, while of some interest in itself, ultimately evades the thrust of explaining something 'frightening to everyone'. By contrast, Cartledge in Waterfield 226–7 meets it head-on. 'The implied fear is of servile insurrection, which actually is not known to have occurred in the Laureium mines until the very end of the second century B.C. On the other hand, many thousands of mine-slaves took advantage of the Spartan occupation of Decelea to run away [see **4.25 Those who**]. Contrast the known (*sc.* Spartan) Helot insurrections.'

Citing Cartledge on this point, Jansen (2007) 398 n.334 expresses disagreement that X. has 'servile insurrection' in mind: '[t]he problem with this interpretation is that we hear of no slave revolts in Attica until the second century B.C. [Diod.Sic. 34.2.19; Athen. *Deipn.* 6.272E–F]. The similarity [of 4.39] with 4.5 is striking…, strongly suggesting that the 'greatest fear' in the minds of the Athenians is over-capitalization.' (Similarly—though without reference to either Cartledge or Jansen, and indeed not even contemplating a non-economic interpretation—Powell (2015) 168–9.) However, while it is undeniable that *some* of the language of 4.5 reappears in 4.39 (chiefly, 'If someone puts in more of them than is sufficient' and 'by not putting in more men than the workings annually demand'), I would still want to insist that the 'most frightening to everyone' element in 4.39 is new. Also, *only* 4.39 speaks explicitly of overcrowding ('crammed too full'). In my judgement that sounds not so much like a term of abstract economic analysis as a description of combustible working conditions.

Cartledge's approach to this passage, then, is not so easily dismissed. But if we are to embrace it, brief expansion is needed. First, everyone (including him: see above) acknowledges that the actuality of organized risings by Athens' chattel-slaves is not attested until very much later than X.'s time. Second, Sparta's Helots—and other subordinated populations of their type: Austin & Vidal-Naquet (1977) 88–9; Garlan (1988) 93–102; Fisher (1995) 32–3—could and did revolt on a regular basis. Third, slaves of both (indeed, all) kinds do, as individuals or in small groups, opportunistically run away; post-413 Attica is the best-known, if extreme, example. A convenient illustration of, and mnemonic for, this distinction comes in two passages of Thucydides: in 4.118.7 a one-year truce between Athens and Sparta makes provision for (free and) slave *deserters* on both sides; in 5.23.3 the subsequent Athens/Sparta alliance envisages only the Spartans being faced with a slave *revolt*. See also e.g. Thuc. 1.139.2 (Megara harbouring runaway Athenian slaves in 432), and generally Ste. Croix (1981) 141–7; Garlan (1988) 176–91; Fisher (1995) 79–85. If it truly was, as orthodoxy holds, a logistical near-impossibility for a heterogeneous slave population like the Athenian one to bring about an authentic mass insurrection, we may wish to say that Cartledge chose the wrong word in reference to the present passage (above). But even short of that, it is not hard to imagine X.'s 'overcrowding' bringing slaves quickly to the end of their tether; likewise the idea of hundreds, or even dozens, of resentful ex-miners at large in southern Attica being 'most frightening to everyone'. Note generally *Hier.*4.3: 'citizens act as unpaid bodyguards for each other against slaves and against criminals, so that no citizen dies a violent death'.

4.40 Thus...the easiest way of doing these things is also the best
A summary (if one were needed) of everything in 4.34–9.

4.40 If, on the other hand, because of the *eisphorai* which have been levied during the war just now, you think that there would be no possibility of further contributions Dakyns translates 'the present war'—but the Social War has already ended. X. himself writes of circumstances 'before the peace' later in this same sentence (see the next lemma), and cf. also 5.11–12. In fact, from Homer onwards the Greek adverb *nyn* had been applied to the immediate past (and the immediate future) as well as to the literal present.

Athenian *eisphorai* in the 360s had been mentioned in 3.7, but X. is now referring to the Social War (357–355) itself. The lack of detail is paralleled in Isoc. 8.19–21, and no relevant information is to be had elsewhere either. The chance preservation of RO 52 (*IG* II^2 123, Harding (1985) no.69) shows an Athenian garrison on the island of Andros (*OCD* 86, *IACP* no.475) being paid for in summer 356 from allied *syntaxeis*, but even if that was not a unique case, implicit in what X. says is that domestic *eisphorai* in Athens had been burdensome.

4.40 Administer the state next year, too, on the basis of the tax-yield before the peace, and invest the surpluses . . . so that the income from them is maximized What X. suggests here about budgetary planning and public spending is noteworthy for its sophistication.

He builds on the idea that, after the burdens of the Social War, no more *extraordinary* taxation will be palatable for a while. Instead, the ordinary, recurrent taxes must suffice (see generally under **3.5 As is plain**); the ones auctioned off by the *pôlêtai* at the beginning of each year. So in this instance 'next year' is 354/3 (Gauthier 172); and it will indeed be a year of surplus(es), for the four reasons stated:

(*i*) 'from the fact that there *is* peace'. X. here regards it as self-evident that peace is less expensive than war, but he will return to the point in 5.11–12.

(*ii*) 'from metics and traders being looked after'. As proposed in Chaps.2–3—though with a new item of vocabulary, here, to describe the policy: see **4.42 We would** (end).

(*iii*) 'from the rise in imports and exports because of the concentration of population'. See already 3.5 for resident and visiting foreigners; and more generally 4.49.

(*iv*) 'from the harbour-dues and the market-revenues being augmented'. On the first of these, *ellimenia*, see under **3.5 As is plain**. The precise sense of the second of them, *agorai* (a more straightforward sense of which will appear in 4.49), is less obvious—and LSJ s.v. is no help. In a different context, the idea of *agorai* 'being augmented' (*auxanesthai*) might have meant physically enlarging them, but surely not here. A possibility is that it summarizes what 3.5 (q.v.) has referred to as 'what is bought, what is sold', i.e. the overall volume of economic transactions, with fiscal consequences, in *agorai*; yet even that does not seem precise enough, in a context where tax revenue to the state is the topic. That sense has a good precedent in Aristoph. *Wasps* 658–60, at 659. Ste. Croix (1972) 278 n.85 persuasively urges that X.'s pairing of *agorai* with *ellimenia* here requires the scope of the latter to be restricted to 'market *revenues or tolls*'; and see now, more fully, Olson (2017).

4.41 Another fear some might have is that this system would be pointless if a war broke out After the universal fear(s) of 4.39, 4.41–8 reverts to what might disturb 'some' of X.'s readers.

It emerges from 4.41–2 as a whole that by 'this system' he means in particular the slave miners. (Gauthier 175 wants to include the 'hardware' of 3.12–14, but that has nothing to do with manpower.)

4.41 But let them consider: if these schemes were in operation, the war would be much more frightening to those initiating it than to Athens For 'let them consider' see again 5.5. The substantive point itself will be underlined at the end of the next section: see **4.42 and put up**.

4.42 what possession is more useful for a war than manpower? Thiel 29 n.1 and Gauthier 176 cite Aristotle's well-known dictum that a slave is a 'sort of living possession' (Aristot. *Pol.*1.1253b32). In the present instance it is the Athenian state itself that has acquired these 'possessions' (4.17, 4.22, 4.39), and X. here takes for granted its right to do something with them that private owners could not: redeploy them in front-line military roles, as required. See under the next two lemmata.

4.42 We would be able to fill many ships by public enrolment. Many men too could fight for the community as foot-soldiers and put up hard opposition to the enemy, if someone looked after them For the Greek here ('We would be able' and 'for the community') see Notes on the Text. The substance can suitably be examined under the two heads indicated.

(1) NAVY. Manning Athenian (war)ships is illustrated at length in lines 12–40 of the 'Themistokles Decree' (ML 23, Fornara (1983) no.55, Johansson (2001)), which looks back from the third century to the Persian invasion crisis of 480. More commonplace instances include one in X. (*Hell.*6.2.11); and see also e.g. Demosth.4.36, Aeschin. 2.133. Each trireme required 170 rowers, plus various others who brought the total complement up to 200 (Morrison, Coates, and Rankov (2000) 107–18). At the time of *Poroi* Athens had almost 300 triremes (283 in the naval list of 357/6, *IG* II^2 1611.5–9). The manpower needs of any fleet that the Athenians were likely actually to deploy in this era—the largest on record, by some distance, is the 120 vessels which fought and lost at Embata in 356 (Rhodes (2010) 275)—thus speak for themselves.

The implications of X.'s phrase 'by public enrolment' (actually a single word in the Greek, δημοσίᾳ; my translation of it stems from the discussion in Gauthier 176) are, by contrast, far from self-evident. However, as general context it is relevant to note that whereas the Athenian state always provided, by conscription or recruitment, any *troops* aboard a trireme (Gabrielsen (1994) 106–7, citing *IG* I^3 60 and Thuc. 8.24.2), finding its *rowers and ancillary personnel* seems normally to have been the responsibility of the trierarch himself. Conscription is attested, but perhaps only in an emergency—of which the classic instance is Arginousai in 406: X. himself reports the decree that ordered the manning of 110 vessels by all men of military age, *slave and free alike* (*Hell.*1.6.24, with Krentz (1989) 151–2). See also e.g. *Hell.*5.4.61, concerning a threat to grain imports in 376. Otherwise, recruitment—via the incentive of pay—of voluntary rowers (whether Athenian citizens or foreign 'mercenaries') had always been the answer. A straightforward reading of Demosth.21.154–5 will suggest that after 357 the state took over responsibility for providing crews (so e.g. Whitehead (1986) 134)), though some question this (Cawkwell (1984) 342–3; Gabrielsen (1994) 108). In any event, as regards *Poroi* 4.42 and X.'s term 'by public enrolment', he seems to be saying that redeploying slave miners could significantly augment the state's ability to man the warships by simple conscription. (The episode described in [Demosth.] 50.6–7 indicates that conscripting *citizens* was harder in practice than theory. A decree had ordered the councillors and demarchs to draw up lists of rowers, but the ones produced by this procedure were few and inadequate, and at least one trierarch had to resort to hiring his own personnel.)

(2) ARMY. Two preliminaries, first. Contrary to Gauthier 176–7 (and Garlan (1988) 176; Gauthier had used the 1972 French version of this), there is nothing in the language or syntax of 4.42 to suggest that A and B here are in an hierarchical order, i.e. that the principal idea is slave rowers, with slave 'footsoldiers' in a second, later category of likelihood ('ensuite seulement'). On the other hand Gauthier is right to insist that 'footsoldiers ('*pezoi*') are not, or not necessarily, to be understood as hoplites (heavily armed infantry troops: *OCD* 704). As a military man, X. would not have abused the lexicon of his profession. He specifies 'hoplites' when that is what he means (2.2 here, q.v., and almost two hundred times elsewhere). When his choice is *pezoi* the scope of that term is deliberately broader; very often (though not here) in distinctions between infantry and cavalry, or terrestrial forces and maritime ones.

Quite possibly, the role which X. has particularly in mind for these slaves is that of peltasts (cf. 4.52). In any event his proposal is a bold one. Garlan (1988) 176 comments that '[t]hese are public slaves, and the only wars in which they are to take part are those of a defensive nature, in which the purpose is to repulse an enemy invasion' (Garlan (1988) 176; again Gauthier endorses the 1972 version). I find this overstated. True, X.'s scenario here is a war which, implicitly, others have begun against Athens (4.41), but the military confrontations that made up any such war would not necessarily be confined to Attica; they could well include aggressive strikes on enemy soil.

Regardless of that, the whole idea of giving these slaves arms and armour and the scope to use them has to be predicated on an assumption that they will loyally fight the state's enemies, and that is where X.'s crucial proviso comes in: 'if someone looked after them'. As Gauthier 177 notes, sometimes, including sometimes in X., *therap-* words (as here) are used in a way which shows the activity concerned in a bad light (e.g. *Hell.*2.3.14: the Athenian oligarchs in 404/3 kowtow to the commander of the Spartan garrison); but contrast e.g. *Cyrop.*8.8.1, where Kyros is said to look after all his subjects as if they were his own children. Here in *Poroi* the concept has appeared already in 4.40, 'from metics and traders being looked after'. To discover what X. meant by that we simply have to (re-)read Chaps.2 and 3. Concerning these public slaves, however, no such detail is given. (Note, besides, another example here of the odd, impersonal phraseology that he had used in Chap.3. See **3.3 suppose that.**) While it is possible that the verb *therapeuein* here means 'train', as it does in a passage of Plato's *Gorgias* about horses (Plat. *Gorg.*516E), the balance of probability within X.'s own usage—much of it concerned with the gods—must be that what he has in mind is something more benevolent, and more psychologically astute, than square-bashing. The guesses of Gauthier 177–8 are as good as any: decent food and clothing, considerate treatment, and the prospect of manumission for exceptional prowess.

4.43 I calculate, personally, that it is feasible not to abandon the silver-mines even while a war is in progress He means a war fought out *in Attica itself*. During the Peloponnesian War, only that late development (**4.25 Those who**) had brought mining to a halt.

4.43 There is of course, near the mines at the sea to the south, a fortress in Anaphlystos For the Greek here ('at the sea to the south') see Notes on the Text.

On Anaphlystos, a constituent deme of the tribe Antiochis, see generally Eliot (1962) 75–109; Traill (1975) 54, 67; Whitehead (1986) 335, 373, 402; Lohmann (1993) 60–74; Bultrighini (2015) 177–205. To judge by its annual allocation of ten seats on the *boulê*, it was a community of considerable size; a small town. Mentions of it in literary sources and in mining leases combine to locate it at one or more of several sites (notably Ag. Georgios) within the valley that still bears its name, Anavysso, to the east of the modern village so called. Unlike Thorikos (see the next lemma), what little remains of fortifications there cannot be dated to the fifth century (despite the impression given in Thiel 30); but they must evidently pre-date *Poroi*.

Modern readers who consult a map of Attica which marks Anaphlystos on it (such as all three of the maps in Traill (1975), or map 3 in *WoA*) may feel that Anaphlystos faces west rather than south—and Thorikos east rather than north, correspondingly. However, Gauthier 178–9 points out that X.'s designations take the larger view, that of where the ultimate destinations of voyages from Attica in these two directions are likely to be: Troizen (*OCD* 1511) or the Cyclades from Anaphlystos; Euboia (*OCD* 543) or the north Aegean from Thorikos.

4.43 there is also a fortress in Thorikos, at the one to the north. They are about eleven kilometres from each other On Thorikos, which belonged to the tribe Akamantis, see in brief *OCD* 1470; also e.g. Traill (1975) 48, 67; Labarbe (1977); Whitehead (1986) 6 and passim; Mussche (1998). In Strab. 9.1.10 one of the twelve ancient Attic towns believed to have been founded by the half-reptilian king Kekrops (*OCD* 294 Ce-),

Thorikos was by this era a five-councillor-sized deme. Its extensive remains, centred on present-day Velatouri, have been studied by Belgian and Dutch archaeologists since the 1950s; they include many generated by the mining industry.

Unlike Anaphlystos (the preceding lemma), a precise date of 410/09 for its fortification is known—from X. himself (*Hell.*1.2.2).

4.44 So suppose there was a third stronghold between them, on the highest point of Besa On Besa see generally Eliot (1962) 117–24; Traill (1975) 54, 69; Whitehead (1986) 373, 402. It was a small (two-councillor-sized) deme belonging, like Anaphlystos, to the Antiochid *phylê*. Mentions of it in literary sources and in mining leases combine to locate its site, very probably, at present-day Synterina. There are remains on the crest of a hill there, with views both west to Anaphlystos and east to Thorikos, which McCredie (1966) 75–7 thought to be Besa's 'stronghold', as X. proposes. But the only certainty is that they *post-*date *Poroi*; Gauthier 179.

It may be relevant to mention here (from another perspective altogether) the demonstration by Rood (2014) that as early as the *Anabasis* X. was portraying himself as someone able to see and appreciate better than others the strategic possibilities of mountainous terrain.

4.44 The works would be unified into a single entity as a result of all the fortresses, and if any enemy activity was noticed, each man could retreat to a place of safety a short distance away In the past this passage has been considered textually deficient. Thiel 20, for example, suggested that a whole line had been lost in transmission: '<so that it would be easy to repel an enemy few in numbers> as a result of all these fortresses'. (This is then the counterpoint to 'an enemy arriving in force' in 4.45, q.v. below.) Nowadays the text as such is regarded as sound. What it means still invites, in part, differing interpretations, but Gauthier 180–2 sorts some of the wheat from the chaff. (In the latter category belongs, for instance, the view first stated by B. Weiske in 1804 and revived by Zurborg and again by Bodei Giglioni: that the 'works' here (*erga*) actually means the 'workers' (*ergatai*). When X. wanted to mention *ergatai*, he did so (4.5, 4.6, 4.22). I agree, and would comment only that Gauthier failed to notice Bodei Giglioni's own change of heart: Bodei Giglioni (1970–1971) 469–70.)

X.'s suggestion of a fort at Besa is such as to create a crooked line of three such forts, running west to east across southern Attica for a total distance of some 10 km., with the main body of *erga* behind it. Jansen (2007) 243 calls this a 'fortified urban center'. However, his later formulation (Jansen (2012) 737) is an 'urban center' with associated 'fortifications', and that second version is much to be preferred, on two counts. First (*a*), while X.'s words do not exclude the possibility that the three fortresses were *linked by connecting walls*, they certainly do not entail it. Second (*b*), even if so, this (loosely) lozenge-shaped 'urban center' would be walled *only on its two north-facing sides*.

A further point arises from *b*. My phrase (in the preceding paragraph) 'with the main body of *erga* behind it' should have added, for clarity's sake: if one approached by land from the north. Obsessed as he was (Gauthier's word) by the Dekeleia episode, X. is visualizing precisely that: a terrestrial enemy attack from the north side. (So again in 4.46–8.) But what of an enemy attack by sea? The possibility is never mentioned. Nor, by association, is the deme and fortress at the southern tip of this inverted triangle: Sounion (*OCD* 1413 Su-), said in Thuc. 8.4 to have been given its fortifications on the coastal promontory in winter 413/12. According to Gauthier 181, X. does nevertheless evoke Sounion *implicitly* in his phrase 'as a result of all the fortresses'. I am sceptical. Given that the aim here is to provide the miners with 'a place of safety a short distance away', the Sounion fort is more likely to have been excluded from mention here as being too far away; so Andrewes in *HCT* 5.11.

4.45 Obviously, an enemy arriving in force would seize any grain or wine or livestock found outside—but after gaining control of silver-bearing ore, what would they have but stones to make use of? 4.47 will again distinguish between small (implicit in 4.44) and full-scale (explicit here) enemy deployments. The distinction may seem banal to the modern reader, who is likely to be a civilian, but military men such as X. and Thucydides knew that it mattered, given the differing responses expected or required from the defenders; cf. e.g. the Spartan King Agis II (*OCD* 39) in Thuc. 8.71, and Gauthier 182.

For loss of livestock see again Thuc. 7.27.5 on Dekeleia after 413: 'all the flocks and beasts of burden were lost'. (Contrast Thuc. 2.14.1 on 431, when, evidently there was more time to ship them to safety.) See also *Mem.*3.6.10–11. Sokrates there politely suggests to young Glaukon of Kollytos (*LGPN* s.v. no.24, *POP* 154–6), the would-be politician, that one of the topics he ought to master is 'defence of the territory', entailing an appreciation of which garrisons are well-placed (and so deserve strengthening) and which could be abandoned. Most scholars who cite this (e.g. Ober (1985) 79; Dorion (2017) 51; Ferrario (2017) 67) omit to mention Glaukon's startling reply: the garrisons should *all* be scrapped, because the consequence of having them is theft from the countryside. Unless the text is faulty there, rural losses (for which cf. also, but more mundanely, *Mem.*2.7.12–14, at 14: the speaking dog in this Aesop-like story earns his keep by deterring thieves) were not confined to occasions of enemy incursion.

The (relative) agricultural barrenness of the Laureion region has been mentioned in passing in 1.5; see at **There is land.** More broadly, Thiel xvi and 30 adduces *Oec.*1.10: with the knowledge of how to play them, pipes (*auloi*) mean wealth; without it, they are 'no more valuable than useless stones'.

4.46 how could an enemy ever make a move in the direction of the mines? I say this because of course Megara etc. Again (cf. 4.44 The works) X. is considering only an overland attack, approaching the mining area from the north.

His expansion of this point chooses the examples of Athens' two nearest terrestrial neighbours—which were nevertheless still some distance away, as indicated: Megara to the south(-west), Thebes to the north. Thiel 31 comments that this choice reflects nothing more than their proximity, not any likelihood that they will actually *be* enemies. In the Megarians' case that is true enough. The contemporary snapshot of them in Isoc. 8.117–18 is one of a people 'living continually at peace' (though a border dispute flared up only a few years later: RO 58 (Harding (1985) no.78), now *IG* II^{3} 292/*AIO*; Papazarkadas (2011) 244–59). But aggression by the Thebans, despite the loss of their larger hegemony, was still a realistic possibility.

4.47 They will be bound to pass Athens X. actually writes 'pass the polis'. He could have been more precise by using the word *asty*, as already in 3.13 and again later in this section (and in 4.51); however, 'polis' in the topographical sense of a state's urban centre is well-attested (see *IACP* 39 with 138–43).

So as not to clutter up his point, X. omits to mention that these enemies will only 'pass Athens' (*en route* to Laureion) if they have managed to break through Athens' border-defences, and the garrisons to which he will make brief allusion in 4.52. See generally Ober (1985), the principal thrust of which (for our purposes here) is that defending Attica's borders—something *not* prioritized in the 'Periklean' strategy for the Peloponnesian War—came to the fore in fourth-century Athenian military thinking, and was implemented from *at least* the 350s onwards. Ober (1985) 127–9 and 116–26, respectively, lists (*a*) the obvious routes from the Megarid into western Attica and (*b*) the more numerous ways into northern Attica from the Theban side. Users of *a* would encounter the fortified deme Eleusis (*OCD* 500; *IACP* no.362). A garrison there is attested in 334/3 (*IG* II^2 1156 lines 36–7); and to the west, i.e. nearer the border itself, were placed several free-standing towers (Ober (1985) 174–8). As to *b*, there was a chain of five forts in all—notably Panakton (*OCD* 1072; Hornblower (1991–2008) 2.428–9)—and, again, towers.

Returning to the present passage itself, the comments of Munn (1993) 27 are apposite. 'In the face of the main force of the enemy in wartime, the safety provided by garrison forts consisted in their security as points of refuge. They were, in effect, independent nodes of local security [cf. 4.44 here: DW], not links in any chain of regional defense. The invasion of an enemy in force, however, was at most a periodic or occasional event. A more prevalent condition of warfare was the threat posed by small raiding parties and freebooters. Under such conditions, forts near the frontiers could serve the defensive interests of the greater territory of Attica by the ability of their garrisons to sound a warning and, in some cases, to challenge and repel such raiders. It is certainly significant, however, that Xenophon regards the city itself as the primary base for troops to repel even small parties of the invading enemy (*Poroi* 4.47). Too often, the garrisons of small towns and forts were ambushed and destroyed when lured out by raiding parties, so that restraint and caution, even against apparently minor incursions, must always have been urged as the wisest policy to garrison commanders.'

4.47 If they are few the likelihood is that they will be destroyed by cavalry and by patrollers On cavalry (2.5) in this regard see already *Hipp.*7 (which mentions Boiotians as opponents; cf. under **4.46 how could**). Thuc. 7.27.5 and (nearer the city) 8.71.2 has illustrative episodes.

On these border 'patrollers', *peripoloi*, see generally Pélékidis (1962) 35–44. X. has not mentioned them before, but he will do so again in 4.52. We first hear of them in 424 (Thuc. 4.67.2 with the note in Hornblower (1991–2008) 2.234–5); again in a fragmentary dossier of decrees from 415 (*IG* I^3 93; ML 78, now OR 171; Fornara (1983) no.146) frs.d&g, lines 3–4; and notoriously in 411, when one of them assassinated the oligarch Phrynichos of Deiradiotai (*LGPN* s.v. no.16). See Thuc. 8.92.2 & 5, with Hornblower (1991–2008) 3.1019–21; *IG* I³ 102 (ML 85, now OR 182; Fornara (1983) no.155); Lys. 13.70–1. 'They probably anticipated the functions of the 18-20-year-old males who would in the fourth century be called ephebes, and were normally stationed on the frontiers of Attica' (Hornblower (1991–2008) 2.234). Though the dating, number and nature of the changes that need to be postulated between 411 and the post-335 system described by ?Aristot. *Ath. Pol.*42.2–5 are all disputed matters (see e.g., in brief, Hansen (1991) 89), X. appears to provide important evidence for one of the intermediate stages. Sekunda (1990) 153 envisages that 'before 335, in the second year of training, those [ephebes] who could afford to provide their own hoplite equipment served as hoplites manning the border-forts of Attica, while those who could not equipped themselves as peltasts [who were lighter-armed: *OCD* 1102] and patrolled the countryside. I further suggest that it was these latter troops who were called *peripoloi*'. (This topic continues in the Comm. to 4.52.)

4.47 They might come in great strength, leaving their own possessions deserted, but that would be problematic for them: Athens town etc. For the reason given. After passing Athens (above, **They will be bound**), the further they proceeded into southern Attica the truer X.'s statement would be, even before they reached Laureion itself.

Though there is no recorded case of the Athenians attacking either Megara or Thebes while the latter's troops were in Attica (let alone southern Attica), the broad principle is exemplified by Thuc. 2.23–5 on 431: getting there by sea, the Athenians attacked Spartan 'Methone' (Mothone: *IACP* no.319), in the absence of the main Spartan/Peloponnesian land army (but Brasidas saved it). Success along the same lines came in 430: Thuc. 2.56. See also several of the stratagems in Polyaenus e.g.: 1.15 (the Spartans and a town in Messenia, eighth century), 1.40.5 (Alkibiades and the outer wall of Syracuse, 415), 1.47.2 (Thrasyllos and Byzantium, 409), 2.1.16 (Agesilaos and Phokaia, *c.* 395), 2.4.1 (Pelopidas in Thessaly, mid-360s), 4.2.8 (Philip and Amphissa, 338).

4.48 how could they *stay*, lacking supplies? Because X. has already given an answer to this question in 4.45 (q.v. above), his tacit background assumption here must be that pickings had been lean. On the general problem see e.g. *Anab.*1.3.11 (without supplies, neither a general nor a private is of any use), *Hipp*.7.9 (the more soldiers there are, the more likely they will scatter in search of supplies).

4.48 For *part* of their force to go and find food would be hazardous, as regards both those making the search and the aims of their mission As in 4.44 (see **The works**), the text here, if we leave it uncorrected as editors nowadays do, yields up its meaning only with some difficulty. The problem is the final phrase, the one I have translated 'and (hazardous as regards) the aims of their mission'. Wilhelm (1934) 51–2 proposed a correction which would visualize the foraging party having already found its *epitêdeia* and now needing to return safely with it (as in e.g. *Hell*.7.1.17). Gauthier 184, usually ready to follow Wilhelm, does not do so in this case.

On 'making the search' for *epitêdeia* cf. already *Hell*.2.1.25.

4.48 having everyone constantly making the search would mean their being blockaded rather than blockading Gauthier 184 adduces Polyb. 1.18.10: while blockading Akragas/Agrigentum (*OCD* 9, *IACP* no.9) in Sicily during the First Punic War the Romans are cut off from their provisions and so become, in equal measure, besiegers and besieged. Gauthier's parallel is a good one, but there are others, because in fact the idea is a *topos*. Rood (1998) 239 with n.36 assembles a second instance in Polybius (1.84.1), two in Diodorus (24.3, 25.4.1), a selection in Roman historians such as Livy (6.33.9), and—most interestingly for our purposes here—two in Thucydides: 4.29.2, 7.11.4. One is tempted to say that Thuc. must be X.'s model. And so he may be, though Rood himself points out that the idea's ultimate origin lies in the *Iliad*. In book 15 there, with Achilles absent, the confident Trojans leave the shelter of their walls and menace the attacker's camp and ships; cf. J. V. Morrison (1994).

Returning to Gauthier 184: he calls Polyb. 1.18.10 an exact parallel with the present passage. So it is, as regards the fundamental idea, reversal-of-fortune or tables-turned (cf. for a different version Thuc. 7.75.7), and also for the Greek verb used, in active and passive voice, to express it. (See also, more broadly, Thuc. 7.47–71 on the Athenians and their allies trapped in the Syracusan Great Harbour in 413.) That said, X.'s turn of phrase here seems to be most noteworthy for its distance from, not closeness to, circumstances such as are described by Polybius, and indeed by Thucydides too. Put simply, this is no blockade/siege situation—on either side. A passage like *Anab*.4.2.15 does show that X. was happy to use the verb *poliorkein* in quite a loose way (it applies there to a situation in which men who had taken a stand on a hill-top were afraid of being surrounded), yet even that conjures up a picture of static encirclement, which does not arise with *Poroi*'s foraging invaders and their adversaries. In truth, X. is using the verb figuratively here.

4.49 the income from the slaves would not be the only thing to enlarge the sustenance for the state For the Greek here ('income') see Notes on the Text.

Sections 4.49–50 as a whole represent a temporary digression from the military theme of 4.41–8, resumed in 4.51–2. See further under **4.51 not only.**

As in 3.7 (q.v.), 'the state' (*polis*) means its citizens (*politai*).

4.49 with a multitude of people gathering around the mines, many revenues would be generated 'A multitude of people', the single Greek noun *polyanthrôpia*, may well be a locution of X.'s own. The only pre-*Poroi* instance of it is also his: *Hell.*5.2.16, in a speech in Sparta in 382, by a representative of Akanthos (*OCD* 2, *IACP* no.559), about the growing size of the Chalkidian League (*OCD* 303). X. will use the related adjective *polyanthrôpos* in 4.50, though that has fifth-century precedents, especially in Thucydides. In any event, one must agree with Gauthier 186 that these 'people gathering' are foreigners and slaves rather than citizens.

Less easy to accept is Gauthier's belief that what X. goes on to evoke in the remainder of 4.49 and in 4.50 is not a concept original to him; rather, that he is simply describing the happy effects that his plans would have on the already existing fiscal yield of the region (Gauthier 186–9). We should distinguish, in my view, between contributory elements which are indeed not new (but enhanced) and a whole which is, or seems, more than the sum of its parts. See further under the next four lemmata, esp. to **4.50 Assuredly**.

An important preliminary point, however, may be addressed here. Jansen (2012) 737 and 738 employs the word Doulopolis, 'Slave-city', for what X. is about to describe here. Jansen is right to credit the term to Gauthier—but Gauthier did not use it in his comments on 4.49–50. Rather, it is a word introduced in his retrospective reflections on *X.'s vision as a whole* (an alarming one to his fellow-citizens: Gauthier 230) of Athens' economic future. That slaves will numerically predominate in the enlarged mining area of southern Attica—so producing what I myself (as indicated in Chap.4 intro.) prefer to call Metallopolis,

'Miners' city'—is of course undeniable; even so, the operations there will require plenty of free personnel also. See further under **4.50 Assuredly**.

Jansen's citation of Anaxandrides fr.4 Kassel-Austin, stray lines from a mid-fourth-century comedy, is nonetheless apposite (Jansen (2012) 738). 'Good sir, no polis of slaves exists, anywhere, but chance can change anyone's condition. Many are they, not free now who will be Sounians tomorrow, and using the agora the day after.' In fact we do hear of places called 'Doulopolis' in Crete, Egypt, and elsewhere, but setting that aside, it is significant that Anaxandrides chose Sounion—on which see already under **4.44 the works**, and again under the next lemma—as the deme, so distant from Athens, where slaves might slip unnoticed into the Athenian citizen-body; cf. Whitehead (1986) 292–3.

4.49 from the market operating there For the Greek here ('operating there') see Notes on the Text.

Substantively speaking, a single 'market' seems to be mentioned (before the textual obscurity arises), and on that basis one would have to concur with Thiel 31 and Gauthier 186–7 that X. has in mind the one in (the deme of) Sounion, implicit in *Hell.*5.1.23 and explicit in *SIG* 913/*IG* II^2 1180 (on a new or enlarged one at just this time, the mid-fourth century). Gauthier surmises, however, that Thorikos (**4.43 there is also**) might play a part too; and despite X.'s singular *agora*, there is merit in the idea. Just one marketplace, in the far south of the mining zone, somehow does not carry conviction. Could X. again (cf. 4.40) be using the word in an unusual way, this time to describe commercial activity as a general phenomenon?

4.49 from public 'houses' near the silver-mines This phrase has generated a wide range of exegesis. The theory of Kahrstedt (1934) 26 that the entirety of Laureion was public property is disproved by ample evidence, including 4.50 here (cf. Bodei Giglioni civ, Gauthier 187). Wilsdorf (1952) 157 supposed that the allusion is to public buildings where officials supervised the registration of lessees and collected relevant taxes; that, however, is not a natural interpretation of X.'s phrase 'revenues from' (cf. Gauthier 187). Three sensible options are left, two of them put forward in the *Poroi* commentaries. Thiel 32 relates the passage to 3.13 (and also to the 'houses' of 4.19, though see the Comm. there), with a comment that in Laureion too, just as in Peiraeius and Athens, there was public accommodation for new settlers. Gauthier himself, without mention of that, envisages these houses as 'state-owned' because they have been subject to confiscation or suchlike and are now being leased to private individuals—specifically, in this Laureion case, to those involved in the mining industry; X. supposes that higher rents could be charged if the industry expands (Gauthier 187).

Neither of these scenarios has a flaw as serious as do the ones summarized above; nevertheless, a more seductive one is to hand. In his study of *SEG* 42.785, the late archaic-period 'stele from the harbour' of Thasos (*OCD* 1449, *IACP* no.526), A. J. Graham draws particular attention to its several provisions about what are referred to as *katoikiai dêmosiai*, public *katoikiai*. These premises, he convincingly argues, are public brothels (Graham (1998), esp.23–39); and during the course of the discussion he suggests that the same interpretation could and should apply to mentions of *oikiai dêmosiai* in three other sources. One is an Athenian decree of 418/17 (*IG* I^3 84; Papazarkadas (2011) 23 and source-index s.v.; OR 167), where the lessee of a piece of extramural sacred land must control rainwater that flows 'between the *oikia dêmosia* and the gates that lead to the baths of Isthmonikos' (for whom, *LGPN* s.v. no.1, see Thuc. 5.18–24: a signatory to the Peace of Nikias and the ensuing Sparta/Athens alliance). The other two occurrences of *oikiai dêmosiai* are both in X.: *Hell.*7.4.37—in Tegea (*OCD* 1435, *IACP* no.297) in 363/2 the aristocrats and their supporters, after arrest, fill up first the prison and then 'the' (singular) *dêmosia oikia*—and the present passage of *Poroi*.

Whatever the identity/use of the Tegean building mentioned, Graham's interpretation of X.'s revenue-generating *oikiai dêmosiai* in Laureion has been well received by e.g. Henry (2002) 219; Rhodes (2010) 371 with 386 (his connection of it with the suggested *katagôgia* of 3.12, not with 4.49, is a mere slip); Glazebrook (2011) 55 n.7; and Papazarkadas (2011) 231—though contrast his 178 n.68. (The contradiction is pointed out by Rousset (2013) 120, himself doubtful—as was Gauthier, *BE* 1999 no.428—about Graham's brothel theory *vis-à-vis* the present passage.) For an '*oikia*' as a place of commercial sex see e.g. X. *Mem.*3.11.4, though there and elsewhere it is the context that establishes that sense (Glazebrook (2011) 35). It would be uphill work to argue that the general context of *Poroi* 4.49 does this; nevertheless the adjective *dêmosios* might give a hint. (See Kapparis (2011) 226–7 on the fact that '[a] large array of terms referring to male and female prostitution suggests an understanding of the brothel as a common place and of the bodies in it as common property'; instances include *damiourgos*, *leôphoros*, and *pandosia* for the person, *koineion* for the place.) As regards a translation of *oikiai dêmosiai* in the present passage: languages such as French (*maison publique*) or Italian (*casa pubblica*) have no equivalent in English, where a 'public house' offers innocent pleasures such as a pint of beer and a snack. Marchant and Waterfield both solve this problem with 'state-owned houses', but to my mind the element of ownership is too restrictive here. My own translation keeps the adjective general and relies on the ambiguity of the noun.

John Graham himself is rightly dubious about the idea that Solon, worried for the rampant libido of young Athenians, had established state-run brothels in the early sixth century: so the claim of Athen. *Deipn.*13.569D–F, quoting the early Hellenistic comic dramatist Philemon (*OCD* 1126 Philemon (2)) and citing also the late Hellenistic poet and antiquarian Nicander of Kolophon (*OCD* 1012–13). Even so, the Athenian state's fiscal interest in prostitution is independently guaranteed by the *pornikon* tax (Aeschin. 1.119; Fawcett (2016) 154, 166).

4.49 and from furnaces Thiel 32 asserts that X. has in mind furnaces (*kaminoi*) that were state-owned and leased to private individuals. Wilsdorf (1952) 157 and 161 speculated that the Athenian state itself had an actual monopoly on such furnaces. The generalization is too much for Gauthier 187–8, who will only go as far as Thiel 32: that X. has in mind here those furnaces which were state-owned (and leased to private individuals). Gauthier claims support for this in the view that X.'s adjective here, 'public', applies not only to the 'houses' (see under the preceding lemma) but also to these 'furnaces'. However, as noted by Graham (1998) 35, X.'s word-order tells strongly against that—and supplementing X.'s text to produce the phrase 'public furnaces' is a question-begging step that has not been advocated since the early nineteenth century (by B. Weiske).

In the light of the general modern view (stemming from Hopper (1953)) that the ancillary activities which supported mining were in private hands, there is thus no good reason to doubt that this was true of the smelting process(es) also. See in any event *IG* II^2 2750, a fourth-century marker-stone 'of a furnace' which *must* be in private ownership (since it has been put up as security: Gauthier 188, and generally Finley (1952) 28–37). Also, when the mine-leasing documents of the *pôlêtai* specify the location of a mine in terms of what adjoins it at ground level, a furnace and its owner are sometimes mentioned: so e.g. in line 54 of the 367/6 leases RO 36 (Austin & Vidal-Naquet (1977) no.95, *Agora* 19 P5).

That said, there is no evidence to shed light on *precisely* what revenue(s) from smelting X. had in mind here; cf. Graham (1998) 36, Powell (2015) 99–100. (And his tailpiece 'all the rest of it' is impenetrability itself.)

4.50 Assuredly, a multitudinous *city* is what would come into being, if organized in the manner described As the gloss in Thiel 32 puts it, what X. is visualizing is the creation, near Athens itself, of a '*nova quasi urbs*'.

Thiel's *quasi* is crucial. Despite using the word *polis*, X. does not mean a new civic community within Attica. But what does he mean instead? The pioneering work of the Copenhagen Polis Centre (directed by M. H. Hansen), from 1993 onwards, has not only shed light on every attested polis or polis-type community but has also probed the meanings and uses of the term *polis* itself. Among other things, Hansen and his colleagues formulated the so-called *Lex Hafniensis de civitate*. This, in application to Hellenic poleis, declares that even when the term is used of a town, an urban centre, it seems to refer 'almost invariably' to a polis in the city-state sense. Only one passage was found which 'flatly contradicts' this: the present one. So Hansen & Nielsen in *IACP* 34 (where *Poroi* '54' should read 4.50), who reiterate the point: '[t]his imaginary nucleated settlement is the only unquestionable instance of a *polis* town which was *not* the centre of a *polis* state'; cf. Gauthier 188, Jansen (2012) 737–8. For '*polis*' in the purely urban sense of the term see *IACP* 39 (*b* there) and passim. (In German, a language which has the capacity to make the distinction, what X. is describing is a *Stadt* but not a *Staat*. In ancient Greek, which lacks that capacity, X.'s use of the term *polis* is viewed by Jansen (2012) 738, reasonably enough, as figurative. See also Powell (2015) 125.)

Had this been otherwise, Gauthier's opinion that there is nothing ground-breaking in X.'s creation (**4.49 with a multitude**) would have been perverse. As it is, when he returns to the question in retrospect he still plays down this 'agglomération industrielle du Laureion' as a phenomenon secondary to the continued existence of *the* polis, Athens itself (Gauthier 188–9). While the point is perfectly valid in its own terms, the *de facto* novelty of X.'s vision—'le développement prodigieux de l'exploitation du Laureion' (Gauthier 189)—still seems to me very striking. To consider population alone (before buildings and other facilities are factored in) establishes the point. X.'s plan envisages an eventual number of slaves three times the size of the citizen-body, thus somewhere between 60,000 and 90,000 (see **4.17 the state**). Add at least 10,000–15,000 free persons, and the total might reach six figures.

As a 'nucleated settlement' (above) this is at any rate much larger than any of the three immediate comparanda:

(*i*) Athens town itself, the *asty*. Hansen in *IACP* 636 does as much as can be done with available evidence and reasonable assumptions. The outcome is 'an urban population of between 47,000 and 56,000 persons in the age of Demosthenes'. We should note, though, that he defines the 'urban population' as Athens *and Peiraeus*. If Peiraieus is kept separate (see *ii* below) this figure is manifestly much lower. For our purposes here there is no need to limit the *asty* to the five demes inside the city walls: Koile, Kollytos, Kydathenaion, Melite, and Skambonidai (Whitehead (1986) 26). One can certainly add Kerameis, which straddled the wall in the north-west quarter, and indeed in general the 'suburbs' (*proasteia*: see e.g. Thuc. 2.34.5, Isoc. 16.13), embracing such demes as Agryle, Alopeke, Ankyle, Diomeia, and Keiriadai. Yet all in all, surely not more than 30,000–40,000.

(*ii*) Peiraieus. See already under *i*. The discussion of this in Garland (2001) 58–61 begins with a 'very conservative estimate' of 30,000 but then, importantly, lays emphasis on the fluctuations, both small- and large(r)-scale.

(*iii*) Acharnai (*OCD* 6). This enormous deme lay north-west of Athens in the foothills of Mt Parnes, around present-day Menidi. See Whitehead (1986) 397–400 (appendix 5); Hornblower (1991–2008) 1.273–4; N. F. Jones (2004) 92–100; and in full now Kellogg (2013). To *quantify* 'enormous', the possible textual problems of Thuc. 2.19.2—where Acharnai is certainly called Attica's largest deme of all—make that a text which is best set aside. A plain fact, by contrast, is Acharnai's annual allocation of no fewer than twenty-two seats on the council; twice the number filled by Eleusis; almost half a tribe's-worth (Oineis, in this instance). Alongside the agricultural activity to be expected in such a location, Acharnai's principal claim to fame was the production of charcoal. This 'industrial' aspect to an otherwise rural community may have led it to support more metics and slaves than other demes in the Attic countryside. Even so, it is hard to imagine a visitor to Acharnai finding more than 5,000–10,000 people there.

4.50 the tracts of land would be no less valuable to the owners there than the ones near town are to theirs In the translation of Waterfield 180, 'valuable to *its* owners' (my emphasis), the only antecedent of 'it' can be the putative polis (see under the preceding lemma). This obliterates the character of X.'s remark. As Gauthier 189 comments, he is viewing matters here, unusually, from the standpoint of 'the owners' of these plots and the economic benefits that they as individuals (as well as the community at large: 4.49) can expect.

Marchant's translation of *chôroi* here as 'building sites' confuses them with the *oikopeda* of 2.5—a point which also answers the contention of Finley (1952) 253 n.50 that there is a conflict between 2.5 (with its implication that intra-mural land is *not* valuable) and the present passage; Gauthier 189. Elsewhere, too, in X. a *chôros* is a tract of land in the countryside (see esp. *Oec*.5.4 and 11.18, where its opposite is the town, *asty*); so Waterfield's '*in and* about Athens' (my emphasis) is again misleading.

4.51 Once the ideas I have expounded are acted on, I agree that Athens would become etc. For the Greek here ('I agree') see Notes on the Text.

Sections 51–2, as Gauthier 190 comments, fit only loosely onto the rest of Chap.4. There is nothing more about the mines, and there are no more *poroi* to propose. Instead, 'the ideas I have expounded' embrace the totality of Chaps.2–4.

4.51 not only better-supplied with sources of income but also better in obedience, better in orderliness, and better in military effectiveness The first of these phrases is one that X. had already used in *Mem*.4.6.14 (the good citizen is the man 'who makes the state better-supplied with sources of income', *euporôtera*). Here it recapitulates the thrust, so far, of the work as a whole.

However, as we see, X. now provides three additional ways—all 'moral' ones—in which Athens will be changed for the better by his ideas. (As with the first way, all three are expressed in the Greek by *eu-* adjectives in the comparative degree: *eupeithestera*, *eutaktotera*, *eupolemôtera*; compare the *eunousteroi* metics of 2.5 & 7.) If seen in the light of *the work as a whole*, i.e. with Chaps.5–6 included, their martial nature might appear surprising, even paradoxical, because those two concluding Chaps. will emphasize that the best way forward for Athens is to embrace peace—and particular sections such as 5.1 and, especially, 6.1 will highlight quite different virtues, in keeping with that eirenic vision. In context here, however, 4.51 still flows from 4.41–8 (after the digression of 4.49–50) and the theme of response to possible military threats.

Gauthier 190–1 demonstrates that light can be shed on both the choice and the association of the three qualities invoked here from three standpoints. One is Sokratic thought. Sokrates in *Mem.*4.4.1 is a paragon of obedience to the officials and the laws, and also, in the military sphere, of orderliness (*eutaxia*, on which see further below). Another is Sparta: see chiefly *Lac.Pol.*8.1 (again, obedience to officials and laws, with *eutaxia* appended) and *Oec.*4.3 (Sparta, though not named, is implicit, and the rare adjective *eupolemos* occurs for the only other time in X.). Third, there is the Athenian *ephebeia* (on which X. will proceed to say more in 4.52). Obedience and orderliness are two of the cardinal virtues of ephebes in Athenian decrees and other documents on stone: see e.g. the earliest extant one of its kind, RO 89 (*IG* II^2 1156, Harding (1985) no.108), ephebes of the tribe Pandionis in 334/3. Note also the *eutaxia* liturgy in *IG* II^2 417, now *IG* II^3 550/*AIO*, apparently from a year or two later; Lambert (2001) 51–9 = Lambert (2012) 224–35.

There is little to add, except that for X. obedience is a (good) attribute of horses (*Symp.*2.10) as well as men. On X.'s abhorrence of *dis*obedience and *dis*order in any context see Dillery (1995) 27–38.

4.52 Those assigned to undergo physical exercise would do this much more diligently if receiving in the gymnasia a sustenance-allowance higher than in the torch-races, under gymnasiarchs For the Greek here ('higher') see Notes on the Text. Earlier in the sentence, Thiel 32 implemented his own belief that the phrase 'in the gymnasia' should be transposed to follow 'physical exercise'. Wilhelm (1934) 36 and Gauthier 191 disagree. In their opinion (which I endorse), 'in the gymnasia' is part of the subordinate clause. (The correctness of this is clearer in the Greek: 'to undergo physical exercise' is the middle-voice verb *gymnazesthai*.)

Concerning substance (of 4.52 as a whole, i.e. including the next lemma): Thiel 32 and Gauthier 192–3 (with 193–5) identify the group(s) concerned—to whom X. applies only the participles and infinitives of verbs, never a noun—as Athens' young ephebes (*ephêboi*), on whom see already above, **4.47 If they** and **4.51 not only**, and generally *OCD* 508. Sekunda (1990) 151–2 concurs: '[t]his passage can hardly be referring to anything other than the ephebate since only the ephebes, at any period in Athenian history, were "ordered" [my 'assigned'] to train in the gymnasia'. Gauthier and Sekunda also note that the 'sustenance-allowance' (*trophê*) mentioned twice here foreshadows the *trophê* (of four *oboloi* a day) provided for the ephebes in the fully organized post-335 system (?Aristot. *Ath.Pol.*42.3).

The rest of what X. says here calls for more context. Gymnasiarchs (*OCD* 638) were rich Athenians appointed each year from the ten tribes to perform the *gymnasiarchia* liturgy—as, for example, the speaker in Lys. 21.3 had done (and also Alkibiades, if his son can be believed: Isoc. 16.35). See also *Oec.*2.6, where Sokrates includes it in a list of the financial burdens imposed by the state on a man like Kritoboulos of Alopeke (*LGPN* s.v. no.4, *APF* 336–7, *POP* 116–19). Specifically, as we observe here, the gymnasiarch's money was spent on an event held at several of Athens' religious festivals, such as the Panathenaia (*OCD* 1073; Parke (1977) 33–50, esp. 45–46): an inter-tribal torch-race (*lampas* or *lampadêdromia*), 'a spectacular ritual race, normally a relay, in which fire was taken from one altar to another . . . It was the form of ritual activity most distinctively associated with the *ephêboi*' (*OCD* 1489; more fully in Sekunda (1990) 153–6).

As to the present passage, then: if we set aside the potentially confusing vocabulary (which might lead the unwary to suppose that the gymnasiarchs played some role in the gymnasia), again Sekunda's comment hits the mark. 'The implication is that, at the time of writing, the ephebes did not carry out any systematic programme of training in the gymnasia because *trophê* was not provided for them on a regular basis, but rather on the whim of the gymnasiarch. Thus the athletic training of the ephebes was suffering because it was under-resourced, and consequently was only carried out intermittently throughout the year. [This aspect of X.'s proposals will] provide funds to improve the standard of ephebic training in the gymnasia' (Sekunda (1990) 151–2; cf. Fisher (1998) 90–1).

See further under the next lemma.

4.52 those assigned to guard-duty in the guard-posts and those assigned to peltast-drill and to patrolling Attica would do all these things better with the sustenance-allowance being distributed in recognition of each of the tasks Dakyns and Marchant both have 'or' patrolling (likewise Schütrumpf: 'oder'), and the same implication of a second and third group is also conveyed by the syntax in Waterfield 180. In X.'s Greek there are just two *in toto*.

As to substance: rather than an empirical approach, as under the preceding lemma, I will begin this one with the bottom line and work backwards. 'The following picture emerges from the evidence. Before [i.e. as well as after] 335 the Athenian ephebate lasted two years. In the first year training consisted simply of athletic training for the three annual torch-races. [...] It should be noted that if first-year ephebic training consisted of training in the gymnasia only, and if attendance was actually compulsory only when the ephebes were training to compete in the three annual torch-races, an ephebe in his first year would be free for a considerable proportion of the year. The second year would consist of military training, either in the garrisons if the ephebe was wealthy enough to provide his own hoplite equipment, or patrolling the countryside in the *peripoloi*, equipped as a peltast, if he was not' (Sekunda (1990) 158). That is the picture, he contends (and I agree) which 'emerges from the evidence'.

Just how much of that evidence is furnished by *Poroi* 4.52, especially the differentiation between the two years and what happened in each of them, we have now seen. The comparandum (to reiterate), for the post-335 system, is ?Aristot. *Ath.Pol.*43.2–5, on which see generally Rhodes (1981) 493–510; cf. also e.g. Habicht (1997) 16 with n.19. (Pursuing the comparison in detail would not be relevant for present purposes. Nevertheless, in response to Sekunda's point that, on his own X.-generated postulates, year-1 ephebes appear to be significantly under-employed, two possibilities proffer themselves: either—despite what X. here suggests—year 1 did also include *military* training, as well as generic athletic and gymnastic exercising; or it did not, and that aspect of the system as a whole was subsequently adjusted. In *Ath. Pol.*43.3–4 the military training is confined, in fact, to year 1: infantry-fighting, archery, javelin-throwing, artillery-work. Also, this first year *begins* with guard-duty in one of the two posts in Peiraieus: Mounychia or Akte. Year 2 is then a year of patrolling 'and' time spent in the guard-posts—presumably the more far-flung ones.)

The task of 'guard-duty in the guard-posts (*phrouria*)' is self-explanatory as far as it goes; cf. generally above, **4.47 They will.** (Later at least, and probably now also, the troops in a *phrourion* were not exclusively rookies: see Demosth. 54.3.) As regards peltast-drill: X. had already used—perhaps coined—the verb *peltazein* in *Anab.*5.8.5, recalling his own conversation with a man whom he asked to identify himself as either hoplite or peltast. (He turned out to be neither, but a muleteer.) In the present context, though, the term surely shifts its sense: from *being* a peltast to *training to be* one. Peltasts (*peltastai*) were named after their distinctive shield, the *peltê*, lighter and more manoeuvrable than the heavy round *aspis* of a hoplite. (*Anab*.6.1.9–10 describes a Mysian who is dancing with a *peltê* in each hand.) In addition their main offensive weapon, the javelin, could kill or wound at much longer range than the hoplite's thrusting-spear. Thuc. 5.10.9 describes a classic instance: Amphipolis 422, with the Athenians on the receiving end. In and after the 390s, under Iphikrates of Rhamnous (*LGPN* s.v. no.4, *OCD* 743, *APF* 248–52), they did master the relevant skills. That must be what X. has in mind here: javelin-throwing in particular, the *Ath.Pol.*'s *akontizein*. (In *Hipp*.1.25 and 6.5 he had stressed the need for practice in effective javelin-throwing from horseback, and cf. generally *Cyrop*.1.2.8 & 12, 1.6.28, 4.3.12.)

On 'guard-duty in the guard-posts' *and* 'patrolling Attica' there is a sensible discussion, citing an array of other evidence, in Hunter (1994) 151–3: 'Appendix [to chap.5]: did ephebes have a role as police?' (Her own answer, after disposing of firm but mistaken versions of a Yes to that question, is that 'they were not police but they did assume some tasks of policing the frontier and the countryside'.)

Gauthier 193 mentions and agrees with the opinion of Reinmuth 123–38—despite the fact that Reinmuth ignored *Poroi*—that the content of ephebic training before and after 335 was the same. Yet X. here says nothing about *hoplite* training, even though he was familiar with *Ath.Pol*.42.3's name for it: *hoplomachia* (see *Anab*.2.1.7, and in general Rawlings (2000) 237–46). Perhaps his phraseology here was not meant to be all-encompassing. But I would think it more probable that the *personal* expertise of the hoplite—hardly expertise of the same order as a peltast's (Lazenby (1991) 103 declares that for a hoplite 'it is obvious from Plato's *Laches* [182A–B] that individual skills were not important')—was something that, in the mid-350s, neither X. nor his city saw as requiring to be taught.

* * * *

Gauthier's endnote (293–5) on the broad significance of what 4.52 reveals about the ephebate at this time *dis*agrees with two other contentions in Reinmuth, likewise on the matter of continuity between the pre- and post-335 systems: (*i*) that under both, the ephebes received *trophê*; and (*ii*) that both were implementations of compulsory military service for all eighteen- to twenty-year-olds, as a prerequisite for entry into full citizenship (Reinmuth 127). In my view he is right to do so.

Concerning *i*: Gauthier 193–4 states that X. attests categorically ('formellement') that the garrison-troops and the patrollers were not already receiving any *trophê*; X.'s suggestion is that in future they should. This is true but overstated; some expansion is necessary. With reference to the garrison-troops and patrollers (and for completeness we should add the peltast-drillers) X. writes of *the* sustenance-allowance. In isolation, that simple definite article could indicate the exact opposite of what Reinmuth and Gauthier envisage. In context, however, these (putatively year-2) proto-ephebes are mentioned only after the mention of 'those assigned to undergo physical exercise', and in their case X. writes of *a* sustenance-allowance. Thus the subsequent phrase '*the* sustenance-allowance' means in effect 'the one already proposed'. (And there is no sign of X.'s proposal having been adopted during the ensuing two decades.)

Concerning *ii*: Gauthier 194–5 begins from the position that the absence of *trophê* before 335 (above, *i*) is in itself explained by the not yet institutionalized character of ephebe-status then: an age-class [cf. *Cyrop*.1.2.4–1.6.26 passim: DW] rather than a statutory period of universal military service. X.'s plan here is to give a sustenance-allowance not to all Athenian eighteen- to twenty-year-olds, but only to those performing the tasks stated. Hence precisely, Gauthier suggests, his avoidance of the noun *ephêboi* in favour of a string of circumlocutory 'those who…' phrases. (In fact *Cyrop*., above, is the only work in which X. does use the word.) This last supposition perhaps goes too far. In 361/0 an honorific decree of the tribe Akamantis refers to *ephêboi* and *neaniskoi* ('young men'), evidently variants of each another, in the same sentence (Reinmuth no.1, lines 15–17). Also, in court in 345, Aeschines famously recalls his two years as a young *peripolos* (at the end of the 370s, if he was born in 390: see Harris (1988)), something for which his 'fellow-ephebes' (*synephêboi*) can vouch (Aeschin. 2.167). Even so, Gauthier's point that after 335 no such para-ephebic vocabulary (as we might term it) was needed, even possible, is a good one.

CHAPTER FIVE

With his detailed ideas fully set out in Chaps.1–4, X. now returns to their underlying character as a peace dividend (4.40); see Jansen (2017).

He begins optimistically enough, by advocating the establishment of a board of peace-custodians (*eirênophylakes*: 5.1), but he then switches into a more defensive mode again (as in 4.34–48) for the remainder of the Chapter. There are concerns that Athens' reputation will be damaged if she becomes wedded to a peace policy. (Roisman (2005) 113 expresses the general point thus: '[t]he Athenians readily admitted that peace was better than war. Nonetheless, war was more prestigious than peace'.) X. feels that he must counter these concerns. First (5.2–4), his argument is that an *economic* resurgence will bring its own kudos, and influence. Then (5.5–7), in response to those who hanker after old-style military might for its own sake, he passes a century and more of history rapidly in review, insisting that the Athenians prospered best when they were *serving* their allies, not browbeating them. Now, therefore, 'an opportunity has come Athens' way: to win the Hellenes back without effort, without danger, and without expense' (5.8). Supporting an autonomous Delphi is central to this (5.9–10).

Two subsidiary worries are addressed in the remaining sections. The notion that war is intrinsically more profitable to Athens than peace is, again, rejected by a consideration of the past as well as the present (5.11–12); and worries that the Athenians, if attacked, would be expected simply to turn the other cheek are allayed. Retaliation would be all the swifter if the aggressors could not create an alliance of Athens' enemies (5.13).

A generation later than X., and perhaps already in his own day, rhetoricians were codifying the arguments that could be made for war and against peace, and vice versa. See Anax. *Ars.Rhet*.2.26–8 and 29–32 (= [Aristot.] *Rhet. ad Alex*.2.1425a9–28 and 1425a29–1425b19). Under the first head we find the very claims that X. does his best to counter here: loss of reputation, of wealth, of power (5.2–5 & 11–12) and righting a wrong (5.13).

Chap.5 overall, on the standard view expressed most recently by Jansen (2007) 257, is 'an impressive piece of Xenophon's anti-imperialist rhetoric'. More exactly perhaps, X. takes over language and tropes from earlier writers who had supported or justified an Athenian imperial stance and re-fashions them in the service of a policy driven by peace (Dillery (1993)) and consent (Farrell (2016)).

Sections 5–13 here have been regularly compared with two speeches in book 6 of *Hell*., those of Kallistratos to the Spartans in 6.3.10–17 and, especially, Prokles of Phleious to the Athenians in 6.5.38–48, with a view to determining how far those two speakers are surrogates for X. himself.

(The orthodox answer is: to a significant extent. For discussion and bibliography see Dillery (1995) 244–49.) If we add into the mix the exchanges between Kyros and Tigranes which fill *Cyrop*.3.1.14–31, fairly characterized by Lendon (2006) as an 'extended theoretical treatment of foreign relations', what emerges is X.'s personal and original contribution to the topic. It differed from (and tacitly rebutted) Thucydides' brutal, pessimistic fear-and-power model, as seen in the Melian Dialogue and elsewhere, in favour of one which assigns a much larger role to such things as loyalty, morale, reciprocity, and (innate or accumulated) superiority. 'In Xenophon ideas and ethics and culture matter: they do not exist merely as a veil to be whisked away, revealing the dark engines of power beneath.... Although Thucydides' account of relations between states is sleeker and more elegant, Xenophon's theory may better describe the Greek world they shared' (Lendon (2006) 82, 98).

* * * *

5.1 the intention that all revenues flow in from the state itself For the Greek here ('from the state itself') see Notes on the Text.

5.1 peace-custodians The term itself is striking and rare, though it would later be used by Aeschines; he scornfully asserts that after the Macedonian victory at Chaironeia in 338 (*OCD* 303) had not, as Demosthenes and others predicted, resulted in Athens' destruction, Demosthenes had wanted to be elected *eirênophylax* (Aeschin. 3.159).

As already noted in the General Intro., section 6, at n.94, Cawkwell (1963) 56 proffers a suggestion about the Aeschines passage. 'Of course this may be mere sarcastic abuse, but it seems natural to connect it with the position Demosthenes held after Chaeronea. Of the two offices attributed to him, the post of *teichopoios* [i/c walls] seems ruled out of consideration, for it was probably not elective [...] I guess therefore that Aeschines referred to his election *epi to theôrikon* for 337/6, and that he chose as a sneer the word used twenty years earlier by Xenophon in proposing a new office to make the most of the peace. Here perhaps as elsewhere in the *Revenues* what Xenophon proposed Eubulus enacted.' The sheer cleverness of this earns it the description 'originale et séduisante' from Gauthier 197–8, but only as a preface to declaring its conclusion a step too far. The Athenians did not, Gauthier insists, create officials called *eirênophylakes* in or after 355. He is nevertheless prepared to salvage from Cawkwell's construct the idea that by the time of Aeschines' remark, 330, it was possible to look back at the early years of the theoric fund and regard its personnel as 'peace-custodians' *de facto*. Perhaps so. However, another line of approach to Aeschin. 3.159 altogether understands *eirênophylax* there as meaning a delegate (*synedros*) to Philip II's 'League of Corinth'. So Ryder (1976); Hammond & Griffith (1979) 644–5; Harris (1994), summarized in Harris (1995) 138–9; Whitehead (2000) 218–19, 448.

See further under the next lemma.

5.1 Such a board of officials, if chosen, would make Athens much more appealing to all people and much more choc-a-bloc with them For the Greek here ('more choc-a-bloc') see Notes on the Text. This adjective, *puknos*, can describe not only (*a*) compactness in space but also (*b*) frequency in time. It is orthodox to categorize the present passage as an instance of *b*: besides LSJ s.v., II.2, see Gauthier 199, following Zurborg (1874) 36 and others. Among translators see e.g. Waterfield 180: 'more frequently visited'. As my own translation indicates (and cf. Marchant: 'more densely thronged'), I advocate the other option. X's usage elsewhere does not settle the matter, but as regards *this passage*, understanding the phrase *pyknoteran eisaphikneisthai* (*poiêseie tên polin*) as meaning '(would make the state) more frequent to visit' seems a great stretch. Under X.'s plan it is not Athens that would be 'more frequent', but *visits* to Athens (like the huntsman's retraced steps in *Kyn*.6.25). LSJ was unable to find a parallel for *pyknos* with such an infinitive. Without a parallel, I consider that 'more *pyknos* to visit' is describing the experience which the visitors themselves will have: a city crowded like a scrum (or an infantry phalanx: so *Anab*.2.3.3, and elsewhere e.g. Hom. *Il*.4.280–2).

This sentence of explanation, as Gauthier 196–7 notes, is enough to falsify the view of Thiel 33 that X.'s board of *eirênophylakes* is intended to arbitrate in inter-state disputes between Athens and other communities. From what X. says here (which is all we have to go by), they are to be Athenians, elected by Athenians, and concerned purely with Athens. (Cawkwell (1963) 56 adds the point that the *thesmothetai* already met the sort of need Thiel has in mind: see ?Aristot. *Ath. Pol*.59.6, and *OCD* 1466.) Much the same consideration, alongside others, militates also against the view of Bodei Giglioni xxxi–xxxiv. Reviving one first propounded in Momigliano (1936) 121, she visualizes these peace-custodians as Panhellenic in conception: nominated by the Athenians but recognized by their allies as guarantors of the peace between them; analogous to the men described in *c*. 331 as 'those in charge of collective security' ([Demosth.] 17.15). Yet these individuals, whoever they are, make a poor fit with the circumstances in which X. was writing *Poroi*. They were imposed by the Macedonian conquerors, not by a defeated polis. In any case, broad as Pan-Hellenism is, it is not as broad as X.'s 'all mankind'.

With flawed exegesis set aside, we can return to 5.1 itself and the inferences that may legitimately be drawn from it. X.'s concern that Athens should present a friendlier face to the world will be repeated, using the same adjective, in 6.1. (There it is only 'the Hellenes' who need to be convinced, but the context explains that restriction: see the Comm. For the same change but in reverse—from 'the Hellenes' to 'all people'—see Isoc. 8.19–21.) Gauthier 198 begins his comment by stating that X. is thinking here of 'étrangers de passage', foreign visitors of all kinds (examples will be given in 5.3–4), but he then muddies the waters by referring to all kinds of 'residents' (plenty of whom will be non-Hellenic: see 2.3). My own view is that foreign residents, metics, are no longer X.'s concern here; in any case, for them another new magistracy, the metic-custodians (*metoikophylakes*), has already been promulgated (2.7). Here by contrast, visitors are the key; the compound verb *eisaphikneisthai* is the one he used in 3.12 when suggesting public hostels for visitors.

That the *metoikophylakes* and the *eirênophylakes* are meant to be *exact* analogues of each other would go too far, for two reasons. There are surely to be more, perhaps many more, of the former; and *metoiko-* and *eirêno-*, the latter so grandiose a prefix, make an unbalanced match. Nonetheless, the view that the essential task of the peace-guardians was 'to make the city more attractive to trade' (Cawkwell (1963) 56) has a lot to recommend it. (Jansen (2007) 259–61, summarized in Jansen (2012) 733 with n.38, provides a useful review of the issue as a whole, but ends with a suggestion of his own that I find far-fetched. When Isoc. 4.175 calls the King of Persia 'guardian of the peace' he does so in a tone of withering scorn; and without the support of that passage—and Plutarch's labelling of the Roman *fetiales* (*OCD* 574), who were priests, as *eirênophylakes*—Jansen's conception of X.'s proposed board as 'a permanent office of diplomats' takes us back too close to Thiel, above.)

5.2 Some might judge that by remaining at peace Athens will be both more powerless and more disesteemed; and of lesser renown in Hellas X. returns to the objection-anticipating mode of 4.34–48 (and earlier).

Translators and commentators have overlooked here the different way in which he describes the three criteria he invokes. The third is straightforward. 'Renown'—being *onomastê*, as it is expressed: a name to conjure with—was precious to any polis, let alone one with such a history as Athens. For Athens to be less *onomastê* means being less so than she ought to be; something that no patriotic Athenian would want, at any time and for any reason. Before describing such a diminution, however, X. uses two adjectives, in the comparative degree, which are already (by their alpha-privative prefixes) the negations of meritorious attributes that belong in the same category as *onomastê*: *adynatôtera* and *adoxotera*—derived from, respectively, the adjective *dynatos* (able, competent, powerful) and the noun *doxa* (esteem, repute, respect). Thus X. is not saying here, simply, that some people are afraid that Athens will have less power and less respect (as well as less renown); rather, that she will lose even more than she has lost already, having lost the Social War.

For a peace—that of 346—described by a hostile critic of it as *adoxos* for Athens, cf. Demosth. 19.97. As regards 355, Isocrates' *On the Peace* is the key text. He writes that Athens needs to recover its *dynamis* (8.6) and to gain 'a better *doxa*' (8.23); and a recurrent theme is how low the Athenians currently stand in the eyes of others (Isoc. 8.19, 29, 31, 125, 142).

5.2 They too, in my opinion, are *mis*judging For the Greek here ('*mis*judging') see Notes on the Text.

5.2 Surely the states that are spoken of as most highly favoured are the ones which remained at peace for the longest time The Greek adjective *eudaimôn* is routinely translated as fortunate, happy, prosperous. In fact, as noted by Cartledge in Waterfield 228, its root-meaning is 'well-favoured by the gods' (the *daimones*), and given X.'s personal piety—see **1.3 the good things**—it seems appropriate to bring out that sense here; cf. generally *Mem*.4.8.3, *Cyrop*.8.1.24, and see 6.1 below for the related participle.

That point aside, Gauthier 199–200 adduces *Mem*.4.4.16–17 as clarification of the present passage. In conversation there with the sophist Hippias of Elis (*OCD* 687 s.v.2, *POP* 168–9), Sokrates declares *homonoia*—literally, being of one mind (*OCD* 700)—to be the great good for states; its concomitant is that everyone obeys the laws, and states where that is so are both the strongest (*ischyrotatai*) and the most highly favoured (*eudaimonestatai*).

5.2 of all states Athens has the best nature to grow in peace-time This is so for reasons set out already, especially in Chap.1, and to be expanded now (5.3–4).

X. really does write 'Athens' here (rather than 'the Athenians' or 'the polis'); noted by Gauthier 200. Whitehead (2006) is a study of the usage in general.

5.3 Would not everyone have need of Athens, if she was maintaining tranquility? Waterfield 180 has 'with the city at peace' (cf. Dakyns), but it is better to choose another form of words, to reflect the fact that X. himself did. Marchant proffers 'if the state is tranquil', which does capture the noun *hêsychia*. 'Athens is to become not just a commercial center, but also one modeled on the Athenian quietist, not "polypragmatist" (an imperial "busybody", *Poroi* 5.3).' So Dillery (2017) 218, context for whose rather telegraphic comment can be found in e.g. Carter (1986), Bauslaugh (1991) part I, and Leigh (2013) chaps.1–2. The Athenians had a long-established reputation for untranquil behaviour to overcome.

5.3. The list starts from ship-owners and merchants Hence the extensive treatment of them already (Chap.3).

The Greek here is more odd than I have made it sound in translation. X. uses the participle 'having started from' in the plural, and this plural must relate grammatically to 'everyone' (see the preceding lemma), as if *they* were making the list. Thiel 34 finds a parallel in Plato's *Republic*: 2.366E.

As regards the list itself, Thiel xix and 34 registers it as a particularly striking example of X.'s liking for trios of things (see already under **1.4 from which**). If we keep in mind—prompted by Gauthier 200—that the initial 'ship-owners and merchants' (*nauklêroi* and *emporoi*) are effectively repeated at the end of 5.4 (q.v. below), the present specimen actually comprises four such trios. The first and second of them concern commercial and 'industrial' activity; the third and fourth turn to intellectual, artistic and religious life (with items 6 and 7—'men able to use their brains and money in investments' and 'craftsmen' effecting a coherent transition). See further in the lemmata below.

At the end of the list (though I will mention it here) Gauthier 204–5 has a supplementary note on 5.1–4 as a whole, pointing out the change of tone it signals. Chaps.1–4 have been all about revenues, but now the focus is on Athens' inherent welfare; and for the first time X. responds to a possible objection not with logical argument but with 'une hymne'.

Dreaming of a possible future, he visualizes an Athens peace-loving, friendly, alluring, happy, affluent. 'Un nouvel âge d'or commence'.

5.3 the men with abundant grain In *Hell.*5.2.16 X. had used, perhaps coined, the abstract noun *polysitia* to describe the ample agricultural food resources available to the Chalkidian League. (The usage is also found, later, in Theophrastus and Strabo.) Here, equally rare, is the (plural) personalization of the concept.

5.3 men with bulk wine, men with premium wine For the Greek here see Notes on the Text. Some editors delete the second element here on the grounds that it was not written by X. but is merely a scribe's addition. So for instance Marchant—hence Waterfield's translation. For reasons pointed out by Herzog (1914) 477, Thiel 34, and Gauthier 200–1, both elements are needed.

(*a*) 'The men with bulk wine' is an unproblematic translation of *hoi polyoinoi*, and the concept itself is self-explanatory. (If Gauthier had translated the word, he would doubtless have written of *vin ordinaire*.) Here again, seemingly, X. is pioneering the word, at least as applied to humans; Thuc. 1.135.8 had called Lampsakos (*OCD* 791, *IACP* no.748) the most *polyoinos* place in its locality.

(*b*) 'The men with premium wine' is an appropriate translation of *hoi hêdyoinoi*. *Anab.*6.4.6 had applied the word *hêdyoinos* (as an adjective) to *vines* growing in abundance in the rich terrain of Kalpe, a promontory on the southern shore of the Black Sea (mentioned several times in *Anab.*6.2–4). Likewise Athen. *Deipn.*1.31B writes that Thrake and its environs 'used to be admired as *hêdyoinos*'. Yet again the application of the term to men with this commodity at their disposal is unique to *Poroi* 5.3. But what is its exact meaning, or connotation? The root-adjective *hêdys* often means sweet in a literal sense; LSJ defines X.'s *hêdyoinoi* as 'dealers in sweet wine'; and for present-day readers wine is 'sweet' if it is not 'dry'. In the present context, though, the contrast is between *poly-* (above, *a*) and *hêdy-*. Also, if an ancient Greek wanted to describe a wine as 'sweet' the adjective *glykys* was the obvious one to use, as e.g. slightly later in that same passage of Athenaeus ('the *glykys* wine called Pollian'; see also 1.30B, 1.32C&F). Either way: while present-day notions of sweetness or dryness in a wine—the latter the result of efficient fermentation of the natural sugars into alcohol—are not entirely unknown (Athen. *Deipn.*1.32F), the main thing a fourth-century Hellene would want to know (and the price would tell him) is whether the drink would be an intrinsically pleasant one, or simply something to wash down plain food and to quench thirst.

5.3 (men) with lots of olive-oil The only instance of this word (in any application) until the Christian era.

The substantive part of it (after the *poly-* prefix) is either *elaia*, the olive-tree and/or its fruit, or *elaion*, the oil pressed from olives (or in other contexts other crops). There is no means of telling which X. meant here. Translators of *Poroi* opt for the second, but contrast LSJ's definition ('owning many oliveyards').

5.3 (men) with lots of sheep Here at last is a term that X. could have borrowed (and probably did) from someone else. Hdt. 5.49 presents a version of what Aristagoras of Miletos (*OCD* 153 Aristagoras (1)) said to the Spartans in 499, when attempting to drum up support for a revolt of the Ionian Hellenes against Persian rule. In it he describes the Phrygians as the most *polyprobatoi* of any people he knows, adding that the Armenians too are *polyprobatoi* (Hdt. 5.49.5–6).

I follow Waterfield 180 in regarding the noun *probata* here as sheep, that being its predominant meaning in Attic prose (see LSJ s.v.). Users of older translations such as Dakyns and Marchant should be aware that their 'cattle' has a wider scope than we usually give it nowadays.

5.3 men able to use their brains and money in investments Thiel 34 understands this phrase to be a periphrasis for bankers, whom others (though never X. himself) would have called *trapezitai* or suchlike. However, Bogaert (1968) 80 n.118 reasonably queried that very point—why use a periphrasis at all?—and urged instead that X.'s phrase be construed more broadly, to include investors of any kind, such as those wanting large returns from maritime loans (3.9 with Comm.). Gauthier 201 agrees, and adds (following Herzog (1914) 477–8) the sort of people mentioned in 4.22, who were looking to the mining industry for their financial returns. See also Millett (1991) 307 n.22, favouring 'maritime credit'.

5.4 craftsmen In *Mem.*3.11.4 (just as in Thuc. 7.27.5: see under **4.25 Those who**) the *cheirotechnai*—literally, men with manual skills—are slaves. Here, by contrast, X. must mean foreigners of free status: so Thiel 34, Gauthier 202. These are the sort of people he is prepared (in *Hipp.*6.1) to credit with intelligence. Thus, as Gauthier remarks, translators—though not the Hellenes themselves—constantly have to wonder whether the topic is artisans or artists. (Here both, according to him.) See also Burford (1972) 13–14; *OCD* 171 (under 'Artists and their work').

5.4 sophists and philosophers This is presented as a single category (linked in the Greek by *te kai*), but Gauthier 202 asks the pertinent question: what is the distinction? The answer is clear enough in general terms if we refer to the 'Sokratic' material in, notably, *Kyn*.13.1–9; see also *Mem*.1.6.13 and 4.1.1 & 8; and generally Dorion (2017) 41–5. X. regards sophists (*OCD* 1381) as charlatans, preying on the naivety of rich young men. Philosophers are authentic sages with only benevolent intentions. (An incidental irony is that X. would have classified Isocrates as a sophist, whereas Isocrates himself stood aloof from them and claimed to teach philosophy. See esp. Isoc. 13 *Against the sophists.*)

5.4 the poets In *Cyrop*.1.6.38 a *poiêtês* is an inventor (of military stratagems), and that root-sense, a maker of something, is also occasionally found in Plato. In context here, though, the word does have the meaning translated (first attested in Hdt. 2.53.3).

See further under the next lemma.

5.4 their production staff X. writes 'those who handle the (affairs) of these men'. Thiel 35 and Gauthier 202–3 take the reasonable view that 'these men' mean only the poets (see the preceding lemma), not any of the earlier categories as well. Hence 'poets and the producers of their plays' (Waterfield 180), unexceptionable as long as we include in 'plays' the genre of dithyramb (*OCD* 469); cf. Gauthier 202 on non-Athenian practictioners of that genre, including Telestes of Selinous (*OCD* 1437).

Marchant's rendering of this whole phrase as 'poets and the people who make use of their work' is reflected in LSJ's classification of the meanings of the verb X. uses here, *metacheirizesthai*; the lexicon places *Poroi* 5.4 under '*practise*, *pursue* an art, study, etc.', a meaning found several times in Plato. However, the only two other instances of the word in X. have the meaning govern/handle/manage: LSJ itself cites *Mem*.1.4.17 (of the mind and the body), and the same is true in *Oec*.14.2 (of a bailiff dealing with an owner's crops). Thus here, as Gauthier says, we should visualize actors, choruses, musicians.

5.4 those desirous of things worth seeing or things worth hearing, whether sacred or celebratory Another of X.'s periphrases, this time for what elsewhere (*Hipp*.3.2 & 5, *Oec*.11.4) he is content to call spectators: *theatai*, a noun connected with the first of the adjectives he uses here. For non-citizens as spectators cf. generally *Mem*. 1.2.61 on Lichas

(*OCD* 832): during the Spartans' midsummer Gymnopaidiai festival he used to give dinners for the *xenoi* who were staying in town.

This *axiotheata*/*axiakousta* coupling (and distinction) is already in *Symp.*4.44: Antisthenes (*OCD* 109 s.v.1, *POP* 35–6) prizes his leisure, which enables him 'to see the things that are worth seeing and to hear the things that are worth hearing'. See also *Oec.*8.4 (on the members of a *choros* being both) and the superlatives in *Lac.Pol.*4.2 (the Spartan lawgiver believed that where the spirit of rivalry, *philoneikia*, was strongest the *choroi* would be most worth hearing and the athletics contests most worth seeing). In *Hier.*1.11 Simonides (*OCD* 1368–9) is made to say that 'in every territory there are things worth seeing, and, in search of each of these, individuals go to any states they want'.

The tailpiece to X.'s phrase also calls for comment. The differentiation, as here, between something that is *hieron* and something that is *hosion* has been routinely represented in English as the sacred/secular divide; so (here) Dakyns, Marchant, Waterfield. Of the two terms it is the second, *hosion*, which presents the problem of definition and perception. Thiel 35 writes: '*hieron* id est, quod deo ab hominibus dicatum est ['that which is devoted to god by men']; *hosion*, id, quod lege divina quadam non scripta sacratur ['that which is hallowed by some unwritten divine law']; deinde, ubi τῷ ἱερῷ opponitur, *profanum* quoque fit ['hence, where its opposite is *hieron*, it also becomes 'profane']'. Gauthier 203 (citing earlier bibliography in French) takes a somewhat different tack: the two terms form a pairing and they both have 'une résonance religieuse', with the distinction being that *hieron* is either sacred by nature or consecrated to gods by men (e.g. objects, animals, sacrifices), while *hosion* is that which is done by men in accordance with religious law or ritual (e.g. an oath, a speech, a form of behaviour). Among Anglophone authorities, Parker contrasts 'sacred' with 'profane' (when mentioning the divisions of items on the agenda of meetings of the citizen assembly: ?Aristot. *Ath.Pol.*43.6, cf. Aeschin. 1.23), but goes on to comment that 'the distinction [is one] which any translation inevitably distorts [. . .] Since *hosia* are things which may be freely discussed or disposed of without offence to the gods [. . .], even the "profane" is defined by direct reference to the sacred' (Parker (1996) 123 with n.9). See also e.g. Parker (1983) appendix 1, Burkert (1985) 269–71, and esp. Connor (1988). Comcomitant with this orthodoxy is, or was, another: that the Athenians, and Hellenes in general, would scarcely have understood a 'secular' domain at all, because '[t]here was no barrier between religion and ordinary life' (Garland (1994) ix;

cf. Parke (1977) 13). Of late, this elusive matter has been re-examined by scholars who do, very broadly speaking, acknowledge 'the secular' in X.'s Athens and elsewhere, and who do for the most part accept 'secular' as a workable translation of *hosios*. See Whitmarsh (2015) chap.1, with the bibliography in n.13 there.

If this is correct, a passage like Isoc. 7.66 on Athens' fifth-century buildings is differentiating between *ta hiera* as temples (as in 4.20, 5.9 and 6.1 here) and *ta hosia* as other public buildings—lawcourts or shipsheds, for instance. Likewise, Demosth. 24.9 denounces Timokrates' law on debtors to the state for depriving two recipients of money that should be theirs: the gods, of *hiera*; the polis, of *hosia*. (The latter passage obviously brings to mind the denarius in the Gospel of Luke (20.24–5): 'render unto Caesar etc.'.) On the other hand, no amount of such examples can efface the fact, evident in LSJ (to look no further), that *hosios* and its cognates do have a lot to do with the gods; cf. Mikalson (2016) appendices 4–5. Within X. himself, witness e.g. *Hell.*4.7.2 (two oracles, those of Zeus at Olympia and Apollo at Delphi, tell the Spartan king Agesipolis that it would be *hosion* for him to refuse a truce proposed by the Argives; cf. generally 7.4.35) and *Cyrop.*8.5.26 (Kyros' father Kambyses tells the Persian elders that whenever Kyros comes to Persia it should be *hosion* for them—'a sacred custom', in the Loeb translation—that he sacrifices *ta hiera* on their behalf).

This is not the place to pursue the general topic any further. (Those wishing to do so could begin with Blok (2010).) With regard to the present passage it must suffice to say that 'sacred or secular' does not seem (to me) quite right; also that 'profane' may mislead twenty-first-century readers who suppose that its only meaning is irreverent, offensive, or suchlike. My translation tries to convey the idea that some of the things X.'s spectators will see and hear are religious through and through; in others the gods are more peripheral. Gauthier 203 confines the first category, in the main, to the inanimate: sanctuaries, temples, statues, dedications; things which, necessarily, would be *axiotheata* but not *axiakousta* (above). Contrast Thiel 35, for whom buildings are *hosia*. Gauthier places in that second category processions and, especially, competitions (athletic, dramatic, musical). This is probably correct, even though a case could be made for classifying as *hiera* the processions (*pompai*) which formed part of most festivals—none more lavish than that of the Panathenaia (as depicted on the Parthenon frieze); see generally Parke (1977) 22–3, Burkert (1985) 99–100. (In X. see *Hipp.*2.1, 3.1–2.) The *hosia* category, in any case, certainly would be exemplified by the competitions (*agônes*) at those festivals which included them. Again the Panathenaia stands out (the partially preserved *IG* II^2 2311 lists the prizes given in *c.* 370; Parke (1977) 35–7 has a summary; see also ?Aristot. *Ath.Pol.*60.3), together with the City Dionysia.

5.4 those needing to sell or buy lots of things quickly See under **5.3 The list**. If the present phrase does pick up '*nauklêroi* and *emporoi*' there, and thus proffer the list's 4 x 3 items in a sort of frame (Gauthier 200), it seems necessary to ask what additional or new point ('Besides') is being made here. The only obvious answer is the 'quickly' element. In general terms this recalls 3.5 (q.v.), perhaps tacitly assuming that the proposal made has been implemented.

5.5 Perhaps nobody contradicts these points For 'contradict' see already 4.10. Here 'these points' encompass everything in 5.3–4, on the blessings of peace for Athens *per se*.

5.5 there *are* some who want Athens to take back its leadership, and they think this objective would be achieved through war rather than through peace In the light of Isoc. 8.5–8, as Gauthier 205–6 remarks, X.'s 'some' might more candidly have been expressed as 'many', or 'the majority'. X. himself will come close (in 6.1) to admitting that it is the rich elite who would be the immediate beneficiaries of an 'anti-war' policy. See further Bodei Giglioni xvii–xix.

The noun (and concept) *hêgemonia*—leadership, command—will be used again later in 5.5, and also at the end of 5.7. Other applications aside (such as the Spartans' position within the Peloponnese), Thuc. 1.95.7 and 1.96.1 had made it, in effect, the technical term for the leadership role recognized by the majority of Hellenic states in the Aegean and coastal Asia Minor. Since its origins in 481, during Xerxes' invasion, it had passed first from Sparta to Athens (cf. Thuc. 6.82.3), back to Sparta in 404 (see below, **5.6 when Athens**), and back to Athens in 377. See generally Wickersham (1994) 81–118. At the end of the Social War, in 355, the Athenians for practical purposes lost it again (despite the continuation, for a further eighteen years, of the rump of the Second Confederacy; Rhodes (2010) 276–8). Hence X.'s phrase here, *tên hêgemonian analabein* (and its variant *anaktâsthai tous Hellênas*; see **5.8 an opportunity**). Compare *Hell.*3.5.10, Theban spokesmen in Athens in 395: 'we all know that you would like to take back (*analabein*) the empire which you once possessed'.

5.5 So let them first consider the Persian wars. Was it by coercing the Hellenes or by benefiting them that we came by the command of the navy and the office of treasurers of the Hellenes? For 'let them consider' see already 4.41.

Ta Mêdika in the (Hellenocentric) sense of 'the Persian war(s)' is first attested in Herodotus (9.64.2), but more copiously throughout Book 1 of Thucydides. In Thuc. 1.14.2 it evidently embraces both of the Persian invasions of Hellas in the first quarter of the fifth century ('just before *ta Mêdika* and the death of Dareios [in 486]'; cf. perhaps 1.97.2), but 1.90.1 has a variant, 'the Persian war', in a narrower reference to Xerxes' invasion of 481–479 (likewise, in various ways, 1.18.3, 1.23.1, 1.41.2, 1.69.1, 1.73.2, 1.97.1, 1.142.7); and in 1.95.7 that same phrase applies to the Hellenic war-effort against Persia *after* 479 (the Spartans no longer wanted to continue it)—which soon saw the creation of the Athenian Empire as described in Thuc. 1.96.

The present passage takes the Thuc. 1.95.7 line, as is apparent from the rhetorical question appended. For the general trope invoked cf. Thuc. 1.75.2, 1.95.1, 1.96.1, and, as Gauthier 206 notes, especially fourth-century oratory. To the passages he cites (Lys. 2.47; Isoc. 4.72, 7.17 & 80, 8.76, 12.67, 16.27) one could add e.g. Isoc. 4.103–6, 8.30. And see further under **5.7 did the Thebans.**

In *Hell.*6.5.34 (summarizing a speech by some Spartans in Athens in 370) X. had coupled together the same two elements of the post-479 era but used loose language: 'the Athenians were chosen commanders of the fleet and custodians of the common money'. Here he is precise. The ten (later twenty) 'treasurers of the Hellenes' (*hellênotamiai*: *OCD* 658), in charge of the cash tribute paid by states who were not contributing warships, are presented in Thuc. 1.96.2 as one of the inaugural institutions of 478/7. Later mentions of them in literary sources occur in Antiph. 5.69–70 (a mysterious scandal in which they were wrongly accused of embezzlement, and executed) and, retrospectively as here, Andoc. 3.38 and ?Aristot. *Ath.Pol.*30.2. There are also numerous attestations in the Athenian 'tribute lists' and other documents on stone; for an instance see *IG* I^{3} 375 (ML 84, now OR 180), Fornara (1983) no.154.

X.'s abstract noun here, *hellênotamieia*, meaning the post of *hellênotamias*, is not found elsewhere. Perhaps it is modelled on *tamieia*—almost as much of a rarity—in *Oec.*7.41. His statement that the Athenians of 478/7 'came by' their naval hegemony is a tolerable summary of the narrative in Thuc. 1.94–6 (which begins with the Spartans in charge); however, that verb is a stretch too far for the *hellênotamiai*. They were Athenians, filling an Athenian-created office (*AO* 8–9).

5.6 when Athens was deprived of the empire, having acquired the reputation of leading it too harshly A roundabout way of referring to the defeat of 404 and the end of the Peloponnesian War. The treaty in which the Athenians were obliged to acquiesce ratified, as a *fait accompli*, the collapse of their Empire (*Hell.*2.2.6–20); and they themselves swore to accept Spartan hegemony.

Marchant translates 'through *seeming* to exercise her authority with excessive harshness' and Waterfield goes even further in that direction with 'for having *supposedly* wielded power with excessive brutality'; my emphasis in both cases. While the aorist participle *doxasa* has that sort of sense in Thuc. 8.96.1 (on the impression made by the Sicilian catastrophe at the time of it), in context here I do not see it as intended to suggest that the perception, in and after 404, of Athens' imperial misbehaviour was mistaken, in X.'s opinion. He is not afraid of plain speaking later in the sentence (see the parenthetical clause in the next lemma); nor had he been in *Hell.*2.2.3 (on the Athenians in 405 bracing themselves for the same sort of treatment as they themselves had meted out to Histiaia, Aigina, Skione, Torone, Melos, 'and many other states') or 2.2.10 for the same in general terms. (In similar vein see Isoc. 8.30–1.)

For aorist or present participles of *dokein* in the sense translated here cf. e.g. *Anab.*1.6.1 (Klearchos); *Hell.*1.1.31 (Hermokrates), 3.1.3 (Tissaphernes), 3.1.8 (Derkylidas), 4.8.31 (Thrasyboulos), 5.3.22, 6.3.7.

5.6 was it not the case that then too—when we refrained from injustice—we again, at the willing instigation of the island-communities, became leaders of the navy? A reference, obviously, to the foundation of the Second Athenian Confederacy in 377: RO 22 (Harding (1985) no.35); Diod.Sic. 15.28–30 (placed a year too late). As Gauthier 207 remarks, X.'s own failure to mention this event—or to chronicle adequately the first fifteen years of the alliance's history—in *Hell.* is a grave deficiency; a Sparta-driven blindspot. Here he makes amends, of a kind.

On 'when we refrained from injustice' see again the words that X. puts into the mouth of the Theban spokesmen in Athens in 395 (*Hell.*3.5.10; above, under 5.5 **there *are* some**): they continue by saying that a resumption of Athenian hegemony is likeliest if the Athenians aid victims of Spartan injustice now (i.e. themselves), and also recollect their own problems in the past, when so many of their downtrodden allies became their enemies. And on that point the best commentary of all is provided by RO 22 itself (above). One of its most striking clauses (lines 19–25) guarantees to any signatory state, present and future, that it will be 'free and autonomous, governed under whatever constitution it wishes, neither receiving a garrison nor submitting to a governor nor paying a tribute, on the same terms as the Chians and the Thebans and the other allies (*sc.* have already signed up to)'. (For Chios see RO 20 (Harding (1985) no.31), from 384; for Thebes see under the next lemma. There were four 'other' founding allies: Byzantium (*IG* II² 41 (Harding (1985) no.34)), Rhodes (Diod.Sic. 15.28.3), and the two principal poleis on Lesbos, Methymna (RO 23 (Harding (1985) no.37)) and Mytilene (again Diod.Sic. 15.28.3, and somehow involved in *IG* II² 40 (Harding (1985) no.33)), an apparent Athens/Thebes alliance.) Though not presented as such, this amounts to a promise of protection against the main elements of 'injustice' in the developed fifth-century Empire. (Lines 25–46 continue the theme.) That the participants in 377 were 'willing'—also in Isoc. 8.30—seems confirmed, again, by this charter/prospectus document and its appended list of almost sixty signatories.

X.'s 'island-communities' (*nêsiôtai*) might seem a peculiar word to choose for them: the 'states' of 1.1. Gauthier 207 calls it an excessive simplification of the facts. That, undeniably, it is; but context and explanation on several levels can be found. The key clause, quoted above, of the charter/prospectus begins by taking pains to stay within the terms of the 386 King's Peace, a.k.a. Peace of Antalkidas (*Hell.*5.1.31). This is expressed by inviting in as members '[*a*] any of the Hellenes or the *barbaroi* living on the mainland or [*b*] the island-communities—those which are not the King's'. (For this same *a*/*b* distinction see Isoc. 8.131–2.) Was X. recollecting the wording of this famous document, on display in the Athenian Agora (lines 63–6)? If he was, he has overlooked the category-*a* allies.

The word *nêsiôtai* was not otherwise a favourite of his. On the contrary, it had otherwise occurred only once, but the passage (*Hell.*3.5.14) is worth examination. In a speech attributed to a Theban spokesman in Athens in 395; urging the Athenians to help Thebes against Sparta, the Thebans' wholeheartedness is promised on the basis that they would be helping themselves, 'not islanders or Syracusans'. These contemptuous comparisons hark back to the latter stages of the Peloponnesian War. From winter 415/14 onwards Syracuse (*OCD* 1420–21, *IACP* no.47) had tried to secure Spartan and Corinthian help against the Athenian invasion-force, help which was indeed forthcoming: Thuc. 6.73.2, 88.7–10, 91.1–5 (speech of Alkibiades), 93.1–3. While there is no mention—and little or no likelihood—of the Thebans having been approached directly on this matter, the 'Peloponnesian League' as a whole must have discussed it; cf. generally Ste. Croix (1972) 101–24. The same is true of the approaches to Sparta by Athens' own allies which began, with the cities of Euboia and Lesbos, in winter 413/12: see Thuc. 8.5.1–2, where in fact 'Boiotian' support (for Lesbos; cf. 3.2.3, 8.100.3) is explicit.

It is relevant to note, furthermore, that in Thuc. 1.81.3 King Archidamos II of Sparta (*OCD* 140) is made to say—perhaps did say—in 432 that Athens' allies, most of them members of her fifth-century Empire, were 'for the most part' *nêsiôtai*; cf. also 6.68.2, 7.20.2, 7.82.1 (and in another genre Aristoph. *Pax* 298). The appendix to Constantakopoulou (2007) chap.3.3 shows that this was far from factually true: 57 out of *c.* 333. But even so, her (persuasive) argument is that the numerical facts were of less importance than what she calls the Empire's 'inherited *nesiotic* character', reflecting the significance of islands in the context of seapower.

In sum: calling these states *nêsiôtai*, as X. did here, had clear fifth-century precedents. That Athenian official language too had by now sanctioned the usage is a possibility that arises from RO 39 (Harding (1985) no.55), an 'imperial' decree concerning the polis of Ioulis, on Keos (*IACP* no.491, cf. *OCD* 299); lines 12–14 mention 'those elected by the demos to exact from the *nêsiôtai* the money they owe'. Without background to X.'s phrase, however, one cannot exclude the possibility that it relates to island-members only—even to Keos only.

5.7 did the Thebans not grant the Athenians leadership over them because they were enjoying benefits? After the jump from 404 to 377 (see under the preceding lemma) X. now backtracks slightly to 379/8, when the Athenians had been asked for, and had given, military aid to expel the Spartan garrison which was in Thebes at that time: *Hell.*5.4.9–10, more explicitly in Diod.Sic. 15.25.1, and see also Din. 1.39. Though the Athenians themselves subsequently regretted this (*Hell.*5.4.19, Plut. *Pelop.*14.1), Athens and Thebes became allies in spring 378: *IG* II^2 40 (Harding (1985) no.33; cf. under the preceding lemma, *re* Mytilene), *Hell.*5.4.34, Diod.Sic. 15.29.7, Plut. *Pelop.*15.1, and see also under the preceding lemma for the retrospective mention of this in RO 22.

The middle/passive participle 'enjoying benefits', *euergetoumenoi*, echoes the active one *euergetountes* (the Athenians benefiting 'the Hellenes') in 5.5. For benefactors cf. also 3.11. Gauthier 212–13, in his analysis of 5.5–10 as a whole, draws particular attention to what he sternly calls X.'s 'utilisation abusive' of the concept of public benefit here. By contrasting war-violence-injustice with peace-benefits-justice, X. gives a (to him) unanswerable riposte to anyone who believes (5.5) that Athenian hegemony must be the outcome of war. No, he says: we have never won it by violence, always by helping people. Gauthier insists that a fully rounded picture should find room for the fact that Athenian 'benefits' often took military form: so in 480–479, 378/7 (*vis-à-vis* Thebes), 369 (*vis-à-vis* Sparta). It was by and for warfare—'par et pour la guerre'—that the Athenians grasped their opportunities for hegemony. See further under **5.9 Suppose**.

5.7 the Spartans...conceded to the Athenians the right to make whatever decisions about the leadership they saw fit not because they had been coerced into this by us but because they were being well-treated We move on another decade, to 369, and to a landscape of Hellas transformed by the Spartans' defeat at Leuktra in 371 (*OCD* 824–5). X. himself, in *Hell.*7.1.1–14, gives quite a lavish account of the alliance concluded in 369 between Sparta 'and her allies' (cf. 7.1.15) and the Athenians, on the initiative of the latter. As X. depicts it, the relevant debate—in the Athenian assembly, but with Spartans and others present and allowed to speak (see generally Hansen (1991) 253, 264)—revolved around the issue of how to share the practicalities of *hêgemonia.* At first a proposal to let the Athenians command at sea (cf. Isoc. 7.65) and the Spartans on land was favoured, but the decision eventually reached (which Thiel 36 calls stupid, Gauthier 207 curious) was for alternation every five days. Diod.Sic. 15.67.1 tells a rather different story, but either way, it is reasonable to suppose (with Gauthier 207) that X.'s summary here reflects the Spartans' willingness to accept the outcome of the vote on that occasion.

The language of this passage continues that of 5.5 ('by coercing the Hellenes or by benefiting them') and the preceding sentence here in 5.7 ('because (the Thebans) were enjoying benefits').

The idea of the Spartans having been 'well-treated' by Athens before this is expressed more extravagantly in Isoc. 8.105. Actual Athenian military action which could be classified as such (so Thiel 36) is recounted in *Hell.*6.5.49: Iphikrates in the Peloponnese in early 369.

5.8 Now, at any rate, turmoil has arisen in Hellas As noted in General Intro., section 3 (at n.25), this noun, *tarachê*, had been one of X.'s descriptors of the unresolved situation after the battle of Mantineia in 362 (*Hell.*7.5.27). Here, however, he applies it to the mid-350s, as does Demosth. 14.36 and, retrospectively, Demosth. 18.18. See also e.g. Isoc. 8.25 and 64.

The view of Thiel 36 that X.'s talk of turmoil had particularly in mind here the central Peloponnese and Thessaly (on the basis of Paus. 4.28.1–2 and Demosth. 2.14, respectively) is not unreasonable in itself but does simply reflect the evidence that happens to have survived. On that basis one could add e.g. Diod.Sic. 15.93.3 (Kerkyra, 361/0) and Demosth. 15, esp. chap.19 there (Rhodes and Mytilene, before 351/0). See further below, **There is.**

5.8 an opportunity has come Athens' way: to gain back the Hellenes without effort, without danger and without expense The word 'opportunity' (*kairos*) is not in the Greek but is implicit in this idiom, already used (as Thiel 36 notes) at the end of *Hipp.*7.4, *ei kairos parapesoi*. Cf. already Thuc. 4.23.2, Isoc. 17.8.

X. uses here the verb (*anaktâsthai*: literally repossess) that Alkibiades casuistically uses to the Spartans in Thuc. 6.92.4: far from attacking somewhere (Athens) that is his homeland, he considers himself as regaining a place that is not. See also e.g. Hdt. 1.61.3 and 3.73.2. Its tone in the present context is not straightforward to assess. The uncompound verb *ktâsthai* means to acquire something which one then owns, as one's *ktêma* (such as the slave manpower in 4.42). That fact could justify understanding the present phrase, *anaktâsthai tous Hellênas*, as more brutal (repossession) than 5.5's *tên hêgemonian analabein*. Yet Attic tragedy—the influence of which on X. we have been noting throughout *Poroi*—has instances of *ktâsthai* applied to acquiring friends (Soph. *Aj.*1360, Eurip. *Orest.*804); and as regards *anaktâsthai*, X. himself exemplifies this in *Cyrop.*1.3.9 and 2.2.10 (and cf. also 7.5.55–6). Accordingly, in the present context it may be that a translation like Waterfield's 'recovering our control over the Greeks' strays too much into the dark side. My own seeks to be neutral (but it too begs a question, because *anaktâsthai* in this application can describe acquiring friends for the first time).

As Gauthier 208 observes, the triad of efforts (*ponoi*), dangers (*kindynoi*), and expense (*dapanê*) had featured more discursively in X.'s portrait of the Spartan Klearchos (*OCD* 329 Clearchus (1)) in

*Anab.*2.6.6–7. Instead of an easy life Klearchos chooses *ponoi*; instead of having money and security, he spends his money on war; finally and above all, he seeks out danger(s). One could adduce *Hell.*3.5.12 too: the Theban spokesmen in Athens in 395 (cf. under **5.6 was it not**) declares that allies of Sparta share in all the *ponoi*, *kindynoi*, and *dapanêmata* but none of the power, prestige, and wealth that success brings. Elsewhere, effort(s) and danger(s) are a regular pairing (*Cyrop.*3.3.8, 4.2.1, 5.5.18; *Hell.*6.1.5–6; *Oec.*6.7); and of course the expense of war is a commonplace, in both X. (e.g. 3.8 and 6.1 here) and other writers since at least the celebrated Thuc. 1.83.2, where wise old King Archidamos of Sparta declares that 'war, for the most part, is not a matter of weapons but of expenditure, which gives the weapons their edge'.

5.8 There is a possibility of trying to arbitrate between the city-states that are making war against one another, and a possibility, too, of bringing about reconciliation in any where people are engaged in factional strife The verb *diallattein* in the sense of 'arbitrate between' (*Hell.*1.6.4 exemplifies another sense) is a technical term in the sphere of arbitration, whether in conflicts between states or within them (the two categories distinguished here: *i* and *ii* below). X. himself knew this perfectly well. When chronicling the civil war which had engulfed Athens after her defeat in the Peloponnesian War, he had written of the military intervention by the Spartan King Pausanias (*OCD* 1096–7 s.v. 2) in 403, and the subsequent 'amnesty'-agreement accepted by both sides, after talks chaired by him and a panel of other Spartans sent to help him in that very aim (*Hell.*2.4.38, cf. ?Aristot. *Ath.Pol.*38.4).

On inter-state arbitration generally see in brief *OCD* 133 (Arbitration, Greek); in full Ager (1996). As the dates of Ager's coverage imply (337–90: earlier material is covered in Piccirilli (1973)), this is quintessentially a phenomenon of the Hellenistic period; even so, its archaic and classical antecedents are well recognized. See e.g.: OR 126 (ML 42; Fornara (1983) no.89), Argos *re* Knossos and Tylissos in Crete, *c.* 450; Thuc. 1.28.1–2, the Corinth/Kerkyra disputes of 433 to be resolved either by impartial Peloponnesian poleis or by the Delphic oracle; Thuc. 5.79.4, in the Argos/Sparta treaty of 418 disputes are to be referred to a third, impartial state; Diod.Sic. 15.18.2–4, the Delphic oracle arbitrates between Klazomenai and Kyme; RO 16 (Harding (1985) no.24), Miletos and Myous, 380s; RO 58 (Harding (1985) no.78), now *IG* II^{3} 292/*AIO* and *I.Eleusis* 144, Athens refers a long-standing border dispute with

Megara (cf. Thuc. 1.139.2) to the Delphic Oracle in 352/1. As regards the present passage:

(*i*) For poleis 'making war' cf. already *Ages.*7.7 (Sparta) and *Mem.*4.4.8 (generic). Gauthier 209 surmises that X. is thinking especially of the Peloponnese, which Demosth. 18.18 retrospectively describes as 'entirely divided' at this time. Diod.Sic. 16.23–39, where we might have hoped to learn of such matters, focuses mostly on Phokis and the Third Sacred War (see below, 5.9–10), but the sudden burst of narrative at 16.39 sees Sparta, in 353, at odds with Megalopolis in Arkadia (*OCD* 924, *IACP* no.282) in a conflict which also drew in, among others, the Argives, Sikyonians, and Messenians, not to mention extra-Peloponnesian interference from Phokis, Thebes, and Thessaly. (See generally, besides, Demosth. 16.)

(*ii*) The other component of turmoil for poleis that X. brings up here is internal *stasis*: see in brief *OCD* 1396; more fully *IACP* 124–9; in detail Lintott (1982) and esp. Gehrke (1985). Thuc. 3.69–85 is a classic study of the phenomenon, with general analysis arising out of a specific case (Kerkyra in 427); and Athens in 403, above, is another well-documented instance. X.'s city itself managed to stay *stasis*-free for the ensuing eighty years, but for many other states in the fourth century it continued to be an endemic problem, with oligarchies ousting democracies or vice versa and hegemonic powers interfering if they saw it as advantageous to do so. In terms of language, one could speak (as X. does here) of individuals engaging in *stasis* 'in' states, but more usually of whole states doing so: *Ages.*1.37, and elsewhere e.g. [X.] *Ath.Pol.*3.10, Thuc. 3.69.2 and 8.95.2, Isoc. 12.100 & 165. (Lys. 2.21 even applies it to Hellas as a whole.) As with *i* above, it is pertinent to ask whether X. has particular poleis (or regions) in mind. Thiel 36 suggested Thessaly, on the basis of Demosth. 2.14 which (in a context of 349/8) apparently mentions recent *stasis* and *tarachê* there. However, Gauthier 209 points out that an emendation of the passage (by the nineteenth-century Dutch scholar C. G. Cobet), accepted in many editions, eliminates the mention of *stasis* there (in favour of 'sickness'). He himself, accordingly, looks once again to the Peloponnese: see above.

Though X. changes his terminology here, from *diallattein* (cf. above) to *synallattein*, Gauthier is almost certainly right to urge that no substantive distinction is intended (even if, here, *synallattein* does not share the status of being a technical term). He cites *Hell.*6.5.8, on the *stasis* in Arkadia in 370: one faction enters into talks 'about *synallagai*' (reconciliation) with the other. One could add *Hell.*2.4.43, on the coda to the Athenian agreement of 403 adduced at the beginning of this lemma. After threatening moves by the oligarchic enclave of Eleusis, more talks are held and Eleusis is persuaded 'to be reconciled'.

5.9 Suppose also that you became conspicuous for striving to make the shrine in Delphi autonomous, as before, not by joining in a war but by going as envoys all over Hellas X. begins here with a three-word phrase, *phaneroi eiête epimeloumenoi*, which will be repeated for emphasis in 5.10 (q.v. below). Its *epimel-* vocabulary, implying a benign but determined concern for something, has already featured in 2.1–2, 3.6, 4.22 and 4.52. In the same general connection, the final participle here, *presbeuontes*, is more 'hands-on' than translations such as Marchant's ('sending embassies') and Waterfield's ('sending delegations') make it sound. Compare Poseidon in Aristoph. *Birds* 1587–8: 'we are come as envoys from the gods, to discuss an end to the war'.

Mentioned again in 6.2, 'the shrine in Delphi' is better known nowadays as the Delphic Oracle (of Apollo). See in brief *OCD* 427–9, with bibliography, and Garland (1994) chap.9; in full e.g. Parke & Wormell (1956); Parke (1967); Fontenrose (1978); Parker (1985); Bowden (2005).

Although Delphi was a (small) polis (*IG* II^2 109a, line 27, and generally *IACP* no.177), it did not control, or even include, the shrine and oracle of Apollo in the same way as (e.g.) Athens did Eleusis, the site of the equally Pan-Hellenic mystery-ceremonies. Instead, Apollo's affairs were administered by an ostensibly ancient body called the Delphic Amphictiony. In X.'s day its twelve 'constituencies' (each with two votes) were tribal groupings—with a clear bias towards central and northern mainland Hellas: Boiotians, Dolopians, Dorians, Ionians (which included Athens), Lokrians, Magnetes, Malians, Oitaians, Perrhaibians, Phthiotians, Phokians, Thessalians (so Aeschin. 2.115; more confusingly in Diod.Sic. 16.29.1). The autonomy which X. speaks of—independence not merely from the polis of Delphi but also and more importantly from other, more powerful states—is something we find upheld in treaties such as the 421 'Peace of Nikias' (Thuc. 5.18.2, with Hornblower (1991–2008) 2.472–3); and theory held that on an ongoing basis it was guaranteed by the existence and operation of the Amphictiony. Practice was often very different. How far back in time X. was reaching with his phrase 'as before' is impossible to tell, but the point is not crucial here. His implicit mention, at the end of this long sentence, of the Phokian seizure of Delphi (see the next lemma) is an allusion to events with their origins in the early 350s but beginning in earnest in, probably, the first half of 356. They would prove to be the preliminary stages of something headlined in Diod.Sic. 16.14.3–5 and then narrated by him, in instalments, between 16.23 and 16.60: the Third Sacred War. See in full Buckler (1989); more briefly Rhodes (2010) 340–3 (and 345–7), esp. 340–2.

According to X. here, the thrust of Athenian policy with regard to this *fait accompli*—the Phokians, under their enterprising generals Philomelos (*OCD* 1133), later the brothers Onomarchos (*OCD* 1039) and Phayllos (*OCD* 1124 Phayllus (2)), and finally Phalaikos (*OCD* 1120), in control of Delphi and its funds—is (or ought to be?) 'not... joining in a war but... sending envoys all over Hellas'. The first of these options must refer to what is recounted in Diod.Sic. 16.25 & 28-31: the initial military responses by the Boiotians and the Lokrians, joined later—once a sacred war (*hieros polemos*), in Apollo's name, had been solemnly declared against Phokis—by others. The alternatives as presented here by X. are either joining in that war or engaging in high-minded Pan-Hellenic diplomacy (cf. Isoc. 8.22). This doubtless sanitizes the choice which the Athenians actually made, and their reasons for making it: good relations with the Phokians (culminating in Diod.Sic. 16.29.1), bad with the Boiotians (as recently as 357: Diod. Sic. 16.7.2); cf. Gauthier 209–10. Besides, as noted already (**5.7 did the Thebans**), what Gauthier 212–13 calls the 'hégémonie pacifique' that X. advocates in 5.5–10 as a whole rhetorically excludes any element of Athenian military power, something that in the actual circumstances of Hellas in the 350s and 340s would surely have been necessary for putting an end to the Third Sacred War, not to mention such other desiderata as suppressing brigandage and piracy (cf. [Demosth.] 7.14–15).

See further under the next lemma.

5.9 Personally, I should not be surprised if you found all the Hellenes unanimous, bound together by oaths and ready to fight as allies against any people who were trying to seize the shrine—once the

Phokians had abandoned it For the Greek here ('anyone who was trying') see Notes on the Text.

X. uses here a trio of descriptors: 'both *homognômones* [adjective] and *synorkoi* [adjective] and *symmachoi* [noun]'. As Gauthier 210 notes, Cobet (see under **5.8 There is**) judged that *synorkos*—not otherwise attested—and *symmachos* are synonymous, and he was inclined to delete 'and *symmachoi*'. Thiel 36 (cf. xx) and Gauthier 210 defend the whole phrase, as being another example of X.'s liking for things in threes, and also (Gauthier) an encapsulation of the three stages that would actually take place in a community visited by one of these putative Athenian envoys: reaching a unanimity of view, swearing oaths to act on it, and finally activating a military coalition. (Note that this talk of fighting does not contradict 'not by joining in a war'. The scenario now is one set in the future. See further below.) With 'all the Hellenes... ready to fight as allies' compare broadly Isoc. 8.136–40, esp. 139.

Both *homognômôn* and its related verb *homognômein* (also used by X.) are first attested in Thucydides: 8.92.2 and 2.97.6 respectively.

5.10 conspicuous for striving to bring about peace through the whole of land and sea On this 'conspicuous for striving' idiom, here repeated for emphasis, see **5.9 Suppose also**. That passage's phrase 'all over Hellas' (*ana tên Hellada*: six times in Herodotus) here re-uses the same preposition but rhetorically enlarges the geographical scope. As Gauthier 210 remarks on 'all the Hellenes' in 5.9 (see the preceding lemma), only the Greeks of the mainland—excluding the Phokians—would be likely to be interested in restoring normality at Delphi; and here X.'s form of words breaks free of prosaic reality altogether.

The phrase 'through the whole of land and sea' reappears (though with a different preposition: *kata* rather than *ana*) in a passage of Hyperides' lost *Delian Speech* (fr.67 Jensen). It tells of Hera, after the birth of Zeus's twin offspring Apollo and Artemis, hounding their mother Leto across the earth (until she eventually found refuge on the small mid-Aegean island of Delos: *OCD* 426–7, *IACP* no.478).

5.10 I personally reckon that the safety of Athens would take pride of place in everyone's prayers, second only to their own communities A more striking formulation than the corresponding thought in Isoc. 8.140: 'who (among the Hellenes) will not praise those responsible for blessings so many and so great?' As Gauthier 211 insists, X. here invokes the norms of ceremonial ritual, of the kind we know marked the opening of proceedings in the Athenian assembly. Aeschin. 1.23 says that *kêryx* (crier/herald) 'prays the traditional prayers' (cf. also Din. 2.14); and the converse of these prayers were the curses formally called down on the heads of traitors and others (Demosth. 19.70 and 23.97, Lyk. *Leok*.31, Din. 2.16). With the help of the parodies in Aristoph. *Thesm*.295–351, Rhodes (1972) 36 offers a reconstruction of the general sense of prayer-plus-curse together. See also Rhodes (1972) 231–5 (on inscriptions which highlight the Athenians' concern for the safety of their own polis), and generally Parker (2005) 99–101.

A comparable depth of evidence is of course lacking for other states, but Gauthier 211 cites an instance which, though Hellenistic in date (after 196), illustrates the very phenomenon that X. has in mind here: a decree of Mytilene (*OCD* 993, *IACP* no.798) orders its *hierokêryx* 'to pray for blessings to come to the Thessalians, after he has prayed for them to come to the polis of the Mytileneans' (*IG* XII.Suppl.3, lines 24–6).

More generally, on the self-interested wisdom of leaders in treating others with solicitude, cf. already e.g. *Cyrop*.1.6.21; *Hier*.11.11–12.

5.11 Some may take a different approach and think that where money is concerned war is more profitable to the state than peace For 'more profitable' see already (in a variety of contexts) *Ages*.11.3, *Anab*.1.9.17, *Cyrop*.4.2.26 & 42, 7.1.18, *Hipp*.5.10, *Oec*.2.18; and cf. also the superlative in 3.1 here.

As regards substance, X.'s view that war is *not* more profitable to Athens than peace is broadly anticipated in the speech he gives to Kallistratos of Aphidna (*LGPN* s.v. no.50, *OCD* 268 Callistratus (2), *APF* 277–82) in Thebes in 371: the Athenians have learned the hard way that aggressive acquisition is unprofitable (*Hell*.6.3.11; Dillery (2017) 218).

5.11 Personally, I know of no better way this could be judged than to consider yet again what happened in past Athenian history A cross-reference back to 5.5–7 in the immediate context, but beyond that, to several sections of Chap.4 (2–3, 13–15, 25, 31). X.'s choice of this doubly compound verb 'consider yet again'—very rare but used three times by Plato—perhaps betrays a worry that not all his readers will share his view that 'yet again' a delve into the past is needed; cf. 4.16 ('But why is it necessary to speak of the old days?').

5.12 Anyone who does this will find, in time past, a great deal of money carried up onto the akropolis during peace, but all this spent up during war For this opening see already *Cyrop*.8.8.27: 'if anyone holds views contrary to mine, by examining the Persians' deeds he will find that they testify in support of my statements'. *Cyrop.*8.8 as a whole, however, is regarded by many as not by X. In any event cf. e.g. Thuc. 5.20.3, 5.26.2–3.

X.'s statement that these sums were *eis tên polin anenechthenta* is understood in a loose way by (e.g.) Marchant and Waterfield, as meaning 'paid into state funds' or suchlike. However, Thiel 37 and Gauthier 213—anticipated, in fact, by Dakyns—construe '*polis*' here in the amply attested sense of (*akro*)*polis*; see generally in the LSJ entry, under I.1. X. had already used this sense at *Anab.*7.1.27 (X. himself, speaking about Athens). While pointing out that in Athenian documents on stone the usage persists well into the fourth century, Gauthier cautiously suggests that because X. is referring here to the past he chose an archaic-sounding term. We might note also that X.'s verb here, *anapherein*, is not the natural one for a process such as allies contributing money to their hegemon. Compare rather e.g. *IG* I^3 52, A.3–4 (ML 58, now OR 144), Fornara (1983) no.119 ('since the three thousand talents voted to Athena have been carried up onto the (akro) polis', *anenenegktai es polin*); also e.g. Andoc. 3.7–8 and Aeschin. 2.174–5 (cited in the LSJ entry on this verb, which classifies the present passage with them). On the treasuries at the summit of the akropolis see in brief Rhodes (1981) 531–2.

The follow-up to saving all this money (pre-431), X. says, was spending it all. The possibility that he might mean *wasting* it all is raised by his use of the compound verb *katadapanân*, in fact twice in this long sentence. It implies more than simple *dapanân* would have implied here: to consume/spend/use either (*a*) totally or (*b*) uselessly. According to LSJ, both senses are attested elsewhere in X. himself, *a* in *Anab.*2.2.11 and *b* in *Cyrop.*6.2.30. However, these examples both come under *a*, in my opinion, as also do *Cyrop.*8.4.6 & 36. In the present context there may be a background implication that money spent on warfare is money down the drain by comparison with the sort of peace-dividend expenditure advocated in e.g. 3.12–13; even so it would have been extreme, especially for a former military man, to characterize spending money to save the polis from defeat and humiliation as squandering it. (For Athens' bankruptcy in 405 see the apocalyptic *Hell.*2.2.10.)

5.12 Because of the war, many sources of revenue were giving out and the ones that did come in were spent up for purposes many and various These *prosodoi* 'giving out' are described by the same verb, used intransitively, that 4.43 had applied to the (non-)cessation of silver-production during a future war. Here, what X. must have primarily in mind is the inevitable fall in the number of free non-citizens in Athens in the mid-350s and the revenues they would have generated (cf. 3.5, and Isoc. 8.20–1).

On 'spent up' see under the preceding lemma.

5.12 ever since there has been peace at sea, the revenues are augmented and the citizens able to use them however they wish For 'augmented' revenues cf. the end of 4.40 (and *Cyrop*.3.2.20).

The idea that Athens' revenues are *already* significantly larger at the time of writing than they had been during the Social War has sometimes been seen as a basis for dating *Poroi* later than the mid-350s. Gauthier 213–14 is adamant that the argument is not cogent. See under **4.40 administer**.

5.13 'Are you really saying', somebody might ask, 'that Athens should remain at peace even with someone who was doing us wrong?' The final appearance of an imaginary interlocutor in the work. It is employed here for a device which (as Thiel 37 and Gauthier 214 note) X. had already used to good effect at the beginning of *Lac. Pol*.14, the chapter which (although misplaced there) questions the assumptions of the rest of that treatise. Cf. more generally *Mem*.1.1.9, *Oec*.6.6. See also e.g. Aeschin. 1.80.

The idea of poleis wronging (*adikein*) each other picks up a topic from 5.6—but here in a grammatically blunter way, as a transitive verb with a direct object. See further under the next lemma.

5.13 we could punish them much more swiftly if *we* had taken the initiative in wronging no-one—because no-one would want to be *their* ally X.'s specific point about allies had been anticipated in *Cyrop*.1.5.13 and esp. *Mem*.2.6.27 (cited by Gauthier 214); and in the context of 355 cf. Isoc. 8.136–40.

More generally, 'punishing' wrongdoers—on an inter-state level—is an identifiable theme in X. (e.g. *Ages*.1.21, *Anab*.5.4.6, 7.7.14, *Hell*. 1.7.24, 4.1.7), just as elsewhere. Here, the scenario is that the Athenians have been at the receiving end of such *adikia* (see the preceding lemma) and they maintain the moral high ground by not having initiated it. On the contrary, the initiative they take is in *not* initiating it. (The verb *hyparchein* with a participle in this sense is registered in LSJ s.v. A.3.a, with examples from X.: *Anab*.2.3.23, 5.5.9. There are earlier instances in Herodotus and Thucydides.) Contrast 1.1, where former Athenian *adikia* towards her imperial allies is mentioned—though only in the mealy-mouthed terms used by apologists for it: see **1.1 to be somewhat.**

Gauthier 214–15, in a ringing conclusion to his comments (esp. at 204–5 and 212–13) on Chap.5, declares that the actual likelihood of Athens having to fight such a defensive war in the near future was small, in X.'s estimation—because only demented malefactors ('des fous criminels') would start one. This goes too far. Those who start wars seldom view themselves in that light. See e.g. Thuc. 1.121.1 (the Corinthians in 432), and more abstractly Thuc. 5.89 in the Melian Dialogue: the Athenian spokesmen will not, they say, make 'a long and untrustworthy speech' about how they were 'wronged'. X. was a much more trusting man than Thucydides, without doubt, but what he says here is fair enough. Anyone attacking Athens after 355 would find it harder to recruit allies if they could not be recruited from states which had suffered from Athenian *adikia*.

CHAPTER SIX

In this brief coda ('chant': Gauthier 216) to the work, X. has two pieces of advice for his fellow-citizens: speed and piety.

First, none of what he has advised 'is impossible, or even difficult'; so in order to seize the cornucopia of benefits which will accrue—6.1 itemizes them—it is necessary to turn thought into action without delay. (X. himself is an old man in a hurry. He wants to see '*now*, in our own time, the city secure and prospering'.) Second, divine blessing must be sought and obtained. Not much has been said about the gods since 1.3–4, as Cartledge in Waterfield 229 comments, but here at the close X. reverts very much to type. Via the oracles of Zeus and Apollo, the Athenian state must have the assurance that specific deities wish it well as it proceeds.

* * * *

6.1 nothing of what I have suggested is impossible, or even difficult Cf. broadly 4.13 (see under **I expect**); also the beginning of 4.18, the end of 4.21, and 4.37.

6.1 we will become more appealing to the Hellenes, we will live in greater security, and we will enhance our glory A last example (if we ignore the remainder of this long sentence) of X's liking for threefold expressions:

(*i*) For 'more appealing' see already 5.1, where likewise this adjective (*prosphilês*) is used with a dative. X. had allowed himself there the luxury of imagining an Athens beloved by all mankind. Here, somewhat more realistically (as the context requires), these warm feelings are confined to Hellas; cf. 5.8–10.

(*ii*) The vision of 'greater security', is related by Thiel 38 to 4.41–8. Gauthier 216, castigating this as an error, again appeals to Chap.5. Both of these antecedents, I would suggest, are relevant. Cf. in any event Isoc. 8.19–20.

(*iii*) *Hipp.*1–2 had already linked the superlative of *prosphilês* (above, *i*) with the superlative of the adjective used here, *eukleês*. (For glory linked with security see *Cyrop.*8.2.22.) Originally Homeric and poetic, its earliest attestations in prose authors are in X. and his contemporary Plato—though before them, the Periklean *Funeral Speech* in Thucydides had spoken of the *eukleia* of the Athenian war-dead on that occasion (Thuc. 2.44.4). In short, the word was a grand, high-flown one. I have suggested under **5.2 Some people** that Athens' stock was very low at this time, and indeed that X. himself acknowledged as much. Here, nevertheless, as he approaches the end of his manifesto, he sets that aside. No matter how the comparative aspect of *euklëesteroi* is construed—more glorious than before (cf. below on festivals); more glorious than others; or both of these—, here is X. the patriot in full cry.

6.1 the common people will have plenty of sustenance, and the rich will be freed from the expense that goes into war X.'s first and only use (in this work) of the noun *dêmos*. In contradistinction, here, to 'the rich', it does require either the adjective I have given it or else recasting as e.g. Waterfield 182 does ('the general populace of Athens'). On 'sustenance' see under **4.33 I have now stated**.

On the expenses of financing war cf. already 3.7–8, 4.40, 5.8. As to the low-key way X. expresses himself here in *Poroi* 6.1, it could hardly be more different from the bitterness he had put into the mouth of some of the elite contributors to *Symp*. Called upon to say what he takes most pride in, the once-rich Charmides (*LGPN* s.v. no.28, *APF* 330–1, *POP* 90–4) nominates his poverty: *Symp*.3.9, expanded (when his turn to speak arrives) at 4.29–33. Freed from, *inter alia*, the constant orders by the state to pay for something, Charmides is no longer the slave (*doulos*) he once felt himself to be. The vocabulary is later taken up by Kallias (III) of Alopeke (*LGPN* s.v. no.84, *APF* 261–9, *POP* 68–74), still a plutocrat at the dramatic date of the work. Commenting on Antisthenes' pride in 'wealth' of the intellectual kind, Kallias can only envy someone 'to whom the state does not issue orders and treat like a *doulos*' (*Symp*.4.45). See generally Tamoulaki (2013).

6.1 Once a large surplus has accrued A happy prospect—though a distant one, as X. has acknowledged in 4.23–4 (in the context set by 4.17) and 4.33–8.

This is X.'s first explicit mention of such a 'surplus' (here in *Poroi*; but at household level see *Cyrop*.3.3.3 and, especially, *Oec*.1.4, 2.10–11, 11.13, 20.21, 21.10). Hitherto he has spoken simply of revenue(s), *prosodoi*, doing so (Gauthier 217 suggests) in order not to distract attention from his primary aim of providing the Athenians with their 'sustenance' (see the preceding lemma). With this established, he can turn, briefly, to additional benefits that his programme would finance.

The next four lemmata address X.'s summary list of the areas—religious, military, civic—where he thinks expenditure is called for. Individually and collectively, they have often been mapped onto the political activity of Euboulos in the period *c*. 355–*c*. 342. In fact, if the evidence does not deceive us, the key period comes later (*c*. 337–*c*. 325), with Lykourgos the central figure: see General Intro., sections 6 and 8.

6.1 we will celebrate festivals even more magnificently than we do now Unlike the three comparative adjectives earlier in the sentence (above, **we will become**), this comparative adverb has a tailpiece which removes any doubt as to what the comparison is.

Though magnificence could of course be displayed in private life by those with enough money (4.8; cf. e.g. Isoc. 16.34, 19.36), in a democratic polis like Athens it was especially appropriate in the public domain and on the occasions of the major festivals. None were grander than the (City) Dionysia and the Panathenaia, the two singled out by Demosthenes in the late 350s in his complaint about the disorganized way in which his fellow-citizens planned, financed and despatched fleets. By comparison, 'the festivals of the Panathenaia and the Dionysia always occur at the right time [. . .], as much money is spent on them as on any single expedition, and they entail as much of a throng and preparation as anything I know of': Demosth. 4.35. Although X.'s 'magnificently' (the adjective *megaloprepês* and its cognates) is quite a rare item of vocabulary in this kind of context, there is an instance of it in [Demosth.] 59.76–7 (from *c.* 340). The passage mentions the ancient shrine of Dionysos-in-the-Marshes, the location of a stone stele recording the role and functions of the 'king' archon (*basileus*) and his wife: 'only once each year is the shrine opened, on the twelfth day of the month Anthesterion. These sacred and solemn rites, for which your ancestors made provision so well and magnificently, you too should strive to maintain.' See generally Mikalson (2016) 252–3.

In public documents of the period, something like the law of *c.* 335 on the 'Little' (= annual, as opposed to quadrennial) Panathenaia uses phrases like 'as well prepared as possible for Athena' and 'as fine as possible for the goddess' (RO 81, now *IG* II^3 447/*AIO*). Another law on religious matters, passed about the same time, concerns the cult ornaments (*kosmoi*) for various deities. It has survived only in fragments but it refers on several occasions to the question—to be decided by 'the god' (cf. 6.2 here)—of whether a given *kosmos* should be made 'larger and more beautiful, or left as it is at present': *IG* II^2 333, now *IG* II^3 445/*AIO*. (The answer to the question, if given, has not been preserved.)

The evident position of X. here that more magnificence in festivals would be a good thing—contrast Isoc. 7.29 (though the particular rhetorical thrust there makes the issue secondary)—is in line with the rest of his wish-list as itemized in the rest of the sentence. We need not suppose that anything specific had provoked it, but note nevertheless Demosth. 22.69–78 (and 24.178) on the alleged thefts by Androtion of Gargettos (*LGPN* s.v. no.3, *OCD* 86, *FGrH* 324), in or before 356/5, as overseer of *pompeia* (cf. *IG* I^3 473, lines 7–8)—items carried in procession, particularly in this instance golden crowns. In any event, X.'s interest in this area was shared by a certain Epikrates (*LGPN* s.v. no.5). In 354/3 he moved a decree calling for a meeting of the *nomothetai* (*OCD* 1019; Hansen (1991) 161–77) about the Panathenaia, 'in order that the offerings are sacrificed, the financing is adequate, and any financial deficiency for the Panathenaia is made good' (Demosth. 24.27, and cf. 24.28 for a phrase that might be quoted from the decree—'as finely as possible'). This man is also identified as the Epikrates who, in that same year, introduced a law concerning the financing of another festival, apparently that of Hephaistos and Athena Hephaistia: Agora Inv.7495, unpublished. See *LGPN* s.v., Jansen (2007) 134, and already in General Intro., section 7, opening para.

6.1 shrines we will keep in good repair This inevitably calls to mind the end of X.'s autobiographical excursus in *Anabasis* book 5. He recounts there how, once he had retrieved (in 396) the booty-money that had been deposited for safekeeping at the shrine of Artemis in Ephesos, he purchased his estate at Skillous (General Intro., section 1) and built on it a small-scale version of the Ephesian Artemision. The inscribed stele there is quoted verbatim. 'Sacred ground, (the possession) of Artemis. He who owns it and takes its produce is to give her a tenth part every year. Out of the residue he is to repair the temple. Should anyone not do these things, it will come to the goddess' attention' (*Anab*.5.3.4–13, at 13; for the 'come to... attention' formula cf. *Hell*.6.4.30).

This parallel/precedent is of especial value because it shows that, for X., the compound verb *episkeuazein* describes paying attention to routine, ongoing maintenance. Translations of the present phrase which use terms like restoration (Dakyns, Marchant), as if of something already seriously dilapidated, thus risk being misleading. Cf. generally e.g. Andoc. 3.14 (triremes), Demosth. 3.29 (roads). That said, X.'s inclusion of this item here does indicate that in his view this sort of good housekeeping had not been adequately kept up in recent times.

6.1 walls and dockyards we will rebuild As with the preceding phrase, it is important to grasp, if we can, the sense of the compound verb X. uses: *anorthoun*. Here, however, the messages (from other evidence) are mixed. X. himself applies it in *Hell*.4.8.12 to the *total rebuilding* of walls (the Long Walls and Peiraieus walls at Athens) which had been demolished. For something equally drastic cf. e.g. Hdt. 1.19.3 and Thuc. 6.88.6: re-building a temple and a camp, respectively, that had been *burned down*. Somewhat less categorical is Hdt. 7.176.5 and 7.208.2 on the wall, meant to keep the Persians at bay, at Thermopylai (*OCD* 1464); *anorthoun* is the verb which describes the treatment the ancient Phokian wall there required in 481, when 'most' of it was fallen ruins. Further along the same spectrum is RO 59, a fourth-century lease of sacred land from Arkesine (*IACP* no.472) on the island of Amorgos (*OCD* 72, *IACP* p.734). One of the recurrent duties of the lessee, on pain of a fine, is to *anorthoun* 'walls that are falling'—meaning in that context, evidently, any walls that do fall in future.

In the light of these examples, it would be sensible to think that X. has in mind here not a single kind of work but a multiplicity—excepting only one (for which there is neither evidence nor probability): replacing walls and dockyards that had entirely vanished. Other than that, the common factor will be, again, that in his estimation more effort was needed in these twin areas, the *teichê* and the *neôria*.

(1) DOCKYARDS. We know that the Peiraieus dockyards were under the day-to-day charge of a 'treasurer [*tamias*] for the *neôria*' and ten *epimelêtai tôn neôriôn* (Hansen (1980) 161 and 157; *AO* 9 and 12); however, decisions about major structural work on or around them will have had to be taken by the assembly, and (since financing would be involved) framed as a law. A client of Dinarchus, speaking in court against Demosthenes in 323, appears to credit Euboulos with creating (*sc.* more) shipsheds, *neôsoikoi* (Din. 1.96). The word that X. uses, *neôria*, features in Aeschin. 3.25: before *c.* 336 the commissioners of the theoric fund—thanks to the stature of Euboulos—also performed other functions such as being in charge of *neôria*. See already on this General Intro., section 6, at n.96). This just might, in some way, be related to X.'s aspiration here; cf. Garland (2001) 43 (but with, at 186, a salutary warning on the rhetorical bias of Din. 1.96, a passage primarily aimed at denigrating the defendant Demosthenes by comparison).

(2) WALLS. They present a more obscure picture, including the matter of who, if anyone, exercised ongoing responsibility for them. Aristot. *Pol.*6.1321b26 includes *teichopoioi*, literally wall-makers, in a list of examples of offices which large democracies will typically have. At three widely separated times we hear of them in Athens: first (*a*), in a fragmentary set of accounts of the *hellênotamiai* from 443/2, *IG* I^3 440; next (*b*) in the wall-rebuilding accounts of 394/3–393/2, *IG* II^2 1658–61; and finally (*c*) in relation to 337/6. (Strange to say, Wycherley (1978) 19 overlooks *a*, and *AO* 15 ignores *b*.) For 337/6 the ten tribes each elected a *teichopoios*—and Pandionis chose Demosthenes. (See Aeschin. 3.14, 17, 23–31; Demosth. 18.55 (a purported document), 113, 118; [Plut.] *Orat.*845F, 851A.) Eclipsing the other nine *teichopoioi* to the extent that even their names are unknown,

Demosthenes had already been the proposer of the decree which set all this up, including 'money for the walls' (Demosth. 18.248; more detail in Aeschin 3.27).

The precise purpose of, and necessity for, *teichopoiia* is not explained in any of those literary contexts, but a degree of light is shed, it is thought, by *IG* II^2 244, now *IG* II^3 429/*AIO*. This is a fourth-century law (or what survives of it) concerning work on, apparently, the Long Walls and Peiraieus walls, i.e. rather than the city-circuit. Several years of such work are envisaged; and at least part of the financing is to come from *eisphorai*. So what is its date? As the stone itself offers none, dating has been based on the most cogent-looking historical context. Traditionally this has always been seen as 337, to match the evidence cited above. Cawkwell (1963) 66 raises the possibility that this orthodoxy is mistaken and that the law belongs instead to 'the period of Eubulus, or if this were unacceptable, the "earlier law" mentioned in line 13 may do so'. (He also draws attention to Aeschin. 1.80: a speech by the defendant Timarchos in 347/6 had alluded to the upkeep—*episkeuê*: cf. under the preceding lemma—of walls and towers.) *IG* II^3 429's 'earlier law' is certainly tantalizing, but the traditional dating of that document itself is reaffirmed in that edition (and in *AIO*); and, as a separate matter, Cawkwell's evidence for a link between Euboulos and walls (Cawkwell (1963) 66 n.108) is evanescent.

6.1 To the priests, the council, the officials and the cavalrymen we will restore their traditional emoluments This concluding item in X.'s wish-list turns from activities and facilities to people, under the four heads given:

(*a*) The 'priests' (*hiereis*) of mid-fourth-century Athens—even if we exclude, as X. himself is certainly excluding, those of imported, non-Hellenic cults that were permitted to operate outside state control—have not been mentioned hitherto. They were a very mixed bag. Its contents embraced women as well as men (if, as here, priestesses were not separately specified, as in *Apol.*13 or *Hell.*6.4.7). And the positions these individuals held were sometimes ancient, sometimes more recent; both hereditary and non-hereditary; and—if the latter—elective or sortitive. Being a (male) priest, moreover, was no private vocation but could be combined perfectly well with public office. Lykourgos of Boutadai (General Intro., section 8) is the paramount example, entitled by his 'clan' (*genos*) descent to be the priest of Poseidon Erechtheus (Parker (1996) 242, 290–4). See further Garland (1990) 77–81.

(*b*) The Kleisthenic 'council' (*boulê*) of Five Hundred has been mentioned at 4.18, q.v. Comm. there. (See also *Hell.*1.4.20, 1.7.3–34 passim, 2.2.15, 2.3.11–12 & 24, 2.3.50–5, 5.2.29–30, 6.4.20, 6.5.33, 7.1.2 & 11; *Hipp.*1.8 & 13, 3.9, 12 & 14; *Oec.*9.15.) There is no possibility that X. is referring, either there or here, to Athens' other, smaller and more ancient 'council', that of the Areopagos (R. W. Wallace (1989); Hansen (1991) 288–95)—even though conservatives among his contemporaries wished to see it re-empowered (Isoc. 7.37–55).

(*c*) The 'officials' (*archai*) ought in the strictest sense to have been described, in context here, as 'the other officials' (because the 500 councillors were also regarded as office-holders: Hansen (1991) 226–7). However, the differentiation here can be paralleled elsewhere (e.g. the document in Demosth. 24.20), and is unproblematic in itself. That X. meant to refer here purely to the nine major archon(te)s—the eponymous archon, the *basileus*, the polemarch and the six *thesmothetai*—is unlikely, given his use of the broader term *archai* (= official positions, but by extension the holders of those positions). There were anything up to 700 of them in total, very often in tribal tens. See Hansen (1980), summarized in Hansen (1991) 239–40.

(*d*) The 'cavalrymen' (*hippeis*) have been mentioned in all but name at 2.5, X.'s proposal to allow (sc. suitable) metics into *to hippikon*; and directly in 4.47. See also e.g. *Hell.*1.1.34, 1.2.16, 1.3.3 & 10, 1.4.21, 1.6.24, 2.3.48, 2.4.2–10, 2.4.24–32, 3.1.4; *Hipp.* passim; and generally Spence (1993) xxi–xxv, 9–17. A reform datable to the 440s or 430s had raised the size of the cavalry corps from the three hundred established in, probably, the 470s, to a figure of 1,000 (100 from each tribe). This 'canonical size' (Bugh (1988) 155) is presupposed by X. in *Hipp.*1.2 ('the number (that is) in accordance with the law'), and that is surely the case here in *Poroi* too.

So far so good. The question now becomes: what does X. mean by restoring, to these four specified categories of Athenian, *ta patria*—literally, their ancestral or traditional things?

I begin with three methodological points. Each is simple, but the first two both have provisos. First: giving something back (the verb is *apodidonai*) to priests, councillors, officials, and cavalrymen must concern, broadly at least, something that they once had. (See e.g. King Archidamos II of Sparta to the Plataians in Thuc. 2.72.3.) There is no intrinsic means, however, of telling how long ago. Second: X.'s *ta patria* in context here (i.e. as an opportunity arising from the accumulation of a large cash surplus) must be things that cost money—or must at least *include* such things. (And because four separate beneficiaries are encompassed in the proposal, all four need not benefit in the same way or ways.) Third: contrary to Jansen (2007) 132–4, who urges that 'To the priests etc.' belongs intimately and explanatorily with everything before it (between 'we will celebrate festivals' and 'walls and dockyards we will rebuild'), this final multi-part element in X.'s long sentence does not look back but adds something new. The sentence's simple paratactic structure demands such an interpretation.

A prefatory issue of another kind is presented by Demosth. 24.96–101. A succession of scholars—Thiel 38, Wilhelm (1934) 33–4, Gauthier 28–9, Jansen (2007) 130 (with n.43) and 132—have drawn attention to correspondences between *Poroi* 6.1 and those six chapters of Demosth. 24 *Against Timokrates*, a speech dating from 354/3. Timokrates of Krioia (*LGPN* s.v. no.63, *APF* 513–14) had introduced a law intended to ease the circumstances of debtors to the Athenian state (a measure now, apparently, being prosecuted as an 'unsuitably framed law': Hansen (1974) 44 with n.21; Hansen (1991) 212—though see below). The particular effects of the law which are castigated in Demosth. 24.96–101 concern the deleterious impact it will have on the public finances. Picked out for special mention in 24.97 are supplementary sums (*proskatablêmata*) 'spent on assembly-meetings, sacrifices, the *boulê*, the cavalrymen, and other matters'. 24.99 refers to the assembly, the *boulê* and the courts having to transact their business without *misthos*, if Timokrates' law goes ahead. 24.101 then claims that Timokrates is ruining everything: 'demos, cavalrymen, *boulê*, *hiera*, *hosia*'. (On these last two see above, **5.4 those keen**.) The reason I adduce Demosth. 24.96–101 here, as a preliminary, is that I do not think it deserves to be part of the four discussions presented below. Taken literally, it would imply that in three out of the four areas mentioned by X. there was already satisfactory provision. However, 'Demosthenes is determined to upset Timocrates' proposal by fair means or foul' in this speech (Rhodes (1972) 151). As a reliable provider of factual information it is best ignored. (MacDowell (2009) 195–6 conjectures that the prosecution of Timokrates never actually came to court.)

* * * *

(1) CAVALRYMEN are a suitable topic with which to begin assessing *Poroi* 6.1 in earnest. Thanks to chance finds on papyrus (parts of Lysias' speech *Against Theozotides*) and on stone (the opening of Theozotides' decree itself: *SEG* 28.46 (Harding (1985) no.8A)), we know that in 403/2 the daily *misthos* of cavalrymen was cut by one-third, from a drachma to four obols: evidence and discussion in Loomis (1998) 45–6 no.19. (The decree bringing about this change was prosecuted as unconstitutional, but the prosecution failed: Hansen (1974) 30 no.5.) This four-obol rate, or its rough equivalent in Aiginetan currency, was still in force in 383: *Hell*.5.2.21–2; Loomis (1998) 49–50 no.25. For the late 360s or early 350s, X.'s statement in *Hipp*.1.19 could equate to four obols a day for a putative 1,000 *hippeis*: Loomis (1998) 51 no.27. On this basis it seems reasonable to think that X. wants to see the restoration of fifth-century rates of gross pay for the cavalrymen: a drachma a day, as in the closing years of the century, if not more. (Loomis (1998) 57 with 43 envisages higher daily rates, up to two drachmas, earlier in the century.) This is the reconstruction suggested by Hansen (19[71–]80) 109 n.6, who also declares that the 'ancestral' rate was indeed restored in *the second half of the 350s*—and thus, quite possibly, prompted by *Poroi* 6.1. His reason for thinking so is that Demosthenes in 351 proposed an expeditionary force, to harass the Macedonians, in which the *hippeis* would be paid at a rate of thirty drachmas a month, i.e. one drachma a day (Demosth. 4.28; Loomis (1998) 52-53 no.29). However, Bugh (1988) 155–6 reports Hansen's second thoughts, communicated to him informally, that Demosthenes was suggesting here an extraordinary expedition which would justify extraordinary pay-rates. 'In the end, we cannot be certain that the four-obol rate was ever restored to one drachma for ordinary cavalry service in the fourth century' (Bugh).

Alongside pay and/or rations, we hear in the fifth century of a cavalryman's 'set-up', *katastasis*. This appears to be a state loan (repaid at the end of his service) intended primarily to help incoming *hippeis*—if they needed such help—to acquire a horse of the necessary quality. See Lys.16.6–7 and the other evidence discussed by Bugh (1988) 52–8 (and 111–14); also Spence (1993) 16, 213 and appendix 4. Very probably the *katastasis*, in X.'s eyes, would have formed part of the cavalry's *ta patria*.

In this instance, however, there is no evidence that either Theozotides or anyone else had taken it away from them.

(2) PRIESTS (male and female) represent an area of Athenian life especially associated with tradition. On *ta patria* in the religious domain see now Mikalson (2016) 110–19. As it happens, the only other occurrence of *ta patria* in X. concerns Kyros' performance of sacrifices 'in accordance with tradition(s)' (*kata ta patria*) as his death approached: *Cyrop*.8.7.1. Though that sheds no light on the present passage, Gauthier 218 adduces an Athenian inscription which does, at least by way of example. In lines 255–8 of *IG* II[2] 1672 (*I.Eleusis* 177), the 329/8 accounts of the overseers of the cults at Eleusis, 'priests and priestesses' are recorded as receiving quantities of barley (from rented land) *kata ta patria*. (See also Papazarkadas (2011) 38–9.)

This category of recipient as a whole, though, is sparsely and randomly documented, as the survey (of the almost entirely epigraphic evidence) in Loomis (1998) 76–87 shows. Besides *misthos*—or what can be understood as such—in a narrow sense, there is reference to 'emoluments (variously called *apometra* or *hier(ei)ôsyna*) paid in money' and also such perquisites as 'choice portions of sacrificial victims and other offerings' (Loomis (1998) 76). A well-known example of the latter is the provision that the priestess of Athena Nike will receive, besides fifty drachmas (a year), 'the legs and skins of the public (sacrificial animals)': *IG* I[3] 35 (ML 44, now OR 156; Fornara (1983) no.93; Loomis (1998) 76 no.2). See also e.g. RO 5, top of face A (Loomis (1998) 81 no.13), preamble to three phratry decrees from Dekeleia, 396/5 and later; RO 37 (Loomis (1998) 82 no.15), decree of the Salaminioi *genos*, 363/2 (Parker (1996) 308–16; M. C. Taylor (1997) 47–63). But overall, what had happened—or was perceived to have happened—in this area, that provoked X. to include it here, is quite impossible to say.

(3) THE COUNCIL, self-evidently, presents a phenomenon with fewer dimensions. It can be inferred from Thuc. 8.69.4 that the oligarchs of 411 abolished the *bouleutikos misthos* payable at that time (whatever it was); except, as ?Aristot. *Ath.Pol.*29.5 clarifies, for the fact that the fifty councillors who served as the *prytaneis* in any given one-tenth of the year were to receive three obols a day. Thereafter, pay for councillors is not mentioned again—apart from here—until *Ath. Pol.*62.2 gives the rates prevailing in the 330s and 320s: five obols a day (for actual attendance, it is presumed), rising to six in that 10% of the year when one's tribe was fulfilling the extra duties of *prytaneis* (*OCD* 1231–2). See generally Loomis (1998) 19–20 nos.16–17, 26 no.30c.

What are we to make, then, of X.'s implicit call here for the *boulê* to have *ta patria* back? First, the evidence for councillors' perquisites, over and above their pay, is slight but does exist. Witness for instance the carefully worded statement in Hansen (19[71–]80) 106–9, at 108 n.5: 'there is nothing to prevent us from assuming' that Isocrates' censure of the 'revenues' (*prosodoi*) and 'profit' (*lêmma*) extracted by office-holders from their offices (Isoc. 7.24–6) embraces the councillors. More substantially, Hansen (19[71–]80) 119 mentions the five portions of roast beef given out to the *prytaneis* at the Panathenaia: RO 81, now *IG* II^3 447/*AIO*. (The bouleutic perquisites mentioned by Rhodes (1972) 14 all belong in the Hellenistic and Roman periods.) Second, if purely *misthos* is at issue here, X.'s complaint is unlikely to have been made if the full *Ath.Pol.* rates were being paid in his day. But what was, instead, being paid is unknown.

(4) Finally, the (other) OFFICIALS. As with priests, above, this is a large and heterogeneous category, poorly and randomly illuminated by evidence. The nine archons are a partial exception. At the time of *Ath.Pol.*62.2 they received four obols a day, out of which, probably, a communal crier/herald (*kêryx*) and piper (*aulêtês*) had to be maintained: Loomis (1998) 26–7 no.30d. Before that, the only quantified reference to their pay is again *Ath.Pol.*29.5: under the oligarchic regime of the Four Hundred (*OCD* 588) they, like the *prytaneis*, were to receive three obols (Loomis (1998) 20 no.17). As regards perquisites: three portions of the Panathenaic beef (above) were theirs in *c.* 335.

This modest haul of data would appear to offer little scope for explaining what X. meant by giving the officials back *ta patria*, at least on the assumption that the 411 oligarchs' abolition of pay (with the two exemptions stated) except for the armed forces no longer held good in the fourth century. For this see e.g. Gauthier 218; Rhodes (1981) 695, and still in Rhodes (2010) 298; also Gabrielsen (1981). However, the opposite assumption is argued for by Hansen (1979), supplemented by Hansen (19[71–]80); and see also D. M. Lewis, reviewing Gabrielsen (1981) in *JHS* 102 (1982) 269. In Hansen's scenario (summarized in Hansen (1991) 240–2), most of the officials did *not* see their pay restored to them when democracy itself was restored in 403/2. Instead, for many of them the important thing was to derive unofficial profit(s) from their tenure; cf. above on Isoc. 7.24–6. Essentially the argument is one of silence either way—but if Hansen is right, a significant pay-off would be the creation of a solid reason why X. said what he did.

6.1 What better course than to take these matters in hand as soon as possible, to enable us to see *now*, in our own time, Athens secure and highly favoured? The idiom 'take *x* in hand' (where *x* is in the dative case—and is not the recipient of a hostile attack, as in Thuc. 4.122.1) is uncommon, but it has a precedent in tragedy (Eurip. *Med.*377).

'Secure' is expressed by the prepositional phrase 'with [= in] security', for which there are precedents in Thucydides (1.130.5, 5.107.1). For 'highly favoured' see under **5.2 Surely the states**. The overtones of divine approval are particularly appropriate here in 6.1–2. (Jansen (2007) 68–9 suppresses them by rendering the participle *eudaimonousan* as 'prosperous'; cf. again 114.)

6.2 If you do take a decision to do these things, my personal advice would be For X. as someone giving 'advice' cf. already 4.30.

'These things' means the entire programme of *Poroi*, now (in the idiom X. uses here) formally adopted as a resolution of the Athenian assembly; cf. Gauthier 221. The boldness of that form of words is subtly offset by its framing in an overtly conditional mode (contrast 4.17 & 51).

The steps advised in 6.2–3 as a whole are an example of the policy credited to Sokrates in *Mem.*1.1.7–9 (here abridged). 'Those who intended to manage both households and states well, he said, had need of divination. It was his opinion that anything like a carpenter's or a bronzesmith's craft [. . .] or how to be a general could be learned and mastered by human intelligence, but he said that the gods reserved to themselves the core matters in these areas; none of them were plain to mankind. [. . .] Even to a politician it is not plain whether being a leader of the state is to *its* advantage [. . .] Those who supposed that none of such things were heaven-sent but that all resulted from human intelligence were irrational, he said—but equally irrational were those who conducted divination on matters which the gods have granted it to humans to decide by learning [. . .] He said that what the gods have granted us to learn we should study, and what is not clear to humans we should try to find out from the gods by divination. This because the gods give signs to those who are in their grace.' (For this final concept cf. *Anab.*6.6.32; *Cyrop.*1.6.2–3 & 46; and outside X. e.g. Soph. *OC* 44.)

The gods' 'signs' were usually to be found in the outcome of animal sacrifices and/or the consultation of oracles, but Hyp. *Eux.* (Whitehead (2000) 153–262) illustrates another medium of transmission: incubation (sleeping overnight in a shrine: *OCD* 731–2) and the dreams experienced during it. (See also lines 36–48 of RO 27, with their commentary at pp.132–3.) Cf. generally *Hipp*.9.9: sacrifices, omens, voices, dreams.

6.2 to send representatives both to Dodona and to Delphi, to ask the gods whether it would be 'preferable and better', 'both now and in time to come', for the polis to be organized on these lines On Delphi see under **5.9 Suppose**. The particular deity consulted there was Apollo. But as we see, X. wants to have the opinion of a plurality of *theoi*, so Apollo's father Zeus is also to be approached, via his oracular shrine—reputedly the oldest in Hellas—at Dodona in Epeiros. See in brief *OCD* 471 (and *IACP* no.93); more fully Parke (1967) 90–3; in full detail Eidinow (2007) chaps.4–6. For the Dodona/Delphi conjunction cf. Demosth. 21.51; Delphi is first-named there. X. himself had never previously mentioned Dodona (and he never at all mentions the celebrated oracle of Ammon in Libya, to which Delphi and Dodona are appended in Aristoph. *Birds* 716), though for questions to Delphi cf. *Anab*.3.1.6 with 6.1.22; *Apol*.14; *Cyrop*.7.2.15 & 18; *Hell*.4.7.2, 6.4.30; *Lac.Pol*.8.5; *Mem*.4.2.24, 4.3.16.

Requesting divine guidance and/or enlisting divine approval in this way was no empty gesture for X. and the bulk of his contemporaries. The solemnity of such oracular consultations is embodied in their ritual language, *which X. twice reproduces here* (6.2–3). The formula 'preferable and better' (already in *Anab*.6.2.15, 7.6.44, and *Lac.Pol*.8.5) is the very phrase used in documents of this kind. Athenian ones include RO 58 (Harding (1985) no.78), now *IG* II^3 292/*AIO* (and *I.Eleusis* 144), the 352/1 consultation of Delphi about sacred land on the border with Megara; and *IG* II^3 445/*AIO* (see under **6.1 we will**). See also RO 50 (Harding (1985) no.67), the 357/6 alliance between Philip II of Macedon and the Chalkidians; *SIG* 1044 (Halikarnassos, fourth or third century), 398 (Kos, 270s), 1158 (Kyzikos, late third century), and the consultation of Dodona by the sick woman Nikokrateia in *SIG* 1161 (fourth or third century) and in several of the transactions collected at *SEG* 15.385–409 (fifth to third centuries). The phrase 'both now and in time to come' also, as Gauthier 219 notes, features in oracular responses: see e.g. *SEG* 15.402 (Dodona, fourth century).

6.3 And if they give their approval, I would then suggest a further question that ought to be asked: which of the gods are the ones we should win over, if we are to do these things in the finest and best way Even winning the favour of Zeus and Apollo—belt and braces—is not enough. Just as Nikokrateia's question to Dodona (see under the preceding lemma) was 'sacrificing to which of the gods' would be 'preferable and better' for the relief of her illness, so too here. Theophrastus' paradigmatic Superstitious Man, *Deisidaimôn*, is also apt to ask this question, after a dream in his case (*Char.*16.11, with Diggle (2004) 368–9), but that fact did not confine it to people at the comical extreme of religiosity; cf. Mikakson (1983) 45.

On this sort of *two-stage* procedure see in brief Gauthier 219–20; in full Bonnechere (2013). X. himself had learned about the convention the hard way. In *Anab.*3.1.5–8 (discussed most recently by Haywood (2016) 88–90) he recalls going to Delphi, on Sokrates' advice, and asking Apollo 'by sacrificing and praying to which of the gods' would he best undertake the expedition with Kyros and return safely. Apollo gave his answer. (It is here unspecified but plural. This appears to conflict with 3.1.12 and esp. 6.1.22, which mention only Zeus Basileus—a strangely Boiotian choice: see Diod.Sic. 15.53.4 and generally M. H. Hansen in *IACP* 446.) But Sokrates was displeased. The young man should have asked first whether it was right for him to make the journey at all. Chastened, X. performed the rituals required—and did come home safe, at least to Hellas.

See also in the same vein Demosth. 43.66: 'sacrificing or praying to which god'. Delphi's answer on that occasion was: to Zeus, Athena, Apollo, Artemis—in fact 'to *all* the Olympian gods and goddesses'. The four consultations reported in Demosth. 21.51–3 resulted in a similarly bet-hedging or scattergun recommendation from Delphi in the second of the two instances given (Dionysos in the first), but somewhat more targeted ones from Dodona: Zeus and Dione; Zeus, Apollo, Dionysos. (On the oracles in Demosth. 43 and 21 see in full Mikalson (2016) appendix 1.) Note also *SEG* 15.386, 395 and 404 (Dodona). More generally cf. e.g. Hdt. 1.67.2 (Delphi: Orestes).

Given the parallels cited above, Robert Parker's view that X. 'here writes as a dreamer' seems harsh (Parker (2005) 110); however, he is right to comment that if enlisting divine approval for constitutional and legislative plans in this elaborate way had been the norm we should have heard about it much more often.

6.3 Once the oracles had named these deities in response, and the sacrifices to them had resulted in good omens, the work could begin, undertaken with divine blessing; thus, in all probability, projects would continue in a manner always 'preferable and better' for the polis X. gives no clue as to who the selected *theoi* might be, and it would be pointless to guess. (The fact that this is a plan for Athens constitutes no reason in itself for thinking that Athena—in any of her cult-manifestations—would feature, with or without others.)

The verb I translate as 'named...in response' is another item of vocabulary from the lexicon of oracular utterances. So in X. (*Anab*.3.1.6 & 8, 5.3.8, *Apol*.14, *Lac.Pol*.8.5) and frequently elsewhere e.g. Hdt. 1.13.2, 2.52.3, 2.139.3, 6.34.2, 9.33.2; Thuc. 1.25.1, 1.118.3, 1.126.4, 2.54.4; Plat. *Apol*.21A; Isoc. 6.17 & 31; Demosth. 21.51; Lyk. *Leok*.105.

For sacrifices resulting in good omens cf. e.g. *Anab*.5.4.22, 7.8.6; *Hell*.3.1.17, 3.3.4, 4.1.22; *Lac.Pol*.13.2. The *Hell*. passages reveal—4.1.22 implicitly—that if at first the omens were unfavourable, sacrificing would or could continue until the situation improved. *Hell*.3.1.17 and *Anab*.6.4.13–6.5.2 describe particularly long-drawn-out and demoralizing episodes of this; cf. also *Anab*.7.1.40–1. (A classic *un*favourable omen would be a discoloured and/or misshapen liver in the sacrificial animal. See generally Burkert (1985) 112–13.) According to Polyaen. *Strat*.3.9.9, the policy of Iphikrates in such circumstances was to vary the other variable: his own plans. X., no doubt, expected all to go smoothly in the present, well-prepared case.

An Athenian decree on stone which includes a provision for obtaining good omens from a sacrifice: *IG* I^3 46 (ML 49, now OR 142; Fornara (1983) no.100), despatch of a colony to Brea (*IACP* no.624) in the (?)430s. Note also e.g. RO 87, recording three decisions taken (in the 330s) by the Klytidai, a constituent (?)tribe of Chios (*OCD* 310–11, *IACP* no.840). The second of them concerns whether to keep their sacred objects dispersed in private homes or collect them in a communal building; the omens were favourable to the latter.

The phrase 'undertaken with divine blessing' renders X.'s 'undertaken with god'. Unsurprisingly, the phrase's origins are poetic: see e.g. Soph. *Aj*.765, 779, *OT* 146; Eurip. *Med*.625 (parodied in Aristoph. *Plut*.114), 802; Pind. *Isthm*.4.5 and 9.1, *Nem*.8.17, *Pyth*.4.260. In X. it became, in its various forms, a signature (cf. Gauthier 220: 'un véritable leitmotiv'): see already *Anab*.2.3.23, 3.1.23, 3.1.42, 3.2.8, 3.2.11, 3.2.15, 5.8.19, 6.5.23, 6.6.33, 7.2.34, 7.3.36–7; *Cyrop*.1.5.14, 2.1.15, 2.3.12, 2.4.14, 4.1.11, 5.2.35, 5.3.19, 5.4.22, 5.5.12 & 19, 6.2.25, 7.5.24 & 70; *Hell*.1.6.11; *Hipp*.5.14, 6.1, 7.3 & 14, 9.2 & 8; *Oec*.6.1, 10.12, 11.20. *Hipp*.9.8 is an especially significant instance, as X. in effect admits there that his readers might be surprised at the great frequency of his exhortations to proceed 'with god'. (If they are, his reply there is simple: danger, in warfare particularly, makes this natural.) This *conditio Jacobaea*—so called from its occurrence in the Epistle of James 4.13–15—might in some authors be discountable as a casual nod to superstition, a verbal tic: 'god willing' (*dis volentibus*), even 'fingers crossed'. Since this is X. and not Isocrates or Plato (let alone Thucydides), a mere throwaway line is not in question.

APPENDIX

[Aristot.] *Oec*.2.1346a25–1353b27

As was noted in the General Intro., section 4, *Poroi* is a work without parallel in classical Hellas. The mid-fourth-century *Poristikê* (*biblos*) of Aeneas 'the Tactician', even if it had survived, would not furnish one; its (generic) subject was military provisioning. The closest comparandum for *Poroi* that we possess is therefore the treatise *Oikonomika*, literally *Household-Management-Matters*, attributed to Aristotle (but actually written by a pupil or other imitator: Pomeroy (1995) 68–9). For the date see further below.

'Closest' comparandum might be more candidly expressed as: least remote. The similarities between this work and *Poroi* are not very close at all. They are close enough nonetheless to be worth examining.

* * * *

Each of [Aristotle]'s surviving two books, as the editions divide them (a third book survives only in Latin versions), has a short, abstract introduction: Austin & Vidal-Naquet (1977) 159–61 nos.1A & B. Book 1, the shorter of the pair, continues on a wholly conceptual, taxonomic plane, and offers no grist to our mill here. But Book 2 soon moves from taxonomy into specifics. After first explaining that *oikonomia* operates on four levels—king, satrap, polis, and (least important) individual—and then asserting that the key principle common to them all is the Aristotelian (or Mickawberesque) one that expenditure must not exceed income, the writer fills the rest of the book with a dossier of summary anecdotes. They relate to a great variety of people, places, and circumstances, but their unifying thread is that they all feature a method of money-raising: *poros chrêmatôn*. (For this term see already General Introduction, section 2.)

The date of [Aristotle]'s material has been variously estimated. Van Groningen & Wartelle (1968) opt for the period 325–275, a position refined by Aperghis (2004) 117–36, with his thesis (originating in Rostovtzeff (1941) 440–6) that [Aristotle] is depicting the Near East under the early Seleukid monarchs. However, if we ignore the generic matter and assess only the historical *exempla*, a different conclusion emerges, as is persuasively demonstrated in Brodersen (2008), again Brodersen (2017). None of the episodes can be shown to post-date 323–322 (the deaths of Alexander and of Aristotle); cf. Swain (2013) 197. The compilation thus 'allows us an insight into the Greek world at the brink of the Hellenistic era' (Brodersen (2017) 63).

Gauthier refers to this catalogue as made up of forty-one 'paragraphes', each containing one or more items (Gauthier 13). Since paragraph layout is a modern editorial choice, it may be better to say that the writer provides (unless further splitting is needed in e.g. **3a***) some *seventy-five illustrations*. Here is my own summary version of the dossier:

1. (1346a32–b6) Kypselos, tyrant of Corinth *c.* 657–627 (*OCD* 405 Cypselus). He fulfils a vow to offer Zeus the Corinthians' entire property, by ten successive years of tithing. As this period progresses the Corinthians recoup the deficit by good use of the other 90%. Date: indeterminable within the timespan of Kypselos' rule.

2. (1346b7–12) Lygdamis, tyrant of Naxos *c.* 545–*c.* 525 (see under *OCD* 1003–4 Naxos (1)). After exiling a faction of the rich, he finds that nobody will buy their property, so he sells most of it back to them. Their unfinished artworks, intended as dedications, are also sold to them (and others), on the inducement of having their names engraved on the offerings. Date: indeterminable within the timespan of Lygdamis' rule.

3a. (1346b13–26) The Byzantines (*OCD* 256 Byzantium, *IACP* no.674). Short of funds on one or more occasions, (*i*) they lease out [or sell: on the disputed interpretation of the verb used here, *apedonto*, see e.g. Rousset (2013) 123 with n.54; Russell (2017) 99 with n.19] communal lands (*temenê dêmosia*)—fertile ones for a limited term, unfertile ones in perpetuity. Lands belonging to cult-organizations and phratries are treated likewise, with the owners compensated in kind in other locations. (*ii*) Activity in markets, fisheries, and places of street entertainment is taxed at 33⅓%. (*iii*) A monopoly concession on money-changing is sold to a single bank. Date: context here in *Oec.* suggests the later sixth century; Russell (2017) 98–104 notes that element *iii* would be surprising so early, but he is ultimately non-committal. (Rihll (1991) 109 n.52 dates element *i* '*c.* 390', without discussion.) See further under **3b**.

3b. (1346b26–9) The Byzantines again. Despite their law requiring citizens to have two citizen parents, they sell citizenship for thirty *mnai* to those who have only one. Date: Russell (2017) 167–74 is again non-committal, while noting that 'the citizenship sale looks forward to the Hellenistic period'; it could be added that a double endogamy law does not seem at all likely before the fifth century, even the fourth (Whitehead (1991) 141, 152).

3c. (1346b29–33) The Byzantines again. During a shortage of food as well as cash, they waylay merchant-ships sailing out of the Black Sea, i.e. fully laden, and (evidently) force them to sell their grain-cargoes cheaply. Later, the traders are allowed a 10% price-rise, but individual retailers end up paying it. See Gabrielsen (2007) 312–13; Russell (2017) 67 and (on the obscure details) 100–2. Date: indeterminable.

3d. (1346b33–47a4) The Byzantines again. After some metics lend money on the security of land, something which (in the event of a default) they could not legally own, it is decreed that *egktêsis*-rights can in effect be bought at a fee of one third the loan's value. Date: indeterminable.

* Cross-references of this kind are to the numbered items below.

4a. (1347a4–8) Hippias, tyrant of Athens 527–510 (*OCD* 687 s.v. no.1). He makes a lot of money by (*sc.* confiscating and then) selling, to the owners of urban buildings, their upper storeys etc. which overhang the main streets. (Whitehead (2003) argues that the parallel anecdote in Polyaen. *Strat*.3.9.30, where the same ploy is attributed to Iphikrates [here **26**], is erroneous.) Date: indeterminable, this and **4b–d** also, within the timespan of Hippias' rule.

4b. (1347a8–11) Hippias again. He nullifies and withdraws the currency, but then reissues it, devalued. See Kroll (2011a) 229–31, citing also two fourth-century episodes (Dionysios, **20h** below; Leukon in Polyaen. *Strat*.6.9.1) of the same generic kind. Date: see **4a.**

4c. (1347a11–14) Hippias again. He permits reluctant trierarchs and other liturgists to commute their service into a monetary payment, while still being commemorated as liturgists. Date: see **4a.**

4d. (1347a14–17) Hippias again. He ordains that on the death of any citizen, and the birth of any child, the priestess of Athena (in effect, the public treasury) is to receive one *obolos*, plus measures of barley and wheat. Date: see **4a.**

5. (1347a18–24) 'The Athenians living in Poteidaia' (*OCD* 1199, *IACP* no.598). Needing money for 'the war', these *epoikoi* or cleruchs 'order everyone not to register all their property in their own deme but plot by plot, place by place'; thus the poor might propose a reduced assessment, and those without land at all would be assessed at two *mnai* per head. 'Thus everyone used to contribute what he had registered'. Date: either 429–405 (the *epoikia*) or 362–351 (the cleruchy). Van Groningen (1933) 76–80 argues for the fifth century (cf. *IACP* 839), Moggi (1979) and Ste. Croix (2004) 59 n.217 for the fourth. N. F. Jones (1987) 266–7 is non-committal.

6. (1347a25–31) The Antissans (on Lesbos: *OCD* 109, *IACP* no.794). Confronted by a cashflow problem at the time of the expensive Dionysos sacrifice, they adopt the solution proposed by a certain Sosipolis: vow to sacrifice double next year, collect what produce there is, and sell it; this realizes a sufficiently large sum to go ahead. Date: indeterminable.

7. (1347a32–b2) The Lampsakenes (*OCD* 791 Lampsacus, *IACP* no.748). When facing a naval attack, they order retailers to sell barley-meal, oil, wine, etc. at greatly inflated prices. The retailers take what they expected, the state the extra. Date: indeterminable.

8. (1347b3–15) The Herakleotes (*OCD* 662–3 Heraclea (3) Pontica, *IACP* no.715). Intending to send a fleet against the Spartokids (*OCD* 1392), they commandeer all available grain, oil, wine, etc. from the sellers, promising to pay later. Merchant-vessels loaded with these commodities accompany the navy to the Crimea, each with a public official on board. There the troops buy what they need from these officials, the officers pay their men with the proceeds. Date: 389–370 (so Burstein (1974) 43–4).

9. (1347b16–19) The Spartans. They raise money through a one-day public fast (cf. generally Plut. *Mor*.64B, Polyaen. *Strat*.1.46), human and animal, for Samian exiles to return to their island (now vacated by Athenian cleruchs). Date: 323 (Shipley (1987) 168).

10. (1347b20–30) The Chalkedonians (*OCD* 303 Chalcedon, *IACP* no.743). Needing to pay a large mercenary force, they compile a list of those (citizens and aliens) who wish to exercise a right of reprisal against any city or individual. This they take as justification to seize passing ships, on their way into the Black Sea (contrast **3c**). Enough money is raised to pay the mercenaries and also to compensate any claimants found to have been the victims of unjust seizure. Date: indeterminable.

11. (1347b31–4) The Kyzikenes (*OCD* 408 Cyzicus, *IACP* no.747). After stasis in which members of the oligarchic faction are defeated and arrested, they are allowed to go into exile on payment of a sum of money to the state. Date: indeterminable (though the period 478–411 has been tentatively suggested: see *IACP* 984).

12. (1347b35–1348a3) The Chians (*OCD* 310–11 Chios, *IACP* no.840). Temporarily in need of funds, they decree that all debtors (identifiable as such from a general register) should pay their debts into the public treasury, which then paid the creditors' interest. Date: indeterminable.

13a. (1348a4–11) Mausolos (*OCD* 914) of Karia. Owing tribute to the Great King, he acquires it by calling together his richest subjects and tricking them: 'planted' individuals profess their eagerness to pay, the rest follow. Date: indeterminable within the timespan of Mausolos' rule (377–353).

13b. (1348a11–17) Mausolos again. He orders the citizens of unfortified Mylasa (*OCD* 988–9, *IACP* no.913), his capital city, to contribute towards wall-building, against a Persian attack; but no wall is built—'the god' deems it inopportune—and he keeps the money. Date: indeterminable within the timespan of Mausolos' rule (though 'in the 360s' according to *IACP* 1129).

14a. (1348a18–23) Kondalos, *hyparchos* for Mausolos (**13a–b**). As general policy he records the names of those who offer to give him livestock when he is travelling; at a subsequent date he takes the animal plus whatever profit it is deemed to have earned. Date: see under **13a**.

14b. (1348a23–5) Kondalos again. He sells, to the state's profit, all trees which either overhang or fall onto royal roads. Date: see under **13a**.

14c. (1348a25–8) Kondalos again. At the death of every soldier he charges a drachma for taking the body out through the gates for burial. Date: see under **13a**.

14d. (1348a28–34) Kondalos again. He spares, for a price, the long hair of the Lykians (*OCD* 869 Lycia), supposedly needed by the King to make hairpieces [or: horse-harness plumes]. (On this and other evidence for Mausolos' acquisition of Lykia see Keen (1998) 172–4.) Date: see under **13a**.

15a. (1348a35–b9) Aristoteles of Rhodes, 'archon' of Phokaia (*OCD* 1138 Phocaea). At a time of stasis he raises money by fooling both factions into giving him some, in return for power; but he keeps the money and reconciles the factions. Date: indeterminable. (Not mentioned in *IACP* no.859.)

15b. (1348b9–16) Aristoteles again. On (?)another occasion he profits from of a large backlog of war-related lawsuits and appeals by hastening them to court and pocketing himself the associated fees, penalties, and other money. (Engelmann (1977) improves the transmitted text.) Date: indeterminable.

16a. (1348b17–22) The Klazomenians (*OCD* 329 Clazomenae, *IACP* no.847). During a shortage of both money and grain, they decree that private citizens with stores of oil should loan it to the state (at interest); grain is then obtained with the oil as security. Date: indeterminable.

16b. (1348b22–32) The Klazomenians again. Needing to pay mercenaries, they strike twenty *talanta* of an iron coinage with a silver face-value; the wealthiest citizens exchange this, at interest, for their silver, and by stages the iron currency is re-exchanged and withdrawn. Date: indeterminable, though probably fourth century (Melville Jones (1986) 121). [The supposed evidence for iron currency in fifth-century Byzantium, still in Figueira (1998) 62, was demolished by Crawford (1982); cf. Russell (2017) 72–3. No actual iron coins of Klazomenai survive; instead there are some from the fourth-century Peloponnese, perhaps including Argos, Megara, Phleious, and Tegea: Melville Jones (1986) 121–2.]

17. (1348b33–49a2) The Selymbrians (*IACP* no.679; not in *OCD*). On one occasion they need money, and have plenty of grain that could be exported—but their own law prohibits this. Their solution is to require each citizen to keep what is needed for one year and surrender the rest at a fixed price; the individual right to export it can then be had on application. Date: indeterminable.

18. (1349a3–8) The Abydenians (*OCD* 1–2 Abydos, *IACP* no.765). With stasis leading to land going out of cultivation, and the city's rich metics refusing to advance any more loans, a decree permits anyone to make loans to the farmers, repayable from the profits of the first year's harvest. Date: indeterminable. (There was a period of stasis in *c.* 360, but not necessarily this one: *IACP* 1003.)

19. (1349a9–13) The Ephesians (*OCD* 509 Ephesus, *IACP* no.844). (*i*) They forbid women to wear gold; instead, it must be loaned to the state. (*ii*) They also offer any citizen the opportunity, for a fixed sum, to have his name inscribed as a pillar-donor in the Artemision. Date: indeterminable (though element *ii* must be either before the fire and destruction of 356 or—more probably?—part of the rebuilding which began in 323.

20a. (1349a14–24) Dionysios (I), tyrant of Syracuse (*OCD* 459–60 s.v. no.1). Claiming an epiphany of Demeter, he commandeers women's jewellery for her, but treats it as a loan to his own treasury. Later, women who wish to wear gold may do so by making an offering of a fixed amount. Date: indeterminable within 406–367, the timespan of Dionysios' rule (though perhaps during the first two decades; cf. **20g**, **20i**).

20b. (2349a24–32) Dionysios again. Wanting to build a trireme-fleet, he claims that a certain city is being offered to him by traitors within, who need to be paid. Money is raised by fixed contributions from the citizens, but returned to them with news that the 'plot' has failed. This confidence trick allows him to raise the money on a later occasion, when he keeps it and builds the fleet. Date: see under **20a**.

20c. (1349a32–6) Dionysios again. Short of silver, he mints a coinage of tin, and sings its praises to the citizens; perforce, they vote to treat it as silver. Date: see under **20a**.

20d. (1349a36–b6) Dionysios again. Faced with the citizens' refusal to contribute, he sells off the palace furnishings, but then takes them back from the purchasers. Date: see under **20a**.

20e. (1349b6–14) Dionysios again. He frees livestock from taxation, so that large numbers of citizens will buy it; he then re-imposes the tax. (Many angry owners kill and sell their beasts. He imposes a daily limit, except for sacrificial victims. They designate *all* their stock sacrificial. He restricts this category to male animals.) Date: see under **20a**.

20f. (1349b14–17) Dionysios again. Ordering lists of all households where the heirs are orphans, he 'uses' their property until the heirs come of age. Date: see under **20a**.

20g. (1349b17–27) Dionysios again. After capturing Rhegion (*OCD* 1274 Rhegium, *IACP* no.68), he offers its inhabitants release on payment of a three-*mnai* premium (and repayment of his war-expenses). He takes the money but sells them anyway. Date: 386 (Diod.Sic. 14.111–12).

20h. (1349b27–33) Dionysios again. He requisitions silver from the citizens and re-mints each one-drachma coin with a face-value of two; this 'repays' the owners for both the present exaction and a previous one. Date: from context here, perhaps the mid-380s.

20i. (1349b33–50a5) Dionysios again. His fleet raids 'Tyrrhenia' (Etruria) and plunders a temple of Leukothea (*OCD* 737–8 Ino-Leucothea; this one was at Pyrgi, *OCD* 1244–5). On top of the communal booty, he duplicitously commandeers, half at a time, what the individual sailors had taken. Date: 384 (Diod.Sic. 15.143–4).

21a. (1350a6–11) The Mendeans (*OCD* 931 Mende, *IACP* no.584). As normal policy they used to levy harbour-dues etc. but simply register, without collecting, the taxes on land and houses; these arrears could then be collected *in extremis*. Date: indeterminable.

21b. (1350a11–15) The Mendeans again. At war with Olynthos (*OCD* 1038, *IACP* no.588) and needing funds, they nationalize slave-holdings (all bar two slaves per household) and sell them. Date: before 348, the Macedonian demolition of Olynthos (Diod.Sic. 16.53.3, etc.).

22. (1350a16–22) Kallistratos of Aphidna (*LGPN* s.v. no.50, *OCD* 268 Callistratus (2), *APF* 277–82). He doubles—from twenty to forty *talanta*—the harbour-dues 'in Macedonia' by significantly reducing the level of sureties demanded from those who wanted to collect them. Date: between 361 (when Kallistratos lost an impeachment-trial and chose exile over the death-penalty) and his unauthorized return, arrest, and execution some years later. See Hansen (1975) 94–5 no.87.

23a. (1350a23–30) Timotheos of Anaphlystos (*LGPN* s.v. no.32, *OCD* Timotheus (2), *APF* 506–12). During his campaign against Olynthos (see **21b**) he runs out of silver currency and issues a bronze one. To meet the troops' complaints he promises that the traders and retailers will accept it. The latter, in turn, are reassured by an instruction to use the bronze coins to buy up commodities; any left over he will exchange for silver. Date: 364/3 (Hammond & Griffith (1979) 186–7).

23b. (1350a30–b4) Timotheos again. During his campaign against Kerkyra (*OCD* 373–4 Corcyra, *IACP* no.123) he is confronted by unpaid, mutinous troops. He pacifies them by saying that pay is coming; meanwhile the three months' worth of grain-rations they already have will be free. Date: 375 (*Hell.*5.4.64–6).

23c. (1350b4–15) Timotheos again. During his siege of Samos (*OCD* 1313–14, *IACP* nos.864–5) he acquires money to pay his troops by selling the besieged Samians their own crops. (Further detail omitted here.) Date: 366–365 (Shipley (1987) 138–40).

24a. (1350b16–30) Datames (*OCD* 415), satrap of Kappadokia. Able to feed but not to pay his mercenaries, he announces that there is plenty of money in a particular stronghold of his. Reaching the place first, he places silver plate on display. The troops cheer up, until told that they must take it to Amisos (*OCD* 70, *IACP* no.712)—many winter-days' journey away—for minting. Date: indeterminable within Datames' period of rule, *c.* 384–362. ('*c.* 370' in *IACP* 954 has no discernible basis.)

24b. (1350b30–2) Datames again. As standing policy, he exercises personal, monopoly control of all the craftsmen in his army and all the retailers accompanying it. Date: see **24a.**

25 (1350b33–51a17) Chabrias of Aixone (*LGPN* s.v. no.2, *OCD* 302–3, *APF* 560–1). When his employer Tachos, king of Egypt, needed funds for a planned expedition, Chabrias has plenty of advice for him. (*i*) Announce the closure of some temples and the dismissal of many of their priests; this prompts money from the latter, a tenth of which is remitted to them, the rest kept. (*ii*) Impose *eisphora*-style levies and (increased?) taxes on buying and selling etc. (*iii*) Requisition all un-coined gold and silver, with compensation out of taxes, via the provincial governors. See generally Ruzicka (2012) 141–2. Date: 362/1 (Diod.Sic. 15.92.3).

26. (1351a18–23) Iphikrates of Rhamnous (*LGPN* s.v. no.4, *OCD* 743, *APF* 248–52). When money for troops is needed by king Kotys (**27**), Iphikrates advises him to order his subjects to grow an extra plot of grain; when sold, this realizes the necessary cash. Date: indeterminable within the period from the early 380s to the late 360s, i.e. that of Iphikrates' association with Kotys, who became his brother-in-law (so *APF* 249, now orthodox, on *kêdestês* in Demosth. 23.129; not son-in-law). The advice need not have been given in person.

27. (1351a24–32) Kotys (I), king of Thrake (see under **26**, and in the Comm. on 3.11). He asks the Perinthians (*OCD* 1107, *IACP* no.678) for an army-raising loan. They refuse, but do agree to his follow-up request, for garrison troops. These he holds hostage until the loan is forthcoming. Date: mid-360s (*CAH* 6.464).

28. (1351a33–7) Mentor (*OCD* 934–5 s.v. no.2) of Rhodes, mercenary leader in Persian service. After capturing Hermias (*OCD* 670 s.v. no.1), tyrant of Atarneus in Mysia, and his strongholds, he leaves their commanders in post. This emboldens them to recover their hidden or exported wealth, whereupon he arrests them and seizes it. Date: 341 (*CAH* 6.94).

29a. (1351b1–6) Memnon (*OCD* 928–9 s.v. no.2) of Rhodes; brother of **28.** After capturing Lampsakos (see **7**) he extracts money from the inhabitants by first levying it from the rich, who are to recoup from the others; then, when that process happens, he commandeers the rest also (as a fixed-term loan). Date: 340s (*IACP* 987).

29b. (1351b6–11) Memnon again. On another occasion he requests contributions from 'the citizens' (of Lampsakos), to be reimbursed from the city's revenues. But when the latter come in, he takes them too—albeit repaying the lenders, later, with interest. Date: see **29a**.

29c. (1351b11–15) Memnon again. His mercenary troops receive no pay or rations for six days each year (viz., one day deducted in each of the six so-called 'hollow', twenty-nine-day months). Date: indeterminable. (NB: Memnon's career extended well before and also well after the Lampsakos period of **29a–b**; he died in 333.)

29d. (1351b15–19) Memnon again. He changes from a system of grain-rations on the second day of every month to one where each month the day is progressively postposed. Date: indeterminable (cf. under **29c**).

30a. (1351b19–28) Charidemos of Oreos in Euboia, later a naturalized Athenian, mercenary general (*OCD* 305–6, *APF* 570–2, *AO* no.637). His small fiefdom in 'Aiolis' (= Troas, *OCD* 1511) being menaced by Artabazos (satrap of Hellespontine Phrygia), he needs money to pay his troops but the citizens' contributions are inadequate. He selects the wealthiest city, from which valuables are to be conducted to safety elsewhere, but he himself appropriates most of them. Date: *c*.360 (Pritchett (1971–1991) 2.85).

30b. (1351b28–35) Charidemos again. He prohibits, on pain of a fine, the keeping of arms in private houses in his cities but does not enforce this until enough people are disregarding it; then there are searches, and fines. Date: see **30**a.

31. (1351b36–52a8) 'A certain Philoxenos', satrap of Karia. He announces a Dionysia festival (presumably in a particular city or cities). Potential liturgists are reluctant to come forward, but do privately agree to pay an even larger sum to avoid serving (cf. **4c**). The ploy is repeated with a second group. Date: 323 (Bosworth (1988) 242, 256–7).

32. (1352a9–15) Euaises(?) the Syrian, satrap of Egypt. After preventing a threatened rebellion among his local officials by arresting and hanging them, he misinforms their relatives that he has imprisoned them. Payment is made to secure release—of their corpses. Date: indeterminable.

33a. (1352a16–23) Kleomenes (*OCD* 332 s.v. Cleomenes (3), satrap of Egypt; in fact a financial administrator). During a scarcity of grain (but an outright famine elsewhere) he first puts a stop to its export altogether (cf. Demosth. 56.7, and **33e** below), then allows it but imposes a heavy duty. Date: 332–323.

33b. (1352a23–28) Kleomenes again. After one of his attendants is taken by a crocodile, considered sacred, he threatens a cull but accepts all the priests' gold instead. Date: see **33a**.

33c. (1352a28–b4) Kleomenes again. Ordered by Alexander to move the market of Kanopos along the coast to a city being settled near Pharos island (*OCD* 60, s.v. Alexandria (1)), he accepts money from priests and residents not to do this, but afterwards demands even more. Date: see **33a**.

33d. (1352b4–14) Kleomenes again. On one occasion, by tricking the parties involved, he lowers the price of a transaction made for him by a subordinate. Date: see **33a**.

33e. (1352b14–20) Kleomenes again. At a time when the market-price of grain is ten drachmas a measure he approaches the growers directly, buys up all they have, and sells it for thirty-two. Date: see **33a**.

33f. (1352b20–5) Kleomenes again. (Essentially a repetition of **25**(i), q.v. Date, if genuine: see **33a**.

34a. (1352b26–33) Antimenes of Rhodes, *hêmiolios* (apparently a financial official; cf. *SEG* 47.1745, line 44, with Jonnes & Ricl (1997) 35–6) at Babylon. He revives an ancient 10% tax on imports. Date: 324–323 (Bosworth (1988) 243).

34b. (1352b33–53a4) Antimenes again. He introduces a slave-registration scheme. Eight drachmas annually, paid to him, insures the owners of runaway slaves their stated value; but it is local governors who must either catch the slaves or reimburse the owners. Date: see **34a**.

35. (1353a5–14) Ophel(l)as of Olynthos, official in Alexander's administration of Egypt. The man he appoints to superintend the revenues of the Athribite nome (in Upper Egypt) is unpopular with other officials, who offer to pay more if he is removed. They do so, but their bugbear stays in post. Date: probably 324–323 (Berve no.599).

36. (1353a15–18) Pythokles of Athens, otherwise unidentifiable (though see below). He proposes to his fellow-citizens that (all) lead from the Laureion mines be bought from the private individuals concerned, at the current price of two drachmas (per unit), and sold at six. Date: in context here perhaps the 320s; alternatively it is this item, not **37**, which begins the miscellaneous addenda to the catalogue. (According to Brodersen (2017) 59, **37–41** are given 'without repeating the details on the tricksters', but in fact that is only certain for **37–39** and **41**, i.e. addenda *to specific entries*.)

37. (1353a19–23) Chabrias addendum (to **25**). Having levied crews for twice as many ships as king Tachos needs, he tells the superfluous men either to serve in place of the others or to provide two months' rations; they choose the latter. Date: see **25**.

38. (1353a24–8) Antimenes addendum (to **34a–b**). Enforcing a law that requires provincial governors to keep the storehouses along royal roads replenished, he sells them what is required. Date: see **34a**.

39. (1353b1–7) Kleomenes addendum (to **33a–f**). He uses further ploys to delay or withhold the troops' monthly pay. Date: see **33a**.

40. (1353b8–19) 'Stabelbios' (as transmitted, but it should be Itabelis, both here and in *Anab*.7.8.15: see Sekunda (1989)), satrap of the Mysians. Lacking pay for his troops, he manoeuvres their officers into dismissing them. Date: *c.* 400.

41. (1353b20–7) Dionysios addendum (to **20a–i**). He has a general policy of appropriating anything of gold or silver (vessels and statue-decoration) from the temples. Date: probably 406–386 (see under **20a**).

* * * *

The material's arrangement is haphazard. This fact appears at its most obvious in the simple tacking-on of **37–41**—perhaps **36** too—as afterthoughts; but on closer inspection (and by adducing external evidence) there are departures from what seems to begin as an attempt at a rough-and-ready chronological order. Such an order is disrupted probably by (e.g.) the early placement of

3a–d (= Austin & Vidal-Naquet (1977) 303–7 no.91A) and certainly by the position of **9**; also by the 'internal' ordering of **23a–c** (= Austin & Vidal-Naquet (1977) 303–7 no.91B).

That apart, the most striking facet of this body of material is its focus on named individuals. This begs obvious comparison with the biography-driven format of Polyaenus' *Stratêgêmata*, Krentz & Wheeler (1994). There, the required cleverness is often displayed in money-raising. Indeed there is a degree of overlap between the two collections in several instances (numbers not in bold are to Polyaenus): so with **4a** (q.v. above), **13a** (7.23.1), **20d** (5.2.19), **20i** (5.2.21), **23a** (3.10.1 & 14), **23c** (3.10.10), **24a** (7.21.1), **25** (3.11.5), and **26** (7.32, but attributed there to Seuthes, a *hyparchos* of Kotys' son and successor Kersebleptes). Nevertheless, from the perspective of a comparison with *Poroi*, individuals and collectivities could serve illustrative purposes equally well as each other, provided their ideas are put forward within the same general circumstances. And that in essence means, in the terms formulated by Gauthier 7–19, *poroi* (and *prosodoi*) aimed not at (*a*) escaping a mere cashflow problem, such as paying impatient mercenaries or an insistent overlord, but at (*b*) bringing about a step-change in the revenue-generating performance of the entity or entities concerned; cf. Gauthier 13 with n.13 (citing our **22**, Kallistratos in Macedonia, as a prime example of *b*).

Of course, this distinction is not always in practice one of chalk vs. cheese. Rather, the data present themselves as more of a continuum, with clear-cut ends and a blurred centre. But given that X.'s own positioning at the *b*-extreme is a constant (Jansen (2007) 737–8), against which to measure everything else, some observations do suggest themselves. I will confine myself, in brief, to four.

(1) Wheeler (2010) 20 speculates that *Poroi* (and Aeneas' *Poristikê*) may have been actual inspirations for [Aristotle]. Seductive at first sight, the idea soon encounters an obstacle: X.'s sheer decency and openness. (Trickery against a military opponent was another matter altogether. On X. in that regard—the writer who makes the first extant mention of *stratêgêmata* (*Mem*.3.5.22)—see Wheeler (1988) 31, 32, 39, 40.) Not for X. the cynic's repertoire of deception and guile which is presented to readers of [Aristotle] (albeit least in the entries concerning whole poleis: Isager (1988) 79–81). Instead of schemes which, as often as not, leave some parties feeling disadvantaged and foolish, X. is the advocate of success through goodwill (*eunoia*) and solicitousness (*epimeleia*) on every level.

(2) X. makes no suggestions on a topic which appears throughout [Aristotle]: altering the currency, by one means or another. (See **4b**, **16b**, **20c**, **20h**, **23a**.) His reason(s) can only be surmised. One might be that this was not a field in which he could lay claim to any expertise. But also, again, the element of sleight-of-hand may have been distasteful to him, and

the association (so often) with short-term expediency. Athenians of his generation could remember the emergency, silver-plated bronze coins which the city had resorted to during the final, desperate years of the Peloponnesian War (and had not withdrawn until 393): Head (1911) 373; Kroll (1976); Dover (1993) 281–2; Figueira (1998) 500–3. Ironically, adjusting the currency in (as Kroll (2011a) 231 emphasizes) an entirely legitimate manner was a step which the Athenians did think necessary, and duly took, in the immediate post-*Poroi* years: see Kroll (2011).

(3) As regards other poleis, the Byzantium dossier (**3a–d**) is not only the fullest of its kind in the collection but does demand direct comparison with *Poroi* and with Athens. Assuming its assertions are true, whatever their date or dates, the striking point is the Byzantines' willingness to circumvent some very fundamental pillars of their constitution and laws in the name of revenue-raising. Landownership rights and even citizenship itself have their price-tickets (more direct and uncomplicated than the Athenians'—and X.'s—mechanisms involving euergetism and the recognition of perceived merit).

(4) Finally: no reader of *Poroi* Chap.4 can fail to be brought up short by [Aristotle's] item **36**, unattested elsewhere. As noted earlier, its position in the dossier immediately before the clear run of unchronological addenda is (or should be) a caveat against placing it in the 320s, purely on the basis of context. It might well, nevertheless, belong there or thereabouts, if (as Boeckh (1886) 42 deemed beyond doubt) this 'Pythokles' is the obvious bearer of that rather commonplace name. Of the twenty or so theoretical possibilities in *LGPN*, there is only one (I believe) who is known ever to have addressed the assembly: no.17. Pythokles (II) Pythodorou from Kedoi was 'active in public affairs after 343 as an adversary of Demosthenes' (*APF* 485), as we see in two of the latter's speeches (Demosth. 18.285, 19.225 & 314; Bosworth (1988) 213), and, later, so closely associated with Phokion (*LGPN* s.v. no.2, *OCD* 1139, *APF* 559–60) as to share his witch-hunt execution in 318 (Plut. *Phok.*35.5; Tritle (1988) 106–7; Habicht (1997) 48–9). Rich enough to be liable for trierarchies, Pythokles has no known link with the mines, but that does not reduce any likelihood that he made this proposal about Laureion's lead—indeed arguably the reverse, if he himself was not one of the *idiôtai* who would have been affected. I say 'would have been' on the assumption—it can be no more—that the plan was not adopted. The opposite view is taken, without discussion, by Gabrielsen (2011) 228 n.38. (Boeckh had been non-committal on all three occasions he mentions the matter.) We need not, though, say 'adversely affected', because the producers would continue, it is stated, to receive the accustomed price. The mark-up to six drachmas (as Boeckh realized) is for the export market. The idea seems a good one, and true to the spirit of *Poroi*.

Bibliography

Abraldes, A. M. (1996) *Pentelethen: The Export of Pentelic Marble and its Use in Architectural and Epigraphical Monuments*, 2 volumes (Diss. Berkeley).

Accame, S. (1941) *La lega ateniese del secolo IV a.C.* (Rome: Angelo Signorelli).

Acton, P. (2014) *Poiesis: Manufacturing in Classical Athens* (Oxford: Oxford University Press).

Adak, M. (2003) *Metöken als Wohltäter Athens. Untersuchungen zum sozialen Austausch zwischen ortsansässigen Fremden und der Bürgergemeinde in klassischer und hellenistischer Zeit (ca. 500–150 v. Chr.)* (Munich: Herbert Utz).

Ager, S. L. (1996) *Interstate Arbitrations in the Greek World, 337–90 BC* (Berkeley and Los Angeles: University of California Press).

Akrigg, B. (2015) 'Metics in Athens', in Taylor and Vlassopoulos (2015) 155–76.

Anderson, J. K. (1974) *Xenophon* (London: Duckworth).

Andreades, A. M. (1933) *A History of Greek Public Finance*, translated and enlarged edition (Cambridge, MA: Harvard University Press).

Aperghis, G. G. (1997–1998) 'A reassessment of the Laurion mining lease records', *BICS* 42: 1–20.

Aperghis, G. G. (2004) *The Seleukid Royal Economy: The Finances and Financial Administration of the Seleukid Empire* (Cambridge: Cambridge University Press).

Archibald, Z. H. (1998) *The Odrysian Kingdom of Thrace: Orpheus Unmasked* (Oxford: Oxford University Press).

Ardaillon, E. (1897) *Les mines du Laurion dans l'Antiquité* (Paris: Fontemoing).

Arnaoutoglou, I. (1998) *Ancient Greek Laws: A Sourcebook* (London and New York: Routledge).

Austin, M. M. (2006) *The Hellenistic World from Alexander to the Roman Conquest: A Selection of Ancient Sources in Translation*, 2nd edition (Cambridge: Cambridge University Press).

Austin, M. M. and Vidal-Naquet, P. (1977) *Economic and Social History of Ancient Greece: An Introduction* (London: Batsford).

Azoulay, V. (2004) *Xénophon et les grâces du pouvoir. De la charis au charisme* (Paris: Publications de la Sorbonne).

Azoulay, V. and Ismard, P. (2011) *Clisthène et Lycurgue d'Athènes: autour du politique dans la cité classique* (Paris: Publications de la Sorbonne).

Badian, E. (2004) 'Xenophon the Athenian', in Tuplin (2004): 33–53.

Bakewell, G. W. (2013) *Aeschylus's* Suppliant Women: *The Tragedy of Immigration* (Madison: University of Wisconsin Press).

Ball, P. (2006) *The Devil's Doctor: Paracelsus and the World of Renaissance Magic and Science* (London: Heinemann).

Barker, E. (1946) *The Politics of Aristotle*, translated with an introduction, notes, and appendices (Oxford: Oxford University Press).
Bauslaugh, R. A. (1991) *The Concept of Neutrality in Classical Greece* (Berkeley and Los Angeles: University of California Press).
Beloch, K. J. (1922) *Griechische Geschichte*, vol. III.1, 2nd edition (Berlin and Leipzig: De Gruyter).
Beresford, J. (2013) *The Ancient Sailing Season* (Leiden: Brill).
Berve, H. (1926) *Das Alexanderreich auf prosopographischer Grundlage*, 2 volumes (Munich: C. H. Beck).
Bettalli, M. (1990) *La difesa di una città assediata* (Pisa: ETS Editrice).
Bissa, E. (2009) *Governmental Intervention in Foreign Trade in Archaic and Classical Greece* (Leiden and Boston: Brill).
Blackman, D. J., Rankov, N. B., and others (2014) *Shipsheds of the Ancient Mediterranean* (Cambridge: Cambridge University Press).
Bloch, D. (2004) 'The date of Xenophon's *Poroi*', *C&M* 55: 5–16.
Blok, J. (2010) 'Deme accounts and the meaning of *hosios*: money in fifth-century Athens', *Mnemosyne* 63: 61–93.
Blok, J. (2017) *Citizenship in Classical Athens* (Cambridge: Cambridge University Press).
Bodei Giglioni, G. (1970–1971) 'Senofonte, *De Vectigalibus* IV 43–44', *Studi Classici e Orientali* 19–20: 465–70.
Boeckh, A. (1886) *Die Staatshaushaltung der Athener,* I, 3rd edition (with notes by M. Fraenkel) (Berlin: G. Reimer).
Bogaert, R. (1968) *Banques et banquiers dans les cités grecques* (Leiden: A. W. Sijthoff).
Bonnechere, P. (2013) 'Oracles et mentalités grecques: la confirmation d'un oracle par une seconde consultation au même sanctuaire', *Kernos* 26: 73–94.
Bosworth, A .B. (1988) *Conquest and Empire: The Reign of Alexander the Great* (Cambridge: Cambridge University Press).
Bowden, H. (2004) 'Xenophon and the scientific study of religion', in Tuplin (2004): 229–46.
Bowden, H. (2005) *Classical Athens and the Delphic Oracle: Divination and Democracy*. Cambridge: Cambridge University Press).
Braund, D. C. (1994) 'The luxuries of Athenian democracy', *G&R* 41: 41–8.
Breitenbach, H. R. (1967) 'Xenophon', in *RE* 9.A.2: 1569–928.
Bresson, A. (2000) *La cité marchande* (Bordeaux: Editions Ausonius).
Bresson, A. (2003) 'Merchants and politics in ancient Greece: social and economic aspects', in C. Zaccagnini, ed., *Mercanti e politica nel mondo antico*, 139–64 (Rome: 'L'Erma' di Bretschneider)
Bresson, A. (2007–2008) *L'économie de la Grèce des cités (fin VIe–Ier siècle a.C.). I: les structures et la production* (2007). *II: les espaces de l'échange* (2008) (Paris: Armand Colin).

Bresson, A. (2016) *The Making of the Ancient Greek Economy: Institutions, Markets, and Growth in the City-states*, translated by Steven Rendall (Princeton: Princeton University Press).
Brinkmann, A. (1912) 'Zu Xenophons *Poroi*', *RhM* 67: 135–7.
Brodersen, K. (2008) 'Nützliche Forschung: ps.-Aristoteles' *Oikonomika* II und die Haushalte griechischer Poleis', in F. Burrer and H. Müller, eds., *Kriegskosten und Kriegsfinanzierung in der Antike*, 106–27 (Darmstadt: Wissenschaftliche Buchgesellschaft).
Brodersen, K. (2010) 'Aegean Greece', in K. H. Kinzl, ed., *A Companion to the Classical Greek World*, 99–114 (Malden and Oxford: Wiley-Blackwell).
Brodersen, K. (2017) 'Poleis on the brink: violence and Greek public finances in ps.-Aristotle's *Oikonomika II*', in M. Champion and L. O'Sullivan, eds., *Cultural Perceptions of Violence in the Hellenistic World*, 58–77 (Abingdon and New York: Routledge).
Brun, P. (1983) *Eisphora—Syntaxis—Stratiotika. Recherches sur les finances militaires d'Athènes au IVe siècle av. J.-C.* (Paris: Les Belles Lettres).
Brun, P. (2003) 'Lycurgue d'Athènes', in G. Lachenaud and D. Longrée, eds., *Grecs et Romains aux prises avec l'histoire: représentations, récits et idéologie*, I: 493–507 (Rennes: Presses Universitaires).
Brun, P. (2005) 'Lycurgue d'Athènes: un législateur?', in P. Sineux, ed., *Le législateur et la loi dans l'Antiquité*, 187–99 (Caen: Presses Universitaires).
Buckler, J. (1989) *Philip II and the Sacred War* (Leiden: Brill).
Bugh, G. R. (1988) *The Horsemen of Athens* (Princeton: Princeton University Press).
Bultrighini, I. (2015) *Demi attici della paralia* (Lanciano: Carabba).
Burford, A. (1969) *The Greek Temple Builders at Epidaurus* (Liverpool: Liverpool University Press).
Burford, A. (1972) *Craftsmen in Greek and Roman Society* (London: Thames & Hudson).
Burke, E. M. (1984) 'Eubulus, Olynthus and Euboea', *TAPhA* 114: 111–20.
Burke, E. M. (1985) 'Lycurgan finances', *GRBS* 26: 251–64.
Burkert, W. (1985) *Greek Religion: Archaic and Classical*, translated by John Raffan (Cambridge, MA: Harvard University Press).
Burstein, S. M. (1974) *Outpost of Hellenism: The Emergence of Heraclea on the Black Sea* (Berkeley and Los Angeles: University of California Press).
Burstein, S. M. (1985) *The Hellenistic Age from the Battle of Ipsos to the death of Kleopatra VII* (Translated Documents of Greece and Rome 3) (Cambridge: Cambridge University Press).
Busolt, G. (1874) *Der zweite athenische Bund* (Leipzig: Teubner).
Calhoun, G. M. (1931) 'Ancient Athenian mining', *JEBH* 3: 333–61.
Camp, J. M. (1974) 'Proxenia for Sopatros of Akragas', *Hesperia* 43: 322–4.
Cargill, J. (1981) *The Second Athenian League: Empire or Free Alliance?* (Berkeley and Los Angeles: University of California Press).

Cargill, J. (1995) *Athenian Settlements of the Fourth Century* BC (Leiden: Brill).
Carter, L. B. (1986) *The Quiet Athenian* (Oxford: Oxford University Press).
Cartledge, P. A. (1987) *Agesilaos and the Crisis of Sparta* (London: Duckworth).
Cartledge, P. A. and Spawforth, A. J. S. (1989) *Hellenistic and Roman Sparta: A Tale of Two Cities* (London and New York: Routledge).
Casson, L. (1991) *The Ancient Mariners: Seafarers and Sea Fighters of the Mediterranean in Ancient Times*, 2nd edition (Princeton: Princeton University Press).
Casson, L. (1995) *Ships and Seamanship in the Ancient World* (Baltimore: Johns Hopkins University Press).
Cautadella, M. R. (1984) 'Per la datazione dei *Poroi*: guerre ed eisphorai', *Sileno* 10: 147–55.
Cawkwell, G. L. (1963) 'Eubulus', *JHS* 83: 47–67. [Reprinted as Cawkwell (2011) chap.15.]
Cawkwell, G. L. (1984) 'Athenian naval power in the fourth century', *CQ* 34: 334–5. [Reprinted as Cawkwell (2011) chap.17.]
Cawkwell, G. L. (2011) *Cyrene to Chaeronea: Selected Essays on Ancient Greek History* (Oxford and New York: Oxford University Press).
Cecchet, L. (2015) *Poverty in Athenian Public Discourse: From the Eve of the Peloponnesian War to the Rise of Macedonia* (Stuttgart: Steiner).
Clerc, M. (1893) *Les métèques athéniens* (Paris: Thorin).
Cohen, E. E. (1973) *Ancient Athenian Maritime Courts* (Princeton: Princeton University Press).
Cohen, E. E. (1992) *Athenian Economy and Society: A Banking Perspective* (Princeton: Princeton University Press).
Cohen, E. E. (2000) *The Athenian Nation* (Princeton: Princeton University Press).
Cohen, E. E. (2008) 'The elasticity of the money-supply at Athens', in W. V. Harris, ed., *The Monetary Systems of the Greeks and Romans*, 66–83 (Oxford: Oxford University Press).
Connor, W. R. (1988) ' "Sacred" and "secular": *hiera kai hosia* and the classical Athenian concept of the state', *AncSoc* 19: 161–88.
Conophagos, C. (1980) *Le Laurium antique* (Athens: Ekdotike Hellados).
Constantakopoulou, C. (2007) *The Dance of the Islands: Insularity, Networks, the Athenian Empire, and the Aegean World* (Oxford: Oxford University Press).
Conwell, D. H. (2008) *Connecting a City to the Sea: The History of the Athenian Long Walls* (Leiden and Boston: Brill).
Cook, B. L. (2009) 'Athenian terms of civic praise in the 330s: Aeschines vs. Demosthenes', *GRBS* 49: 31–52.
Crawford, M. H. (1982) '*Sidareoi* at Byzantium', *Athenaeum* 60: 276.
Crawford, M. H. and Whitehead, D. (1983) *Archaic and Classical Greece: A Selection of Ancient Sources in Translation* (Cambridge: Cambridge University Press).

Crosby, M. (1950) 'The leases of the Laureion mines', *Hesperia* 19: 189–312.

Crowley, J. (2012) *The Psychology of the Athenian Hoplite: The Culture of Combat in Classical Athens* (Cambridge: Cambridge University Press).

Cunningham, C. J. K. (1967) 'The silver mines of Laureion', *G&R* 14: 145–56.

Dalby, A. (2002) *Dangerous Tastes: The Story of Spices* (Berkeley and Los Angeles: University of California Press).

Daly, K. F. (2007) 'Two inscriptions from the Athenian Agora', *Hesperia* 76: 539–54.

Daniel, R. (2007) '*Oikopeda* in Xenophon, Diodorus Siculus and elsewhere', *ZPE* 159: 61–9.

Davidson, J. (1990) 'Isocrates against imperialism: an analysis of the *De Pace*', *Historia* 39: 20–36.

Davies, J. K. (1981) *Wealth and the Power of Wealth in Classical Athens* (New York: Arno Press).

Davies, J. K. (1993) *Democracy and Classical Greece*, 2nd edition (London: Fontana).

Davis, G. (2014) 'Mining money in late archaic Athens', *Historia* 63: 257–77.

Delebecque, E. (1957) *Essai sur la vie de Xénophon* (Paris: C. Klincksieck).

De Martinis, L. (2013) 'Licurgo tra tradizione e innovazione', *Nuova Secondaria* 8: 24–54.

Demetriou, D. (2012) *Negotiating Identity in the Ancient Mediterranean: The Archaic and Classical Multi-ethnic Emporia* (Cambridge: Cambridge University Press).

Diehl, C. (1888) *Quo tempore qua mente scriptus sit libellus qui* Poroi *inscribitur* (Paris: Berger-Levrault).

Diggle, J. (2004) *Theophrastus*, Characters, edited with an introduction, translation and commentary (Cambridge: Cambridge University Press).

Diller, A. (1937) *Race Mixture among the Greeks before Alexander* (Urbana: University of Illinois Press).

Dillery, J. (1993) 'Xenophon's *Poroi* and Athenian imperialism', *Historia* 42: 1–11.

Dillery, J. (1995) *Xenophon and the History of His Times* (London and New York: Routledge).

Dillery, J. (2017) 'Xenophon: the small works', in Flower (2017): 195–219.

Domingo Gygax, M. (2016) *Benefaction and Rewards in the Ancient Greek City: The Origins of Euergetism* (Cambridge: Cambridge University Press).

Dorion, L.-A. (2017) 'Xenophon and Greek philosophy', in Flower (2017): 37–56.

Dover, K. J. (1974) *Greek Popular Morality in the Time of Plato and Aristotle* (Oxford: Blackwell). [Reprinted Indianapolis: Hackett, 1994.]

Dover, K. J. (1993) *Aristophanes:* Frogs, edited with introduction and commentary (Oxford: Oxford University Press).

Duncan-Jones, R. P. (1980) 'Metic numbers in Periclean Athens', *Chiron* 10: 101–9.

Dušanič, S. (1982) 'Plato's Atlantis', *L'Antiquité Classique* 51: 25–52.

Edwards, M. J. (1994) *The Attic Orators* (Bristol: Bristol Classical Press).
Eidinow, E. (2007) *Oracles, Curses, and Risk among the Ancient Greeks* (Oxford: Oxford University Press).
Eliot, C. W. J. (1962) *Coastal Demes of Attika: A Study in the Policy of Kleisthenes* (Toronto: University of Toronto Press).
Ellis Jones, J. (1982) 'The Laureion silver mines: a review of recent researches and results', *G&R* 29: 169–83.
Engelmann, H. (1977) 'Ps.-Aristoteles über Prozesse in Phokaia', *ZPE* 24: 226.
Engen, D. T. (2010) *Honor and Profit: Athenian Trade Policy and the Economy and Society of Greece, 415–307 BCE* (Ann Arbor: University of Michigan Press).
Fachard, S. and Pirisino, D. (2015) 'Routes out of Attica', in M. M. Miles, ed., *Autopsy in Athens: Recent Archaeological Research on Athens and Attica*, 139–53 (Oxford: Oxbow Books).
Faraguna, M. (1992) *Atene nell' età di Alessandro: problemi politici, economici, finanziari* (Rome: Accademia Nazionale dei Lincei).
Faraguna, M. (2011) 'Lykourgan Athens?', in Azoulay and Ismard (2011): 67–88.
Farrell, C. A. (2012) *Xenophon in Context: Advising Athens and Democracy* (Diss. KCL).
Farrell, C. A. (2016) 'Xenophon *Poroi* 5: securing a "more just" Athenian hegemony', *Polis* 33: 331–55.
Fawcett, P. W. (2006) *Athenian Taxation from the Pisistratids to Lycurgus, 550–325 BC* (Diss. Durham. Online at http://etheses.dur.ac.uk).
Fawcett, P. W. (2016) '"When I squeeze you with *eisphorai*": taxes and tax policy in classical Athens', *Hesperia* 85: 153–99.
Ferrario, S. B. (2017) 'Xenophon and Greek political thought', in Flower (2017): 57–83.
Figueira, T. J. (1998) *The Power of Money: Coinage and Politics in the Athenian Empire* (Philadelphia: University of Pennsylvania Press).
Figueira, T. J. (2012) 'Economic thought and economic fact in the works of Xenophon', in Tuplin and Hobden (2012): 514–31.
Finley, M. I. (1952) *Studies in Land and Credit in Ancient Athens 500–200 BC: The* horos-*inscriptions* (New Brunswick: Rutgers University Press). [Reprinted New York: Arno Press, 1973.]
Finley, M. I. (1985) *The Ancient Economy*, 2nd edition (London: Hogarth Press).
Fisher, N. R. E. (1995) *Slavery in Classical Greece*, reprinted with corrections (Bristol: Bristol Classical Press).
Fisher, N. R. E. (1998) 'Gymnasia and the democratic values of leisure', in P. A. Cartledge, P. C. Millett, and S. Von Reden, eds., *Kosmos: Essays in Order, Conflict and Community in Classical Athens*, 84–104 (Cambridge: Cambridge University Press).
Fisher, N. R. E. (2001) *Aeschines,* Against Timarchos, translated with introduction and commentary (Oxford: Oxford University Press).

Flower, M. A. (1994) *Theopompus of Chios: History and Rhetoric in the Fourth Century BC* (Oxford: Oxford University Press).

Flower, M. A. (2016) 'Piety in Xenophon's theory of leadership', in R. F. Buxton, ed., *Aspects of Leadership in Xenophon*, 85–119 (Newcastle: Histos).

Flower, M. A., ed. (2017) *The Cambridge Companion to Xenophon* (Cambridge: Cambridge University Press).

Fontenrose, J. (1978) *The Delphic Oracle: Its Responses and Operations* (Berkeley and Los Angeles: University of California Press).

Fornara, C. W. (1983) *Archaic Times to the End of the Peloponnesian War* (Translated Documents of Greece and Rome, 1), 2nd edition (Cambridge: Cambridge University Press).

French, A. (1964) *The Growth of the Athenian Economy* (London: Routledge & Kegan Paul).

Gabrielsen, V. (1981) *Remuneration of State Officials in Fourth-century BC Athens* (Odense: Odense University Press).

Gabrielsen, V. (1994) *Financing the Athenian Fleet: Public Taxation and Social Relations* (Baltimore and London: Johns Hopkins University Press).

Gabrielsen, V. (2007) 'Trade and tribute: Byzantion and the Black Sea straits', in V. Gabrielsen and J. Lund, eds., *The Black Sea in Antiquity: Regional and Interregional Economic Exchanges*, 287–324 (Aarhus: Aarhus University Press).

Gabrielsen, V. (2011) 'Profitable partnerships: monopolies, traders, kings, and cities', in Z. H. Archibald, J. K. Davies, and V. Gabrielsen, eds., *The Economies of Hellenistic Societies, Third to First Centuries BC*, 216–50 (Oxford: Oxford University Press).

Garlan, Y. (1972) 'Les esclaves grecs en temps de guerre', in *Actes du colloque d'histoire sociale de 1970 à Besançon*, 29–62 (Paris: Presses Universitaires de Franche-Comté).

Garlan, Y. (1988) *Slavery in Ancient Greece*, revised and expanded edition, translated by J. Lloyd (Ithaca and London: Cornell University Press).

Garland, R. (1990) 'Priests and power in classical Athens', in M. Beard and J. North, eds., *Pagan Priests*, 73–91. Ithaca: Cornell University Press and London: Duckworth).

Garland, R. (1994) *Religion and the Greeks* (Bristol: Bristol Classical Press).

Garland, R. (2001) *The Piraeus*, 2nd edition (London: Duckworth).

Garland, R. (2014) *Wandering Greeks: The Ancient Greek Diaspora from the Age of Homer to the Death of Alexander the Great* (Princeton: Princeton University Press).

Garnsey, P. D. A. (1988) *Famine and Food Supply in the Graeco-Roman World* (Cambridge: Cambridge University Press).

Gauthier, P. (1972) *SYMBOLA. Les étrangers et la justice dans les cités grecques* (Nancy: Université de Nancy).

Gauthier, P. (1975) 'Les ports d' l'Empire et l'*Agora* athénienne: à propos du "Décret Mégarien"', *Historia* 24: 498–503.

Gauthier, P. (1984 [2010]) 'Le programme de Xénophon dans les *Poroi*', *RPh* 58: 181–99. [2010 English version, 'Xenophon's programme in the *Poroi*', which I cite, in V. J. Gray, ed., *Oxford Readings in Classical Studies: Xenophon*, chap.4 (Oxford: Oxford University Press).]

Gehrke, H. J. (1985) *Stasis: Untersuchungen zu den inneren Kriegen in in den griechischen Staaten des 5. Und 4. Jahrhunderts v.Chr.* (Munich: C. H. Beck).

Gernet, L. (1955) *Droit et société dans la grèce ancienne* (Paris: Receuil Sirey).

Gillis, D. (1970) 'The structure of arguments in Isocrates' *De pace*', *Philologus* 114: 195–210.

Glazebrook, A. (2011) '*Porneion*: prostitution in Athenian civic space', in Glazebrook and Henry (2011): 34–59.

Glazebrook, A. and Henry, M. M., eds. (2011) *Greek Prostitutes in the Ancient Mediterranean, 800 BCE–200 CE* (Madison: University of Wisconsin Press).

Godin, B. (2015) *Innovation Contested: The Idea of Innovation Over the Centuries* (New York and Abingdon: Routledge).

Gomme, A. W. (1946) 'The slave population of Athens', *JHS* 66: 127–9.

Graham, A. J. (1998) 'The woman at the window: observations on the "stele from the harbour" of Thasos', *JHS* 118: 22–40.

Gray, V. J. (2006) Review of Azoulay (2004) in *CR* 56: 43–5.

Gray, V. J. (2007) *Xenophon on Government* (Cambridge: Cambridge University Press).

Gray, V. J. (2011) *Xenophon's Mirror of Princes: Reading the Reflections* (Oxford: Oxford University Press).

Green, P. (1994) 'Text and context in the matter of Xenophon's exile', in I. Worthington, ed., *Ventures into Greek History*, 215–27 (Oxford: Clarendon). [Reprinted as chap.6 in P. Green, *From Ikaria to the Stars: Classical Mythification, Ancient and Modern* (Austin: University of Texas Press, 2004).]

Griffith, G. T. (1978) 'Athens in the fourth century', in P. D. A. Garnsey and C. R. Whittaker, eds., *Imperialism in the Ancient World*, 127–44 (Cambridge: Cambridge University Press).

Habicht, C. (1997) *Athens from Alexander to Antony* (Cambridge, MA and London: Harvard University Press).

Hakkarainen, M. (1997) 'Private wealth in the Athenian public sphere during the late classical and early Hellenistic period', in J. Försén, ed., *Early Hellenistic Athens: Symptoms of a Change*, 1–32 (Helsinki: Finnish Institute).

Hall, E. (1989) *Inventing the Barbarian: Greek Self-definition Through Tragedy* (Oxford: Oxford University Press).

Hall, J. M. (1999) Review of Hunt (1998) in *CPh* 94: 461–6.

Hammond, N. G. L. and Griffith, G. T. (1979) *A History of Macedonia II: 550–336 BC* (Oxford: Oxford University Press).

Hansen, M. H. (1974) *The Sovereignty of the People's Court in Athens and the Public Action Against Unconstitutional Proposals* (Odense: Odense University Press).

Hansen, M. H. (1975) Eisangelia. *The Sovereignty of the People's Court in Athens in the Fourth Century* BC *and the Impeachment of Generals and Politicians* (Odense: Odense University Press).

Hansen, M. H. (1976) Apagoge, Endeixis *and* Ephegesis *against* Kakourgoi, Atimoi *and* Pheugontes: *A Study in the Administration of Justice in the Fourth Century* BC (Odense: Odense University Press).

Hansen, M. H. (1979) '*Misthos* for magistrates in classical Athens', *SO* 54: 5–22.

Hansen, M. H. (19[71–]80) 'Perquisites for magistrates in classical Athens', *C&M* 32: 107–25.

Hansen, M. H. (1980) 'Seven hundred *archai* in classical Athens', *GRBS* 21: 151–73.

Hansen, M. H. (1985) *Demography and Democracy: The Number of Athenian Citizens in the Fourth Century* BC (Herning: Systime).

Hansen, M. H. (1991) *The Athenian Democracy in the Age of Demosthenes*, translated by J. A. Crook (Oxford: Blackwell).

Hanson, V. D. (1989) *The Western Way of War: Infantry Battle in Classical Greece* (New York: Knopf).

Hanson, V. D. (1999) *The Other Greeks: The Family Farm and the Agrarian Roots of Western Civilization*, 2nd edition, with a new preface and bibliographic essay (Berkeley and Los Angeles: University of California Press).

Harding, P. (1973) 'The purpose of Isocrates' *Archidamus* and *On the peace*', *CSCA* 6: 137–49.

Harding, P. (1985) *From the End of the Peloponnesian War to the Battle of Ipsus* (Translated Documents of Greece and Rome 2) (Cambridge: Cambridge University Press).

Harris, E. M. (1988) 'When was Aeschines born?', *CPh* 83: 211–14.

Harris, E. M. (1994) 'Demosthenes loses a friend and Nausicles gains a position: a prosopographical note on Athenian politics after Chaeronea', *Historia* 43: 378–84.

Harris, E. M. (1995) *Aeschines and Athenian Politics* (New York and Oxford: Oxford University Press).

Harris, E. M. (2012) 'Homer, Hesiod, and the "origins" of Greek slavery', *REA* 114: 1–22.

Harris, E. M., Lewis, D., and Woolmer, M., eds. (2015) *The Ancient Greek Economy: Markets, Households and City-states* (Cambridge: Cambridge University Press).

Harrison, A. R. W. (1968) *The Law of Athens I: Family and Property* (Oxford: Oxford University Press). [2nd edition 1998: London: Bristol Classical Press and Indianapolis: Hackett].

Harrison, A. R. W. (1971) *The Law of Athens II: Procedure* (Oxford: Oxford University Press). [2nd edition 1998: London: Bristol Classical Press and Indianapolis: Hackett.]

Hasebroek, J. (1933) *Trade and Politics in Ancient Greece*, translated (from the original *Staat und Handel im alten Griechenland*) by L. M. Fraser and D. C. MacGregor (London: G. Bell & Sons). [Reprinted 1965: New York: Biblo and Tannen.]

Haywood, J. (2016) 'Divine narratives in Xenophon's *Anabasis*', *Histos* 10: 85–110.

Head, B. V. (1911) *Historia Numorum: A Manual of Greek Numismatics* (Oxford: Clarendon). [Reprinted 1991: Amsterdam: Hakkert.]

Henry, A. S. (1983) *Honours and Privileges in Athenian Decrees* (Hildesheim: G. Olms).

Henry, A. S. (1996) 'The hortatory intention in Athenian state decrees', *ZPE* 112: 105–19.

Henry, A. S. (2002) 'Hookers and lookers: prostitution and soliciting in late archaic Thasos', *ABSA* 97: 217–21.

Herzog, R. (1914) 'Zu Xenophons *Poroi*', in *Festgabe Hugo Blümner*, 469–80 (Zurich: Buchdruckerei Berichthaus).

Hochschultz, B. (2007) *Kallistratos von Aphidnai: Untersuchungen zu seiner politischen Biographie* (Munich: Herbert Utz).

Holzapfel, L. (1882) 'Über die Abfassungszeit der dem Xenophon zugeschriebenen *Poroi*', *Philologus* 41: 242–69.

Hopper, R. J. (1953) 'The Attic silver mines in the fourth century BC', *ABSA* 48: 200–54.

Hopper, R. J. (1961) 'The mines and miners of ancient Athens', *G&R* 8: 138–51.

Hopper, R. J. (1968) 'The Laureion mines: a reconsideration', *ABSA* 63: 293–326.

Hopper, R. J. (1979) *Trade and Industry in Classical Greece* (London: Thames & Hudson).

Hornblower, S. (1991–2008) *A Commentary on Thucydides*, 3 volumes (Oxford: Oxford University Press).

Hornblower, S. (2002) *The Greek World 479–323 BC*, 3rd edition (London and New York: Routledge).

Howgego, C. (1995) *Ancient History from Coins* (London: Routledge).

Humphreys, S. C. (1985) 'Lycurgus of Boutadae: an Athenian Aristocrat', in J. W. Eadie and J. Ober, eds., *The Craft of the Ancient Historian: Essays in Honor of Chester G. Starr*, 199–252 (Lanham: University Press of America). [Reprinted 2004 with 'Afterword' as chap.3 of her *The Strangeness of Gods: Historical Perspectives on the Interpretation of Athenian Religion* (Oxford: Oxford University Press).]

Hunt, P. (1998) *Slaves, Warfare, and Ideology in the Greek Historians* (Cambridge: Cambridge University Press).

Hunt, P. (2006) 'Arming slaves and helots in classical Greece', in C. L. Brown and P. D. Morgan, eds., *Arming Slaves: From Classical Times to the Modern Age*, 14–39 (New Haven: Yale University Press).

Hunt, P. (2015) 'Trojan slaves in classical Athens', in Taylor and Vlassopoulos (2015) 128–54.

Hunter, V. J. (1994) *Policing Athens: Social Control in the Attic Lawsuits, 420–320 BC* (Princeton: Princeton University Press).

Hunter, V. J. (2000) 'Introduction: status distinctions in Athenian law', in Hunter and Edmondson (2000): 1–19.

Hunter, V. J. (2006) 'Pittalacus and Eucles: slaves in the public service of Athens', *Mouseion* 6: 1–13.

Hunter, V. J. and Edmondson, J. (2000) *Law and Social Status in Classical Athens* (Oxford: Oxford University Press).

Hurwit, J. M. (1999) *The Athenian Acropolis: History, Mythology, and Archaeology from the Neolithic Era to the Present* (Cambridge: Cambridge University Press).

Isager, S. (1988) 'Once upon a time. On the interpretation of [Aristotle], *Oikonomika* II', in A. Damsgaard-Madsen, E. Christiansen, and E. Hallager, eds., *Studies in Ancient History and Numismatics Presented to Rudi Thomsen*, 77–83 (Aarhus: Aarhus University Press).

Isager, S. and Hansen, M. H. (1975) *Aspects of Athenian Society in the Fourth Century BC* (Odense: Odense University Press).

Isager, S. and Skydsgaard, J. E. (1992) *Ancient Greek Agriculture: An Introduction* (London and New York: Routledge).

Ismard, P. (2015) *La démocratie contre les experts. Les esclaves publics en Grèce ancienne* (Paris: Seuil).

Jaeger, W. W. (1938) *Demosthenes: The Origin and Growth of his Policy* (Berkeley: University of California Press).

Jansen, J. N. (2007) *After Empire: Xenophon's* Poroi *and the Reorientation of Athens' Political Economy* (Diss. Austin. Online at http://repositories.lib.utexas.edu).

Jansen, J. N. (2012) 'Strangers incorporated: outsiders in Xenophon's *Poroi*', in Tuplin and Hobden (2012) 725–59.

Jansen, J. N. (2017) 'Beyond war, imperialism, and Panhellenism: Xenophon's eirenic thought', in E. P. Moloney and M. Stuart Williams, eds., *Peace and Reconciliation in the Classical World*, 255–70 (Abingdon and New York: Routledge).

Johansson, M. (2001) 'The inscription from Troizen: a decree of Themistocles?', *ZPE* 137: 69–92.

Johnstone, S. (2003) 'Women, property, and surveillance in classical Athens', *CSCA* 22: 247–74.

Jones, A. H. M. (1969) *Athenian Democracy* (Oxford: Blackwell).

Jones, C. P. (1987) 'Stigma: tattooing and branding in Graeco-Roman antiquity', *JRS* 77: 139–55.

Jones, N. F. (1987) *Public Organization in Ancient Greece: A Documentary Study* (Philadelphia: American Philosophical Society).

Jones, N. F. (1990) 'The organization of the Kretan City in Plato's *Laws*', *CW* 83: 473–92.
Jones, N. F. (1995) 'The Athenian phylai as associations: disposition, function, and purpose', *Hesperia* 64: 503–42.
Jones, N. F. (2004) *Rural Athens Under the Democracy* (Philadelphia: Pennsylvania University Press).
Jonnes, L. and Ricl, M. (1997) 'A new royal inscription from Phrygia Paroreios: Eumenes II grants Tyriaion the status of a polis', *EA* 29: 1–30.
Kahrstedt, U. (1934) *Staatsgebiet und Staatsangehörige in Athen* (Stuttgart: W. Kohlhammer).
Kallet, L. (2001) *Money and the Corrosion of Power in Thucydides: The Sicilian Expedition and its Aftermath* (Berkeley and Los Angeles: University of California Press).
Kamen, D. (2013) *Status in Classical Athens* (Princeton: Princeton University Press).
Kamen, D. (2016) 'Manumission and slave-allowances in classical Athens', *Historia* 65: 413–26.
Kapparis, K. A. (2002) *Abortion in the Ancient World* (London: Duckworth).
Kapparis, K. A. (2005) 'Immigration and citizenship procedures in Athenian law', *RIDA* 42: 71–113.
Kapparis, K. A. (2011) 'The terminology of prostitution in the Ancient Greek World', in Glazebrook and Henry (2011): 222–55.
Kears, M. J. (2013) *Metics and Identity in Democratic Athens* (Diss. Birmingham. Online at http://etheses.bham.ac.uk).
Keen, A. G. (1998) *Dynastic Lycia: A Political History of the Lycians and Their Relations with Foreign Powers, c. 545–362 BC* (Leiden: Brill).
Kellogg, D. L. (2013) *Marathon Fighters and Men of Maple: Ancient Acharnai* (Oxford: Oxford University Press).
Kennedy, R. F. (2014) *Immigrant Women in Athens: Gender, Ethnicity, and Citizenship in the Classical City* (New York and Abingdon: Routledge).
Koerte, A. (1902) 'Ein Gesetz des Redners Lykurgos', *RhM* 36: 625–7.
Krentz, P. (1989) *Xenophon,* Hellenika *I–II.3.10*, edited with an introduction, translation and commentary (Warminster: Aris & Phillips).
Krentz, P. (1995) *Xenophon,* Hellenika *II.3.11–IV.2.8*, edited with an introduction, translation and commentary (Warminster: Aris & Phillips).
Krentz, P. and Wheeler, E. L. (1994) *Polyaenus, Stratagems of War*, edited and translated, 2 volumes (Chicago: Ares).
Kroeker, R. (2009) 'Xenophon as a critic of the Athenian democracy', *HPTh* 30: 198–228.
Kroll, J. H. (1972) *Athenian Bronze Allotment Plates* (Cambridge, MA: Harvard University Press).
Kroll, J. H. (1976) 'Aristophanes' *ponêra chalkia*: a reply', *GRBS* 17: 329–41.
Kroll, J. H. (2001) 'A small find of silver bullion from Egypt', *AJN* 13: 1–20.

Kroll, J. H. (2011a) 'The re-minting of Athenian silver coinage, 353 BC', *Hesperia* 80: 229–59.
Kroll, J. H. (2011b) 'Athenian tetradrachm coinage of the first half of the fourth century BC', *RBN* 157: 3–26.
Kuenzi, A. (1923) *EPIDOSIS* (Bern: P. Haupt).
Kyle, D. G. (1993) *Athletics in Ancient Athens*, 2nd edition (Leiden: Brill).
Labarbe, J. (1977) *Thorikos: les testimonia* (Ghent: Comite des Fouilles Belges en Grèce).
Lambert, S. D. (1997) *Rationes Centesimarum: Sales of Public Land in Lykourgan Athens* (Amsterdam: Gieben).
Lambert, S. D. (2001) 'Ten notes on Attic inscriptions', *ZPE* 135: 51–62.
Lambert, S. D. (2006) 'Athenian state laws and decrees 352/1–322/1, III: decrees honouring foreigners, A: citizenship, proxeny and euergesy', *ZPE* 158: 115–58.
Lambert, S. D. (2007) 'Athenian state laws and decrees 352/1–322/1, III: decrees honouring foreigners, B: other awards', *ZPE* 159: 101–54.
Lambert, S. D. (2010) 'Athens, Sokles, and the exploitation of an Attic resource (*IG* II^2 411)', in Sekunda (2010): 114–25.
Lambert, S. D. (2011a) 'What was the point of inscribed honorific decrees in classical Athens?', in S. D. Lambert, ed., *Sociable Man: Essays on Greek Social Behaviour in Honour of Nick Fisher*, 193–214 (Swansea: Classical Press of Wales).
Lambert, S. D. (2011b) 'Some political shifts in Lykourgan Athens', in Azoulay and Ismard (2011): 175–90.
Lambert, S. D. (2012) *Inscribed Athenian Laws and Decrees 352/1–322/1: Epigraphical essays* (Leiden: Brill).
Lambert, S. D. (2015) 'The inscribed version of the decree honouring Lykourgos of Boutadai (*IG* II^2 457 and 3207)', *AIO* Papers no.6.
Lane, F. C. (1973) *Venice: A Maritime Republic* (Baltimore and London: Johns Hopkins University Press).
Lane Fox, R., ed. (2004) *The Long March: Xenophon and the Ten Thousand* (New Haven: Yale University Press).
Lauffer, S. (1955–1956) *Die Bergwerkssklaven von Laureion* (Wiesbaden: Steiner). [There is a second edition (1979), but I cite the first to preserve the chronological relationship between *Bergwerkssklaven* and Gauthier's *Commentaire*.]
Lauffer, S. (1975) 'Das Bergbauprogramm in Xenophons *Poroi*', *Miscellanea Graeca* 1: 171–205.
Lazenby, J. F. (1991) 'The killing zone', in V. D. Hanson, ed., *Hoplites: The Classical Greek Battle Experience*, 87–109 (London and New York: Routledge).
Leigh, M. (2013) *From Polypragmon to Curiosus: Ancient Concepts of Curious and Meddlesome Behaviour* (Oxford: Oxford University Press)
Lendon, J. E. (2006) 'Xenophon and the alternative to realist foreign policy: *Cyropaedia* 3.1.14–31', *JHS* 126: 82–98.

Lewis, D. (2011) 'Near eastern slaves in classical Attica and the slave trade with Persian territories', *CQ* 61: 91–113.
Lewis, D. M. (1955) 'The public seal of Athens', *Phoenix* 9: 32–4.
Lewis, D. M. (1968) 'New evidence for the gold-silver ratio', in C. M. Kraay and G. K. Jenkins, eds., *Essays in Greek Coinage Presented to Stanley Robinson*, 105–10 (Oxford: Oxford University Press).
Lewis, D. M. (1990) 'Public property in the city', in Murray and Price (1990): 245–63.
Lewis, D. M. (1997) 'On the financial offices of Eubulus and Lycurgus', in P. J. Rhodes, ed., *Selected Papers [of D. M. Lewis] in Greek and Near Eastern History*, 212–29 (Cambridge: Cambridge University Press).
Lewis, J. D. (2009) 'Xenophon's *Poroi* and the foundations of political economy', *Polis* 26: 370–88.
Lewis, S. (1996) *News and Society in the Greek Polis* (London: Duckworth).
Liddel, P. (2007) *Civic Obligation and Individual Liberty in Ancient Athens* (Oxford: Oxford University Press)
Liddel, P. (2016) 'Honorific decrees of fourth-century Athens: trends, perceptions, controversies', in C. Tiersch, ed., *Die athenische Demokratie im 4. Jahrhundert. Zwischen Modernisierung und Tradition*, 335–58 (Stuttgart: Steiner).
Lintott, A. W. (1982) *Violence, Civil Strife and Revolution in the Classical City, 750–330 BC* (London: Croom Helm).
Lohmann, H. (1993) *Atene. Forschungen zur Siedlungs- und Wirtschaftsstruktur des klassischen Attika* (Cologne: Böhlau).
Loomis, W. T. (1998) *Wages, Welfare Costs and Inflation in Classical Athens* (Ann Arbor: University of Michigan Press).
Loraux, N. (1986) *The Invention of Athens: The Funeral Oration in the Classical City*, translated by A. Sheridan (Cambridge, MA: Harvard University Press).
Lu, H. (2015) *Xenophon's Theory of Moral Education* (Newcastle upon Tyne: Cambridge Scholars Publishing).
Luccioni, J. (1948) *Les idées politiques et sociales de Xénophon* (Paris: Ophrys Editions).
McCredie, J. R. (1966) *Fortified Military Camps in Attica* (Princeton: Princeton University Press).
MacDonald, C. (1961) 'The ancient mine-workings of Laureion', *G&R* 8: 19–21.
MacDowell, D. M. (1978) *The Law in Classical Athens* (London: Thames & Hudson).
MacDowell, D. M. (1986) *Spartan Law* (Edinburgh: Scottish Academic Press).
MacDowell, D. M. (2009) *Demosthenes the Orator* (Oxford: Oxford University Press).
Mansouri, S. (2011) *Athènes vue par ses métèques (ve et ive siècle av. J.-C.)* (Paris: Tallandier).

Marsden, E. W. (1969) *Greek and Roman Artillery: Historical Development* (Oxford: Oxford University Press).
Marshall, F. H. (1905) *The Second Athenian Confederacy* (Cambridge: Cambridge University Press).
Mathieu, G. (1925) *Les idées politiques d'Isocrate* (Paris: Les Belles Lettres).
Meiggs, R. (1972) *The Athenian Empire* (Oxford: Oxford University Press).
Melville Jones, J. (1986) *A Dictionary of Ancient Greek Coins* (London: Seaby).
Melville Jones, J. (2007) *Testimonia Numaria: Greek and Latin Texts Concerning Ancient Greek Coinage, II: Addenda and Commentary* (London: Spink).
Meyer, E. A. (2010) *Metics and the Athenian* Phialai-*Inscriptions: A Study in Athenian Epigraphy and Law* (Stuttgart: Steiner).
Meyer, E. A. (2013) 'Inscriptions as honours and the Athenian epigraphic habit', *Historia* 62: 453–505.
Michelini, A. N. (1998) 'Isocrates' civic invective: *Acharnians* and *On the peace*', *TAPhA* 128: 115–33.
Michell, H. (1940) *The Economics of Ancient Greece* (Cambridge: Cambridge University Press).
Migeotte, L. (1984) *L'emprunt public dans les cités grecques: recueil des documents et analyse critique* (Quebec: Éditions du Sphinx and Paris: Les Belles Lettres).
Migeotte, L. (1992) *Les souscriptions publiques dans las cités grecques*. Geneva and Quebec.
Mikalson, J. D. (1983) *Athenian Popular Religion* (Chapel Hill and London: University of North Carolina Press).
Mikalson, J. D. (2016) *New Aspects of Religion in Ancient Athens: Honors, Authorities, Esthetics, and Society* (Leiden: Brill).
Miller, J. (2016) 'Euergetism, agonism, and democracy: the hortatory intention in late classical and early Hellenistic Athenian honorific decrees', *Hesperia* 85: 385–435.
Miller, S. G. (1978) *The Prytaneion: Its Function and Architectural Form* (Berkeley and Los Angeles: University of California Press).
Millett, P. C. (1980) 'Note on a Greek text relating to credit transactions', *PCPhS* 26: 67–9.
Millett, P. C. (1983) 'Maritime loans and the structure of credit in fourth-century Athens', in P. Garnsey, K. Hopkins, and C. R. Whittaker, eds., *Trade in the Ancient Economy*, 36–52 (Berkeley and Los Angeles: University of California Press).
Millett, P. C. (1991) *Lending and Borrowing in Ancient Athens* (Cambridge: Cambridge University Press).
Millett, P. C. (2001) 'Productive to some purpose? The problem of ancient economic growth', in D. J. Mattingly and J. B. Salmon, eds., *Economies Beyond Agriculture in the Classical World*, 17–37 (London and New York: Routledge).

Mitchel, F. W. (1973) *Lykourgan Athens: 338–322. Lectures in Memory of Louise Taft Semple* 2, 165–214 (Cincinnati: University of Cincinnati).
Moggi, M. (1979) 'L'eisphora dei coloni ateniesi a Potidea ([Aristot.] *Oec.* 2.2.5 [1347a]', *QUCC* 1: 137–42.
Momigliano, A. D. (1936) 'Per la storia della pubblicistica sulla *koinê eirênê* nel IV secolo a.C.', *ASNP* 5: 97–136. [Reprinted in his *Terzo contributo alla storia degli studi classici e del mondo antico*, 457–87 (1966, Rome: Edizioni di Storia e Letteratura).]
Moreno, A. (2007) *Feeding the Democracy: The Athenian Grain Supply in the Fifth and Fourth Centuries* BC (Oxford: Oxford University Press).
Morin, D. et al. (2012) 'The Laurion shafts, Greece: ventilation systems and mining technology in antiquity', *Historical Metallurgy* 46: 9–18.
Morrison, J. V. (1994) 'Thematic inversion in the *Iliad*: the Greeks under siege', *GRBS* 35: 209–27.
Morrison, J. S., Coates, J. J., and Rankov, N. B. (2000) *The Athenian Trireme: The History and Reconstruction of an Ancient Greek Warship*, 2nd edition (Cambridge: Cambridge University Press).
Morrow, G. R. (1960) *Plato's Cretan City* (Princeton: Princeton University Press).
Moysey, R. A. (1982) 'Isocrates' *On the Peace*: rhetorical exercise or political advice?', *AJAH* 7: 118–27.
Müller, C. (2011) 'Autopsy of a crisis: wealth, Protogenes, and the city of Olbia in c. 200 BC', in Z. H. Archibald, J. K. Davies, and V. Gabrielsen, eds., *The Economies of Hellenistic Societies, Third to First Centuries* BC, 324–44 (Oxford: Oxford University Press).
Munn, M. H. (1993) *The Defense of Attica: The Dema Wall and the Boiotian War of 378–375* BC (Berkeley and Los Angeles: University of California Press).
Murray, O. and Price, S., eds. (1990) *The Greek City from Homer to Alexander* (Oxford: Oxford University Press).
Murray, W. M. (2012) *The Age of Titans: The Rise and Fall of the Great Hellenistic Navies* (Oxford: Oxford University Press).
Mussche, H. F. (1998) *Thorikos: A Mining Town in Ancient Attika* (Leuven: Peeters).
Nemeth, G. (2001) 'Metics in Athens', *AAHung* 41: 331–48.
Nenci, G. (1993) '*Oikopedon* e *gêpedon*. Contributo al lessico urbanistico greco', *Annales littéraires de l'Université de Besançon* 491: 273–86.
North, D. C. (1981) *Structure and Change in Economic History* (New York: W. W. Norton).
North, D. C. (1990) *Institutions, Institutional Change and Economic Performance* (Cambridge: Cambridge University Press).
North, D. C. (2005) *Understanding the Process of Economic Change* (Princeton: Princeton University Press).

Ober, J. (1985) *Fortress Attica: Defense of the Athenian Land Frontier 404–322 BC* (Leiden: Brill).
Ober, J. (1989) *Mass and Elite in Democratic Athens: Rhetoric, Ideology, and the Power of the People* (Princeton: Princeton University Press).
Ober, J. (2008) *Democracy and Knowledge: Innovation and Learning in Classical Athens* (Princeton: Princeton University Press).
Ober, J. (2015a) 'Classical Athens', in A. Monson and W. Scheidel, eds., *Fiscal Regimes and the Political Economy of Pre-Modern States*, 492–522 (Cambridge: Cambridge University Press).
Ober, J. (2015b) *The Rise and Fall of Classical Greece* (Princeton: Princeton University Press).
Ober, J. (2017) 'Inequality in late-classical democratic Athens: evidence and models', in G. C. Bitros and N. C. Kyriazis, eds., *Democracy and an Open-Economy World Order*, 125–46 (Cham: Springer).
Oliver, G. J. (2007) *War, Food, and Politics in Early Hellenistic Athens* (Oxford: Oxford University Press).
Oliver, G. J. (2011) 'Before "Lykourgan Athens": the origins of change', in Azoulay and Ismard (2011): 119–31.
Olson, S. D. (2017) 'Some overlooked Athenian economic vocabulary (ἀγοραί and λιμένες)', *Prometheus* 43: 87–8.
Osborne, M. J. (1981–1983) *Naturalization in Athens*, 4 volumes (Brussels: Academie voor Wetenschappen, Letteren en Schone Kunsten).
Osborne, R. G. (1985) *Demos: The Discovery of Classical Attika* (Cambridge: Cambridge University Press).
Osborne, R. G. (1987) *Classical Landscape with Figures: The Ancient Greek City and its Countryside* (London: George Philip).
Osborne, R. G. (1995) 'The economics and politics of slavery at Athens', in A. Powell, ed., *The Greek World*, 27–43 (London and New York: Routledge).
Osborne, R. G. (2000) *Classical Greece, 500–323 BC* (Oxford: Oxford University Press).
Osborne, R. G. (2004) *Greek History* (London: Routledge).
O'Sullivan, L. (2001) 'Philochorus, Pollux, and the *nomophulakes* of Demetrius of Phalerum', *JHS* 121: 51–62.
O'Sullivan, L. (2009) *The Regime of Demetrius of Phalerum in Athens 317–307 BCE: A Philosopher in Politics* (Leiden and Boston: Brill).
Papazarkadas, N. (2011) *Sacred and Public Land in Ancient Athens* (Oxford: Oxford University Press).
Parke, H. W. (1933) *Greek Mercenary Soldiers: From the Earliest Times to the Battle of Ipsus* (Oxford: Oxford University Press).
Parke, H. W. (1967) *Greek Oracles* (London: Hutchinson).
Parke, H. W. (1977) *Festivals of the Athenians* (London: Thames & Hudson).
Parke, H. W. and Wormell, D. E. W. (1956) *The Delphic Oracle*, 3 volumes (Oxford: Blackwell).

Parker, R. C. T. (1983) *Miasma: Pollution and Purification in Early Greek Religion* (Oxford: Oxford University Press).
Parker, R. C. T. (1985) 'Greek states and Greek oracles', in P. Cartledge and D. Harvey, eds., *Crux: Essays Presented to G. E. M. de Ste. Croix on his 75th Birthday*, 298–326 (Exeter: Imprint Academic).
Parker, R. C. T. (1996) *Athenian Religion: A History* (Oxford: Oxford University Press).
Parker, R. C. T. (2004) 'One man's piety: the religious dimension of the *Anabasis*', in Lane Fox (2004): 131–53.
Parker, R. C. T. (2005) *Polytheism and Society at Athens* (Oxford: Oxford University Press).
Patterson, C. J. (2000) 'The hospitality of Athenian justice: the metic in court', in Hunter and Edmondson (2000): 93–112.
Pečírka, J. (1966) *The Formula for the Grant of Enktesis in Attic Inscriptions* (Prague: Charles University).
Pélékidis, C. (1962) *Histoire de l'éphébie attique* (Paris: E. de Boccard).
Perrin, B. (1902) 'The Nikias of Pasiphon and Plutarch', *TAPhA* 33: 139–49.
Phillips, T. (2016) *Pindar's Library: Performance Poetry and Material Texts* (Oxford: Oxford University Press).
Piccirilli, L. (1973) *Gli arbitrati interstatali greci, I: dalle origini al 338 a.C.* (Pisa: Edizioni Marlin).
Pickard-Cambridge, A. W. (1988) *The Dramatic Festivals of Athens*, 2nd edition revised by J. Gould and D. M. Lewis (1968), with Supplement (1988) (Oxford: Oxford University Press).
Pomeroy, S. B. (1994) *Xenophon,* Oeconomicus: *A Social and Historical Commentary* (Oxford: Oxford University Press).
Powell, J. (2015) *Risk, Rationality and Enterprise in Fourth-Century Attica* (Diss. Birkbeck. Online at http://bbktheses.da.ulcc.ac.uk).
Pownall, F. (2004) *Lessons from the Past: The Moral Use of History in Fourth-century Prose* (Ann Arbor: University of Michigan Press).
Pritchard, D. M. (2015) *Public Spending and Democracy in Classical Athens* (Austin: University of Texas Press).
Pritchett, W. K. (1971–1991) *The Greek State at War*, 5 volumes (Berkeley and Los Angeles: University of California Press).
Rawlings, L. P. (2000) 'Alternative agonies: hoplite martial and combat experiences beyond the phalanx', in H. Van Wees, ed., *War and Violence in Ancient Greece*, 233–59 (Swansea: Classical Press of Wales)
Reed, C. M. (2003) *Maritime Traders in the Ancient Greek World* (Cambridge: Cambridge University Press).
Rhodes. P. J. (1972) *The Athenian Boule* (Oxford: Oxford University Press).
Rhodes, P. J. (1979–1980) 'Athenian democracy after 403 BC', *CJ* 75: 305–23.
Rhodes, P. J. (1981) *A Commentary on the Aristotelian Athenaion Politeia* (Oxford: Oxford University Press).

Rhodes, P. J. (2007) *The Greek City States: A Source Book*, 2nd edition (Cambridge: Cambridge University Press).
Rhodes, P. J. (2010) *A History of the Classical Greek World 478–323 BC*, 2nd edition (Malden and Oxford: Wiley-Blackwell).
Rhodes, P. J. (2013a) 'The organization of Athenian public finance', *G&R* 60: 203–31.
Rhodes, P. J. (2013b) 'The alleged failure of Athens in the fourth century', *Electrum* 19: 111–29.
Rhodes, P. J. (2015) 'Directions in the study of Athenian democracy', *SCI* 34: 49–68.
Rhodes, P. J. with D. M. Lewis (1997) *The Decrees of the Greek States* (Oxford: Oxford University Press).
Rihll, T. E. (1991) '*Hektêmoroi*: partners in crime?', *JHS* 111: 101–27.
Rihll, T. E. (2007) *The Catapult: A History* (Yardley: Westholme).
Rihll, T. E. (2010a) 'Athens' silver springs', in Sekunda (2010): 65–75.
Rihll, T. E. (2010b) 'Skilled slaves and the economy: the silver mines of the Laurion', in H. Heinen, ed., *Antike Sklaverei, Ruckblick und Ausblick. Neue Beiträge zur Forschungsgeschichte und zur Erschliessung der archäologischen Zeugnisse*, 203–20 (Stuttgart: Steiner).
Rihll, T. E. (2011) 'Classical Athens', in K. Bradley and P. Cartledge, eds., *The Cambridge World History of Slavery, I: The Ancient Mediterranean World*, 48–73 (Cambridge: Cambridge University Press).
Roisman, J. (2005) *The Rhetoric of Manhood: Masculinity in the Attic Orators* (Berkeley and Los Angeles: University of California Press).
Roisman, J. and Worthington, I. (with Waterfield, R.) (2015) *Lives of the Attic Orators: Texts from pseudo-Plutarch, Photius, and the Suda* (Oxford: Oxford University Press).
Rood, T. (1998) 'Thucydides and his predecessors', *Histos* 2: 230–67.
Rood, T. (2014) 'Space and landscape in Xenophon's *Anabasis*', in K. Gilhuly and N. Worman, eds., *Space, Place, and Landscape in Ancient Greek Literature and Culture*, 63–93 (Cambridge and New York: Cambridge University Press).
Roscalla, F. (2004) '*Kalokagathia* e *kaloi kagathoi* in Senofonte', in Tuplin (2004) 115–24.
Rostovtzeff, M. I. (1941) *Social and Economic History of the Hellenistic World*, 3 volumes (Oxford: Oxford University Press).
Rousset, D. (2013) 'Sacred property and public property in the Greek city', *JHS* 133: 113–33.
Roy, J. (1998) 'The threat from the Piraeus', in P. Cartledge, P. Millett, and S. Von Reden, eds., *Kosmos: Essays in Order, Conflict and Community in Classical Athens*, 191–202 (Cambridge: Cambridge University Press).
Runciman, W. G. (1990) 'Doomed to extinction: the *polis* as an evolutionary dead-end', in Murray and Price (1990): 347–67.

Russell, T. (2017) *Byzantium and the Bosporus: A Historical Study, From the Seventh Century* BC *until the Foundation of Constantinople* (Oxford: Oxford University Press).
Ruzicka, S. (2012) *Trouble in the West: Egypt and the Persian Empire, 525–332* BC (Oxford: Oxford University Press)
Ryder, T. T. B. (1965) *Koine Eirene: General Peace and Local Independence in Ancient Greece* (Oxford: Oxford University Press).
Ryder, T. T. B. (1976) 'Demosthenes and Philip's Peace of 338/7 BC', *CQ* 26: 85–7.
Ste. Croix, G. E. M. de (1953) 'Demosthenes' *timêma* and the Athenian *eisphora* in the fourth century BC', *C&M* 14: 30–70.
Ste. Croix, G. E. M. de (1972) *The Origins of the Peloponnesian War* (London: Duckworth).
Ste. Croix, G. E. M. de (1981) *The Class Struggle in the Ancient Greek World* (London: Duckworth).
Ste. Croix, G. E. M. de (2004) *Athenian Democratic Origins and Other Essays*, edited by D. Harvey and R. Parker, with the assistance of P. Thonemann (Oxford: Oxford University Press).
Saliou, C. (2015) 'Architecture and society', in P. Destrée and P. Murray, eds., *A Companion to Ancient Aesthetics*, 128–39 (Malden and Oxford: Wiley-Blackwell).
Sallares, R. (1991) *The Ecology of the Ancient Greek World* (London: Duckworth).
Saunders, T. J. (1970) Plato, *The Laws*, translated with an introduction (Penguin Classics) (Harmondsworth: Penguin).
Scafuro, A. C. (2009) 'The crowning of Amphiaraos', in L. Mitchell and L. Rubinstein, eds., *Greek History and Epigraphy: Essays in Honour of P. J. Rhodes*, 59–86 (Swansea: Classical Press of Wales).
Schorn, S. (2006) 'Zur Authentizität und Datierung von Xenophons *Poroi*', *WJA* 30: 25–40.
Schorn, S. (2011) 'Xenophons *Poroi* als philosophische Schrift', *Historia* 60: 65–93.
Schorn, S. (2012) 'The philosophical background of Xenophon's *Poroi*', in Tuplin and Hobden (2012): 689–724 [an English version of Schorn (2011)].
Schütrumpf, E. (1995) 'Politische Reformmodelle im vierten Jahrhundert', in W. Eder, ed., *Die athenische Demokratie im 4. Jahrhundert v. Chr.*, 271–301 (Stuttgart: Steiner).
Schütrumpf, E. (2010) 'Xenophon (2)', in *BNP* 15.824–33.
Schwahn, W. (1931) 'Die xenophontische *Poroi* und die athenische Industrie im vierten Jahrhundert', *RhM* 80: 252–78.
Schwenk, C. J. (1985) *Athens in the Age of Alexander: The Dated Laws and Decrees of 'the Lykourgan era', 338–322* BC (Chicago: Ares).
Seaford, R. A. S. (1982) 'The date of Euripides' *Cyclops*', *JHS* 102: 161–72.
Seager, R. J. (2001) 'Xenophon and Athenian democratic ideology', *CQ* 51: 385–97.

Sealey, R. (1955) 'Athens after the Social War', *JHS* 75: 74–81. [Reprinted in Sealey (1967): 164–82.]
Sealey, R. (1956) 'Callistratus of Aphidna and his contemporaries', *Historia* 5: 178–203. [Reprinted in Sealey (1967): 133–63.]
Sealey, R. (1967) *Essays in Greek Politics* (New York: Maryland Books).
Sealey, R. (1993) *Demosthenes and His Time: A Study in Defeat* (Oxford and New York: Oxford University Press).
Sekunda, N. V. (1989) 'Itabelis and the satrapy of Mysia', *AJAH* 14: 73–102.
Sekunda, N. V. (1990) '*IG* II^2 1250: a decree concerning the lampadephoroi of the tribe Aiantis', *ZPE* 83: 149–82.
Sekunda. N. V., ed. (2010) *Ergasteria: Works Presented to John Ellis Jones on his 80th Birthday* (Gdansk: Akanthina).
Shipley, G. (1987) *A History of Samos, 800–188* BC (Oxford: Oxford University Press).
Shipton, K. M. W. (1998) 'The prices of the Athenian silver mines', *ZPE* 120: 57–63.
Sinclair, R. K. (1988) *Democracy and Participation in Athens* (Cambridge: Cambridge University Press).
Sosin, J. D. (2004) 'An endowed peace', *MH* 61: 2–8.
Sosin, J. D. (2015) '"Those who live apart" were mercenaries', *Historia* 64: 413–18.
Sosin, J. D. (2016) 'A metic was a metic', *Historia* 65: 2–13.
Spence, I. G. (1993) *The Cavalry of Classical Greece: A Social and Military History with Particular Reference to Athens* (Oxford: Oxford University Press).
Stadter, P. A. (1989) *A Commentary on Plutarch's* Pericles (Chapel Hill: University of North Carolina Press).
Stroud, R. S. (1971) 'Theozotides and the Athenian orphans', *Hesperia* 40: 280–301.
Stroud, R. S. (1974) 'An Athenian law on silver coinage', *Hesperia* 43: 157–88.
Stroud, R. S. (1998) *The Athenian Grain-Tax Law of 374/3* BC (Princeton: American School of Classical Studies at Athens).
Sturz, F. W. (1802) *Lexicon Xenophonteum*, 4 volumes (Leipzig: Libraria Gleditschia). [Reprinted 1964: Hildesheim: Olms.]
Stylianou, P. J. (1998) *A Historical Commentary on Diodorus Siculus Book 15* (Oxford: Oxford University Press).
Swain, S. (2013) *Economy, Family, and Society from Rome to Islam: A Critical Edition, English Translation, and Study of Bryson's* Management of the Estate (Cambridge: Cambridge University Press).
Tamoulaki, M. (2013) 'A citizen as slave of the state? Oligarchic perceptions of democracy in Xenophon', *GRBS* 53: 31–50.
Taşliklioğlu, Z. and Frisch, P. (1975) 'New inscriptions from the Troad', *ZPE* 17: 101–14.

Taylor, C. (2017) *Poverty, Wealth, and Well-Being: Experiencing* Penia *in Democratic Athens* (Oxford: Oxford University Press).

Taylor, C. and Vlassopoulos, K. eds. (2015) *Communities and Networks in the Ancient Greek World* (Oxford: Oxford University Press).

Taylor, M. C. (1997) *Salamis and the Salaminioi: The History of An Unofficial Athenian Demos* (Amsterdam: J. C. Gieben).

Theocharaki, A. M. (2011) 'The ancient circuit wall of Athens: its changing course and phases of construction', *Hesperia* 80: 71–156.

Thomas, R. (1989) *Oral Tradition and Written Record in Classical Athens* (Cambridge: Cambridge University Press).

Thompson, W. E. (1982) 'The Athenian entrepreneur', *L'Antiquité Classique* 51: 53–85.

Thomsen, R. (1964) *Eisphora: A Study of Direct Taxation in Ancient Athens* (Copenhagen: Gyldendalske Boghandel).

Thonemann, P. (2012) Review of P. Gauthier, *Études d'histoire et d'institutions grecques: choix d'écrits. Edité et indexé par D. Rousset* (Geneva 2011), in *Klio* 94: 523–5.

Thür, G. (1989) 'Wo wohnen die Metöken?', in W. Schuller, W. Hoepfner, and E. L. Schwandner, eds., *Demokratie und Architektur*, 117–21 (Munich: Deutsche Kunstverlag).

Todd, S. C. (1993) *The Shape of Athenian Law* (Oxford: Oxford University Press).

Tracy, S. V. (1995) *Athenian Democracy in Transition: Attic Letter-cutters of 340 to 290* BC (Berkeley and Los Angeles: University of California Press).

Traill, J. S. (1975) *The Political Organization of Attica* (Princeton: American School of Classical Studies at Athens).

Tritle, L. A. (1988) *Phocion the Good* (London and Sydney: Croom Helm).

Tuplin, C. J. (1987) 'Xenophon's exile again', in M. Whitby, P. Hardie, and M. Whitby, eds., *Homo Viator: Classical Essays for John Bramble*, 59–68 (Bristol: Bristol Classical Press).

Tuplin, C. J. (1993) *The Failings of Empire: A Reading of Xenophon* Hellenica *2.3.11–7.5.27* (Stuttgart: Steiner).

Tuplin, C. J., ed. (2004) *Xenophon and his World: Papers from a Conference Held in Liverpool in January 1999* (Stuttgart: Steiner).

Tuplin, C. J. (2012) 'Xenophon (1)', in *OCD* 1580–3.

Tuplin, C .J. (2017) 'Xenophon and Athens', in Flower (2017): 338–59.

Tuplin, C. J. and Hobden, F. E., eds. (2012) *Xenophon: Ethical Principles and Historical Enquiry* (Leiden: Brill).

Van Alfen, P. G. (2012) 'Xenophon *Poroi* 3.2 and Athenian "owls" in Aegean-Near Eastern long distance trade', in M. Asolati and G. Gorini, eds., *I ritrovamenti monetali e i processi storico-economici nel mondo antico*, 11–32 (Padua: Esedra).

Van Groningen, B. A. (1933) *Aristote: Le second livre de l'Économique* (Leiden: Sijthoff).

Van Groningen, B. A. and Wartelle, A. (1968) *Aristote: Économique* (Paris: Les Belles Lettres).

Van Wees, H. (2011) 'Demetrius and Draco: Athens' property classes and population in and before 317 BC', *JHS* 131: 95–114.

Veligianni-Terzi, C. (1997) *Wertbegriffe in den attischen Ehrendekreten der klassischen Zeit* (Stuttgart: Steiner).

Vélissaropoulos, J. (1980) *Les nauclères grecs* (Paris: Minard).

Vlassopoulos, K. (2013) *Greeks and Barbarians* (Cambridge: Cambridge University Press).

Von der Lieck, K. (1933) *Die Xenophontische Schrift von der Einkünften* (Diss. Cologne).

Von Reden, S. (1995) 'The Piraeus—a world apart', *G&R* 42: 24–37.

Wallace, R. W. (1989) *The Areopagos Council to 307 BC* (Baltimore: Johns Hopkins University Press).

Wallace, W. P. (1949) 'The public seal of Athens', *Phoenix* 3: 70–3.

Waterfield, R. A. H. (2006) *Xenophon's Retreat: Greece, Persia, and the End of the Golden Age* (Cambridge, MA: Harvard University Press).

Watson, J. (2010) 'The origin of metic status at Athens', *CCJ* 56: 259–78.

Welwei, K.-W. (1974) *Unfreie im antiken Kriegsdienst, 1: Athen und Sparta* (Wiesbaden: Steiner).

Welwei, K.-W. (1977) *Unfreie im antiken Kriegsdienst, 2: die kleineren und mittleren griechischen Staaten und die hellenistischen Reiche* (Wiesbaden: Steiner).

Westermann, W. L. (1941) 'Athenaeus and the slaves of Athens', *HSCPh* suppl. vol.: 451–70. [Reprinted 1959 in M. I. Finley, ed., *Slavery in Classical Antiquity: Views and Controversies*, 73–92 (Cambridge: Cambridge University Press).]

Westermann, W. L. (1955) *The Slave Systems of Greek and Roman Antiquity* (Philadelphia: American Philosophical Society).

Wheeler, E. L. (1988) *Stratagem and the Vocabulary of Military Trickery* (Leiden: Brill).

Wheeler, E. L. (2010) 'Polyaenus: *scriptor militaris*', in K. Brodersen, ed., *Polyaenus: New Studies*, 7–54 (Berlin: Verlag Antike).

Whitby, M. (1998) 'The grain trade of Athens in the fourth century BC', in H. Parkins and C. Smith, eds., *Trade, Traders and the Ancient City*, 102–28 (London and New York: Routledge).

Whitehead, D. (1977) *The Ideology of the Athenian Metic* (Cambridge: Cambridge Philological Society).

Whitehead, D. (1978) '*Isoteleia*: a metaphor in Xenophon', *Eirene* 16: 19–22.

Whitehead, D. (1981) 'Xenocrates the metic', *RhM* 124: 223–44.

Whitehead, D. (1983) 'Competitive outlay and community profit: *philotimia* in democratic Athens', *C&M* 34: 55–74.

Whitehead, D. (1986) *The Demes of Attica 508/7–c.250 BC: A Political and Social Study* (Princeton: Princeton University Press).

Whitehead, D. (1990) *Aineias the Tactician, How to Survive under Siege*, translated with introduction and commentary (Oxford: Oxford University Press). [Reissued 2001 with corrigenda and addenda (Bristol: Bristol Classical Press).]

Whitehead (1991) 'Norms of citizenship in ancient Greece', in A. Molho, K. Raaflaub, and J. Emlen, eds., *City-States in Classical Antiquity and Medieval Italy*, 135–54 (Ann Arbor: University of Michigan Press).

Whitehead, D. (1993) 'Cardinal Virtues: the language of public approbation in democratic Athens', *C&M* 44: 37–75.

Whitehead, D. (2000) *Hypereides: The Forensic Speeches*, translated with introduction and commentary (Oxford: Oxford University Press).

Whitehead, D. (2003) 'Polyaenus on Iphicrates', *CQ* 53: 613–16.

Whitehead, D. (2006) 'Polis-toponyms as personal entities (in Thucydides and elsewhere)', *MH* 53: 1–11.

Whitehead, D. (2009) 'Spiteful Heaven: residual belief in divine *phthonos* in post-fifth-century Greece', *AAHung* 49: 327–33.

Whitmarsh, T. (2015) *Battling the Gods: Atheism in the Ancient World* (New York: Knopf).

Wickersham, J. (1994) *Hegemony and Greek Historians* (Lanham and London: Rowman & Littlefield).

Wijma, S. M. (2014) *Embracing the Immigrant: The Participation of Metics in Athenian Polis Religion* (Stuttgart: Steiner).

Wilamowitz-Moellendorff, U. von (1887) 'Demotika der attischen Metoeken', *Hermes* 22: 107–28, 211–59.

Wilhelm, A. (1934) 'Untersuchungen zu Xenophons *Poroi*', *WS* 61: 18–56.

Wilsdorf, H. (1952) *Bergleute und Hüttenmänner im Altertum bis zum Gange der römischen Republik: ihre wirtschaftliche, soziale und juristische Lage* (Berlin: Akademie Verlag).

Wilson, C. H. (1970) 'Athenian military finances, 378/7 to the peace of 375', *Athenaeum* 48: 302–26.

Wood, E. M. (1988) *Peasant-Citizen and Slave: The Foundations of Athenian Democracy* (London and New York: Verso).

Woodhead, A. G. (1981) *The Study of Greek Inscriptions*, 2nd edition (Cambridge: Cambridge University Press).

Woolmer, M. (2015) '*Emporoi kai kapeloi*: redefining commercial roles in classical Greece', *JAH* 3: 150–72.

Worthington, I. (1993) *A Historical Commentary on Dinarchus* (Ann Arbor: University of Michigan Press).

Worthington, I. (2013) *Demosthenes of Athens and the Fall of Classical Greece* (Oxford: Oxford University Press).

Wycherley, R. E. (1978) *The Stones of Athens* (Princeton: Princeton University Press).

Wyse, W. (1904) *The Speeches of Isaeus,* with critical and explanatory notes (Cambridge: Cambridge University Press).

Zelnick-Abramovitz, R. (2005) *Not Wholly Free: The Concept of Manumission and the Status of Manumitted Slaves in the Ancient Greek World* (Leiden and Boston: Brill).

Zurborg, A. (1874) *De Xenophontis libello qui* Poroi *inscribitur* (Berlin: W. Weber).

Index

Athens is not indexed here, though individual Athenians are. The entry for one of them, X. himself, is selective.

Ostensibly geographical entries such as 'Abydos', immediately below, do subsume their collective citizen-bodies (or inhabitants at large) but do not systematically extend to named individuals from that place. The same applies to generic entries: 'kings', 'satraps', and suchlike.